SHAKESPEARE AND DONNE

SHAKESPEARE AND DONNE

Generic Hybrids and the Cultural Imaginary

Edited by Judith H. Anderson and Jennifer C. Vaught

Fordham University Press
New York 2013

Copyright © 2013 Fordham University Press

All rights reserved. No part of this publication may be reproduced, stored in a retrieval system, or transmitted in any form or by any means—electronic, mechanical, photocopy, recording, or any other—except for brief quotations in printed reviews, without the prior permission of the publisher.

Fordham University Press has no responsibility for the persistence or accuracy of URLs for external or third-party Internet websites referred to in this publication and does not guarantee that any content on such websites is, or will remain, accurate or appropriate.

Fordham University Press also publishes its books in a variety of electronic formats. Some content that appears in print may not be available in electronic books.

Library of Congress Cataloging-in-Publication Data

Shakespeare and Donne : generic hybrids and the cultural imaginary / edited by Judith H. Anderson and Jennifer C. Vaught. — First edition.
　　　pages cm
　Includes bibliographical references and index.
　ISBN 978-0-8232-5125-4 (cloth : alk. paper)
　1. Shakespeare, William, 1564–1616—Literary style. 2. Donne, John, 1572–1631—Literary style. 3. Shakespeare, William, 1564–1616—Criticism and interpretation. 4. Donne, John, 1572–1631—Criticism and interpretation. I. Anderson, Judith H., editor of compilation. II. Vaught, Jennifer C., editor of compilation.
　　PR3072.S336 2013
　　822.3'3—dc23

2012048080

Printed in the United States of America

15 14 13   5 4 3 2 1

First edition

In Memory of Marshall Grossman

Contents

Introduction
   Judith H. Anderson and Jennifer C. Vaught   1

PART I: TIME, LOVE, SEX, AND DEATH

1. Sites of Death as Sites of Interaction in Donne and Shakespeare
    Matthias Bauer and Angelika Zirker   17

2. "Nothing like the Sun": Transcending Time and Change in Donne's Love Lyrics and Shakespeare's Plays
    Catherine Gimelli Martin   38

3. "None Do Slacken, None Can Die": *Die* Puns and Embodied Time in Donne and Shakespeare
    Jennifer Pacenza   61

PART II: MORAL, PUBLIC, AND SPATIAL IMAGINARIES

4. Donne, Shakespeare, and the Interrogative Conscience
    Mary Blackstone and Jeanne Shami   85

5. Mapping the Celestial in Shakespeare's *Tempest* and the Writings of John Donne
    Douglas Trevor   111

PART III: NAMES, PUNS, AND MORE

6. Inserting *Me*: Some Instances of Predication and the Privation of the Private Self in Shakespeare and Donne
    Marshall Grossman   133

Improper Nouns: A Response to Marshall Grossman
David Lee Miller 141

7. Aspects, Physiognomy, and the Pun: A Reading of Sonnet 135 and "A Valediction: Of Weeping"
Julian Lamb 148

PART IV: REALMS OF PRIVACY AND IMAGINATION

8. Fantasies of Private Language in "The Phoenix and Turtle" and "The Ecstasy"
Anita Gilman Sherman 169

9. Working Imagination in the Early Modern Period: Donne's Secular and Religious Lyrics and Shakespeare's Hamlet, Macbeth, and Leontes
Judith H. Anderson 185

Notes 221
List of Contributors 279
Index 283

SHAKESPEARE AND DONNE

Introduction

JUDITH H. ANDERSON AND JENNIFER C. VAUGHT

Shakespeare and Donne: Generic Hybrids and the Cultural Imaginary is a collection of essays that focus on textual and contextual intersections between these early modern writers. Although Shakespeare and Donne were both Londoners and nearly exact contemporaries, the one a poet-playwright and the other a poet-priest, just a single book, Anita Gilman Sherman's *Skepticism and Memory in Shakespeare and Donne* (2007) has recently centered on them.[1] In more than fifty years, the only predecessor of Sherman's book has been Patrick Crutwell's *Shakespearean Moment and Its Place in the Poetry of the 17th Century* (1954), and it is so despite its title, which signals a primary focus on Shakespeare.[2] A number of thematic books on poetics, inwardness, death, politics, religion, melancholy, and even science in recent decades have included separate chapters on Donne and on Shakespeare and in this way have indicated their mutual pertinence, but the primary interest of these studies has been thematic, regardless of whether to some extent also formal, historical, or cultural, and, on the whole, they have not offered sustained attention to relations or comparisons between the two writers. While thus contiguous, the writings of the two have remained nonetheless separate, their mutual relevance more incidental than important and focal.

The basic premise of the present volume is that comparative exploration of the various writings of Shakespeare and Donne can be illuminating, offering fresh insight both into these and into the culture they reflect and engage. The youthful Donne was noted to be "a great frequenter of Playes," and years later, while he was dean of St. Paul's Cathedral, his daughter Constance married Edward Alleyn, the actor, theatrical entrepreneur, and founder of Dulwich College, who was known for his performance of Marlovian roles as the "'Roscius of his Age.'"[3] Such a marriage suggests the social and cultural intersections that a historicized, dynamic conception of genre might be thought to include as well. Donne himself was also a celebrated performer as a preacher of sermons in St. Paul's and other London venues.[4] He, too, regularly addressed an audience. His poems have been noted for their dramatization of a speaking voice or, alternatively, for the pure play of various cultural voices within them. His writings, like Shakespeare's, reflect and engage the religious and political controversies of their time, which were arguably intensified for both writers by their being apostate sons of Catholic parentage. Death, desire, and identity were constant themes for both, and language was virtually their obsession.

Both Shakespeare and Donne wrote in a variety of lyrical, dramatic, satirical, and distinctively mixed modes. In this sense, both writers were themselves generic hybrids. Even in their poems and soliloquies, the latter found in sermons as well as in plays, their personae are masks and often multivoiced ones that draw on an extensive repertoire of cultural allusion, one certainly not restricted to a single mode or genre. In Shakespeare's *Tragical History of Hamlet*, a title already generically mixed, Polonius's notoriously comic catalogue of "tragedy, comedy, history, pastoral, pastoral-comical, historical-pastoral, scene individable or poem unlimited" is a theater in-joke with more than a little relevance to Shakespeare's own deliberate and often self-reflexive mixtures of mode and genre, which are especially conspicuous in his incorporation of songs and sonnets into the plays.[5] (Should an echo of the familiar title under which Donne's love lyrics were gathered in 1635 be noticed in the preceding sentence, so much the better.) The mixing of roles, voices, and forms is sufficiently pronounced in the fiction of both poets—that is, in their making (< Greek *poiein*, "produce, invent, create, make")—to have led to comparisons of either's work to the shifting, visual illusions of M. C. Escher.[6]

Shakespeare and Donne are alike in transgressing generic boundaries, and a volume that puts them together might be said to do so as well. While every genre has conventions and social and material conditions, generic isolation, like generic stasis, seldom happens in practice. The cross-fertilizing of writings in different modes and genres is to a considerable extent what reinvigorates them. Even new genres and modes or those thought at the time to be new have rhizomatous root systems. Already established genres, that is, old genres, are also constantly in flux, or as Alastair Fowler has put it, "the character of genres is that they change."[7] Fowler primarily intends historical change over centuries, whereas our focus is on the relative immediacy of cultural cross-fertilization—something that is currently in the cultural winds even more than it is deliberate. In fact, we have made evidence of cultural cross-fertilization, owing largely to the cultural winds, the major focus of our collection. Questions of direct influence and actual borrowings, though ever welcome and never irrelevant, are incidental to this focus, as is a literalized search for hybrids in full bloom—newly invented generic formations or whole hybrid products—as apart from hybrid producers and dynamic processes of hybridization.

The essays that follow center on relationships between the writings of Shakespeare and Donne that are broadly cultural, theoretical, and imaginative. They are suggestive at once within an early modern context and within our own critical one. Not surprisingly, our collection particularly emphasizes the intersection of physical or material dimensions of experience with nonphysical or transcendent ones, whether these are moral, intellectual, or religious. It also juxtaposes lyric and sermons interactively with narrative and plays. Performance and audience number among its concerns, as recurrently do the cultural themes of skepticism and imagination and various philosophies of thought, sensation, and meaning: for example, those of Aristotle, Ludwig Wittgenstein, Stanley Cavell, Saul Kripke, Giorgio Agamben, Brian Massumi, and Michel Serres. Another conspicuous emphasis in the volume is on language and relatedly on rhetoric: naming and punning (especially "Will," "Donne," and "More"), public and private discourse, figures, tropes, and styles. Besides philosophies of mind and language, theoretical orientations in the volume encompass intertextuality, feminism and sexuality studies, reception and performance, and various historicisms.

The authors of these essays bring a variety of backgrounds to the collection that merits mention. One authorial pair in Canada combines a practicing dramaturge with an authority on sermons; another pair teaches in Germany and collaborates on a well-known critical journal with a dialogic orientation; a third contributor is an Australian teaching in Hong Kong. By permission of the author's estate, a fourth contribution to the volume is posthumous. This last essay, by Marshall Grossman, to whose memory our volume is dedicated, was written for a seminar of the Shakespeare Association of America, and it was to have been revised and enlarged for our collection. We think it well worth publishing despite its unfinished form, and, accordingly, we asked David Lee Miller to write a reflective essay to accompany and situate it. The essays of Grossman and Miller effectually constitute another pair of contributors to the volume. The rest of the authors, like those already mentioned, represent a further variety of critical allegiances and positions within the academy. As far as we know, excepting Sherman, no contributor has previously and focally compared Shakespeare and Donne in a single article, chapter, or book, something we mention to highlight the extent to which this collection is exploratory.[8]

The first three essays of the volume center on the intersection of time, love, sex, and death and therefore on the conjunction and disjunction of mortality and, if not of traditional immortality, of something, somehow more lasting. The opening essay, by Matthias Bauer and Angelika Zirker, concerns "Sites of Death as Sites of Interaction in Donne and Shakespeare." This essay is at once intertextual and broadly intergeneric. In it Bauer and Zirker draw extensively on familiar topoi treating life in the grave—the couplings of womb and tomb, for the obvious example—to argue that one aspect of this topic, the site of death as a specific place of interaction, distinguishes the practice of Shakespeare and Donne from that of their contemporaries. Bauer and Zirker show that the practice of these two writers is distinctive to a significant extent and in explicit ways—enough so, they suggest, as to indicate that, for Donne, the gravesite as an intermediate phase is actually "inspired, as well as elucidated, by a dialogue with Shakespeare." Their essay focuses on two of Donne's poems and three of Shakespeare's plays: Donne's lyric "The Extasie" in relation to the fatal tomb scene in Shakespeare's *Romeo and Juliet* and Donne's verse letter "Epitaph on Himselfe" in relation to the epilogues of *A Midsummer Night's Dream* and *The Tempest*.[9]

The very pairing of "The Extasie" with *Romeo and Juliet* is novel, enabling the perception of surprising and pervasive links between these works. Donne's striking verbal coinage "interinanimates," expressing the effect of mutual love on the two lovers' souls, is a multiple pun (the life-giving "animate," the life-canceling and/or inwardly vitalizing "inanimate," the preposition and/or verb "inter," the suspension [soul-sleep?] of "interim," the coupling of "mates") that can be read simultaneously as death in life and life in death—as the sepulchral death of the individual souls and their rebirth as one abler soul. Comparably, in the tomb of death, Romeo and Juliet want, by kisses or inanimating breath, to establish a further connection, an exchange of souls, and a new life within death. While we might interpret such similarity as the ironic exposure of the symbolic possibilities of Donne to the bodily enactment of Shakespearean drama, the strongly affective dimensions of language in Shakespeare's staged performance resist our doing so, especially if we happen also to recall that this poet of tragic death is the same one who in time will write the end of *The Winter's Tale*. Hardly by coincidence, it seems, Bauer and Zirker also observe an analogous, transformative interaction between the onlooker (and reader) in "The Extasie" and those who witness and memorialize the lovers' deaths in *Romeo and Juliet*. The end of *The Winter's Tale*, which enacts rebirth and offers to its witnesses a new beginning, comes again to mind.

Whereas both these works, "The Extasie" and *Romeo and Juliet*, memorialize—even monumentalize—the lovers in everyday life, Donne's "Epitaph on Himselfe" and the epilogues in Shakespeare's *Dream* and *Tempest*, as Bauer and Zirker show, alike address a general audience from a world of shadows, sleep, and death that is markedly separated from everyday existence. These addresses offer betterment—a mutual "mending"—to speaker and audience. Like many of Donne's other poems, as well as his sermon *Deaths Duell* and his *Devotions*, Shakespeare's epilogues, like his lyrical *Phoenix and Turtle*, are liminal texts that variously link the play world to the ordinary one and the living to the dead. Moreover, like "The Extasie" and *Romeo and Juliet*, they pivot on a site where death meets a possibility beyond it—an actual place and a literary topos that are quite simply *between*. In such a state of relationship, of confluence and virtuality, we might recognize the *prepositionality* proposed by the philosopher, scientist, and mathematician Michel Serres and thus glance ahead to the third essay in our opening group, by Jennifer Pacenza, whose concerns overlap those of both the essays that precede it.[10]

In the second essay of the volume, "'Nothing like the Sun': Transcending Time and Change in Donne's Love Lyrics and Shakespeare's Plays," Catherine Gimelli Martin engages the relation of change and loss to a desire for undying love, as do Bauer and Zirker, but she sharply reevaluates it. She identifies this desire with the *hieros gamos*, or sacred marriage, that figures a perfected, timeless, transcendent union. Writing as a feminist, however, she exposes the negative side of monumentality and associates its stasis with a control that is absolute. Martin distrusts the sincerity of Donne's youthful protestations of libertinism and skepticism and aligns them with those of Benedick in Shakespeare's *Much Ado about Nothing*. In addition, she contrasts Donne's desire to control time and transcend mutability in mature poems such as "The Good-Morrow," "A Lecture upon the Shadow," and "A Valediction Forbidding Mourning" with Shakespeare's mockery of this desire, his depiction of changelessness as an impossible dream. Her argument concentrates on what she sees as Donne's and Shakespeare's vastly different masculine responses to the cultural figure of the fickle woman. Although both writers create male personae who share "misogynistic fears of female betrayal" that result in various degrees of insecurity and skepticism, Shakespeare, again in contrast to Donne, explores "the dark side of a male desire for unchanging love." In *Much Ado about Nothing*, *Othello*, and *The Winter's Tale*, he memorably depicts male jealousy, not female betrayal, as the more likely, more potent, more destructive evil. Martin argues that Othello's desire to entomb Desdemona in the "monumental alabaster" of her own flesh reflects his perverse need to ensure her irreversible constancy through her death. The corrosive, deathly cynicism of Iago, to whom time itself is a fickle whore, not a fertile healer, is what catalyzes Othello's fateful doubting of Desdemona. Unlike Donne, Shakespeare examines in both comic and tragic plots the damaging results of men's trying to control the women they love, their attempt to find a stable anchor in female immobility, and thus their ultimately humbling and futile efforts to transcend time and change. While Martin softens her criticism of Donne's perceived idealism and absolutism in the end, her challenge to it abides. The contrast between the essays of Bauer and Zirker and Martin is provocative in the best sense of this word.

The next essay, Jennifer Pacenza's "'None Do Slacken, None Can Die': *Die* Puns and Embodied Time in Donne and Shakespeare," analyzes how both writers attempt to transcend linear time through their puns and other erotically charged expressions of imagination, including sheer phantasy. This essay is the most speculative in the volume. Pacenza focuses on Donne's *Songs and Sonnets* and Shakespeare's sonnets, those in which the two poets reveal the immortalizing, yet humanly experienced, power of perpetual sexual moments. Pacenza defines these as "embodied time." Her essay draws on the theoretical work of Massumi and Serres to explore the middle ground between binaries, a generative terrain that produces a mixing rather than a separation of ontological concepts—a space of orgasmic virtuality and pure potentiality. Like Bauer and Zirker's essay, Pacenza's engages the interaction between life and death and the analogous movement into and out of the womb and the tomb. Through poetic imagination and the potential at once in bodily pleasure and in language itself—in her argument the combined emphases of Thomas Laqueur, Massumi, and Serres—Donne and Shakespeare are seen to escape linearity by rearranging time in all its multiplicity and mingling of past, present, and future. In contrast to a focus on orgasmic and actual dying in Donne's *Songs and Sonnets*, in Shakespeare's sonnets Pacenza finds a greater concern with time itself, although this concern is inevitably and inextricably linked to death as well.

Shakespeare's first fifteen sonnets to the Young Man exhibit a specifically masturbatory language that perpetuates his youth and beauty through "asexual replication," as Pacenza conceives it. Such replication is distinguished from physical procreation and likened to the poetic trope of a virgin birth. As trope, it is also analogous to the real birth by the Blessed Virgin, both with respect to its inspirited origin and to its phantasied result. At the same time, this metaphorized result remains grounded in and referable to physical pleasures and acts. In these sonnets, the resulting creation of offspring that duplicate their single parent—each offshoot a sort of clone in an age when genetic replication happened only in the test tube of imagination—"saves the Young Man from the ravages of time" by perpetuating embodied memories of him. These memories are both phantasied to be real and realized as poems. Visible just beyond Pacenza's present argument, not to mention Martin's *hieros gamos* and the gravesite of Bauer and Zirker, lies the embodied, orgasmic virtuality of Cleopatra's imaginatively potent, climactic death scene in Shakespeare's *Antony and Cleopatra*.

The next two essays in our volume might be taken together as moral, public, and spatial imaginaries insofar as they range from explorations of the heart and mind to explorations of outer space. The first of these, Mary Blackstone and Jeanne Shami's essay "Donne, Shakespeare, and the Interrogative Conscience," addresses the performative dimensions of the pulpit and the theater, comparable venues that appealed to elite as well as to popular, live audiences. This essay shares an awareness of reception and specifically of audience that is likewise found in Bauer and Zirker's and also shares a broadly historical orientation with the essay by Douglas Trevor, which immediately follows it. As Blackstone and Shami explain, sermongoers and playgoers commonly experienced an interrogation of their religious beliefs, political allegiances, and cultural values that influenced their private examination of their souls and the way they constructed a sense of self. Blackstone and Shami focus on two of Donne's priestly performances at court—his Lenten sermon of 1617–1618 and the sermon on Mark 4:24 that he preached to Charles I in 1617—and comparatively on Shakespeare's *Henry V*, all of which use "some of the same rhetorical, dramaturgical, and performative mechanisms." Each of these persuasive, propagandistic texts includes variations of tone that appeal to listeners from positions of nearness and distance, from an intimacy inviting self-reflection to the reinforcement of public commonalities such as nationalism. As this reinforcement suggests, Shakespeare and Donne both qualify, in terms Blackstone and Shami borrow from Daniel Lerner and Anthony D. Smith, as "Transitionals," or "men-in-motion," historical figures positioned at a point of engagement between private and public, old and new values, new hopes and old traditions.[11] We might refigure the fluid relationship between such paired terms as a kind of hybridizing conceived as a continuing and provisional process.

Donne's and Shakespeare's mutual interest in affecting and influencing their audiences often found a complementary response in these audiences' active engagement. Blackstone and Shami suggest that the medial space of the stage and the pulpit could even reverse the relationship of agent and audience. For instance, Charles I became the admonishing preacher and Donne the auditor when the king expressed concerns about his 1627 sermon and requested a full-text version, much to Donne's surprise, since Donne feared he might lose his position as royal chaplain. Situations and roles mirror one another in other ways as well insofar as actors rely on "their mimetic skills" and spectators imaginatively "imitate what they are seeing." Variously, Shakespeare and Donne made compelling use of their understanding of cognitive processes to bridge the gap between the body of the performer and the mind of the audience. Other rhetorical and performative methods in *Henry V* and the sermons also affected the viewing public, such as the creation of an impression of presentness and of the shifting perspectives associated with diverse voices or characters. The popularity of both writers, along with their engagement of "the interrogative conscience of their age," resulted in their attaining what Blackstone and Shami rightly describe as the "pinnacle of influence" in "mass media: in the theater, the pulpit, and print publications."

Space travel and global, otherworldly cartography are focal in Douglas Trevor's essay "Mapping the Celestial in Shakespeare's *Tempest* and the Writings of John Donne," the second essay in this grouping. Trevor offers a revisionary reading of *The Tempest* that critiques European imperialism from the perspective of Caliban, insomuch as he is a "mooncalf." He argues that Caliban, like his mother Sycorax, exhibits a close association with the lunar and that the resulting depiction of him as far more exotic, strange, and monstrous than any other early modern imagining of a native American figure challenges the usual connection of Caliban only with the New World. The precedent of sea voyages to foreign lands, as well as of Galileo's telescope, led many to wonder whether the moon were inhabited and could be visited through space travel, as illustrated, for example, by John Lyly's *Endymion, the Man in the Moon*. The moon functions as a kind of rhetorical, celestial map in *The Tempest* and as a means for Caliban to envision liberation from his servitude to Prospero and Miranda. Trevor subsequently associates Donne's interest in celestial maps with their exposure of "the fault lines of human knowledge" and connects these to Montaigne's moderate skepticism in "An Apologie of Raymond Sebond." His examination of Donne's prose works and several of his poems, especially "The Good-Morrow" and "Hymne to God, my God in my Sicknesse," accentuates both the entwining of the cartographic with the skeptical impulse and the poet-priest's Montaignian "sense of earthly inconstancy," a dimension of Donne's love lyrics that Martin's essay also addresses. Like Montaigne, Donne endorses the value of subjectivity, a private, interior realm for exploration that is potentially revelatory like the heavens and thus moderates his skepticism. Again like Montaigne, he considers human intelligence and knowledge "stubbornly provisional," temporal, and characteristic of the limited, yet still valuable, perspective afforded by studying the earth and its inhabitants.

Introducing a group of three essays on names, puns, and (punningly) more, Marshall Grossman's essay "Inserting *Me*: Some Instances of Predication and the Privation of the Private Self in Shakespeare and Donne" attributes to Donne and to Shakespeare the realization that "the self can be possessed and confirmed only through and as acts of predication." In these acts, "the immediacy of the self is sacrificed to the hegemony of its signifiers." Although Grossman intends to study the workings of this dual realization of possession and loss in Donne's Holy Sonnets and Shakespeare's

Will sonnets, he begins by analyzing two familiar exchanges in *Hamlet* in which the public and private dimensions of language conflict: one exchange involves the word "father," the other the word "son." He wants to establish the basic recognition in Shakespeare's text that literature "can tell a common truth only by representing particulars, which must belie their particularized circumstances." The space for what Grossman considers "authentic being" lies (a pun he exploits) only between such "dissonant linguistic predications," between a public language and a private one. The play between proper name and common use/usage, between *Will* and *will* in Shakespeare's punning sonnets becomes for him the place where words cannot be separated and truth can be told only by lying. The struggle for selfhood in these sonnets finds its parallel in Donne's, when the latter poet struggles "to surrender the self to the Holy Spirit" without also losing his "subjective voice." Grossman's eventual goal is to recover what the late Joel Fineman meant when he wrote that the reader of literature experiences "'the desire of the homosexual for the heterosexual'" or, refigured, that "'of the man to be sodomized by the woman.'" Equipped with these premises, Grossman proceeds with a metrically, linguistically, and grammatically significant analysis of Donne's sonnets "As due by many titles" and "Batter my heart." From these, he turns to the best known of Shakespeare's Will sonnets, number 135, signaling his desire to read it in the highly suggestive context he has presented. Because of death, his reading was not completed.

David Lee Miller's contribution bears the title "Improper Nouns: A Response to Marshall Grossman." Miller's essay reflects on the multiple ironies of its own insertion with respect not only to Marshall's title but also to the latter's lifelong meditation on Fineman's career. He turns from these to the aporetic relation of private self and public speech, self-immediacy and signification. The basic question Miller would ask Grossman's essay concerns the shift "from the intensely carnal and secular interest of Shakespeare's sonnets to the sacred context of Donne's." Calling Luther's "theological grammar" to mind, Miller notes the rigorous analysis that early modern theology brought to a text—one to rival the rigor of modern systems of psychoanalysis and language philosophy. He considers Donne's pronouns further by glancing at the medieval poet Alain de Lille and at John Milton before returning to Grossman's association of resistance, excess, and masculine self-possession with the final pun on "more" in Donne's "Hymn to God the Father." In Donne's grammatical and pronominal equivocations and in poignant counterpoint to the essay by Bauer and Zirker, Miller finds "a failure of the imagination faced with death," and he wonders elegiacally at the end, as did the poets he treats, about the extent to which words can outlast their speakers by opening themselves to the "unknowable force of the Other."

Titled "Aspects, Physiognomy, and the Pun: A Reading of Sonnet 135 and 'A Valediction: Of Weeping,'" Julian Lamb's witty essay might, in one sense, be seen to pick up where Grossman's and Miller's ended, but where Grossman cites Kripke and, via Fineman, implicitly Jacques Lacan, Lamb's approach to naming and punning predominantly derives from Wittengenstein's notion of family resemblances. Invoking and assessing an impressive array of other modern theorists of the pun—William Empson, Jonathan Culler, Derek Attridge, Catherine Bates, Stephen Booth—Lamb also utilizes Wittengenstein's famed duck-rabbit picture and discussion of the dawning, or recognition of a (physiognomical) aspect. He explains that the puns on proper names that he engages—Will, Donne, More (Donne's wife Ann)—"make us aware of the inert and unchanging homophone from which meanings emerge, but which is not itself meaningful."[12] He works with proper names precisely because their identification with their bearers makes the work of the pun more powerful: if a pun is ordinarily conceived as being like the breaking of white light by a prism into its constituent colors, Lamb tells us, he would reverse the process.

Like Grossman, Lamb approaches Shakespeare's Sonnet 135 by way of Shakespearean drama, here the passage in *Henry V* that plays outrageously with the word "mock" in the context of rebounding tennis balls. Having acknowledged that this wordplay is *antanaclasis* and not truly punning, Lamb soon changes his tack to suggest that the repetitions leading us to see a word as an object effectually dissolve its physiognomy and radically alter the work of the pun. A similar but more extensively refined argument pertains to Shakespeare's Will/will before Lamb turns to "Emblems of More." He finds the crux of this pun in Donne's "Valediction: Of Weeping" in the uncertainty of whether "more" will mean "More" after separation, a question that mirrors our deciding where and when the common word puns on the proper one (or vice versa). Qualifying David J. Leigh's reading of "A Hymn to God the Father," Lamb also hears "a contrapuntal voice" in the final pun of Donne's hymn: "Under the infinitely perceptive readership of God the Father, every word becomes a cognizance, an object enclosing unknown meanings, always signifying in excess of what a speaker intends, always signifying more."

The essay by Anita Gilman Sherman titled "Fantasies of Private Language in 'The Phoenix and Turtle' and 'The Ecstasy'" begins a grouping of two essays on realms of privacy and imagination that extend the linguistic interests of the previous grouping but also shift more emphatically inward. Sherman's essay clearly shares ground with Grossman's and Miller's, but instead of centering on puns, it engages the relation of intimacy and privacy to public conventions such as genre and ritual and to other externalized expressions, including bodily ones. Another essay with which Sherman's is therefore linked to an extent is that by Blackstone and Shami, on the engagement of the individual conscience by the public forms of plays and sermons. Sherman's essay, like her book on Shakespeare and Donne, is fundamentally informed by the philosophy of Wittgenstein's talented interpreter Stanley Cavell, which she knows broadly and in depth. Whereas Donne, she tells us, in "The Ecstasy" "offers a fiction of interanimate legibility" to combat "the 'loneliness' of skepticism," in "The Phoenix and Turtle," Shakespeare offers "a chorus of voices witnessing as outsiders to a relationship so ineffable that language itself is stymied." In sum, these metaphysical poems explore "the problems of privacy and hyperbolic language" fueled by skepticism, a subject to which both Trevor and our final essayist, Judith H. Anderson, attend as well. Theatricality, exhibitionism, mythologizing, omniscience, and fantasied reciprocity all play into Sherman's analysis. Many of these concerns also strike a chord with Martin's essay insofar as Sherman observes that "the wish for perfect understanding bears an uneasy resemblance" both to God's uniquely privileged ability to read innermost thoughts and to "a desire for possession of the beloved." The outcomes of ecstasy in the poems Sherman examines differ radically, as do the personae of the two poets, the one self-effacing, the other "ostentatiously present," but she locates the essential difference less in personality or plot than in "discrepant stances toward language." Shakespeare's lyric makes genre, for all its publicity, meaningfully resist interpretation, whereas Donne's, for all its openness, asks readers to understand "a private language in action."

The final contribution to our collection, Judith Anderson's, is titled "Working Imagination in the Early Modern Period: Donne's Secular and Religious Lyrics and Shakespeare's Hamlet, Macbeth, and Leontes."

Anderson takes the Aristotelian tradition of faculty psychology to be the basic, fullest, and most important one in the early modern period, although it is one that mixes variously with others, such as the medical and Neoplatonic traditions. Aristotle's noncommittal skepticism about the reliability of the images that imagination processes touches the very foundation of the Aristotelian system for knowledge with a tinge of doubt, a fact that Anderson connects to early modern developments in optics. Referring to the Aristotelian tradition and examining salient instances of intensely imaginative work in Shakespeare's plays and Donne's lyrics, she brings into sharp relief the careful and urgent attention to the mind's operations in their writings. For Shakespeare, she first considers two soliloquies comparatively—Hamlet's after the Player's recitation of the murder of Priam and Macbeth's dagger soliloquy—and then moves to the virtual soliloquy by Leontes in which he manifestly becomes the plaything of images generated by an imaginative faculty run wild: "Affection!—thy intention stabs the centre." Anderson also invokes arguments based on the earliest texts of *Hamlet* that the Prince's soliloquies are "movable or even detachable" to underwrite her comparison of "this dramatic, subjective, imaginative form with like expressions in other genres," Donne's lyrics being the cases in point. For Donne, she selects as an instance of "love, death, and more," what is arguably his signature lyric, "The Canonization"; to represent "psychic modeling and motivation," she selects the affective and cognitive landscapes of "A Nocturnal upon S. Lucy's Day," "Good Friday, 1613," and a Holy Sonnet, and she discusses two lyrics about dreaming that attend to the fuzzy borders of sleep and waking and bear as well on the plight of Leontes.

Anderson's cognitive, formal, and cultural concerns are so broad and basic that they might, in a sense, be said to inform the whole volume. Ideas about the workings of the faculty of imagination underlie its more specific cultural manifestations and exhibit similarities that these manifestations, however important, can obscure. For example, much as techniques of religious meditation reveal about Donne's lyrics, their formulas and sectarianisms tend to conceal more basic psychological and epistemic similarities between his work and Shakespeare's, and much as traditional generic assumptions and material conditions of performance reveal about Shakespeare's plays, they can become obstacles to grasping the relation of his work to the forms and the conditions of reception that pertain to Donne's. In both instances, the danger is that a more inclusive or more fundamental picture of the cultural surround is simply pushed off limits. A relation to the whole is arguably evident in Anderson's qualified use of the historian Stuart Clark's characterization of early modern culture as visual. As she observes, this period might rather "be *seen* as imaginative not least because of the relation of sense (eyesight) to imagination (interior impression)." Clark recurrently designates as "seeing"—his quotation marks signaling interpretation, perception, vision (or visions), and the like—what is actually translative and tropic; indeed, such "seeing" is itself imaginative, "a connection between inside and outside, external object and interior representation." Let imagination, then, be the culminating note on which we end.

PART I   Time, Love, Sex, and Death

1. Sites of Death as Sites of Interaction in Donne and Shakespeare

MATTHIAS BAUER AND ANGELIKA ZIRKER

If there is a motif that runs like a thread through all of John Donne's writings, it is the awareness of death and its impact on life. Donne's portrait in a shroud, the frontispiece to his most famous sermon, "Deaths Duell," which became the model of his epitaph in St. Paul's Cathedral, is the visible sign of this constant awareness.[1] It shows the living Donne awaiting his deliverance from "the manifold deaths of this *world*" and visualizes his notion of a paradoxical interdependence of *exitus* and *introitus*, of going out and going in, which characterizes the relation of life and death:

> But then this *exitus a morte*, is but *introitus in mortem*, this *issue*, this deliverance *from* that *death*, the death of the *wombe*, is an *entrance*, a delivering over to *another death*, the manifold deaths of this *world*.[2]

Life and death are described as movements from and into rooms: just as the womb is a tomblike container if we are not delivered from it at birth ("The *wombe* which should be the *house of life*, becomes *death* it selfe, if *God* leave us there"), the world in which we live "is but an *universall church-yard*, but our *common grave*," if we are not delivered from it (232, 234).[3] This second delivery is of course all-decisive, and, accordingly, the site connected to it deserves our special consideration: the *exitus* from the deaths of this world "is an *entrance* into the *death of corruption* and *putrefaction* and *vermiculation* and *incineration*, and dispersion in and from the *grave*, in which every dead man dyes over againe" (236). Except for the happy few that will be alive at the second coming, all human beings must undergo this third process of dying, the site of which is the grave. But just as the other two phases imply both death and life, the dying over again in the grave is a form of life, too, a "dissolution" and a "sleeping" preparing for the final *exitus/introitus* into eternal life (238). It is this phase and this site, in its intermediate position between life on earth and eternal life, that preoccupied Donne's imagination. And it is his conceptualization of this site and phase, we would like to suggest, that is inspired, as well as elucidated, by a dialogue with Shakespeare.

This dialogue concerning "life in the grave" is embedded in a wide context of theological as well as literary utterances concerning the nature of death. Nevertheless, it seems both possible and fruitful to focus on one specific aspect of the topic in which a characteristic connection between Shakespeare and Donne becomes visible: the representation of the site of death (a grave, a monument, and the like) as a place of interaction. Taking our cue from two poems by Donne, "The Extasie" and "Epitaph on Him-selfe," we will see that the eschatological dimension of this interaction is inextricably linked with a poetological one and in particular with a notion of dramatic self-reflection. For, in these poems, the grave or monument is the site where the most intense exchange between human actors takes place, and it is the site where an interaction between the living and the dead is realized. In each case, a change or metamorphosis is brought about, and in each case verbal art plays a decisive role in the process. Last but not least, the dialogue between the two poets will reveal a mutually illuminating relationship between the epitaph and the epilogue.

Loving Interinanimation and the Site of Death

Both poets prototypically conceived the exchange that takes place at the site of death as the union of lovers. This union is experienced as an ecstasy both in "The Extasie" and in *Romeo and Juliet*. Yet, while Donne focuses on the similitude to death in his poem, Shakespeare's lovers "really" do die on the stage, and their death is final.

"The Extasie" starts with the lovers sitting on a bank, with their "hands firmly cimented" and their "eye-beames twisted," which are the only "meanes to make us one" (5, 7, 10).[4] But this description concerns their bodies only—their souls have left them and "hung 'twixt her, and mee," for in the manner of "two equal Armies, Fate / suspends uncertaine victorie" (13–16). The souls have left their bodies "to advance their state," which implies that this was impossible as long as they were part of the body (15).

The separation of body and soul, however, means death; that the lovers appear as if dead becomes obvious in stanza five:[5]

> And whil'st our soules negotiate there,
> Wee like sepulchral statues lay;
> All day, the same our postures were,
> And wee said nothing, all the day.
>
> (16–20)

The lovers have become "like sepulchral statues"; they can no longer change their postures and appear as inanimate, very much in the manner of recumbent effigies.[6]

The lovers' bed—the bank on which they lie is described in terms of "a pillow on a bed" (1)—becomes their deathbed.[7] The identity of love and death, as expressed, for instance, by Ronsard in his *Sonnets pour Hélène* ("Car l'Amour et la Mort n'est qu'une mesme chose"[8]), has found what is probably its most famous expression in the ending of Shakespeare's *Romeo and Juliet*. In the poem, the ecstasy experienced by the lovers is a rehearsal of death, whereas on the stage, death becomes a kind of ecstasy: the lovers are united in death and thus are able to experience fulfillment, even if not in this life.[9]

After Juliet has taken the potion, which will make her "appear like dead," she is entombed in her family's monument (IV.i.99).[10] The news of her death reaches Romeo through Balthasar, who tells him, "Her body sleeps in Capel's monument, / And her immortal part with angels lives" (V.i.18–19). Balthasar describes her death as the separation of body and soul.[11] But this description contains a contradiction, a paradox even: if her soul is "immortal," then the implication is that her body is mortal; if this is the case, however, then why does it "sleep"? Not only does Balthasar's statement contain dramatic irony—as, indeed, Juliet is only asleep, which is known to the audience—but he also refers to Juliet's intermediary state here. Body and soul are separated and personified, and as such they await Judgment Day, when the body will "awake" to be again united with the soul.[12]

When Romeo enters the tomb, he thinks that Juliet is dead, whereas, in fact, she is only a "poor living corse, clos'd in a dead man's tomb" (V.ii.30), as Friar Laurence describes her state. Juliet is still alive but also resembles a recumbent effigy.[13] Ironically, Romeo addresses her as dead but still resembling life in her beauty: "O my love, my wife, / Death that hath suck'd the honey of thy breath / Hath had no power yet upon thy beauty" (V.iii.91-93).[14] Romeo's tragic error serves to point out that the intermediate state in which he finds Juliet is a likeness not only of the transition from life to death, the "*entrance* into the *death of corruption*" but also—Juliet does not show any marks of corruption—of the transition to life in death. Indeed, she awakes shortly afterward, only to make us realize that her sleep and her awakening were but a foreshadowing of the real death that is to follow.[15] This likeness of sleep to death—and of death to sleep—can be linked to the paradox of life in death and death in life as Shakespeare used it to characterize Lucrece's transitional state shortly before she is raped:[16]

> . . . life's triumph in the map of death,
> And death's dim look in life's mortality.
> Each in her sleep themselves so beautify,
> As if between them twain there were no strife,
> But that life liv'd in death, and death in life.[17]

Donne describes life and death in these terms in "Deaths Duell," when he writes that birth is "*exitus a morte*" and "*introitus in mortem*," and the lovers in "The Extasie" likewise represent the image of "life liv'd in death, and death in life" as their souls live on while their bodies are dead, and the whole moment of ecstasy is like some death in life—a paradox that Donne dwells on extensively in "Deaths Duell." In both the poem and Donne's sermon, the life found in death is the better life, but in "The Extasie," this "death" is understood as a foreshadowing only. In "Deaths Duell," Donne refers to the death that awaits all human beings at the end of their lives. Romeo is confronted with this death when he enters the monument of the Capulets. In different ways, all three texts present death as a similitude—even *Romeo and Juliet*, in spite of its tragic finality in this play.

At first entering the monument, Romeo regards it as a "triumphant grave" (V.iii.83). It is not so much a place of darkness (and death) as a place of light: "For here lies Juliet, and her beauty makes / This vault a feasting presence, full of light" (85–86). She transforms the grave into a lantern,[18] into a "presence" rather than an absence, and by this imagery Romeo evokes life after death. His description of the vault as a "feasting presence," more-

over, calls to mind the banquet in heaven as described in Psalm 23:5—
"Thou preparest a table before me"—and in Luke 12:37—"he [the Lord]
shall gird himself, and make them to sit down to meat, and will come forth
and serve them."[19] Thus, Juliet's resurrection—which shortly afterward is
foreshadowed when she "rises" and also when "her statue" is "raise[d]"—is
prefigured in Romeo's perception of her tomb (V.iii.147, 289).[20]

He goes on to exclaim, "Death lie thou there, by a dead man interred"
(87). Death is either "buried" itself and therefore dead—similarly to the
ending of Shakespeare's Sonnet 146, "And death once dead, there's no
more dying then," which is a direct allusion to 1 Corinthians 15:54,[21] and
to Donne's Holy Sonnet "Death be not proud": "Death shall be no more,
Death thou shalt die"—or the place is representative of death and marked
by its presence as it lies there "interred." But it is also interred by "a dead
man," and given that Romeo comes to the tomb to kill himself, he regards
himself as such: he is a "dead man," while Juliet is a "living corse." It is
not entirely clear which meaning—death or life—is predominant here;
what we find is some intermediary state, and the tomb has both qualities,
those of life and of death, which is already expressed by Romeo when he
enters the tomb of the Capulets:

> Thou detestable maw, thou womb of death
> Gorg'd with the dearest morsel of the earth,
> Thus I enforce thy rotten jaws to open,
> And in despite I'll cram thee with more food.
>
> (V.iii.45–48)

It is clear from this passage that Romeo wants to join his wife in death and
therefore "cram" the tomb with yet another inhabitant. The words "womb
of death" are particularly striking in this passage as it is not entirely clear
what they mean. Gibbons in his annotation glosses "womb" as belly, following the semantic field of eating, which is prevalent in the passage.[22]
Depending on whether we read "of death" as a *genitivus subiectivus* or a *genitivus obiectivus*, however, the expression has more than that meaning alone
and therefore contains a double movement. In the first case, as a *genitivus
subiectivus*, the words denote a womb that belongs to death; in the second,
as a *genitivus obiectivus*, it is a womb that issues death or that means death.[23]
If Juliet finds herself in a womb of death in the first sense, she must be

delivered forth from there to another life; that is, the womb produces life. Donne describes birth as an *"exitus à morte uteri"* in "Deaths Duell" (232: margin).[24]

The reading as a *genitivus obiectivus*, however, seems to be more common in the context of Shakespeare's work, for example, in *Richard III*, when the Duchess of York curses her son Richard and his deeds by exclaiming "o my accursed womb, the bed of death."[25] Her womb has brought forth death in delivering Richard. Margaret later takes up a very similar image when she addresses the Duchess in the following terms: "From forth the kennel of thy womb hath crept / a hell-hound that doth hunt us all to death" (IV.iv.47–48).[26] She also uses the image of Richard as a harbinger of death who stems from his mother's womb, which hence leads to death rather than life.

When Richard addresses Elizabeth about his wish to marry her daughter, he uses the imagery of the womb in more organic and positive terms. To Elizabeth, mourning the loss of her children, Richard replies, "But in your daughter's womb I bury them, / Where, in that nest of spicery, they will breed / Selves of themselves, to your recomforture" (IV.iv.423–25), which implies some sort of "re"turn and exchange. In this play, the womb is both a place of death and of life and birth.[27]

The doubling of the *genitivus subiectivus* and *genitivus obiectivus* results in the double interpretation of the "womb of death." This double movement between life and death can be found not only in "Deaths Duell" but also in the meditation of Donne's eighteenth *Devotion*: "[I]n her [our natural mother's] womb we grew, and when she was delivered of us, we were planted in some place, in some calling in the world; in the womb of the earth we diminish, and when she is delivered of us, our grave opened for another; we are not transplanted, but transported, and our dust blown away with profane dust, with every wind."[28] While we grow in the womb of our "naturall Mother," we "diminish" in "the womb of the earth"—as Friar Laurence has it, "the earth that's nature's mother is her tomb / What is her burying grave, that is her womb" (II.iii.5-6).[29] In this passage, our mother's womb delivers us into the world, and we are delivered from there again into another womb, that of the earth. First we grow, then we diminish, but both processes are not in themselves final. The site of death is therefore full of life.

In Donne's poem, the two lovers are "*like* sepulchral statues," and while their bodies lie on the bank,[30] their two souls are active; they "negotiate" and interact:

> When love, with one another so
> Interinanimates two soules,
> That abler soule, which thence doth flow,
> Defects of lonelinesse controules.
>
> (41–44)[31]

In his *Pseudo-Martyr*, Donne wrote, "God inanimates . . . every man with one soul."[32] In "The Extasie," Donne introduces a new compound based on this verb by adding the prefix "inter-."[33] The meaning of "in-" as "into" in "God inanimates" is supplemented by another meaning of "in-," namely, the sense of negation; the verbalized adjective can therefore mean both "with life" and "lifeless." By the addition of "inter-," the word takes on a different meaning yet, especially so if one reads the poem in light of the site of death as a site of interaction and exchange. In "interinanimation," "inter" as a preposition thus evokes "inter" as a verb, and vice versa.[34] It is love that "interinanimates two souls," which can be interpreted either as the death of the individual souls—they are inanimate—and their emergence as one, like the sepulchral statues that are "cemented" (5) and "*inter*graft" (9) together, or as a process in which they give life to one another through love (very much as God inanimates man, that is, gives a soul to man), and a new soul is "born" from the two.[35] Interinanimation can thus be read as the process in which the souls are given souls, and this results in their becoming one "abler soul"; line 59—"Soe soule into the soule may flow"—can then be read like an explanation of the procedure.[36] What is more, by verbalizing the adjective "inanimate," Donne stresses the very fact that even—or especially—in death, the souls are very much alive.

Just as the soul leaves the dying body in a breath,[37] the kiss may be a way in which interinanimation is realized.[38] Romeo closes his farewell speech with a "last embrace" and a "righteous kiss"; it is "with a kiss" that he dies (113–14, 120). As before Death "hath suck'd the honey of [Juliet's] breath," it is now as if Romeo wants to give up his soul by kissing her for a last time (92). But his kiss is "righteous," which refers to his suspicion that "Death is amorous" and keeps Juliet "in dark to be his paramour" (103–5).

With his own lips, the "doors of breath," Romeo "seal[s]" a "dateless bargain to engrossing Death" (114–15). His kiss is inanimating—it makes him lifeless, but at the same time, he dies "with a kiss" and thus finds life, namely in the union with Juliet.[39] Similarly Juliet, in kissing Romeo's lips, dies "with a restorative" (164, 166). By their kisses they want to establish a further connection, an exchange of their souls, and a new life in death.

Being "inanimate" therefore refers not only to a state of being but also to an activity. By creating a new compound, Donne offers diverse options for dividing or composing its elements. One can read it not only as "inter-inanimates" but also as "interin-animates." The verb "animates" contains the soul, "anima," as well as "any mates," which shows the exemplarity of the two lovers presented in the poem. If we then continue to read "interin" as "interim," we are reminded of the intermediate state of the souls after death, called *refrigerium interim* by Tertullian and others, in which they are waiting for the resurrection of the body.[40] This intermediate state is caused by the ecstasy of the lovers, the (temporal) separation of body and soul. The action between the souls is one of giving life to and taking it away from each other.

In "The Extasie," the separation of body and soul and the process of interinanimation result in the soul's becoming "abler" than the two separate souls before; it becomes "pure" (65), which implies that it has achieved its aim to "advance" its state.[41] This advancement takes place while the bodies of the lovers are "dead," as in a tomb. The emblem of lovers in a tomb has been used to symbolize the alchemical opus, which is why "The Extasie" has been read in light of alchemy.[42] In an alchemical context, the processes in the tomb are not restricted to putrefaction, as they result in purification.[43]

In Donne's poem this purification is not limited to the soul/s alone. It is extended to a bystander who is introduced in stanzas six and seven in terms of an analogous process:

> If any, so by love refin'd,
> That he soules language understood,
> And by good love were grown all minde,
> Within convenient distance stood,
>
> He (though he knew not which soule spake,
> Because both meant, both spake the same)

Might thence a new concoction take,
And part farre purer than he came.

(21–28)

The concoction (that is, "perfection, refinement, purification") that takes place between the two souls is also transmitted to the listener who has "heard this dialogue of one" (73–74).[44]

A similar effect on the audience is shown in the ending of *Romeo and Juliet*. There, the site of death is, first and foremost, one of interaction between the lovers when Romeo and Juliet kill themselves: their ecstasy and union in death are based on their interaction while still alive. But the site of death also becomes a site of interaction with and of those who witness their death. At the end, their families erect the statues of the lovers as a sign of reconciliation.[45] Montague says, "For I will raise her statue in pure gold," to which Capulet responds, "As rich shall Romeo's by his lady's lie" (298, 302). They thereby also enact an exchange as each does not erect a statue for his own child but for his former enemy's: Montague for Juliet and Capulet for Romeo. The lovers' union in life as well as in death is therefore indicated by sepulchral statues.[46]

In *Romeo and Juliet*, as in "The Extasie," the effect of the death scene is thus modeled within the text itself. In both cases it is the effect of a similitude: while in the poem the speaker establishes the likeness of the lovers and the sepulchral statues, in the play we witness the "dismal scene" (IV.iii.19) of the lovers' death in the lifelikeness of dramatic action. In *Romeo and Juliet* as well as in "The Extasie" the lovers experience an ecstasy, which in the one case implies that they gain life by becoming one in death and that they become the protagonists of "their story of [. . .] woe" (V.iii.308), while in the other it means an interinanimation that results in an "abler soul" (43). In both texts, the lovers' fulfillment is shown to be an interaction with and in death, in each case linked to a specific site.

The Site of Death as a Poetic Parable

In "The Extasie" the lovers, who lie on the bank "like sepulchral statues," anticipate death, the moment and the place when and where the souls are liberated from the body. Their union is figuratively a foreshadowing of the time when they will actually be in the grave. There is a difference between the two states, even though it is small, which is observed by the witnessing lover, who hears "this dialogue of one," that is, the souls talking to each other as well as the poem itself. He "mark[s]" the lovers and "shall see / Small change, when we'are to bodies gone" (75–76).[47] The ecstasy of love thus appears as a rehearsal of death, which to the lover who stands "Within convenient distance" (24) is a very special *memento mori*. The situation is enhanced by the ambiguity of "to bodies gone": on the one hand, this phrase refers to the return of the lovers' souls to their bodies, which thus become the book in which we can read the mystery of love grown in the souls; on the other hand, it refers to the lovers' souls not really changing much from their ecstatic state, when they will have actually died and their human selves become corpses. In the first perspective, the lovers become a living monument; their living bodies are the book in which love is revealed,[48] and the reunion of body and soul evokes the final restoration from death at the end of the world;[49] in the second perspective, the lovers become something so entirely spiritual that anyone who is a "lover such as we" (73) will notice their celestial, rather than physical, state. Accordingly, Donne has his speaker present a double vision of life after death: one in which body and soul are transformed and reunited and another in which the soul is so refined that it leaves behind all material substance.

In "The Extasie," the lovers' becoming a monument has poetological implications. The likeness to death, which is brought about by the lovers' ecstasy, becomes a poetic likeness that is to provide insight into the nature of love and death.[50] By including an audience in the poem, Donne provides a link between the event and the poetic text. The site of death as a site of interaction is thus witnessed by readers who are to see and to remember. This is similar to the golden sepulchral statues, whose erection is announced at the end of *Romeo and Juliet*: still within the play, we are reminded to mark and remember the uniqueness as well as the parabolic nature of the lovers' reunion in death.

The transformation into the work of art that is in each case evoked adds a dimension to the reversal of the life-death relationship that takes place at the site of death. This transformation is an attempt to give a local and temporal habitation to the transition from a life that is death to a death that is life and where the *introitus in mortem* becomes an *exitus a morte*. As we have seen in "The Extasie," the site of death is the site of the poem itself, a notion that inevitably evokes the context of Shakespeare's sonnets and of *The*

Phoenix and Turtle. Whereas Donne, implicitly or explicitly, conceives of this added dimension in terms of the epitaph, which is a text that reflects on the lover's life and its transformation, Shakespeare's sonnets constantly refer to this life as the result of the poetic act itself. Whereas in "The Extasie" the living lovers are turned into a monument, in Shakespeare's sonnets it is the poem as monument that brings about the lovers' life.

Thus in Sonnet 18 the valley of the shadow of death is replaced with the site of the sonnet itself, in which there is life in death, a growing to (musical) time. Similarly, in *The Phoenix and Turtle* the poem appears as a funereal site and as "this urn" (65) (comparable to the "well-wrought urn" in "The Canonization"), in which a metamorphosis into the life of poetic rhythm takes place. Not only is the body transformed in the poem, but the poem itself may also present parts of the body, and in particular the head, as sites of death from which life may issue. An example is the "fairly common" image of the brain as a womb, which is quite unconventionally evoked in Sonnet 86, where the rival poet's "proud full sail of his great verse, / . . . did my ripe thoughts in my brain in-hearse, / Making their tomb the womb wherein they grew" (Duncan-Jones, *Sonnets*, 282n). Depending on whether "tomb" or "womb" is considered the object that is turned into something else, we get either an idea of the brain as a womb in which the thoughts grow but then die (because, as in Donne's "Deaths Duell," it is like a mother's womb, from which there is no *exitus a morte*) or an idea of the brain as a tomb in which there is nevertheless life and in which thoughts grow because they cannot go out.

In Sonnet 81, there are even two such sites of death, the eyes and the mouth. The poem begins by describing a situation not entirely unlike the monument scene in *Romeo and Juliet*, in which the speaker and his beloved addressee are envisaged as being alternatively living and dead: "Or I shall live, your epitaph to make; / Or you survive, when I in earth am rotten";[51] one of the differences from Romeo and Juliet's situation being the asymmetry of the relationship, consisting in the fact that the speaker will devote his life to the setting up of an epitaph, whereas the addressee will just go on living. This asymmetry leads to a shifting interaction. While the poet-speaker at first refers to the composition of an epitaph, that is, a commemorative text, he then replaces "epitaph" with "monument"—the difference being that the latter is the container of the dead person himself: "Your monument shall be my gentle verse." This difference may be conventionally neglected (in the light of the *exegi monumentum* topos, for example) since a monument also has a commemorative function, but to Shakespeare, who shows life within the monument in his plays, the distinction is marked. "When you entombed in men's eyes shall lie" clearly shows the replacement, which is also a result of the reading process ("Which eyes not yet created shall o'er-read"): reading the epitaph leads to an actual "in-hearsing" of the addressee in the eyes of the reader. This change implies a change from death to life, which is then stressed by changing the image of the monument from eyes to mouth:[52]

> And tongues to be your being shall rehearse,
> When all the breathers of this world are dead.
> You still shall live, such virtue hath my pen,
> Where breath most breathes, even in the mouths of men.[53]

The interaction that marks this site of death is a change from in-hearsing to re-hearsing, a pun that offers, as it were, Shakespeare's poetological program in a nutshell.[54]

The idea of the poem itself being the tomb and of the spectator or reader having power over the life of the dead is by no means alien to Donne, but it takes a somewhat different form. Among his verse letters to the Countess of Bedford, there is one that gives evidence of his particular preoccupation with the sites of death and the "dispersion in and from the *grave*, in which every dead man dyes over againe" ("Deaths Duell," 236). In the first, dedicatory part of the "Epitaph on Himselfe" the speaker addresses the Countess in a way that plays with the traditions of the tomb and the epitaph as a receptacle and a text documenting, as well as serving to ensure, the fame of the deceased:

> Madame,
> That I might make your Cabinet my tombe,
> And for my fame, which I love next my soule,
> Next to my soule provide the happiest roome,
> Admit to that place this last funerall Scrowle.
> Others by Testament give Legacies, but I
> Dying, of you doe beg a Legacie.[55]

The site of death is expressly regarded as a "case for the safe custody of jewels, or other valuables, letters, documents, etc.," that is, a "Cabinet"

(OED, *n*. 5.a.). The speaker thus identifies with his "Scrowle," since it is preserved by the Countess, becomes the basis of his fame. The "happiest roome" (implying the familiar pun on "stanza") is where the speaker wishes to see both his writing and his soul maintained after his death; it is a receptacle reserved, in neighboring compartments or drawers, for both worldly reputation and spiritual welfare.[56] The conventional flattery of dedicatory verse apart, it is quite remarkable that Donne represents the addressee as the one who ensures what the speaker will be. The giving (of the scroll) is in fact a getting (of fame and a happy room for the soul), an interaction that goes beyond the hopes for worldly preferment obtained in exchange for devoting one's literary skills to a noble patron.[57] This idea is then developed in the epitaph itself, addressed to readers in general:

Omnibus

My Fortune and my choice this custome break,
When we are speechlesse grown, to make stones speak,
Though no stone tell thee what I was, yet thou
In my graves inside see what thou art now: 10
Yet thou'art not yet so good, till death us lay
To ripe and mellow here, we'are stubborne Clay.
Parents make us earth, and soules dignify
Us to be glasse; here to grow gold we lie.
Whilst in our soules sinne bred and pamper'd is,
Our soules become wormeaten carkases;
So we our selves miraculously destroy.
Here bodies with lesse miracle enjoy
Such priviledges, enabled here to scale
Heaven, when the Trumpets ayre shall them exhale. 20
Heare this, and mend thy selfe, and thou mendst me,
By making me being dead, doe good to thee,
And thinke me well compos'd, that I could now
A last-sicke hour to syllables allow.

Right from the beginning the speaker draws attention to the uncommon nature of this epitaph. This is not the usual inscription on a tombstone or monument that tells us about the life of the person buried in the grave but rather has the dead himself speak.[58] All in all, this is less exceptional than it may appear, for Donne here varies another tradition, the *quod tu es, ego fui; quod ego sum, tu eris* of monumental inscriptions and murals.[59] The variation, however, is characteristic. His speaker does not say "As ye are now so once were we" but rather "As you are now so I am" or even "As you are now so I will be," for if we assume that the speaker is the same as the one of the dedicatory opening, he is still alive but anticipates his death. This is confirmed at the end of the poem, when the speaker refers to himself as "being dead" but simultaneously refers to the present moment, "now," in which he finds himself on his deathbed but still alive (in his "last-sicke hour") as the writer of this very epitaph. The poem serves as an example of the general observation made by the speaker of Donne's *Devotions*: "A sicke bed, is a grave; and all that the patient saies there, is but a varying of his owne *Epitaph*" (15).

This paradoxical inversion of states and stages can be elucidated in several ways. The first is the concept presented by Donne in the "Deaths Duell" sermon quoted earlier: if the world is but a common grave, the tomb makes us realize not just what we will be but also what we are, namely, dead. Furthermore, if death is neither the end nor yet immediately the "*introitus in vitam*, . . . an entrance into everlasting life," if it is some intermediary state in which we are temporally entombed, just as we were in our mother's womb and as we were in life, it is not absurd to assume that the dead person speaks ("Deaths Duell," 231). Thus the blending of the speaker as a person preparing for his death and the speaker as a person addressing us from the grave makes sense. In particular, the speaker presents an interaction between soul and body that undergoes a transformation between the moment of entombment and the moment when "the Trumpets ayre shall them [the bodies] exhale." The speaker describes the soul (in life) as a container in which sin is pampered and which accordingly decays, becomes "wormeaten"—another example of the world of the living being a grave. Ironically, this is called a "miraculous" process—miraculous indeed, for the soul is actually, as we have just read in the poem, created to "dignifie / Us to be glasse" (13–14).[60] By breeding sin during life on earth, it surprisingly manages to act against its very nature. This perversion is contrasted with the tomb, in which a change for the better takes place. Whereas we have unnaturally destroyed ourselves in life (destroyed our souls, by pampering sin), it is "lesse miracle" (18)—because it is natural—that the body is destroyed in the grave, that is, enjoys the same "priviledges" that (ironically, "miraculously") the soul did on earth. This destruction will enable the bodies "to scale / Heaven" when the world ends, for when they have become dust it will be able to undergo the alchemical process of exhalation set about by "the Trumpets ayre" (20).[61] While there is thus an inverted relation between the tomb and the grave of the world, there is also an implicit analogy between the tomb and the first of the three graves mentioned in "Deaths Duell," that is, the womb, for the grave is not just the site where the body dissolves but also a place where we lie "to grow gold" (14). Just as "we" means our souls when "we our selves miraculously destroy" in life, "we" means the souls when "here to grow gold we lie" in the grave. Accordingly, what the readers will "see" when they look into the grave is a very special *memento mori* that is not so much a reminder of one's final dissolution as the vision of a future state in which the dissolution of the body becomes a privilege, for it entails a ripening and mellowing of our selves to becoming "good" and "gold."[62]

This representation of the grave as not just a place where our bodies are turned to dust but also a place where we grow into a better substance takes us to the second way of explaining the characteristic inversion of states and stages.[63] We take note of the fact that the speaker plays a role, addressing first, prologuelike, his noble dedicatee but then "Omnibus," the audience in general. He speaks to us in the role of a dead man, for our benefit. We are reminded of Donne's portrait as a living man dressed up in his shroud. In the light of this speech, his earlier desire for "fame" turns out to be ironical, too, for there is nothing of worldly reputation, no telling of what the speaker is or was but rather a message about the time after death; his fame is thus truly a *"sermo hominum"* serving *"Omnibus"* rather than his own status.[64] At the end of the speech, which is to be heard ("Heare this") rather than read (the "Scrowle" then becomes a script for oral delivery), Donne's persona refers to its effect upon the audience: "Heare this, and mend thy selfe, and thou mendst me, / By making me being dead, do good to thee, / And thinke me well compos'd." Again the speaker and his verbal composition become one: he is "compos'd" in a triple sense—in being calmly prepared for death, in turning to earth (becoming "compost"), and in becoming a well-ordered poetic text.[65] We think that all three senses are implied when it comes to the complex interaction of a mutual mending of speaker and audience. It is the speaker's preparedness for death that serves as a model for us; it is his future/present state of turning into gold that gives us hope, and it is the poem itself that will do us good.

Joshua Scodel has pointed out that the mutuality of effect—it is not just the living who are to be improved but the dead as well—is utterly exceptional among poetic (and actual) epitaphs in early modern England.[66] He has ascribed this to a Catholic conviction still lingering with Donne at the time of composition that accepts or even demands prayers for the dead, who may thus be helped in their state of purgatory. We will come back to this but would first like to suggest another context, which in our view is (even) more pertinent. The cluster of words and concepts focusing on "mending," on thinking and acting, and on the interaction between the inhabitants of a world of death and ourselves as a living audience recalls Puck's epilogue to *A Midsummer Night's Dream*:[67]

> If we shadows have offended,
> Think but this, and all is mended,
> That you have but slumb'red here
> While these visions did appear.
> And this weak and idle theme,
> No more yielding but a dream,
> Gentles, do not reprehend.
> If you pardon, we will mend.
> And, as I am an honest Puck,
> If we have unearned luck
> Now to scape the serpent's tongue,
> We will make amends ere long;
> Else the Puck a liar call.
> So, good night unto you all.
> Give me your hands, if we be friends,
> And Robin shall restore amends.
> *[Exit.]*[68]

The verbal link between the two texts is enhanced by the similarity of the speakers' situations: Both address a general audience as if from the nether world, from the world of shadows. In each case there is an insurmountable gap between the speaker and his audience: the dramatic character belongs to a sphere as strictly separate from everyday life as the world of the dead is separate from the world of the living. What will happen if you mingle the two has been unforgettably shown by Shakespeare's and Donne's contemporaries Beaumont and Fletcher in *The Knight of the Burning Pestle*.

And yet the epilogue is a genre that is positioned on the very border between the two worlds:[69] Puck's outstretched hand, a sign of solidarity between the "shadows" and us, is to bridge the gap. The analogy between the transition from play world to real world and the transition from the world of the dead to the world of the living (or vice versa) is underlined by the fact that Puck evokes the prototypical simile of death, namely, sleep. When Puck says that we "have but slumbered here" while witnessing the play, his very expression "but slumbered" does not primarily mean that we should imagine having been asleep (while in fact we were awake). At least partly due to the fact that a similar collocation, "but sleepeth," is closely linked to Jesus's calling the dead back to life, Puck's words evoke the notion that we have been dead but this death has not really meant death but a sleep from which we will wake.[70] Paradoxically, however, Puck indicates that we are now returning to our waking life and simultaneously says "good night unto [us] all": we are to sleep or to die, now the life of the play has come to its end.[71] This is the very paradox Donne evokes in his "Deaths Duell" sermon, where he speaks of the "sleeping" in the grave, which is a delivery from "the deaths of this world," or as Sir Thomas Browne put it in *Religio Medici*: "We tearme sleepe a death, and yet it is waking that kils us, and destroyes those spirits that are the house of life."[72] Puck, as one of the spirits belonging to that site of sleep or death, or house of life, the "little room confining mighty men," will disappear at the very moment when he has spoken the epilogue, but he announces that he will come to life again.[73] Accordingly, Donne's "*exitus a morte*, [which] is but *introitus in mortem*," has its exact parallel on the stage, where the exit of an actor is but a "going in" (compare Romeo's "going in the vault" [V.iii.275]) and where the outside may always become an inside and vice versa—analogous to "in mortality" and "immortality" being, as it were, the same thing, composed of the same "syllables."[74]

Just as Donne's sickbed is a liminal site where what the patient says is "a varying of his owne *Epitaph*," that is, a site which "is a grave," and our "nights bed is a *Type* of the *grave*," the epilogue marks the grave of the dramatic characters' lives, while the play is the shadow (or "type") of death (and life) (*Devotions*, 15). This notion of the epilogue's marking the transition from life to death and vice versa is found in *The Phoenix and Turtle* as well, where the epitaph-like Threnos is announced as "chorus" to the "tragic scene" of the Phoenix and the Dove (52). The idea of the epilogue as a speech marking such a transition is by no means restricted to Shakespeare, however. We see it, for example, in Shakespeare's and Donne's contemporary, Thomas Dekker, whose "Epilogue at Court," which concludes *Old Fortunatus* (1600), asks the Queen to revive the players whose lives end with the ending of the play:

> O deere Goddesse,
> Breathe life in our nombd spirits with one smile,
> And from this cold earth, we with liueley soules
> Shal rise like men (new-borne) and make heau'n sound
> With Hymes sung to thy name.[75]

In anticipation of that kind of death, the prologue to *The Shoemaker's Holiday*, "*pronounced before the Queen's Majesty*," presents the actors as being positioned on the verge of life and death, and asking the Queen for her life-giving grace:

> our hap is such
> That to ourselves ourselves no help can bring,
> But needs must perish if your saint-like ears,
> Locking the temple where all mercy sits,
> Refuse the tribute of our begging tongues.
> Oh, grant, bright mirror of true chastity,
> From those life-breathing stars your sun-like eyes
> One gracious smile; for your celestial breath
> Must send us life, or sentence us to death.[76]

The analogy to the Last Judgment is obvious, with the Queen as the ruler of the audience in the position of God, whose mercy is implored. The liminal texts (prologues/epilogues) enhance the ubiquitous simile of the world as a stage (or life as a play) by including the transition to the afterlife. In Dekker's case, the interaction is limited to the sovereign's deciding about the fates of the shadows, who will be restored to life if they happen to elicit "One gracious smile."

In Donne and Shakespeare, the conceit is more complex. Apart from the fact that it is not just the one privileged person (the Countess of Bedford or the Queen) but *Omnes*, or the audience in general, who are addressed and involved, the issue is not just one of the speaker's finding grace but also one of giving and taking, of "mending" and a mutual influence (Scodel,

English Poetic Epitaph, 126). Puck's outstretched hand also signals an interaction and exchange rather than simply the grace given to the dead by the divine audience. Shakespeare similarly evokes such an exchange in the epilogue to *All's Well* when he has the King, who is now a beggar (that is, when he has put off the part he played in life), say, "Ours be your patience then, and yours our parts / Your gentle hands lend us, and take our hearts."[77] Apart from the fact that Patience is proverbially linked to the *monument*, this appears as a version of the *ego sum quod tu eris* topos, in which the two sides are shown to profit from each other.[78]

In the case of Puck, the actor's "mending" will be due to the audience's "pardon" ("If you pardon, we will mend"), which on one level suggests an improvement of the actors' performance if they are gracefully given a chance to perform again. On another level, evoked by the life-stage analogy, however, the epilogue alludes to a mutual mending of actors and audiences in the aftermath of the play. Robin's promise to "restore amends"[79] primarily means that he will "give back"[80] amends; that is, not only is he the one who needs pardon and promises to "make amends," but he will also give back those amends or improvement, implying that it is we who will mend, too.[81] Accordingly, his phrase also rings with an echo from the *Book of Common Prayer*, "Restore thou them that be penitent."[82] This mutuality of improvement is corroborated by the facts that not only will the audience's pardon allow the mending of future performances but also that our thinking will bring about the mending of the performance just witnessed; that is to say, this amending refers to the actors as well as the audience: "Think but this, and all is mended / That you have but slumbered here."[83] The prologuelike Chorus to *Henry V* similarly tells us to "piece out" the "imperfections" of the actors "by our thoughts" while gently hearing the play: the "pardon" the Chorus asks for and the mending of what we see on the stage are realized by our own imaginations. If we look at the role assigned to the audience in the prologues and epilogues mentioned earlier, it is partly that of the strict judge who is asked for pardon, partly that of the patient authority who is promised improvement, and partly that of a coactor who will bring about the mending himself and participate in the transformation. Donne assigns all of these roles to his interlocutors as well.

Donne's "Epitaph on Himselfe" is, or so it seems, more straightforwardly instructive:

> Heare this, and mend thyself, and thou mend'st me,
> By making me being dead, do good to thee,
> And think me well compos'd . . .

The listener is asked to mend himself as a result of the *memento mori* he has just heard. By doing so, however, he mends the person to whom he has listened. This is where we come back to the suggestion that the poem presents a remnant or an imaginative transformation of Donne's earlier Catholic convictions by evincing the notion of the living improving the fate of the dead by praying for them.[84] Apart from the fact that Donne, even in his most official function as dean of St. Paul's, would have found the wish to pray for the dead understandable, though scripture does not warrant such a prayer,[85] the speaker of the "Epitaph on Himselfe" does not actually ask his audience to pray for him. The mending of the speaker by the audience consists in the listener's mending himself; it is quite similar to what we hear in Puck's epilogue to *A Midsummer Night's Dream* and the Chorus as prologue in *Henry V*: just as we are asked to "piece out" the "imperfections" of the actor "with our thoughts," so we are asked to mend the speaker and ourselves and "think him well composed." Thinking good of the dead will make us better and will also make the dead better than they were, putting us in a position of the one who will "be the first / To see our best side, not our worst."[86]

In both Shakespeare and Donne, the notion of faults and shortcomings to overcome is closely linked with the notion of imaginative art and composition, and both are linked with death. Thus Hippolyta perceptively remarks, "It must be your imagination then," when she responds to Theseus's observation about the imperfect actors of *Pyramus and Thisbe*: "The best in this kind are but shadows; and the worst are no worse, if imagination amend them" (V.i.205–6). Even here we see the connotation of death in the reference to "shadows" that may be "amended." What happens after death can, to the human mind, at best be the matter of an imaginative *compositio loci* evoked by a site of death such as the grave, the tomb, the sickbed;[87] we see this in the speaker's playing the role of a dead man in "Epitaph on Himselfe" and, to give just one other example, in the speaker of the Holy Sonnet "At the round earth's" presenting the "imagin'd corners" of the world in his vision of the end of days, which comes to focus on "this lowly ground" where he presumably lies; the sickbed as the entry into death is the counterpart to the site where God "came to breath into *Man* the breath of life . . . [and] found him flat upon the ground" (*Devotions*, 15).

Toward the end of *The Tempest*, Prospero announces that "every third thought / Shall be my grave."[88] It is quite in keeping with this announcement that in his epilogue he presents himself in some state of bondage that he hopes is intermediate as he asks the audience, "But release me from my bands / With the help of your good hands." The situational context identifies this intervention as the peal of applause, while at the same time the notion of prayer at the point of transition to the world of death is evoked:

And my ending is despair,
Unless I be reliev'd by prayer,
Which pierces so, that it assaults
Mercy itself, and frees all faults.
As you from crimes would pardon'd be,
Let your indulgence set me free.

In particular, the use of the word "indulgence" has led to the interpretation of the epilogue as an injunction to pray for a soul in purgatory.[89] This is by no means certain since the speaker does not unambiguously present himself as "dead" but wishes to prevent a death in despair. Nor does he present his state as that of cleansing fire. What seems certain, however, is that the speaker desires to be set free, that is, finds himself in a state from which he has to be delivered. "This bare island" is, or may become, a site of death, but this site is also, as an image of the stage, a site of life. Prospero's final exit is thus both an "*exitus a morte*" and an "*introitus in mortem*," but in each case it is presented as a simile evoking the "power to give us an *issue* and deliverance, even then when wee are brought to the jawes and teeth of death, and to the lippes of that whirlepoole, the grave. And so in this acceptation, this *exitus mortis*, this *issue of death* is *liberatio a morte, a deliverance from death*" ("Deaths Duell," 230).

2. "Nothing like the Sun": Transcending Time and Change in Donne's Love Lyrics and Shakespeare's Plays

CATHERINE GIMELLI MARTIN

> Where's that palace whereinto foul things
> Sometimes intrude not? Who has that breast so pure . . . ?
> *The Tragedy of Othello*

Kathryn Kremen defines the Western conception of the *hieros gamos* (sacred marriage) as a way of imagining the "sexual union of man and woman on earth" to be a prefiguration of "the hypostatical union in body and soul of man and the Godhead in heaven."[1] Even completely nonreligious love lyrics such as Shakespeare's Sonnet 116 often reflect this idealized vision of sexuality: "[N]o impediment to the marriage of true minds" exists for soul mates whose love conquers age, time, and every other barrier. Donne's love lyrics alternatively express this ideal in spiritual as well as in secular terms, but both poets pose significant challenges to Jonathan Dollimore's claim that the Western love lyric inevitably exalts mutability. Yet the poets themselves are mutable: Donne's imaginative efforts to transcend time and change seem to accompany his monogamous maturity, while Shakespeare's mature period produces new and far darker insights into the male desire for unchanging love. Quite possibly influenced by Montaigne, Shakespeare's middle and late tragedies frequently represent this desire as a deluded and potentially fatal quest.[2] His critique is perhaps most obvious in *Othello*, where, from the moment the tragic hero hails his reunion with Desdemona as a miraculous escape from chance and time, he begins to go astray. After their joint deliverance from the storm, he proclaims that "My soul hath her content so absolute / That not another comfort like to this / Succeeds in unknown fate," and so to die now " 'Twere . . . to be most happy" (II.i.190–92, 188–89). This eerie foreshadowing of Othello's fatal end is produced not only by the audience's awareness of Iago's plotting but also by Desdemona's rejection of her husband's wish to stop time. Representing a healthier, growth-oriented attitude toward love, she instead prays, "The heavens forbid / But that our loves and comforts should increase / Even as our days do grow" (II.i.192–94).[3]

Donne's mature poems side much more closely with Othello in wishing to transcend not just the "rags of time" ("The Sunne Rising," 10) but also any resemblance to "dull sublunary lovers love" ("A Valediction Forbidding Mourning," 13).[4] This half-wistful, half-boastful hope is countered only in his devotional poems, which frequently confess his inability to maintain constancy to himself, much less to his fellows or to God; yet even here, change is clearly his enemy, not a fact of life, still less a source of celebration as his libertine lyrics preach. In "The Litanie," very like Othello, the speaker longs to die "To this world, ere this world doe bid us goe" (180), making a premature departure that would purge or at least "rectifie those Labyrinths" of our minds and hearts so "That beauty, paradises flower / For physicke made, from poison be exempt" (218, 237–38). By this means all beautiful, earthly things would be purified in the inviolable "palace" that Iago (rightly for once) declares incompatible with life in this world. Yet Iago's remark is partly disingenuous since his real purpose is to make Othello yearn for the spotless life and perfect "content" that his "poisonous" bride has supposedly destroyed (II.i.195). He thus urges Othello to contain or purge, not multiply or expand, the "beautiful" but all too carnal passions so that, as Donne hopes, "Natures nothing, be not nothing" in the hereafter ("Litanie," 241). Earthly love is not thereby ruled out as an image or a promise of heavenly "bloom," but it *is* limited to a still and full inversion of nothing, a self-enclosed point in the divine circumference of Being. Under Iago's malign influence, Othello begins to worship his image of an eternal palace guarded by those "ever-burning lights above" in "yond marble heavens," or what Plato would call a "moving image of eternity" (*Timaeus* 37d). Hypnotically repeating Iago's own words (III.iii.460, 463), he lights the "flaming minister" or torch that will lead him to where he will extinguish Desdemona's all-too-imperfect "light." Fatuously mistaking this murder for a service to the "chaste stars" above, he "quenches" or entombs his pathetically innocent bride in the "monumental alabaster" of her own flesh, thereby fulfilling a tragic "cause" very far from the just one he believes it to be (V.ii.1–5, 8).

Donne's "Litanie" can be read as deliberately renouncing the message of his earlier libertine lyrics, poems like "Womans constancy," "The Indifferent," and most of his elegies. There the free-thinking "Jack" Donne repeatedly mocks both pre- and postmarital chastity as a mere "fetish" or an addiction to unthinking custom, urbanely defending his right and even duty to change his affections as fast as the fickle females he admires and seeks. Elegy XVII follows this pattern until its very end, when the speaker suddenly craves "stillness" or constancy, not change. If Robert Ellrodt is right about its early date of composition, Donne quite possibly had this end in sight all along, yet the poem itself at first offers little overt warning as to his abrupt change of heart.[5] It begins in the same libertine line of thought that Elegie III consistently maintains: since "waters stincke soone, if in one place they bide," fluidity or "Change" (the third elegy's subtitle) not only prevents stagnation but also provides an indispensable "nursery / Of musicke, joy, life, and eternity" (31, 35–36). Elegie XVII opens by extending this analogy to the heavens themselves: "The heavens rejoyce in motion, why should I / Abjure my so much lov'd variety, / And not with many youth and love divide?" (1–3). Here the transience of all earthly things is actually part of their glory, as the seemingly stable sun itself teaches. Its free-roaming chariot shows that "Pleasure is none, if not diversifi'd," for Apollo sits securely "in the chaire of light" only to "flame into what else soever doth seem bright" on earth. In the higher heavens as well, our sun is never "contented at one Signe to Inne" but "ends his year and with a new beginnes" (4–8). In general, then, both elegies argue that "All things doe willingly in change delight, / The fruitfull mother of our appetite," and that all humans once acknowledged this fact in the "golden age" of Saturn (9–10). Then the rule of "liberty" prevailed as our happy "Syres . . . / . . . held plurality of loves no crime!" (49, 37–38). Yet in Elegy XVII these conventional libertine apologies conclude with a major qualification. As Ellrodt and other critics surveyed in the Donne *Variorum* recognize, the poet now contemplates exchanging "plurality" for constancy, perhaps in anticipation of lifelong monogamy with Ann More.[6]

This sudden reversal of lifestyle is ironically set up with a libertine boast just before the poem's conclusion: "Onely some few strong in themselves and free / Retain the seeds of antient liberty,"

> Amongst which troop although I am the least
> Yet equall in perfection with the best,
> I glory in subjection of his [Love's] hand,
> Nor ever did decline his least command.
>
> (61–62, 67–70)

Love's "hand" here refers to the fickle, free-roaming Cupid, who, once the age of Saturn expired, sadly lost his "daring armes," his roving "eyes," "awfull wings," and "sinewy bow," to foolish "opinion," "A monster in no certain shape attir'd" at first, but soon after a stern dictator of "manners and laws to nations" (50–59). Even now, however, and "in spight of modern censures," the speaker and a "few" other daring souls continue "avowing [Cupid] / Their Soveraigne, all service him allowing," and obey his "message[s]" in "whatever forme" they take (61–66, 71). This "vow" of unflagging obedience, even bondage to his sovereign, precipitates Donne's abrupt *volta*, which suddenly hails an entirely new kind of freedom that will end his long and well-"loved service" to his former master (74). Like the speaker's previous "allegiance," this new service is nevertheless described as natural, a simple result of growing maturity: because all earthly things are subject to change, bondage to the classical or golden age Cupid is equally "temporary," ending when "firmer age returnes our liberties" (47, 75–76).

Here one kind of freedom naturally cancels another; free-ranging love may be lovely for awhile, but it inhibits new kinds of "messages" from women capable and worthy of sexual fidelity. From this new perspective, mutability itself might become a fetish, an addiction to whimsical love that denies one's innate "right" to emotional peace. Since for everything there is a season, stability now represents the return of liberty, not its loss, for the mature speaker foresees that soon he

> Shall not so easily be to change dispos'd
> Nor to the art of severall eyes obeying,
> But beauty with true worth securely weighing,
> Which being found assembled in some one
> Wee'l leave her ever, and love her alone.
>
> (78–82)

The elegy's final couplet obviously represents something of a crux, which several manuscripts solve by replacing the word "leave" with "love." That would certainly make sense in light of the poem's stated goal of loving one woman and "her alone," yet the *Variorum* points out that the original word was probably "leave" and that even if it is left standing, the meaning remains essentially the same: Donne proposes forever to "leave" change, here implicitly personified as the conventionally fickle woman whose opposite is the solid beauty and truth he must and will faithfully love.[7]

Like the North Star in Shakespeare's Sonnet 116, faithful love was often imagined as a stable pole or an emotional anchor, which "A Valediction" famously turns into the central foot or axis of its two-footed compass. Although this poem, too, is not without its cruxes, readers almost universally agree that the central foot guiding its twin to make a perfect circle represents the female lover or wife, most probably Ann herself, who frequently endured the "mournful" separations condoled in the poem. It thus bestows great honor and importance upon this "some one" of "true worth" who stays behind as the wandering foot revolves around her without ever truly departing, joined to her at their central, upright axis. Yet it also binds her to staggering responsibilities: while her mate remains free to circle their figurative globe, she must supply the gravitation that grounds and guides their companionate marriage. In more philosophical terms, this makes her analogous to the Platonic world soul, sometimes symbolized as the root or tree of earthly life, the "crown" of which is the divine flower of godlike, usually male, perfection. Traditionally, the world soul guides the seasonal world of becoming and change, while the changeless deity reciprocally guides it and perfects their circle. Much like the two legs of Donne's compass, then, these mythic partners perform a semipagan version of the *hieros gamos*, achieving the combination of stillness and motion that in the *Timaeus* at once imitates and anticipates eternity. In "A Valediction," this balance can be sustained only if the female partner recognizes her "natural" limit, which is at once to follow and to anchor the moving leg completing their circle. Much like Dante's Beatrice, she "stands" in the virginal center or "fixt foot" of their universe, "hearken[ing] after" her mate until he "comes home" to its still point (27–31).

In "A Lecture upon the Shadow" this point is alternatively figured as the full sun or circle of noon, so that just as the two-legged compass moves only to close or complete its perfect form, the lovers of "A Lecture" obey different motions until, much like the two hands on a clock, they meet upright at noon.[8] Both love lyrics thus at once recognize and cancel the Petrarchan convention of prolonging intense emotion through suffering, denial, and only temporarily reawakened hope, the topos that Dollimore considers central to Western love literature.[9] Both poems recognize the sufferings and "shadows" that have intensified the lovers' devotion and longed-for reunion, but like Shakespeare's Sonnet 116, they imagine these woes as illusory and "immature" in comparison to their regular revolution around the stable center formed by mutual love. In this essentially geocentric erotic universe, the male sun circles the female earth until they achieve a perfect alignment, eclipsing all below and replacing it with a transcendent heaven-on-earth. This erotic ideal implicitly confirms Marjorie Nicolson's thesis that like many of his contemporaries, Donne bitterly resented the "breaking" of the perfect, heavenly circles long thought to enclose the earth and align it with the highest, empyreal sphere.[10] Unlike the irregular "new astronomy" protested in Donne's *Anniversaries*, his ideal lovers imitate the perfect motions of Elizabeth Drury's saintly soul and become new and more circular suns and moons to each other. As in "A Valediction," their circles protect them from emotional pain, including the literally "unspeakable" pain of separation, placing them in a higher orbit where all "trepidation" is harmless or "innocent" of disturbance (5–6, 11–12). Transient things may have "elemented" their love, but unlike "dull sublunary lovers," they have become "so much refin'd" as no longer to know what their elements are (13–18). What they do know is that their new "matter" is some quintessential substance surpassing the highest element of fire itself: "Like gold to ayery thinnesse beate," it fixes or joins their single or uniform soul even when their bodies remain apart (24).

Despite all this "centering," no sexual pun on the woman's "Centrique part" seems intended (as it is in *Loves Progress*, 36) since the spiritual "mystery" of their union hallows their love, much as the "ridle" of the Phoenix does in "The Canonization": "we two being one, are it. / So, to one neutrall thing both sexes fit, / Wee dye and rise the same." If they cannot "live by love," they can at least "dye" for it, reborn in some erotic literary "heaven" (23–28). Precisely like the lovers of "The Good-morrow," this couple exults in the perfect complementarity or "mirroring" that Othello longs for but fails to achieve and that leads to his fatal rejection of the real world of difference, accident, and uncertainty.[11] Yet Donne refuses to see anything fatal in his need for a totalizing love capable of conquering flux itself:

> Loves riddles are, that though thy heart depart,
> It stayes at home, and thou with losing savest it:
> But wee will have a way more liberall,
> Then changing hearts, to joyne them, so wee shall
>   Be one, and one anothers All.
>
>   ("Loves infinitenesse," 29–33)

Here, as in "A Valediction," love allows the partners to regard difference or change as an illusion, merely an imperfect apprehension of their expansion and contraction into a higher substance. Like the meek, they inherit the earth by losing themselves in a greater whole, so that, like the pair in "The Sunne Rising," neither dawn nor any other change threatens them with separation. Instead, it marks an endless rebeginning, not a "nowhere" of loss but an everywhere of plenitude within the perfect circle of a Ptolemaic lovers' "heaven." In this case, however, their comfortable circle has become technically smaller, not "infinite," but still "all" as the sun outside revolves around them, while inside their joint principality she becomes "all States," "all Princes," he (21).

"A Lecture" varies this motif by asking the sun not to shrink its orbit but actually to "Stand still." Exchanging dawn for noon, the lovers nevertheless bask in the same "full constant light" that can at once eclipse the sun's power and figuratively reenact the birth of light and, by extension, love's divine fire. Donne's recurrent light imagery clearly connects the first fruition of love in "The Sunne Rising" to its maturity in "A Lecture": both couples displace the sun's motion and, with it, time and change, so any deviation from their new circle "is night" ("Lecture," 25, 26). Like the reunited "twins" of "A Valediction" or the intertwined "eye-beames" of the lovers in "The Extasie," master and pupil in "A Lecture" achieve a "quintessence" of light dispelling all the shadows, clouds, or impermanent illusions of their previous lives (7). In the "brave clearnesse" of their noon, all their former "disguises" and "cares," dark doubts and stratagems, evaporate before "the high'st degree" of solar perfection, the all-seeing (and seen) sun, from which they must never depart (8–12). Within this charmed circle, they neither decline "westwardly" with the sun nor experience its afternoon shadows, which aptly represent afterthoughts, new fears, lies, or compromises. Forever maintaining a vertical and upright relation to heaven nevertheless means confining themselves to a space and time beyond whose "first minute" lies utter eclipse (19, 26), a fearful decline from their lofty pinnacle.

"The Good-morrow" supplements this "dreame" of full being by depicting newly awakened lovers casting off their slow-growing, shadowy past in favor of a newly enlightened present (7). Technically an aubade like "The Sunne Rising," this poem also testifies to their escape from the equivalent of Plato's cave and entry into an infinitely larger, yet (once again) smaller sphere.[12] In their smallest space, "our waking soules" see only each other, not "out of feare" but because "love, all love of other sights controules, / And makes one little roome, an every where" (9–11). Yet, as in the related love lyrics discussed earlier, this self-enclosure is not just a contraction but also a simultaneous expansion. Enlightening and improving not just their "little roome" but the globe itself as well, the pair now forms "two better hemispheares / Without sharpe North, without declining West," a world benignly limited to the eastern land of the rising sun and the sunny climate of the benign south (17–18). Very like the two legs of Donne's famous compass, they thereby create a space so perfectly circular and "so alike, that none doe slacken, none can die." Like the sun reflecting light onto the moon, one lover sees "my face in thine eye, [as] thine in mine appears," so that once more, no earthly shadows can intervene (15, 21).

A merely literary (as opposed to biographical) essay cannot fully explain Donne's apparently sudden departure from amorous changeability, but in light of the poems considered earlier, it is not unreasonable to suppose that, like Shakespeare's Benedick in *Much Ado about Nothing*, he unwittingly wanted constancy all along. Before finding "some one" he can trust, Benedick contentedly remains an attractive lady's man committed to bachelorhood not just by natural vigor and love of "sport" but also by fears of female fickleness and potential infidelity. This fear of love provides one of Shakespeare's great themes not just in innumerable sonnets but also notably in *King Lear*, as Stanley Cavell has so eloquently shown.[13] Poems like Donne's "The Indifferent" exorcise these apprehensions by praising inconstancy, for the most obvious way to remain uncommitted is by pursuing "loose" or libertine women, an especially safe option if they are already married, like the female speaker of "Confined Love." One manuscript identifies her as "the worthiest of all my lov my virtuous Mrs P" (Patrides, *John Donne*, 82n1), but even if that attribution is incorrect, she is clearly a spouse questioning why she should not "shine" on many men when the "Sunne, Moone, or Starres" are not "by law forbidden, / To smile where they list, or lend away their light?" (8–9). For if neither of these "lords" of the universe nor the birds and beasts below are "chidden" for roaming (10), why should fair women be "lock[ed] up" any more than "faire ship[s]" or "faire houses" (15–18)? The "correct" libertine answer is that custom decrees it even though "nature" dictates otherwise, and nature should be followed: "Good is not good, unlesse / A thousand it possesse" (19–20). Unlike God, Mother Nature says go and be fruitful unto all.

Still another strategy is suggested in Donne's Holy Sonnet III, which claims that he knowingly pursued unattainable objects of desire, women perhaps like the unwilling virgin of "The Flea" or like the originally aloof and mistrustful Beatrice of *Much Ado about Nothing*. Alternatively, Donne's sonnet may simply allude to the conventional Petrarchan lady who demands the tribute of endless "sighes and teares," which he belatedly laments spending "in vaine" on "my idolatry" of such females. He seems especially bitter that these tears, unlike the "past joys" of other sinners—drunkards, thieves, lechers, and boasters, who can at least recall past pleasure as some "reliefe / Of comming ills"—were not only joyless but entirely "waste[d]" on cold mistresses. "The Indifferent" nicely sums up another avoidance strategy in boasting that—again very like Shakespeare's Benedick—the speaker can enjoy "all ladies" (I.i.119), but he pursues only women whom he is already planning to reject or exchange for another partner. In "The Indifferent," this point is driven home by Donne's "Venus," who warns that "perversely" faithful women will be punished by loving only unfaithful men (27). Shakespeare's Beatrice seems to have learned this lesson well, as she distrusts all men and despises the "curse" of marriage after being cruelly deserted by the flirtatious Benedick in some previous phase of their courtship. Now forewarned, she tartly justifies her taunting of the returned war hero by complaining that when he last lent her his heart and she "doubly" returned his affection, she found that he had "won it of me with false dice": his heart remained "single" (II.i.263–65). This remark obliquely alludes to giving or receiving the losing throw of "snake eyes" in dice, two singles, since Roman times, the "dog's throw." A little earlier in Act II the masked Beatrice revenges this "singling" of her by replying to the masked Benedick's request concerning his reputation that he is a mere "jester" in whom "none but libertines delight" since his "commendation is not in his wit, but in his villainy" (131–34).

How seriously we should take Beatrice's retorts is difficult to gauge; she is partly paying back Benedick's most recent accusations of disdainfulness and borrowed wit, the latter (he insultingly claims) cribbed from the crude "comic book," a *Hundred Merry Tales* (II.i.123–25). In any case, it is her attack (not his) that strikes home; he immediately repeats her taunts, with embellishments, to Don Pedro, indignantly describing her as the very embodiment of "Lady Disdain," the name by which he defensively greets her as soon as they meet (I.i.112). Benedick thus makes himself, not Beatrice (as Don Pedro believes her to be: II.i.224–26), the wronged party, claiming that he would gladly travel to the ends of the earth to prove her a harpy, essentially the same voyage the speaker of Donne's "Goe and catche a falling star" proposes to "prove" woman's universal untrustworthiness:

> Will your grace command me any service to the world's end? I will go on the slightest errand now to the Antipodes that you can devise to send me on, I will fetch you a toothpicker now from the furthest inch of Asia, bring you the length of Prester John's foot, fetch you a hair off the Great Cham's beard, do you any embassage to the Pygmies, rather than hold three words conference with this harpy. You have no employment for me? [II.i.249-57].

Comic hyperboles of this sort are relatively commonplace during the period, but the fact that both Shakespeare and Donne refer almost exclusively to mythic "proofs" of their conviction that women are faithless harpies or hypocrites suggests similarities not just in technique but also in perspective. Benedick promises to bring back the "length of Prester John's foot"; Donne vows to deliver the knowledge of "who cleft the Divels foot"; Benedick offers to travel to "the furthest inch of Asia," Donne to "Ride ten thousand daies and nights"; Benedick volunteers to visit the "Pygmies," Donne to visit the singing "Mermaides"; and both would make these voyages to "keep off envies stinging"—the evil mythically represented by harpies. True, Donne alone claims the impossibility of finding anything that can "advance an honest minde" in fair women—and Beatrice would undoubtedly be considered fair "were [she] not possessed with a fury"—but even more than women's dubious chastity, Benedick seems to resent the lack of "fair" or unclouded, unbiased minds in the "fair sex," another by no means uncommon opinion (I.i.182–83).

The close link between libertinism and misogyny or at least misogynistic fears of female betrayal or "disdain" is thus clearly of mutual interest to both poets, who differ chiefly in their methods of resolving these fears. Throughout the first half of *Much Ado*, Shakespeare comically uses Benedick to embody "typical" male weaknesses, particularly his "hard heart" or desire to be beloved without loving in return (I.i.118–21). Nor is this strictly personal; he mercilessly twits his infatuated friend Claudio for wondering whether worthy women can be "bought" at any price rather than, like a good bachelor, "wear[ing] his cap with suspicion, as he does" (173, 189): "That a woman conceived me, I thank her; that she brought me up, I likewise give her most humble thanks; but that I will have a recheat winded in my forehead, or hang my bugle in an invisible baldrick, all women shall pardon me. Because I will not do them the wrong to mistrust any, I will do myself the right to trust none; and the fine is (for which I may go the finer), I will live a bachelor" (227–34). His fears of cuckoldry are so obvious here that his main difference from the speaker of Donne's libertine lyrics is that Benedick wants nothing at all to do with the blind Cupid of Elegy XVII except perhaps to challenge him to a duel or hang his image on the door of a brothel (36–39, 240–41). Yet he is by no means blind to beauty or even, as the audience soon intuits, to Beatrice's somewhat malicious verbal charms; this lady's man protesteth too much fully to be believed. If he were naturally impervious or promiscuous, he might be more circumspect, just as, if Donne were a natural-born libertine, he might have profited better by feigning romantic notions of undying love than by paying so much homage to the fashionable male cult of inconstancy.

In most respects, then, the semi-insecure cynic who speaks Donne's harshest *Songs and Sonets* and Shakespeare's Benedick are nearly identical. Shakespeare sets up the latter for a comic fall wittily but tenuously warded off by Donne's persona, who similarly flaunts his clever avoidance of commitment. Just as Donne predicts his conversion in Elegy XVII, moreover, Benedick's friends predict his turnabout once he is assured that Beatrice secretly loves him.[14] Differing experiences of life or other external influences nevertheless cause Shakespeare and Donne to develop very different appraisals of mutability: Donne's major love lyrics eloquently defend the eternal, mutual commitment abandoned in most of Shakespeare's later sonnets, which, like Sonnet 138, reject the ideal of Sonnet 116 in favor of accepting the uncertainties of lying with those who lie.[15] Benedick hardly looks forward to sharing that fate, but the plot of *Much Ado* does force him to abandon his desire for secure, "untainted" bachelorhood and adopt far more liberal attitudes toward instability and change. He enters into marriage with Beatrice without any promises or other guarantees that his reputation will never be sullied by the infidelity he so obviously fears in advising Claudio against taking his sudden "leap of faith." Claudio at first simply avoids confronting such fears, but, once ignited, they produce drastic personality changes with potentially tragic consequences. As in *Othello*, these "typical" masculine fears prove groundless, thereby implying that male jealousy is a more potent and likelier danger than female infidelity. This point is particularly evident in *Much Ado*, which provides far more circumstantial and "ocular" evidence against the innocent Hero than there actually is against Desdemona. By this means both plays variously, if effectively, plead for reasonable doubt or uncertainty as necessary ingredients of strong, enduring, and charitable relationships.

Much Ado "proves" this necessity by placing poor Hero in a situation where two men very close to her, Don Pedro and Claudio, are certain that they have seen her passionate midnight meeting with some unknown secret lover. Hero survives mainly because she had not yet married Claudio or "destroyed" his reputation, while the equally innocent Desdemona dies on the basis of incredibly flimsy, hearsay evidence, and Cassio's mere possession of her handkerchief. Taken as a whole, these plays stress the wisdom of suspending jealous doubt by demonstrating the peculiar unreliability of majority opinion: everyone but Othello and the pseudo-"honest" Iago affirms Desdemona's innocence, everyone but Beatrice believes in Hero's guilt, and no one but the fool, Dogberry, really gets the facts right.[16] True, Beatrice's conviction is partly supported by the friar called in to marry Hero, who finds some "proof" of innocence in her swoon, but neither he nor Beatrice has any real means of explaining how or why both Don Pedro and Claudio could be "honestly" wrong in accusing her. Supporting Beatrice therefore strongly tests both Benedick's commitment to her and his reformed male psychology, his newly acquired questioning of the all-too-common assumption that all fair women are liable to sexual infidelity regardless of upbringing, character, or demonstrated values. This assumption does much of the dirty work in Othello's tragedy, but Benedick flatly rejects it as he reluctantly but resolutely accepts the sharp price Beatrice imposes upon her love: to champion her cousin Hero by challenging his former best friend and comrade, Claudio, to a duel. Although the audience's knowledge of Hero's innocence and Don John's scheme seems to justify this abrupt about-face, the strong element of pure luck in the plot also makes his sacrifice very real: the duel would have proceeded, and Benedick or Claudio been killed had not the utterly incompetent Dogberry and his illiterate watchmen "miraculously" apprehended Don John's main accomplice, Borachio.

Borachio's oral confession serves a crucial function in invalidating the seemingly flawless "ocular" proof of Hero's infidelity, which in turn validates Benedick's apparently groundless but, by that very measure, almost Christian and certainly "unseen" faith in both cousins. Yet, while Borachio's revelation that he and Hero's unwitting waiting woman Margaret, dressed in Hero's clothes, staged the seduction of "Hero," should remind us that sight is a much less reliable organ than generally believed, it actually proves nothing about Beatrice beyond her loyalty to Hero and her innate resistance to the unjust social power of false accusation. In regard to Benedick, however, the same results are not guaranteed: events suggest that he should maintain his faith in a woman whose kinship-loyalty will probably extend to her husband, but, otherwise, there is no resolution, no plighting of unbreakable troths or perfect conjunctions such as Donne delights in imagining. Quite the opposite: Beatrice and Benedick end up complaining of being tricked into loving each other, as they partly are—or at least tricked *out* of their proud resistance to one another's attractions—until written proof of their affections emerges. Even then, Benedick does not so much affirm faith in his bride as renounce his former opposition to marriage in general: "In brief, since I do purpose to marry, I will think nothing to any purpose that the world can say against it; and therefore never flout at me for what I have said against it, for man is a giddy thing, and this my conclusion" (V.iv.103–7).

More remarkably still—even for a sex comedy of this kind—the newly committed Benedick seems less smitten with Beatrice's womanly virtues than simply willing to give up his obsession with cuckoldry. His last act is to advise the Prince himself to "get thee a wife" since "there is no staff more reverend than one tipped with horn" (V.iv.120–22). This joke seems to have no very serious point (cuckoldry, if proven, still quite obviously matters) except to suggest that wise men who carry staffs should look for horn there, not on their heads, where they are much less likely to find it; or, if they do find it there, they perhaps prove wisest who refuse to be demeaned by it—as in Sonnet 138, openness or pure willingness to trust is all. This point becomes less comic (Benedick speaks somewhat in jest) when applied to Othello, who rules out the possibility of trusting without solid proof as soon as the question of Desdemona's fidelity is raised and in the process unwittingly prevents anything like a fair trial for his wife. Too insecure and too desirous of quick solutions or sudden closure to weigh the slight evidence against her accurately, Othello prefers the easily obtained, "probable," but wholly manufactured evidence offered by Iago's insinuations and manipulations. Othello's complete disregard for the central thesis of *Much Ado* and so much of Shakespeare's work—that appearances can be fatally deceptive—also by contrast validates Benedick's newfound awareness that outward and even mutual assurances are less important than inner trust and contentment. By extension, it also contrasts with Donne's need to preserve love in the kind of pristine condition Othello so deeply desires, needs, and demands. Of course, it is principally Iago who sparks these needs, apparently because, like the younger Donne or at least his persona, he considers faithful love nothing but an oxymoron unless passion is fueled by the constant, faithless change Dollimore considers essential to it. Iago, in fact, sets the stage for the tragedy by "teaching" first Roderigo and then Othello that the "sport" innately requires a change of partners and, in particular, that women's love "feeds" on constant variety. Even more than the honor-bound, ultrapatriarchal males of *Much Ado*, then, his character unites misogyny pure and simple—women in his view are both vastly inferior to men and innately "deserving" of punishment—with extreme skepticism about pure love, emotional purity, and even "real" but changeable emotions.

Iago's attitudes are most fully explored at the end of the first act of *Othello* as he schools Roderigo in a value system directly opposed to the lessons learned by Benedick: rather than "suffer" either love, doubt, or any potential alteration of reputation, the wise man pays love's material "price" in jewels or other forms of legal, not emotional, "tender." This course is wise in every sense since for Iago no emotion other than lust is natural, and even lust can be manipulated, inhibited, or encouraged as occasion suits or, to adopt his gardening metaphor, scanted or "manured" (I.iii.324). An extreme Stoic—as many Renaissance libertines were believed to be—he argues that if we "had not one scale of reason to poise another of sensuality, the blood and baseness of our natures would conduct us to most prepost'rous conclusions. But we have reason to cool our raging motions, our carnal stings or unbitted lusts; whereof I take this that you call love to be a sect or scion" (326–32). As for love and "Virtue? A fig!" they are no more than a "lust of the blood and permission of the will" to deceive ourselves and otherwise mere misnomers (319, 334–35). Unless such deceptions are recognized, mere emotional desire is foolish and unprofitable unless it achieves its proper end, which is pleasure, just as mere virtue is useless unless directed toward attaining some material reward.

As for faithful marriage, it is part hypocritical "sanctimony" and part a "frail vow" between men and women who little know that what joined them is merely sex, a temporarily "luscious" food that becomes bitter as poison as soon as the body is "sated" with it, as Desdemona must soon be with Othello's body (347–53). To make "money" or profit from these desires should be the only goal of "reasonable" men capable of restraining their own, and Iago proves himself just such a man by making money from Roderigo's cupidity. As for "pimping" a woman he has no real control over, that seems only "right" to Iago, for, as he soon reveals (supposedly in jest) to Desdemona and later to Othello, all women are prostitutes: there is no real difference between Othello's "saintly" wife and Cassio's "strumpet," Bianca, who, though a lower-class and extramarital lover, like Desdemona "falsely" denies being a prostitute simply because she loves. She also believes Cassio will marry her (IV.i.127–29), and although he has no such intentions (as she may suspect), she can stoutly proclaim her "honesty" when Iago questions her on the attempted murder of Cassio, which he himself arranged (V.i.117–25). In thus portraying still another of Iago's female victims, this scene gains some sympathy not just for "supersubtle Venetian" women but also for women in general, including his wife, Emilia, all of whom he describes as pretending pure motives and undying love but eager to "change for youth" when bored, as they soon will be (I.iii.348–54).

This ideology allows Iago to make mutability at once his primary weapon and target, a force with which to threaten men and contain women by making it essentially evil, female, but also conquerable by male "heroes," such as he himself is. As he chillingly tells Roderigo, "There are many events in the womb of time, which will be delivered" in due course to the man who waits and plans how to turn "free and open nature[s]" like that of the "foolish" Moor and his one-time rival, the unsuspecting gull Roderigo, to his own advantage (I.iii.367–68, 391). In a very real sense, then, to Iago, time itself is a whore, one he ironically uses to produce his "legitimate" son, revenge on his real or imagined enemies. Although the audience understands before Iago utters these words that Othello's passion for Desdemona is his chief vulnerability, the fatal weakness linked to it does not really lie in his nature. Othello seems initially far less suspicious of women in general or fearful of taking a wife than either Iago or even Benedick. Of Desdemona, he early declares that he would stake his "life upon her faith!"—words that carry a bitter ring for those already suspecting that he will do just that in all the wrong senses (294). Nevertheless, until Iago interferes, there is nothing to contradict Othello's stated intention of becoming the carefree husband Benedick at last promises to be:

> 'Tis not to make me jealous
> To say my wife is fair, feeds well, loves company,
> Is free of speech, sings, plays, and dances;
> Where virtue is, these are more virtuous.
> (III.iii.183–86)

Even when Othello fails to live up to this liberal standard, his failure is not so much due to misogyny or even misanthropy as to a different, genderless vulnerability: his partial loss of confidence in his character judgment after Cassio gravely belies the great faith he has placed in him.

Significantly, even this real disappointment is partly due to false appearances, in this case to a little interlude ocularly staged by Iago, much as Hero's pseudoseduction was staged by Don John and Borachio. By exploiting Cassio's "secret" susceptibility to drink—a more real flaw than Hero's simple lack of suspicion, but hardly the deeply rooted vice Iago makes it appear—he cleverly surrounds him with the kind of doubt that Othello will soon transfer to Desdemona. Iago easily arouses it merely because neither Cassio nor Desdemona is or can be precisely what Othello wishes them to be: changeless, or at least absolutely "true" to their assigned roles. Iago emphasizes this changeability and all that it implies by reminding Othello that Cassio earlier served as a go-between during his secret courtship of Desdemona (III.iii.94–100), a mission meant to imply their (but strangely enough, not Othello's own) liability to duplicity. Claudio first harbors similar doubts about Hero's constancy when he suspects that the go-between in their courtship, Don Pedro, may have caused the maid to fall more in love with the messenger than with the intended man. For Othello especially, however, this potential confusion of signifiers with signifieds amplifies the doubts already ignited by Iago's stated belief that people and especially women should be but are often not what they seem, a form of doubt from which Othello automatically excludes himself since he knows his own mind. To determine Desdemona's mind, he therefore demands the collapse of signifiers into signifieds, or what he simplistically regards as self-evident "ocular proof." Yet here again, the actual or imagined desires of Donne's speakers are ironically similar, to obtain "ocular proof" from mirroring eyes, minds, and hearts. He may be too clever to demand mere circumstantial evidence such as "magical" handkerchiefs, but some critics see the "masculine persuasive force" of Donne's rhetoric exerting similarly decisive control over his love objects.[17]

There is of course no evidence that Donne ever followed Othello in exchanging his "free and open" nature for the false comforts of a Machiavellian tyrant, thereby becoming the manipulator of consequences that Iago "honestly" approves both in principle and in order to line his purse if not with the promotion and money he wants, then with the revenge he so devoutly desires and achieves. Iago's techniques in attaining these ends are generally well known: by constantly harping on his own and his "friend" Cassio's honesty, which only he, Iago, has "definitely" proven in the course of many battles, he implicitly forces Othello to doubt Cassio's far more scanty and short-lived appearance of loyalty and probity, which remains either untried or, as shown in the barroom scene, untrustworthy. He cleverly hides his own, far greater untrustworthiness both by "kindly" taking Cassio's side and warning Othello against the sexual jealousy he may feel for his beautiful wife. Given the high social price Desdemona has paid to be with him, this possibility has not yet really entered Othello's mind, but Iago arouses the "monster" by reminding him that her faithfulness to him meant deceiving her father. Her love thus rests on a proven—as opposed to a possible—propensity to deception that may turn against *him*. Although ungrateful and even disloyal to his love, this line of reasoning is not fatal in itself, but its chief corollaries are, for Iago can now draw Othello into disavowing jealousy in terms that predictably renounce any kind of change:

> Think'st thou I'd make a life of jealousy,
> To follow still the changes of the moon
> With fresh suspicions? No! To be once in doubt
> Is once to be resolved. Exchange me for a goat
> When I shall turn the business of my soul
> To such exsufflicate and blowed surmises,
> Matching thy inference . . .
> Nor from mine own weak merits will I draw
> The smallest fear or doubt of her revolt,
> For she had eyes, and chose me. No Iago;
> I'll see before I doubt; when I doubt, prove;
> And on the proof there is no more but this—
> Away at once with love or jealousy!
>
> (III.iii.177–83, 187–92)

On these few lines rest the crux of the drama since they provide all the clues needed for Iago's plot to take its final shape. No wonder he is "glad of this; for now I shall have reason / To show the love and duty that I bear you / With franker spirit" (III.iii.193–95). That is, he can now present "ocular proof" of the suspicions Othello refuses to harbor in unresolved form. He does this first, as we have seen, by arguing that Othello's confidence is poorly grounded on Desdemona's outward appearance, her falsifiable "ocular" expressions, since "She did deceive her father, marrying you; / And when she seemed to shake and fear your looks, / She loved them most" (III.iii.206–8). Second and most tragically, he can offer Othello another more "objective" ocular path to certitude. The sudden change in character of which many critics complain in the general is thus not sudden at all; Othello still desires to be a free and open husband but not to a wife free and open to deception and, worse, to the adultery he now begins to associate with the smallest of untruths.[18] Unlike Benedick, who freely participates in the Friar's deception about Hero's death in order to buy time to prove her innocence, but very like the speaker of Donne's "A Lecture," Othello can justify deception only in the interest of a secret courtship aimed at attaining honest marriage; after that, or even as a result of that, all "disguises" must disappear, something that in Desdemona's case proves impossible since Iago surrounds her with fabricated but plausible "disguises" once his wife pilfers her handkerchief and Desdemona insists (perhaps with honest conviction) that it has not been lost even though she cannot produce it. Her quandary at its unexpected disappearance suggests that the absolute mutuality demanded in Donne's love lyrics must ever prove a human impossibility; even the most honest love can be ignorantly misled, appear untrue, and sometimes harbor the fears that the compass concept in his "Valediction" would banish. Given her simultaneous innocence and ignorance, Desdemona is doomed even before Iago uses Cassio's possession of her handkerchief to prove a nonexistent liaison between them, for just as he promises he would, Othello begins banishing her from his heart as soon as his doubts fail to disappear. When they do not and cannot, he prematurely declares, "She's gone. I am abused, and my relief / Must be to loathe her" (III.iii.267–68).

Perhaps the cruelest part of Othello's ordeal is that he can never really loathe Desdemona, which is why he must kill her. He takes an important step in that direction as he realizes that the supreme "curse of marriage" is "that we can call these delicate creatures ours, / And not their appetites!" (III.iii.268–70). Forced to relinquish a form of control that he never really possessed, he vows to "whistle her off" to the winds of perpetual change once her inconstancy is proven; those changeable winds represent his version of hell when they should instead exemplify the natural flux of human emotions (262). Soon afterward he begins tragically preferring the dead to the living woman, the absolutely still and motionless Desdemona lit only by his own torch or candlelight to the wife capable of "lighting" wherever she wishes. Seeking to preserve her in a state as lifeless and "smooth as monumental alabaster," as we have seen, he anoints himself the priest who must sacrifice his wife to the cause of the "chaste stars," which forbid her to "betray more men" (V.ii.1–6). The "flaming minister" of light (8) held over her bed represents to him the will of those fixed stars or immutable realm above, yet he initially hesitates since he knows that he may put her light out but not restore it, may ensure her changelessness only through irreversible death. Really nothing like the sun, the all-too-human Othello can no more revive her "vital growth" after forever stopping her at the peak of noon or midnight than he can control the processes of time and change, which will aptly enough restore her innocence and prove his guilt. Yet the temptation permanently to "preserve" her proves too great: he chooses to "love thee after" as he sees her now, beautifully immobile (V.ii.14, 19).

As we have seen, the same desire for static perfection darkens the comic men of *Much Ado*, particularly Don Pedro, Claudio, and Hero's Brabantio-like (if comic) father. Both her betrothed and her father similarly enter a tragic world where the difficulties of distinguishing appearance from reality propel them toward changeless certitude. Believing that Hero's "outward graces" have belied the carnal "thoughts and counsels of thy heart," Claudio cynically vows from then on to renounce love and beware beauty as a sure indicator of mutability and even "pure impiety" (IV.i.103):[19]

> For thee I'll lock up all the gates of love,
> And on my eyelids shall conjecture hang,
> To turn all beauty into thoughts of harm,
> And never shall it more be gracious.
>
> (IV.i.104–7)

Sharing Othello's false conviction of "fickle" female guilt, Claudio vows to make himself, not Hero, a living tomb that will "never more" admit light or beauty, yet if their wedding had taken place, his solution to the problems of time, doubt, and change might have proved as violent as Othello's. That solution is represented by Leonato, who wishes Hero to die with her shame:

> Do not live, Hero, do not ope thine eyes,
> For, did I think thou wouldst not quickly die,
> Thought I thy spirits were stronger than thy shames,
> Myself would on the rearward of reproaches
> Strike at thy life. Grieved I, I had but one? . . .
> And mine that I was proud on—mine so much
> That I myself was to myself not mine,
> Valuing of her—why she, O, she is fall'n
> Into a pit of ink, that the wide sea
> Hath drops too few to wash her clean again,
> And salt too little which may season give
> To her foul tainted flesh!
>
> (IV.i.123–27, 137–43)

Leonato's absolute certainty that his daughter is now stained black as ink initially leads him to abandon the processes of time, in which she may be cleared—the course adopted by the Friar, Benedick, and Beatrice. These processes run their course too late to save Desdemona, while here they ensure that the tomb of Leonato's daughter will be empty, but his initial desire for her early death is all too real. Simply suspecting his "monument" of female perfection of any flaw makes him jump to the conclusion that only death can purify her. Figuratively stopped at midnight, she has fallen into a "pit" too deep to be excavated by any earthly means, forever a devilish "black weed" like Desdemona (IV.ii.69).[20] Washing or salting may be a means of "preserving" virtue in a world of time and change, but Leonato believes that the only proper condition for daughterly or wifely beauty is literally statuesque: if not honorably married, she must be immobilized and shut away from sight in a monument no wandering eye can penetrate. Thus Shakespeare's comedy and his tragedy alike suggest that whether young, old, or middle aged, the typical male problem is not that their mistresses' eyes are nothing like the sun but that, like the wandering sun of *The First Anniversarie*, their eyes might stop revolving only around them or their duly chosen sons-in-laws.

Balthassar's song in *Much Ado* slightly varies this situation by warning ladies that men were "deceivers ever," erring wanderers with "one foot in sea, and one on shore / To one thing constant never" (II.iii.61–63). Yet that is only half the story; the other half is that men wish to leave behind a stable anchor, a perfectly immobile female who might, they fear, stray off course in their absence. If she does, they will readily cast her into an utter deep, the darkness in which Desdemona dies and Hero swoons. By showing the damage done by this male desire for total control, Shakespeare warns through both his comic and tragic plots that such fixations cannot heighten but only tighten and ultimately deaden a circle of love that naturally resists closure. By ignoring that "fact of life," both Othello and Leonato become sadly obsessed with "put[ting] out the light" (*Othello* V.ii.7), joint obsessions that invert but also strangely reflect Donne's fantasy of causing his erotic suns and moons to revolve in perfect circles around or—at the very least— with him. Yet this stark contrast may also be made to seem less damning to the passionate Donne. Innumerable critics have followed G. Wilson Knight in admiring the "Othello music," the great charm and mysterious poise behind all of Othello's speech acts, including his most violent expressions, while innumerable others have speculated what his marriage might have been like without Iago's evil influence, his dark embodiment of the worst side of the male psyche.[21] Following Carol Thomas Neely's incisive evaluation of Desdemona as Othello's "perfectly" courageous yet modest counterpart—and more her father's daughter than Neely or most other feminist critics might credit, a true admirer of military virtue—one might imagine a tragically silenced "Desdemona music," a soprano to Othello's base, with or without minor chords.[22] In that case, we can imagine a marriage not very different from the one Donne sought and seems fortunately to have found, a marriage more traditional than most female readers could any longer approve, but a harmonious union or reciprocal circling of balanced yet shifting planetary bodies that, even at this late date, has not entirely lost its appeal.

This argument may be further extended by suggesting that Donne did not escape the potentially tragic flaws in his love life—his major love lyrics dwell mainly on external obstacles, not internal flaws—merely by happy accident. More than one literary critic, including me, has noted strong dialogic implications in these lyrics despite their lack of any overt feminine voice. From this perspective, Donne's contrast with Shakespeare's tragic or even tragic-comic characters becomes obvious: unlike Donne's poetic persona or Shakespeare's Benedick, these characters—Othello, Brabantio, and Claudio—all pervert the art of dialogue. Donne's lyrics, on the other hand, are in many ways antimonological, implying multiple and even competing voices within their narrative structure. Heather Dubrow finds that the poet's insistence on exerting powerful control over his "plots" ultimately undermines them by emphasizing "how hypothetical and hence volatile and even fragile their own stories are, recalling too that *story* often alludes to one possible interpretation among many." This inherent instability is also heightened by Donne's hyperbolic attempts to predict or control the future of his narratives, "to assert knowledge of the unknowable, control over the uncontrollable," thus innately revealing the paradoxes and problems underlying his endeavor.[23] Ben Saunders goes still further in this direction by arguing that even Donne's most securely gendered lyric voices ultimately prove as unstable as the mind-body distinctions he consistently attempts to transcend. In the last analysis, the "reflected and reflexive gaze" of the imaginary "ideal 'I' . . . (re)discovered in the meeting of lovers' eyes" is not really a form of "magic" wherein the fragmented self becomes everything since "the nothing [always] shows through."[24]

Saunders's interpretation has a decidedly postmodern ring, but a similar case can be made simply by observing the inherent riskiness, the sense of gambling against all odds at the heart of Donne's major love lyrics and his elegies alike.[25] Oddly like "The Flea" and other seduction poems, the serious lyrics often suggest an unspoken boast or dare to "say it isn't so," to deflate his imagined states of perfect reciprocity or ideal enclosure and regard them as mystifications or wishful hyperboles that human reality can never really support. Although Donne generally refrains from overtly daring his audience not to credit his "fantasy" as Shakespeare does in Sonnet 116, he often implies something very like the speaker's boast, "If this be error, and upon me proved, / I never writ, nor no man ever loved." In both, we find an open or implicit desire for writing itself to become part of an undeniable "proof" of the all-too-familiar yet always mysterious act of loving. As in this sonnet, that proof ultimately rests on a mere speech act supported by slippery signifiers referring either to an unknowable future where none "alters when it alteration finds" or to a semimysterious "star" providing "an ever-fixèd mark" despite "tempests," which would actually make it invisible. For those reasons alone, their hearers' responses must prove as ambiguous and unpredictable as the future itself: for some, the only rejoinder can be (like that of the nameless lady in "The Flea") that the poet's "proof" is utter nonsense; for others, that the speaker's illogical and circular demonstrations may fall short of objective truth but still testify to a known or knowable emotional reality; for still others, that since time itself is somehow circular, despite alteration and change, true lovers do discover a changeless state not in any constant "sphere" perhaps but rather in the recursive reality most of us at times experience.

These options hardly exhaust the plethora of potential responses, which vary not just with individual listeners but also with each individual's varying emotional state or circumstance. Even so, Shakespeare's and Donne's passionate persuasive force convinces most readers that the ancient human desire for undying love is both normal and "real" for lovers in some phases of their relationship, not just its beginning but also its middle and its actual or potential end as they depart for foreign shores. If Shakespeare alone explores the potentially tragic consequences of this desire, as he does when Othello tries to make an extraordinary moment of loving reunion into the undying constant of his marital life, that may well be because dramatic narrative is his stock in trade, whereas for Donne, it was only one tool in his astonishing panoply of poetic resources.

3.   "None Do Slacken, None Can Die":
     Die Puns and Embodied Time in Donne
     and Shakespeare

JENNIFER PACENZA

The last stanza of Donne's dawn song "The Good Morrow" asserts that the love between the poet and his beloved shall never die as do loves "not mixed equally."[1] Instead, Donne's speaker posits, "If our two loves be one, or, thou and I / Love so alike, that none do slacken, none can die." Their love is a balanced mix of humors that will allow it to live forever as a unified and perfected body. More important, though, the ending pun on *die* heightens the morbid eroticism of the final stanza. Obviously, Donne is using this image to express never-ending love. But why place the line's final emphasis on the word "die"? According to Ramie Targoff, the power of Donne's love poetry stems not from "his joyful assurance that his love will endure" but from the "special urgency and force" of "the difficulty of sustaining such a union."[2] But in "The Good Morrow," *die* does not automatically show the imminent end of love or the sex act. Through the more salacious meaning of *die*, Donne can imagine a sexual encounter where "none do slacken, none can die." The perpetual, preorgasmic sexual embrace created through *die* allows his lovers to escape the confines of time. These moments reside in the momentary interval between "the beginning of the bodily event and its completion in an outwardly directed, active expression" of Brian Massumi's virtual, a precognitive realm of possibility. Throughout *Songs and Sonnets*, Donne uses imagery of suspended sexual animation as a way to imagine escaping the destructive passage of time, but he is not alone in this imaginative use of *die*. Shakespeare uses the same pun to create autoerotic, perpetual sexual moments in the first fifteen sonnets to the Young Man. Just as the bedroom in "The Good Morrow" becomes an everywhere full of possibility, so Donne's and Shakespeare's works, by exploring the middle space between mortal and orgasmic death (whether the latter is imminent or actually consummated), become containers of pure potentiality that utilize the *die* pun as an escape from the confines and damages of linear time through what I term "embodied time."

The writings of Donne and Shakespeare are rife with *die* puns. Donne uses some form of the word *death* (death, die, dying, kill, and murder) 61 times in the *Songs and Sonnets*; however, Shakespeare uses *death* and its variants only 49 times in his whole sonnet cycle even though the cycle is longer than Donne's work.[3] Both these authors utilize the pun to varying degrees of seriousness and salaciousness. The frequency with which they utilize *die* makes its usage more than mere wordplay. For these two writers, the two elements of the *die* pun create a mutually constitutive relationship that borders on the synonymous, causing death to become eroticized and the erotic to become deathlike.

The meanings of the *die/die* pun are common knowledge among those well versed in early modern literature. Many theories exist for the origin of the phrase "little death" to mean orgasm. The most prevalent stems from classical medicine; Aristotle, and later Galen, argue that, because semen is reconstituted blood, orgasm causes a release of life-giving blood; too much blood loss would be deadly. In other texts, Galen states that the ejaculation of semen, which occurs in both sexes, releases a bit of the soul or spirit, leading to other well-known puns: spirit/semen and inspire/inseminate.[4] Like Aristotle and Galen, Jonathan Margolis, author of *O: The Intimate History of the Orgasm*, speaks only to the physiological reactions of orgasm. For Margolis, understanding orgasmic pleasure as purely a physiological response frees sexual pleasure from confining political and religious discourse. In a scathing reaction to Margolis's book, the sex historian Thomas Laqueur insists that orgasm is more than just a physical reaction to stimuli. Accordingly, Laqueur believes that depicting orgasmic pleasure as the sole reason for sexual consummation diminishes the symbolic power of orgasm. The little death is "the bodily signal of a cycle of mortality and generation," which is an end in and of itself. To take the love and passion out of orgasm is to discount the power of sexual pleasure, or as Laqueur stresses, "Nowhere more than in the sharp, sweet, ephemeral, melting quality of orgasm are the great tropes of birth and death more clearly inscribed on the body."[5] As Laqueur emphasizes, orgasm has physiological, cultural, and symbolic value; thus, equating orgasm solely with the physiological response it engenders diminishes its transformative power.

Through the use of the *die* pun, Donne and Shakespeare demonstrate the transformative power of orgasm; the pun represents the "excluded middle" between two physiological processes: death and orgasm. According to Massumi, typical binary thinking, like that represented in traditional interpretations of the *die* pun, allows only for "'displacement,' but not transformation." True embodied experience of either death or orgasm occurs in the realm of the virtual, or the "half-second lapse between the beginning of the bodily event and its completion in an outwardly directed, active expression." The virtual, Massumi explains, forces the body to exist within "a lived paradox where what are opposites coexist, coalesce, and connect." The virtual is a wholly unique "temporal structure, in which past and future brush shoulders with no mediating present . . . and where half-actualized actions and expressions arise like waves on a sea to which most [of these actions and expressions] no sooner return." For Massumi, embodied action arises from a sea of possible embodied responses that may never become fully manifest. For Donne and Shakespeare, the continued insistence on the embodied and poetic manifestation of orgasmic pleasure stresses its superiority over those other "half-actualized actions and expressions." Past ontological classification attempts to fix the body in a grid of predefined binaries of signification; I would argue that the *die/die* pun has been interpreted as just such a binary. To be stuck in this grid, to be stuck between death and orgasm, between the big death and the little one is not to focus on the body's movement between the categories but instead "only its beginning and endpoints." The virtual, as it applies to the sexual pleasure described in these poems, allows for the body to exist in "a form of superlinear abstraction," where it can feel the pleasure of the orgasmic event while simultaneously existing outside the temporal moment of the orgasmic event. The body then exists within the excluded middle of binary thinking.[6] For Massumi, the virtual is a permanent and undeniable lived experience that disavows the power of language to contain the body in ontological categories.

Given the body's natural ability to reside within the excluded middle of the binary, do the numerous *die* puns in Donne's and Shakespeare's poems signal their poetic attempts to contain the uncontainable? Absolutely not. In fact, the perpetual sexual moments created through the *die* pun represent the excluded middle, the erotic, embodied experience of sex that linear time denies. The *die* pun poetically realizes an embodied experience expressed by the loose, liquid, and tangential places residing in what Michel Serres calls "the hyphen between terms." Like Massumi, Serres explores the middle ground between binaries, but whereas Massumi's exploration is embodied, Serres's is linguistic and conceptual. Linguistic binaries, according to Serres, deny intellectual possibility. Exploring the hyphen between terms allows Serres to combat the stifling effects of binary thinking by allowing the concepts to mix together instead of separating into individual ontological entities. The hyphen is the place of genesis, creation, and potentiality because it leads to the "dual unveiling" of both terms.[7] The "dual unveiling" of death and orgasm allows Donne and Shakespeare to create a space that frees the body from linear time.

Donne's and Shakespeare's perpetual sexual moments, which I have called embodied time, live within the virtual hyphen of the pun. As mentioned earlier, they represent the excluded middle between two physiological processes, death and orgasm, which, seemingly, can exist only in linear time. The opposing ends of the *die/die* binary, death and orgasm, are bounded in time because the body is temporally bound. The body is birthed into existence and eventually dies (as exemplified by the birth and death dates engraved on headstones); accordingly, the sex act begins with arousal and ends with orgasm. Viewed this way, life becomes a movement from birth to death, and sex a movement from arousal to completed orgasm, both of which focus only on the end points. The lost middle, the actual experience of living or of the sex act, is denied by linear time. For that reason, time plays an important role in both poets' works. In the entirety of Shakespeare's sonnet cycle, for example, there are 87 occurrences of the word *time*. Although in Donne's *Songs and Sonnets* there are many fewer actual instances of *time*, the entire collection of lyrics containing only 11 occurrences, other words denoting the passage or counting of time (day, month, year, minute, hour) are definitely more numerous. *Songs and Sonnets* includes 58 references to the measurement of time, but still this total is paled by the sheer number of references to counting time in Shakespeare's Sonnets—73 occurrences. Of course, within both Donne's and Shakespeare's poetry, sex, death, and time are interrelated, and excising one, the pleasures of sex, for example, from this triumvirate is seemingly impossible. The only choice, then, is to work through time, to utilize time itself to defeat time. Again, by creating these perpetual sexual moments, Donne and Shakespeare create a virtual space necessary for reclaiming the lost middle, freeing the body from its temporal bounds, and enabling embodied time.

Embodied time, as represented in these particular poems, is an event that takes place in the "superlinear abstraction" of Massumi's virtual, where death and orgasm, like the body itself, are "as immediately abstract as [they are] concrete" (31).

Not all sexual encounters create perpetual moments of embodied time, however. For Donne, experiencing embodied time, and thus removing the body from linear time, requires the emotions of love and passion. "The Good Morrow" illustrates this need by comparing those sexual encounters defined by lust and those defined by love: "If ever any beauty I did see, / Which I desired, and got, 'twas but a dream of thee." The sexual pleasures Donne's speaker "got" earlier in life were but childish and devoid of love. The past tense of "got" places the speaker's past sexual encounters within linear time. Through these lustful sexual conquests the speaker was able to achieve physiological orgasm, but it was only a "dream" of dying with the orgasmic pleasure that allows for the "waking [of] souls" and accompanies the realization of embodied time. Even in Shakespeare's masturbatory sonnets, the perpetual sexual moments signify not only the Young Man's "self-love" (3.8), his narcissistic passion, but also the Shakespearean speaker's own devout passion for the Young Man, which causes him to create embodied time imagined through masturbation-induced asexual replication. Through the *die* pun, the speaker uses autoerotic orgasm to combat the permanence of mortal death even as he urges the Young Man to accept orgasmic death in order to procreate. These perpetual sexual moments, embodied time, live within "the hyphen" of the pun. As I have proposed, they allow for reclamation of the lived experience of death and orgasm typically relegated to the excluded middle. Donne and Shakespeare use these moments to preserve their experience of love from the ravages of "time's scythe" (Shakespeare, 12.13).

At this point, it may seem that in combating one binary (*die/die*) I am creating another (linear time/embodied time), but my phrasing here is mostly an attempt to name a poetic reality that seems to be completely atemporal, as traditional categories of transcendence are not because they are tied to linear time. Serres distinguishes several time-oriented binaries in his theories on time: episodic/linear, momentary/everlasting, discontinuous/continuous. Serres is dissatisfied with these options, however, as he is with all binary thinking. Binary options are reductive in his view, and they cannot fully account for the complexities of time:

> Time is a tatter and it is sporadic. It solidifies like a crystal or vanishes like a vapor. It is an unintegrable multiplicity, endowed, here and there, with unities, there and here deprived of snapshot moments. It is not a flux that can be differentiated into tiny little fluxions, although it can become one and then become fringed in differentials, it is, for the most part, a sumless aggregate, a bundle of dispersed fluctuations. It is not a set, although it can become one, it goes in bursts [*Genesis*, 116].

In his poetic way, Serres denies the linearity of time. It can be a "tatter," "sporadic," crystalline, vaporous, multiple, unified, fluctuating, or stable. Time can be any combination of these qualities, an "aggregate" of conceptions of time, and it can also be none of these. Like orgasm, time "goes in bursts"; therefore, seeing time only as linear denies the possibility of multiplicity, which for Serres is denial of the true nature of time.

In their battles against the ravages of time, Donne and Shakespeare use poetry to imagine a version of time that is similar to Serres's and allows for a pure multiplicity. Both poets and, I would argue, Serres, too, rearrange time through the use of language. As Serres points out, once time has become a pure potentiality, a percolation where the past mingles with the present and future, "Language . . . is suddenly bereft of possibilities for eliminating. It cannot put anything outside or inside a boundary, it cannot draw a boundary" (*Genesis*, 116).[8] As Massumi's virtual frees the body, Serres's aggregate time frees language from its linear constraints. The poets' logic works similarly but uses the aggregate nature of language to create time unbounded by linearity. Putting Serres, Donne, and Shakespeare into conversation emphasizes the mutually constitutive relationship between time and language, which can be used either to confine or, as all three writers advocate, to liberate. Both poets use the *die* pun to liberate the body from linear time, thus creating the perpetual sexual moments that represent embodied time—time unbounded but physically experienced through poetic pleasure. While each author imagines nonlinear time in multiple ways, reading Donne and Shakespeare through the concept of embodied time relieves death and orgasm of their temporal nature, allowing them to become virtually synonymous.

"The Good Morrow" contains the most overt instance of embodied time in either Donne or Shakespeare. Within just a few lines, Donne uses the intermingled meanings inherent in the *die/die* pun to transform linear time into embodied time. "Good Morrow," the poem and the phrase, comes to symbolize a simultaneous collapse and expansion of time through language. In wishing "good morrow to [their] . . . waking souls" (8), the speaker is bidding "good morrow" not only to this day but also to all subsequent days in a desire for an eternal continuation of love's bliss.[9] The lovers' "waking souls" are waking not only to the promise of a new day but also to the pure potentiality of desire unconfined by time.

While the day already holds the potential for collapsing time, only sexual pleasure, as represented in the *die* pun, can truly create embodied time. At the end of "The Good Morrow," Donne's speaker speculates, "If our two loves be one, or, thou and I / Love so alike, that none do slacken, none can die." Despite or maybe because of the explicit salaciousness of the final pun, many critics find it unsettling and therefore deny the transcendent power of sex. For example, Anne Ferry has found that the *die* pun "creates a conflict" within the poem: "[T]he meanings cancel each other as desirable possibilities of escape from mortality."[10] Combating Ferry's reading, R. E. Pritchard, though, uses the sexual meaning of "die" to link the poem to both nonorgasmic, tantric sex and Plato's spheroid humans. Ultimately, however, Pritchard reads Donne's lovers as initiators of a "catalytic miracle, cancelling the effects of the Fall" and initiating "the new paradise of immortal love."[11] Although Pritchard's reading ascribes transcendental power to sex, transcendence is accomplished only after the active physical expression that for Massumi resides outside the realm of the virtual; thus, the transcendence is spiritually or mentally realized but cannot be physically so. The meaning of the line also does not depend on historical or literary contextualization even though these connections are highly enlightening. For Donne, the word *die* itself has the power to encompass both meanings; the pun gives sex transcendent power. Death and orgasm do not cancel each other out; instead, they work together to create a new *poetic* reality that is physically, passionately realized through the suspension of both types of death. Prior to reaching orgasmic climax, time erupts into one of its nonlinear bursts. The poetic reality in "The Good Morrow" disrupts linear time, allowing for a perpetual, preorgasmic moment of unadulterated, uninterrupted pleasure. The experience of such pleasure allows the speaker and his beloved to reside within the excluded middle, which exists only in embodied time.

In "The Good Morrow" and in his poetry generally, Donne uses the *die/die* pun to highlight the suspension of linear time necessary for creating an afterlife that exists for the lovers both before and after mortal death. Ramie Targoff argues that even though Donne continually worries about the state of love in the afterlife, "he never dares to imagine a real afterlife for love." While Targoff might be unable to "imagine a real afterlife for . . . [Donne's] love," Donne is able to use the embodied experience of the *die* pun's excluded middle to remove himself and his beloved from linear time and imagine his love itself as an afterlife. The embodied experience of orgasm, which happens within linear time, escapes linear time through a simultaneous invocation of mortal death in the pun. The resulting atemporality of orgasm imbues the pun with the imaginative capacity to deny mortal death. The linguistic conflation of meaning allows for a death that is not death, a removal from linear time while living. The coupling of *die* (death) and *die* (orgasm) within Donne's "Good Morrow" leads both to a conflation of these two concepts and to their atemporal transcendence; therefore, the pun no longer becomes a salacious joke but an ontological definition of how Donne perceives both the embodied sexual experience and the imagined afterlife that it simultaneously figures and achieves, anticipates and makes present.

Donne's obsessive punning in "The Paradox" explores the seemingly paradoxical, interdependent relationship between death and orgasm to figure and achieve an embodied sexual afterlife. The poem's dizzying wordplay embellishes the problems and possibilities of the *die* pun and finds that the only way to save love in this paradox is to compress the pun's two meanings: "I cannot say I loved, for who can say / He was killed yesterday?" Because love in this poem refers to both emotional and physical passion, the speaker denies the possibility for love to exist or for sex to occur when to love is to be "killed." The murdered man, who has ceased to live, cannot say afterward that he loved. As opposed to actual death, which "kills with too much cold," love kills "with excess of heat." Even this description of the way death kills can be read erotically. In true Petrarchan fashion, death is caused by either lover's coldness, which greatly contrasts with common early modern medical theories where the heat of sexual passion can physiologically bring about death as well. "How can all this be possible?" Donne's speaker seems to ask: "We die but once, and who loved last did die / He that saith twice, doth lie." In this dizzying collection of puns on *die*, *love*, and *lie*, Donne's witty speaker slyly suggests that the finality of actual death, not orgasm, denies the possibility of ever loving again. Those who say they have loved twice do "lie," meaning both "tell untruths" and "lie in a sexual embrace." But the *die/die* pun allows for an image of something akin to the undead: "Here dead men speak their last, and so do I; / Love-slain, lo, here I lie." In the last line the speaker holds himself up for display, but for what purpose? Through the excessive punning on *die*, the speaker's body becomes the embodiment of the hyphen between the two meanings. Paradoxically, he is both dead and undead, alive and lacking life, truthful and lying, heated with love and cold with death. Through sexualized death within the context of this particular poem, the speaker's body has become pure potentiality, the essence of embodied time.

While orgasmic pleasure is an important element for creating embodied time, the achievement of embodied time can continue to provide pleasure even outside the bedroom. In Donne's poetry, emotional love, not just physical passion, disengages the lovers from linear time to experience embodied time. In the first stanza of "The Sun Rising," Donne's speaker asserts that true love does not feel the ravages of time: "Love, all alike, no season knows, nor clime, / Nor hours, days, months, which are the rags of time." The unitary measurements of time—the hour, day, and month—are time's refuse. To escape "the rags of time," love itself must provide its own version of time, as further exemplified in "The Anniversary," in which the anniversary of the lovers' first year together is both celebratory and mournful because it acknowledges a landmark occasion that looks forward to more years together even while mourning the present loss of one year. Donne acknowledges this loss of time: "[T]he sun itself, . . . Is elder by a year, now, than it was" and "All other things, to their destruction draw" (4–6). In order to combat this loss, he imagines love allowing the perpetuity of the momentary because "love hath no decay" (7). Time is unable to affect their love because love manipulates the linearity of time by creating one perpetual moment: "Running [time] . . . never runs from us away, / But truly keeps his first, last, everlasting day" (9–10). Time continues to run, and the lovers run with it because love "no tomorrow hath, nor yesterday" (8). Love allows for both a compression and an expansion of time that characterizes love's lived afterlife in embodied time.

Love's lived afterlife can be denied by the possibly finite nature of love—whether idealized Platonic love, bawdy sexualized love, or a combination of both; however, as can be seen in "Lovers' Infiniteness," true love's amount cannot be reckoned, to borrow at once a word and a sentiment that Shakespeare's Antony will express.[12] The speaker in "Lover's Infiniteness" both bemoans his inability to "have thee all" and admits that he "would not have all yet, / He that hath all can have no more" (11, 23–24). The speaker is torn between two versions of the "all" that he envisions. "All" refers to "the entire amount." It is this version of "all" that he invokes in his complaint, "If yet I have not all thy love, / Dear, I shall never have it all" (1–2). To have all the woman's love, the speaker would have her "entirely" and "totally."[13] In this case, the "all" is full. It contains within it all of the woman's body, mind, and love. Yet, the ability to possess all of the woman ultimately puts a limit on love's infiniteness. To have all and to possess all deny the possibility of more love; as a result, love's amount is limited by complete possession. With this realization, the signifier "all" becomes empty, allowing love itself to become an empty signifier because, as the speaker imagines, the lady can give only a finite amount of love to the speaker. Still, the passage of time may allow that "New love created be" within the beloved's heart for another man. Since the "New love created" did not exist prior to the lady's original gift of all her love to the speaker, she technically would not be disavowing the "all" the speaker still possesses. The threat, then, is not just one of amount but of temporality. The "all" previously given is the extent of the "all" that was available up until that particular, present moment. However, the future, the passage of time, poses a threat to the amount of the previous "all." As time progresses, the lady can create new love that is no longer part of that time-bounded "all" given previously. Even though linear time seems boundless, the speaker is conceiving of time as encapsulated moments, so that in giving "all," the beloved destroys the infiniteness of love itself.

As in "The Anniversary," Donne uses a conflation of time and bodies to reconcile simultaneous fullness and emptiness within the realm of love's "all." The title—"Lovers' Infiniteness"—refers to a complete and total expansion of the lovers themselves. Donne is able to solve "Love's Riddles" and escape the bounded "all" through "a way more liberal, / Than changing hearts, to join them, so we shall / Be one, and one another's all." Donne's solution is highly "liberal" because it frees love from the restraints of both time and the body. True exchange of hearts is not possible because "though thy heart depart, / It stays at home." The heart cannot literally be given away because extracting the heart from the body would lead to physical death. To escape the confines of the body, the speaker imagines that he will "be" his beloved's heart, and she will "be" his. The metaphorical overlay of hearts on bodies allows for the hearts themselves to be both embodied and disembodied. The simultaneous embodiment and disembodiment of the hearts allows the two lovers to "be one." They are able to escape the boundaries of their individual bodies and become one unified being, imagined in a sexual embrace. The solution of being "one another's all" might pose similar temporal problems that allow for both the fullness and emptiness of the "all." Donne denies these problems by signifying not only the lovers' embodied transcendence but also a simultaneous compression and expansion of time when he begins the final line of the poem with "be." While "be" is grammatically paired with "shall" in the previous line, implying a sense of futurity, the line's initial emphasis on "be" highlights, as well, the verb's perpetual present. Therefore, the speaker manipulates temporality by extending the present moment indefinitely while simultaneously compressing the future into a perpetual, present moment. The lovers exist within an eternal present characterized by the transcendent mixing of their two bodies.

The eternal present created by embodied time cannot be disrupted, not even by death. Orgasmic pleasure and emotional love imbue the lovers' bodies with a potentiality that has the ability to deny physical death the power to separate them, as is illustrated in "The Dissolution." Given the pun on "more" at the end of the poem, "The Dissolution" is typically said to commemorate the death of Donne's wife, Ann More. Read through the concept of embodied time, however, the poem becomes even more than just a commemorative piece. Because of Donne's insistence on using the *die* pun, dying—to cease living—and dying—to achieve orgasm—become inseparable; they both lead to a dissolution of the body:

all which die
To their first elements resolve;
And we were mutual elements to us,
And made of one another.

Donne's description of love in these lines is reminiscent of the humors in "The Good Morrow," which are "mixed equally" and keep a "love so alike" from dying (in both its literal senses). When the beloved dies and dissolves into her constituent elements in this poem, however, the elements stay with the speaker: "My body then doth hers involve, / And those things whereof

I consist, hereby / In me abundant grow." His body does "Receive more." The dissolution of Ann More's body does not mean the dissolution of their love, and it certainly does not deny love's afterlife, as Targoff argues. Instead, the lovers remain one until Donne is able to (re)consummate his marriage with More in the afterlife.

As stated earlier, Donne is not the only poet to use the *die* pun imaginatively to create transcendent, yet still embodied, sexual passion freed from linear time. Shakespeare's use of perpetual sexual moments, like Donne's in the *Songs and Sonnets*, disengages death from the bounds of linear time, thus creating embodied time. But instead of imagining embodied time within the context of the reciprocal love and passion of heterosexual coupling, Shakespeare's speaker provides an autoerotic alternative through the masturbatory language and represented acts that pervade these poems. In Shakespeare's first fifteen sonnets, imminent death is a problem that haunts the speaker and his beloved. To combat the effects of "time's scythe," the speaker tries to convince the Young Man to create an heir, but the beloved is loath to give up his self-love.[14] The Petrarchan conceits within these poems describe a youth overflowing with sexual energy that he chooses to use only on himself. Unlike the perpetual sexual moments that create embodied time in Donne's poetry, however, Shakespeare's sonnets do not capture a sustained moment. Instead, the perpetual sexual moments of embodied time are created through the Young Man's self-sufficient, seemingly never-ending replication phantasied as possible through the physical pleasure of masturbatory orgasms. These imagined moments of self-replication through masturbation coexist with professions of the realistic need for heterosexual procreation. The Young Man's self-love, then, becomes both deviant, culminating in unproductive masturbatory acts, and ideal, resulting in embodied time through imagined self-replication, not heterosexual reproduction.

Most literary critics ignore or treat Shakespeare's use of masturbatory language within the *Sonnets* as a fleeting, humorous aside. Bruce Smith, a major voice in early modern sexuality studies, discusses masturbation and its historical relationship to sodomy in his book *Homosexual Desire in Shakespeare's England* but fails to connect Shakespeare's sonnets with masturbation.[15] In their editions of Shakespeare's collected sonnets, Stephen Booth and Helen Vendler both note that Sonnet 4's "traffike with thy selfe alone" refers to masturbation. While Booth does not make much of the reference,

Vendler delves a little deeper by naming that particular line as an "early parody of the many true reciprocities envisaged in the sequence."[16] For Vendler, the allusion to masturbation shows the ridiculousness of the act when compared to the "true reciprocities," a phrase that emphasizes her own bias against masturbation as a valuable topic of sexuality studies. In another book that is ostensibly about sex in Shakespeare, masturbation is not even sexy enough to constitute in-depth analysis; Stanley Wells's *Looking for Sex in Shakespeare* barely mentions it.[17] Perhaps these critics consider masturbation benign—a childish hobby that will eventually be replaced by interpersonal sexual relationships—and, therefore, not taboo enough for critical inquiry.[18] However, the references to masturbation collapse the distinctions between death and orgasm in the sonnets to create more than just an immature joke; as I have earlier suggested, masturbation allows Shakespeare to imagine the Young Man's escape from linear time through a form of asexual replication even as he urges the youth to produce an heir through heterosexual reproduction; this escape through replication does not replace procreation; instead, the two exist simultaneously.

The asexuality in the sonnets is analogous to that studied in biology and zoology, especially the form of asexual reproduction known as *parthenogenesis*. Biologically speaking, asexual reproduction, generally, is the ability of an animal or a plant to create offspring without sexual congress or without contributions from both the male and the female of the species. Parthenogenesis, which comes from the Greek for "virgin birth," is the ability to procreate asexually. Animals that can procreate by parthenogenesis are gendered female, and so they do not have hermaphroditic sex organs as some asexual creatures do. Instead, the female, by either choice or necessity, creates a fully fledged embryo without the assistance of the male of the same species. The resulting offspring is a genetic duplicate because, instead of mixing male and female DNA, the female parent passes on the entirety of her genetic material to her offspring, barring any embryonic defects or genetic mutations.

While parthenogenetic asexual reproduction might seem completely anachronistic, the concept of virgin birth, stemming from Christian belief, pervades Renaissance poetry. Although Shakespeare would have known nothing about parthenogenesis, DNA, or genetic duplication, virgin birth is nonetheless a vital poetic trope for poetic creation in the works of the time: the virgin poet is fictively inseminated/inspired by the muses from on high.[19] For a familiar instance of the trope, Sir Philip Sidney utilizes birth images several times in *Astrophil and Stella* to depict the creative process that leads to poetry. The most outright example occurs in the first sonnet of the sequence, where Sidney describes himself as "great with child to speak, and helpless in my throes."[20] The poet imagines himself inspired/inseminated by love's pain and woe. Inspiration metaphorically impregnates him, and the creation of poetry becomes like the throes of childbirth. Sidney's poetic child is a virgin birth because, although he is inspired by his love, the inspiration comes from a lack of actual heterosexual consummation. He must give birth to his poetry exactly because his beloved will not return his love. For Sidney, the creative process, then, becomes a form of virgin birth. Perhaps, then, Shakespeare's speaker uses masturbatory imagery to imagine a procreative possibility not available through traditional heterosexual coupling.

Besides being an important literary trope for Shakespeare and his contemporaries, virgin birth, more specifically parthenogenesis, provides a modern metaphor that thus helps the reader envision the paradoxical, metaphorical reality Shakespeare attempts to create in his masturbatory poems. By emphasizing the Young Man's masturbatory habits, the speaker imagines a way for the beloved to have offspring without the aid of a woman. Typical biological procreation, according to Renaissance medicine, occurs when male and female semen join within the uterus. The male semen provides the form of the embryo and the motion required for life, and the female semen provides the material substance of the embryo, which is molded and shaped by the male semen.[21] Therefore, the created offspring, as in our modern understanding of sexual procreation, is a mixture of physical, mental, and emotional aspects of both the mother and the father. In his own way, Shakespeare's speaker, like Donne's in "The Good Morrow," questions the vitality of a love that is "not mixed equally," a love that does not result in a perfected, unified humoral body, whether metaphorical or physical. In Shakespeare's poems specifically, heterosexual procreation is depicted as contaminating the perfect balance of humors that creates the Young Man. By imagining masturbation as a form of parthenogenic asexual replication, Shakespeare's speaker gives the Young Man the ability to create imagined offspring through the physical pleasure of masturbation. The offspring's balanced humoral material is untainted by the addition of female semen and, consequently, by negative feminine aspects. Thus the offspring would be an exact, self-inspired (self-spirited/inseminated) duplicate. The images of masturbation that pervade the first fifteen sonnets create a metaphorical reality that denies the power of death through replication of the Young Man and thus denies the linearity of time through masturbation-induced immortality.

Even though the masturbatory language ultimately inspires the creation of imagined offspring, in the first sonnets of the sequence the speaker also condemns the wastefulness of the Young Man's masturbatory self-love, as illustrated in Sonnet 3, where an unmistakable reference to masturbation is embedded in a plea to engage in heterosexual procreation: "Die single and thine Image dies with thee." On the surface, the quoted line posits that if the Young Man dies single or unmarried, then he will not beget a legitimate heir to continue the family line. Because of the pun inherent in the word *die*, however, the speaker also warns the young man not to "die" or have an orgasm alone; in other words, the young man should choose the more productive orgasmic pleasure one attains during heterosexual sex rather than the nonproductive orgasmic pleasure of masturbation. According to Martin Luther, masturbation, or more generally spilling the seed outside the womb, killed the child before it even had a chance to be born; thus masturbation was for him fundamentally the same as abortion (Laqueur, *Solitary*, 127–28). The Young Man, then, is aborting his heir, and through the metaphoricity of the rhyme pair "womb" and "tomb" in lines 5 and 7 of this sonnet, his body implicitly becomes a receptacle to hold both types of spirit, his own semen and the immortal spirit of his dead baby. His body possesses the ability both figuratively to conceive (that is, to inspire) and literally to kill a child, making his own body similar to the "un-eared wombe[s]" of his dismissed female lovers. Like the conflation of *die/die* in Donne's poetry, the Young Man's masturbatory dying single allows for both kinds of death: orgasm, which creates (whether physical or poetic) life, and death, which destroys these biological and poetic life forms. Because the Young Man's body contains both kinds of death, it exists within the excluded middle of the pun. The physical pleasure of masturbatory dying, though single, still allows for the superlinear abstraction necessary for removal from linear time and the creation of embodied time. Even though embodied time is not yet fully realized here, Sonnet 3 does disengage the

Young Man's body from linear time, a disengagement that is necessary for poetically imagining the beloved's masturbatory habits as protection from "time's scythe."

Shakespeare's use of the *die* pun—as Laqueur argues about the little death more generally—illustrates the metaphorical and embodied "cycle of mortality and generation" attained through the Young Man's nongenerative, yet productive, masturbation. When Shakespeare's speaker worries about the effects of dying single, he simultaneously creates two options for expressing and figuring this cycle. The sonnets have an ability to uphold both of these seemingly paradoxical generative options, as they famously do many other paradoxes. From the beginning of the sequence, Shakespeare's speaker imagines his beloved capable of parthenogenetic replication, as well as of biological reproduction. Despite the apparent, negative effect dying single may have on heterosexual coupling and the offspring it would produce, the speaker's attitude toward the Young Man's autoerotic inclinations, spurred on by his own androgynous beauty, is more complex and ambiguous than may at first be evident. Even though the first sonnet uses the social "we" to reprove the young man's actions, as well as the language of shame and usury in sonnets two and four, respectively, the sonnets do not simply or unambiguously condemn this solitary sex act. On the contrary, they meld the profane and the divine in the image of a sexually self-sufficient youth who can replicate himself through traffic with himself alone. Such a reading, queer and against the grain, is consistent with the overt theme of immortality through poetry, which pervades the sonnets.

Although the Young Man's masturbatory self-love incites the speaker's criticism, this criticism is tempered by the speaker's efforts creatively to transform dying single into an alternative possibility for producing an heir, if only imaginatively. According to Petrarchan conventions, the beloved is the poet's great foe because she will not return his love; her "fair cruelty"[22] impedes the heterosexual coupling necessary for the marital contract. Shakespeare's speaker revises Petrarchan conceits in order to critique his beloved's autoerotic tendencies. In the first sonnet of the sequence the Young Man becomes his own "foe" and is "too cruell" to his own "sweet selfe" because he is "contracted to [his] . . . owne bright eyes" (1.8, 5). He wants to marry only himself, yet within his self-marriage, the marital debt must still be paid or desire satisfied. Through traffic with himself alone, the beloved "Feed'st [his] . . . lights flame with selfe substantiall fewell."

His narcissism acts as "fewell" for his own erotic desire, which therefore makes it "selfe substantiall"—that is, self-sufficient and, simultaneously, seemingly never-ending. For a moment grounded in the physical experience of autoerotic pleasure, masturbation and replication replace heterosexual procreation, imaginatively trumping it.

Again, even while the poet repeatedly warns that the Young Man will not profit from masturbation because it will make "famine where aboundance lies," he cleverly shifts the youth's masturbatory self-love into a form of parthenogenetic asexual rebirth that is reminiscent of Donne's afterlife through orgasmic death. Instead of envisioning (as does Donne's speaker in "The Good Morrow") an embodied afterlife as a perpetual, preorgasmic sexual embrace between two people, Shakespeare's speaker combats death by making the pleasures of dying single a metaphor for an autoerotic, asexual replication that sustains the Young Man's youth and beauty and shows that "selfe substantiall" masturbation is hardly "Profitles." Less openly, if no less originally than Donne, he creates in these sonnets a perpetual, embodied experience of orgasmic pleasure.

As opposed to Donne's creation of embodied time through heterosexual coupling, Shakespeare's speaker creates an imagined reality where the Young Man's dying single results in the asexual creation of a child. In Sonnet 2, the speaker unsuccessfully tries to scare the Young Man into having a child by reminding him that one day he will grow old, his beauty will diminish, and he will have nothing to show for his "lusty daies":

> Then being askt, where all thy beautie lies—
> . . . . ,
> How much more praise deserv'd thy beauties use,
> If thou couldst answere this faire childe of mine
> Shall sum my count, and make my old excuse
> Prooving his beautie by succession thine.
> This were to be new made when thou art ould,
> And see thy blood warme when thou feel'st it could.

If the Young Man has a legitimate heir, the child will inherit not only his wealth but also his warm blood and beauty, thus ensuring their continued existence and allowing both father and son to profit from this relationship. Because "this faire childe of mine / Shall sum my count," the imagined son will also be an embodiment of the profit that the Young Man is currently spending on himself. The child would also seem to inherit his father's masturbatory habits. When the speaker answers his own hypothetical question, he states that the child will "make . . . [the Young Man's] old excuse," which Stephen Booth analyzes as a justification for the Young Man's venery during his youth but, considering the references to dying single in these sonnets, could also be interpreted as the child's taking up the same narcissistic, masturbatory practices that used to occupy his father when he was young. The child, then, becomes not just the Young Man's comfort in old age but also a warm copy of the Young Man himself—*redidivus*. He is "new made" with the birth of a child, predilection for "selfe substantiall fewell" and all. With this image of rebirth, Shakespeare compresses the present, embodied within the Young Man, and the future, represented by the child. Through this imagery he invokes both linear time, through succession, and nonlinear time, through compression, in order to manipulate both kinds of time. His simultaneous handling of linear and nonlinear time, succession and compression, further denies time's destructive scythe, allowing both father and son imaginatively and physically to live in the "pastnesses opening directly onto a future" of Massumi's virtual (30). Like Donne's images of the overlaying of the lovers' hearts onto each other's bodies in "Lovers' Infiniteness," the father and the child can live within a compression of linear temporalities; they, too, can run with running time.

The conflation of the Young Man with his offspring culminates in another variant form of asexual replication, one that is minimally orgasmic but nonetheless results in an embodied divinity in Sonnet 7. In a seemingly uncomplicated, extended metaphor, the speaker compares the Young Man to the sun, a comparison intended as evidence that the Young Man should propagate. Booth sums up the typical interpretation of this sonnet: "[T]he poem implies [the equation] between the sun's cyclical birth, death, and rebirth and human victory over mortality by procreation" (143). Because the Young Man becomes like the sun, a previously unnoticed promise of parthenogenetic asexual rebirth arises. Practically, the comparison between the Young Man creating an heir and the rebirth of the sun does not work because the same sun that, "Like feeble age . . . reeleth from the day" and sinks down into "his low tract" the night before, "Lifts vp his burning head" the next morning. In other words, the sun does not have an heir who newly makes the trek every day. Even though the word "sun" is never used in this sonnet, the poem makes a rhetorical link between the sun and the Young Man. With the adverbial use of *so*, "So thou" (13), the speaker identifies the Young Man as like the sun. If the Young Man is the sun, he is also the son in this common Renaissance pun. Again, such conflation in the image compresses present and future time, but through it, Shakespeare also incorporates the past. The sun, which existed before the birth of the Young Man and his child and will ultimately exist after they have died, represents both the rigid counting of linear time and a perpetual timelessness. Through this metaphor, then, both father and son are able to transcend the binary of time and perpetuity to exist within the perpetual present of embodied time.

The rhetorical mixing of the Young Man and his future son has divine, not to mention blasphemous, results because of an additional connection between the sun and the Son of God within this sonnet. The pun on "sun" and "son" ties the Young Man to the Son of God; Booth believes that the "Christian references never solidify" (143). Yet Booth does not take into account that they are pointing to a controversial but desired similarity between the Young Man and a self-sufficient God. According to a perversely literal reading of John's gospel, God and Jesus are one: "In the beginning was the Word and the Word was with God, and the Word was God . . . And the Word became flesh and dwelt among us, and we beheld His glory, the glory as of the only begotten Son of the Father, full of grace and truth."[23] Since both God and Jesus are synonymous with the Word, as if John were conflating Father and Son, Jesus becomes the fleshly incarnation of God instead of a separate being (an idea resonant with, if not identical to, some form of Gnostic Docetism or Monophysitism, heresies known to the Renaissance). The conflation of the Young Man and his future child mirrors the conflation of the God and Jesus found in John. Because of the constant comparison of the Young Man to both God and Jesus throughout the sonnet, the Young Man becomes both the father, who should "get a sonne," and the son, who is to be gotten, whether through parthenogenetic replication or through heterosexual reproduction. Both options at once exist within the imaginative wording of the poem and are grounded in the embodied, sexual pleasure of trafficking with himself alone.

By making the Young Man and his future child one, the speaker emphasizes his own desires not merely that the Young Man procreate but also that he replicate himself to create another self who has all the physical and personality traits of the original, which, according to my argument, include his narcissistic masturbatory habits. The speaker wants the Young Man to "breed an other thee" (6.7). Importantly, the speaker does not say that he wants the Young Man to have a child but "an other thee." In an image that might remind the modern reader of cloning, the speaker pictures the Young Man making "an other selfe" (10.13) or perhaps even ten: "Or ten times happier be it ten for one, / Ten times thy selfe were happier then thou art, / If ten of thine ten times refigur'd thee" (6.8–10). Again the emphasis is not on the individual personality or beauties of the child but the numerous identical Young Men the Young Man should create, disseminating himself by dying single.

Perhaps it is wishful thinking on the speaker's part, but he uses the masturbation imagery and conflation of the Young Man with his future child to entertain the possibility of the Young Man asexually replicating through a phantasied form of parthenogenesis because only then will the child be *exactly* like the father, only then could the speaker's desires be fulfilled: "then you were / Your selfe again after your selfes decease" (13.6–7). The physical pleasures of masturbatory death/orgasm, then, become an ideal way to imagine this generative possibility of denying mortal death even though, ironically, it is a nongenerative form of sexuality. Using masturbation to create the imaginative possibility of perpetually embodied time allows the speaker to disengage the Young Man from the ravages of time and preserve him "so long as men can breathe or eyes can see" (18.13). So long as the masturbatory poems exist, future readers can celebrate the Young Man's unique beauty, along with the speaker, thus creating another form of asexual replication through the solitary pleasures of reading.

For both Donne and Shakespeare, death, an inescapable aspect of linear time, is an ever-present threat to the love between the lover and his beloved. In their poems, both imaginatively combat the threat of mortal death through salvific, orgasmic death. For Donne, the preorgasmic pleasure that creates embodied time or the temporal, superlinear abstraction created by the compression and expansion of linear temporalities provides both an imagined disengagement from linear time during life and suggests a physical, passionate, and pleasure-filled afterlife for love. Donne uses the *die* pun to create—in a phrase I have earlier borrowed from Serres—a "dual unveiling" of mortal death and orgasmic death and envisions both forms of death as an embodied experience that transcends time itself. For the poet-speaker of Shakespeare's sonnets, however, a heterosexual consummation—one that results in orgasm—between himself and his beloved is impossible because the youth was "prickt . . . out for womens pleasure" (20.13). Shakespeare's use, or creation, of embodied time, therefore, differs greatly from Donne's. The poet does not suggest homoerotic sex as a viable option for transcending temporal constraints. Heterosexual sex between the Young Man and a woman also seems fraught with complications because the addition of a woman causes a triangulation of desire that detracts from the relationship between the poet and the beloved. Shakespeare then imagines autoerotic desire and pleasure as a viable option, metaphorically speaking, for the creation of embodied time. Masturbatory pleasure also allows the poet to imagine a metaphorical parthenogenesis that saves the Young Man from the ravages of time through replication, not reproduction. In this way, the beloved transcends linear time through the physical pleasures of trafficking with himself, thus achieving an embodied immortality. Unlike Donne, Shakespeare does not create an embodied afterlife for his love; doing so is not necessary. If his poetic imaginings become a reality, the beloved will never die. The beloved will be replicated by each subsequent reading. The solitary pleasure of reading the poems provides another manifestation, albeit not necessarily orgasmic, of physical pleasure that, according to the speaker, will lead to the imagined replication of the Young Man.

For Donne and Shakespeare, language, specifically the *die/die* pun, is a vehicle for the manipulation of both meaning and time. As Serres explains, "Language describes many areas of mixture where the multiple is gathered without necessarily being sorted through some unitary wicket" (*Genesis*, 103). Time is one of these. Language is the way we measure and construct time; thus language is also the key to deconstructing it, allowing both figurative and literal transcendence. Puns, as these two poets deploy them, deny both a unifying central meaning and diametrically opposed binary meanings. Instead, they create a multiplicity of meanings manifested in embodied time.

PART II   Moral, Public, and Spatial Imaginaries

4. Donne, Shakespeare, and the Interrogative Conscience

MARY BLACKSTONE AND JEANNE SHAMI

Born within eight years of each other, Shakespeare and Donne grew up under the terms of the Elizabethan Settlement, as a result of which the monarch's governance of all things political, social, and cultural merged with the governance of religious belief and practice through the Act of Uniformity and mandated use of the *Book of Common Prayer*. As Patrick Collinson has observed, however, Elizabeth's best intentions of bringing "settlement" to years of religious turmoil and effecting uniformity and commonality of religious belief among her subjects must be delineated from the grassroots reality of diverse religious allegiances and practices throughout her reign and that of her seventeenth-century Stuart successors: "The result was an Established Church that stood firm on the basis of the Elizabethan Settlement, but which would never again embrace the whole nation."[1] Rather than being generally or casually touched by the religio-political turmoil of their day, Shakespeare and Donne shared a particular divergence from the uniformity of settlement. While admittedly better documented for Donne's higher-profile family than for Shakespeare's, both families retained an allegiance to Catholicism, and what little we can deduce regarding their education suggests that individuals who harbored some form of Catholic belief, even Jesuits, figured among their teachers and early influences.[2]

A third commonality also links Shakespeare and Donne in the sociopolitical, secular sphere. Ultimately, they both rose through the support of members of the nobility and the Privy Council to enjoy the patronage of James I, whose role as monarch, like that of Elizabeth, encompassed responsibilities as supreme governor of the Church of England. Royal patronage brought both Shakespeare and Donne not only social advancement but also public responsibilities in the performance and popular negotiation of an interconnected set of hegemonic values, including political and national allegiance, social mores, personal identity, and religious beliefs. As a member of the King's Men and especially as one of their principal playwrights, Shakespeare could have been expected to articulate points of view aligned with James's agenda, whether the company was performing at court, in its London playhouses, or on tour in the provinces. As royal chaplain, later dean of St. Paul's, and one of the best-known preachers of his day, Donne could have been expected to promote allegiance to the king and compliance with Church of England doctrine, whether preaching before the king at court, publicly at Paul's Cross, or to his congregation at St. Dunstan's-in-the-West or visiting patrons and friends in the countryside.

Contemporary accounts and more recent scholarship have often cast playwright/players and preachers in opposing roles. In Donne's case, it has been argued that the performative dimension of his preaching was in fact influenced by his knowledge of theater, but he appears to be an exception to the increasingly antagonistic positions taken by players and preachers in the late sixteenth and seventeenth centuries.[3] This antipathy derived in part from a fundamental commonality. The pulpit and the theater were both performative venues that appealed to a broad cross-section of early modern society from the lowly apprentice to the court elite. They were major competitors whose success depended on their capacity to engage an audience and whose live performances in a primarily illiterate society, along with extended distribution in print, could approach the impact of twenty-first-century mass media in their contribution to the development of shared values and identity.[4] Although more recent Shakespearean and Donnean scholarship has interested itself in the performative dimension of their work, over time, studies of both have tended to focus on the content and substance of their work in print more than the performative and persuasive mechanisms employed in the texts to appeal to live audiences. Clearly there were significant differences between Donne's sermons and Shakespeare's plays, but given the performative success enjoyed by Shakespeare and Donne as contemporaries in two rival disciplines, this survey of their approaches to engaging an audience is concerned with providing a snapshot of some of the commonalities across performative genres and their impact on early modern audiences.

Inasmuch as theatrical and homiletic performances were thought to be competing for the same audiences in early modern England (a result, it has been argued, of the liturgical vacuum created by focus on the word rather than on ritual in post-Reformation churches: Crockett, *Play of Paradox*, 33), an appreciation of how those audiences participated in these performances can tell us much about early modern sensibilities and the role of public performance in shaping them. What exactly was the experience of a playgoer or sermongoer, a spectator or a listener engaged in the "arts of hearing"? Moreover, how does this contribute to our understanding of the ability of both plays and sermons to interrogate moral, political, and cultural values, engage the consciences of audiences in the processes of examining the state of their souls or constructing a sense of self, and probe the cultural anxieties of an age in which the participants' identities were being fashioned as both individuals and as subjects of church and state? Although there are clearly significant differences between Shakespeare's plays and Donne's sermons, here we focus on the ways they engaged these audiences through similarly experiential processes by activating the individual as well as the collective conscience in a performative journey. Both types of performance led the audience to experiences such as anxiety, conflict, interrogation, empathy, enmity, and fear in a context of crisis and climax. Although both sermon and play offered the obligatory resolution or denouement, their ultimate effect is one of active, ongoing engagement engendered through the manipulation of mechanisms promoting distance or empathy. These in turn set in motion a potentially transformative process of reflection and questioning that could extend beyond the particular performance. Here we are concerned less with the content of their work and more with understanding similarities in the way in which Donne, Shakespeare, and their audiences achieved this engagement.

Performance Texts and Their Commonalities

We have focused on three works that reveal several common characteristics: two Donne sermons and *The Life of Henry V*.[5] The first sermon takes as its text Luke 23:40, the words of the repentant thief crucified with Christ. Delivered during Lent on February 20, 1617/1618, it was preached at Whitehall but without the king in attendance apparently because of his "former nights watching" at a performance of *The Masque of Mountebanks* as presented by "the gentlemen of Gray's Inn."[6] The second sermon, also Lenten, is a more politically motivated piece based on Mark 4:24 ("Take heed what you heare"), which was preached to King Charles I at Whitehall on April 1, 1627. *Henry V*, thought to have been written and first performed between 1598 and 1599, most likely at the new Globe Theatre, was subsequently performed at court in January 1605. We therefore focus specifically on parallel "performance" texts of each work—not only the surviving printed texts but also the full performative experience encompassing performer and court audience and potentially even extending through audience response beyond the venue or the temporal boundaries of the actual event.

Beyond related venues and audiences these three performance texts have been chosen because they display other commonalities. As the capstone to the three *Henry IV* and *Henry V* plays, the conversion in *Henry V* of Prince Hal from Falstaff's comrade in crime to a Christian king has been closely linked to the Vice figure/Everyman conflict of the medieval morality play with its roots in didactic, homiletic tradition.[7] Having been critically regarded and/or produced as overt pieces of propaganda, *Henry V* and the sermons, particularly the later sermon, also share rhetorical elements that have been linked to a persuasive agenda.[8] More generally, as a history play rather than a tragedy or a comedy, the play highlights an essential commonality of approach with sermon literature in that both Shakespeare and Donne are interpreting apparently stable historical texts—the Bible and the English chronicles—in an effort to make their immediate and current application readily apparent and to engage an audience in actively applying them at both personal and collective levels. In these three performative pieces we can in fact see Donne and Shakespeare selecting texts that lead to related thematic materials as well as to dramatic, conflicted, dialogic, and questioning moments with especially strong performative potential and elements that can contribute to a highly participatory and innately metaperformative experience for the audience.

Donne makes it clear that he expects his congregations to play an active, participatory role in the performance of sermons. Their vocation while they are at church is to be hearers and thereby doers of the Word: "Hath God made this World his Theatre, . . . that man may represent God in his conversation; and wilt thou play no part? But think that thou only wast made to pass thy time merrily, and to be the only spectator upon this Theatre? Is the world a great and harmonious Organ, where all parts are play'd, and all play parts; and must thou only sit idle and hear it?" (1.207). Perhaps the most metatheatrical of Shakespeare's plays, *Henry V*, foregrounds the discrepancy between the stage and the chronicle accounts to emphasize the extent to which Shakespeare wishes to motivate his audience to "piece out our imperfections with your thoughts," "thoughts that now must deck our kings, / Carry them here and there, jumping o'er times" (Prologue, 23, 28–29). This shared focus on audience participation serves to frame the propagandist and conformist intentions commonly ascribed to the play and the later sermon in particular. The reception of the 1627 sermon and the highly divergent interpretation and reception of *Henry V* during more than 400 years of performance history reveal a volatile instability in received meaning, particularly when the audience is motivated self-consciously to participate in "producing" the performance themselves.

Court Audiences and Performance Spaces

Although Donne did deliver sermons for more mixed (St. Paul's Cross) and popular (St. Dunstan's-in-the-West) congregations, they were intended for one performance and one particular audience only, whereas *Henry V* was presumably written for multiple performances, first at the public playhouse and only later at court. By focusing on the court audiences that these sermons and the play have in common, however, we are highlighting both the potential diversity within court audiences and the clear understanding on the part of Donne and Shakespeare of commonalities in the way individuals within an audience generally engage with public performance. Peter McCullough has demonstrated that preachers at court performed in a complex social space, and John Astington has noted that "the performative dynamics of sermons at court were comparable to those of theatrical entertainment."[9] If a sermon was preached in the Chapel Royal (with a capacity of 500 auditors), one could expect that the king, if in attendance, had taken his seat in the royal closet, an elevated chamber over the body of the chapel that emphasized his royal supremacy both by its physical distance and by its symbolically significant screen of latticed windows. Once the monarch was seated, the rest of the entourage descended the stairs to sit in the stalls reserved for court officers and titled nobility, who were separated on either side of the chapel by sex. Staff from below stairs were also allowed into the chapel, as were knights and gentry, and it appears that movable benches supplied the necessary seating. If court sermons were preached in the outdoor Preaching Place, this venue could accommodate up to 2,000 spectators across a broad spectrum that could include the king, courtiers, privy councillors, gentry, commoners, and clergy (McCullough, *Sermons at Court*, 42–49). Astington has likewise done a detailed study of seating and audience dynamics for plays with reference to extant drawings and records of performances, which reveal a similar arrangement for seating the monarch (in a central, raised position) and the same array of individuals associated with the court seated in degrees or possibly standing as appropriate to their status. The capacity of the Jacobean court spaces commonly used by players would have been similar to the capacity of the private theaters like Blackfriars. They probably ranged from a few hundred at most in the great chamber to considerably more in the hall, where, for a performance of the King's Men in 1613, it was reported that "many hundreds of people stood attending the same."[10] Unlike the "accidental" audiences of the public playhouses, the audiences for both sermons and plays would have been to some degree integral in their shared relationship to the court and the king, but they were still of mixed backgrounds and likely to experience the events in particular ways. Just as the physical location in which the sermon was preached and the relative physical relationship between preacher, king, and the various degrees of the congregation would generate much different experiences in the auditors/spectators, so, too, would the physical dynamics of playgoers at court have influenced the nature of their engagement with the performances of players and king and the impact of those performances on them.[11]

Nearness and Distance

Intriguingly, though, both Donne and Shakespeare cultivated a persuasive mode of performance that blurred the complex divisions within and among the spectators, the performers, and the characters or personae presented. Appealing to the individual as well as the collectivized congregation or audience, Donne and Shakespeare engaged audiences by varying the tone of their performance from intimate and introverted moments generating self-reflection to high rhetorical constructions reinforcing group commonalities such as nationalism and Christianity. At one end of the spectrum Donne argued that "It is not the depth, nor the wit, nor the eloquence of the Preacher that pierces us, but his nearenesse; that he speaks to my conscience, as though he had been behinde the hangings when I sinned, and as though he had read the book of the day of Judgement already" (3.142).[12] When the preacher achieves nearness, the listeners—who must cooperate in the process—hear "the Sermon of the Sermon" (rather than merely its logic, rhetoric, or ethics: 7.293)—as in the case of the 1627 sermon where Donne warns both whispering and silent critics of the king, "That which thy heart hath said, though the Law have not, though the Jury have not, though the Peers have not, God hath heard thee say" (7.408). This experience, this moment, is intensely personal, although, paradoxically, it is achieved only within the communal preaching situation. As Donne explains in his Christmas 1629 sermon—specifically in the context of whether congregants should sit or kneel—"I would speake so, as the congregation should not know whom I meane; but so, as that they whom it concernes, might know I meane them" (8.152). This targeted nearness, a sniper's assault on the particular sin of a particular sinner that is camouflaged by the more general moral point, required rhetorical skill, tact, and deft assurance in walking the line between revelation and recognition, which would accomplish for each sinner exactly that conversion or transformation born of surprise, shock, and relief. The relief is based on the hearers' realization that, charitably, the sermon resists particular revilings, something James's *Directions to Preachers* in 1622 had attempted to eradicate from sermons, but at the same time, the hearers recognize the close call and can resolve to reform their ways.

This appeal to the individual conscience and a sense of self had its counterpart in Shakespeare's soliloquies, where the individual spectator vicariously experiences the interior deliberations of key characters—often at transformative moments of crisis. In *Henry V* these moments of nearness feature a spectrum of characters, ranging from the king himself to the boy who decides to abandon his service to Nym, Bardolph, and Pistol because "they will steal anything, and call it purchase" and because "they would have me as familiar with men's pockets as their gloves or their handkerchers; which makes much against my manhood" (V.ii.44, 49–52). Henry's soliloquy before the Battle of Agincourt is situated at the dark and introspective heart of the play. Emphasizing his aloneness and isolation, Henry eloquently strips away the external "ceremony" of kingship and emphasizes his fundamental kinship with "the wretched slave." Yet this speech must really be seen as the climax to the previous scenes in Act IV, in which Henry enacts the performative and transformative impulses of the preacher who seeks nearness with the individuals in his congregation. Shakespeare's is a more complicated relationship of engagement with the audience than that of Donne because Henry V as preacher speaks only indirectly to the audience through his appeals to his men, with whom an audience may identify. Through this identification, however, a similar emphasis is placed on nearness, personal reflection, and the individual conscience. After drawing a moral lesson from the French enemy, who "are our outward consciences, / And preachers to us all," Henry dons Sir Thomas Erpingham's cloak and sets off on his own because "I and my bosom must debate awhile, / And then I would no other company" (IV.i.8–9, 31–32). This speech frames all of what leads up to his soliloquy in an introspective mode while simultaneously conjuring up a complex overlay of "a little touch of Harry in the night," whose conversion from an Eastcheap specialist in highway robbery to a Christian king prepares him to meet the ordinary soldier literally on common ground (IV.Chorus.47). Clearly a man of many parts, Henry as Harry dons a disguise that allows him to achieve the "nearnesse" of the preacher "behind the hangings" as well as the kind of direct access Charles would have envied in dealing with the "whisperers" Donne exposes in 1627.

Despite Henry's lack of success in "converting" the doubting soldiers to his point of view, his performance the night before the Battle of Agincourt establishes the interconnection between Donne's concept of nearness and the rhetorical device of common ground, suggesting a performative interest in transformation or conversion shared by both Donne and Shakespeare. However, in the extroverted St. Crispin's Day speech, which follows Henry's soliloquy closely, he also establishes common ground with the ultimate objective of transforming his dejected army to embrace a collective nationalism and an expansive vision of "We few, we happy few, we band of brothers," who will be remembered "From this day to the ending of the world" (IV.ii.58, 60). In comparatively few lines, Henry goes from establishing nearness with individual soldiers and spectators to publicly reasserting his position of authority with an appeal to the collective consciousness of his men and the audience.

A close look simply at the rhetorical use of pronouns in this speech reveals how carefully Shakespeare could craft such speeches for the persuasive effect of strategically shifting the relative nearness or distance of the audience offstage as well as onstage and thereby attempting to manipulate levels of empathy and sympathy.[13] Henry begins by establishing first-person common ground with his men through the projection of his ambitions for honor onto the ideal common soldier and the nationalistic audience that his speech labors to construct. Moving antithetically to the third person, "he which hath no stomach to this fight," Henry separates himself and the ideal soldier from the fearful soldier and opens up the possibility for further separation by encouraging such men to leave—yet again demonstrating that he is "no tyrant, but a Christian king" (I.ii.241). In contrast, he proceeds to lead his army in imagining the personal and national pride they will enjoy after the battle. He aligns the royal "we" with the man "that shall see this day, and live old age, / . . . And say, 'Tomorrow is Saint Crispian'" (IV.iii.28, 44, 46). By the time he has imagined how they will all be remembered he can confidently shift to the all-encompassing hegemonic "we":

> We few, we happy few, we band of brothers;
> For he to-day that sheds his blood with me
> Shall be my brother; be he ne'er so vile
> This day shall gentle his condition:
> And gentlemen in England now a-bed
> Shall think themselves accurs'd they were not here.
>
> (IV.iii.60–65)

The powerful identification Henry achieves through the hegemonic "we" is strengthened further by contrasting third-person references to individuals who will regret not sharing in the honor derived from the battle. That anyone would even consider early in this speech taking Henry up on his offer of a passport and money to depart before the fight is unthinkable once he has started on this extroverted and confidently persuasive performance, and it is easy to imagine his onstage audience leading Elizabethan theater audiences in enthusiastic cheers in response to it. Yet such a defection is momentarily unthinkable only because of the way the speech positions both subject and audience member relative to the speaker.

Like Shakespeare, who appeals to his audiences through identification with Henry's shifting persona and/or stage audiences, in his Lenten sermon of 1617/1618 (in the absence of the king), Donne approaches audience engagement by constantly situating the relative positions of preacher and congregant on a continuum of nearness and distance. He uses many of the same rhetorical devices as Shakespeare, such as shifting pronouns, interrogative or imperative sentence structure, and common ground. For instance, at the end of the sermon Donne uses the familiar "thou" in establishing an interrogatory "nearnesse" with individual congregants and sets himself up on comparatively common ground: "[W]hy doest thou insult upon him [Christ], revile him, who art in as ill state as he? thou seest him, (who, though thou knowest it not, hath other manner of assurances, then thou canst have) in Agonies, in Feares, in Complaints, in Lamentations: Why fearest not thou, being under the same condemnation? . . . Thou hast no better a life then I, thou art no farther from thy death then I; and the consideration of my condemnation, hath brought me to fear God: why shouldst not thou feare, being under the same condemnation? . . . why shouldst thou not fear now? why shouldst thou not go so far towards thy conversion this minute?" (1.266–67).

In the very next sentence, however, Donne steps back to conclude the sermon with a collectivizing (and climactic) appeal to the congregation that he constructs as containing both Christ and the good thief from the crucifixion:

To end all, it is all our cases; we are all under the same condemnation . . . what sin soever God hath found in any, he may find in us; either that we have falne into it by our misuse of his grace, or should fall into it, if he should withdraw his grace. In those that are damned before, we are damned in Effigie; such as we are, are damned; and we might be, but that he which was *Medius inter personas divinas*, in his glory, in heaven; and *Medius inter prophetas*, in his Transfiguration in Mount *Thabor*; and *Medius inter Latrones*, in his Humiliation in this text, is *Medius inter nos*, in the midst of the Christian Church, in the midst of us, in this Congregation, and takes into his own mouth now, the words which he put into the thiefs mouth then, and more: . . . since I have done and suffered so much to rescue you from this condemnation, *Nonne timetis*? will ye not fear the Lord, but choose still to be under the same condemnation? [1.267].

Participants and Performers

By constantly shifting the relative nearness or distance experienced by their audiences, Shakespeare and Donne not only cut across the social complexity of the court through appeals to the individual and the collective but also heighten audience involvement through the resulting experiential and participatory dimension of these shifts. The persuasive interest in transformation and conversion in *Henry V* and the sermons contributes to an actively engaged audience. Herbert Blau regards the most fundamental ingredient of performance as "the audience, projecting there upon the empty space, where there is nothing either good or bad but thinking makes it so," and Roger Scruton has argued that emotional response to a work of art "is a function not of the assertedness of its core of thought, but rather of the degree of 'imaginative involvement' that is experienced."[14] As we have already seen, Shakespeare and Donne appear to have shared these perceptions. Donne demanded of individuals in his congregations that they not simply watch or listen but also engage as players in God's theater of the world, and Shakespeare's Chorus repeatedly demands that playgoers activate their "imaginary forces" (Prologue, 18) to complete the performance of *Henry V*.[15] Both Donne and Shakespeare construct their audiences in the active rather than the passive voice. They are to think of themselves as subjects rather than objects within the performance texts. For these early modern spectators, then, performances of the sermons and the play constituted events in which audience members, as well as actors, were metamorphosed to productive or performative roles beyond the passive consumption of a text.

The social dynamics at court, then, provide a good example of the way in which the roles and relationships within and among spectators, performers, and the characters or personae presented can merge in performance. To begin with, seated in a raised, central location, the king constituted a powerful performative presence even from behind the lattice windows in the Chapel Royal. His performance—whether apparently critical, positively responsive, apparently uninterested—would have been as important as the play or sermon to the other members of the audience and perhaps even more important to the preacher or players, who became spectators themselves as they watched for his reactions. Even when he was not present for the Lenten sermon, he would have had an impact on the dynamics of the performance as everyone would have been aware of his absence, and some would no doubt have recalled his performance at the masque the night before.[16] In his Lenten sermon of 1627, Donne draws particular attention to the complicated performative roles and relationships negotiated by preacher, king, and a congregation of subjects in the context of any sermon:

> And into this part I enter with such a protestation, as perchance may not become me: That this is the first time in all my life . . . that in the exercise of my Ministery, I wished the King away; That ever I had any kinde of loathnesse that the King should hear all that I sayd. Here, for a little while, it will be a little otherwise; because in this branch, I am led, to speak of some particular duties of subjects; and in my poor way, I have thought it somewhat an Eccentrique motion, and off of the naturall Poles, to speake of the Duties of subjects before the King, or of the duties of Kings, in publike and popular Congregations [7.403].

Any time a speaker invokes an "I" accompanied by a confessional tone it is likely to shock an audience into full alert, but when Donne simultaneously also singled out one of his congregation—his most important performative counterpart, the king—the level of engagement must have been electric. Yet the King's Men were in a similar position when invited to perform the roles of *Henry V* and his subjects before James, another Christian king (though not perhaps to be classified as a "plain soldier" [V.ii.153]), and his subjects. For this occasion, when they did in fact have a monarch "to behold the swelling scene" (Prologue, 4), they must have used a prologue different from the one that accompanies the extant version of the play, and it would no doubt have addressed the same complicated relationship between a performer/subject presenting king and subjects to a performer/king and other participants/subjects. The full performance text of the 1627 sermon further illuminates the genuine importance of the roles played by the early modern audience versus today's largely passive/responsive audiences in the popular theater. Although we are uncertain of the precise reason, the king and Bishop William Laud responded to the sermon with concerns and asked Donne to provide a full text for examination. Rather than suspicion and displeasure, Donne had expected praise, or at least affirmation, from Charles for the sermon's condemnation of the king's courtly critics, and so Donne responded to the concerns with extreme surprise, fear of subsequently appearing before the king or even being seen with others of the court, and possibly even anxieties about losing his position as royal chaplain to Charles.[17] Ultimately, the king did not pursue the matter further, but this extreme example of audience "participation" in a courtly performance text demonstrates that its role was far from passive or inconsequential.

Presence and Mediality

The physical, social, and performative dynamics of these three events at court suggest that participants were less aware of any dichotomies between performance and life, performer and audience, observer and observed, subject and object than they were of what Erika Fischer-Lichte calls a sense of "co-presence." Drawing on the work of John L. Austin, Fischer-Lichte observes that the performative tends "to destabilize and even collapse binary oppositions," with actors like Donne becoming spectators and spectators like Charles and Laud becoming actors and that consequently theater takes place in a medial position "*between* the actors and spectators, and even between the spectators themselves."[18] Blau has similarly situated theater "in the middle distance, between elsewhere and nowhere, the semblance of an act and the resemblance of an image" (218). We argue that this mediality applied as well in the context of the sermons and that the particular spatial and social orientation of the participants in all three court performances constituted what Peter Brook has described as "a practical difference between actor and audience, not a fundamental one" with respect to performative dynamics—or, as we shall see, the attribution of meaning.[19]

Recent scholarship in the field of cognitive studies reinforces the blurred nature of performative dynamics and extends it to encompass audience perceptions of the performance of characters as they may have been presented on stage or in the pulpit. Drawing from the studies of cognitive scientists, Bruce McConachie notes that critically constructed dichotomies such as auditor and spectator, hearing and seeing, and body and mind break down under scientific scrutiny. He also notes that "when engaged in the performance of a play, spectators usually experience 'actor/characters' as a blend, not as separate entities." He describes a process whereby individuals "watching others act in intentional ways" generate "visuomotor representations" that mirror the actions of the performer/character and "stimulate empathy, typically the first step toward our emotional and social engagements in the theatre" (56, 63). By embodying or simulating "the experiences of actor/characters in their own minds" spectators are able to "read their [the actors'/characters'] minds" and "ascribe beliefs, desires, intentions, and emotions to them." This empathy enables audience members "to judge onstage actions" and "form feelings of sympathy or antipathy for many actor/characters."[20]

What emerges from an understanding of human cognitive processes, then, is that, like playwrights and actors who have been perceived as dependent on their mimetic skills, so, too, are spectators dependent on their capacity imaginatively to imitate what they are seeing. Describing a similar process, Fischer-Lichte also identifies the sense of self that derives from the blurring of mind and body that occurs when spectators "experience the performer as well as themselves as embodied minds" (99). Although clearly the visual dimensions of Donne's performances as preacher were of a different order from those of *Henry V* as performed by the King's Men, the processes McConachie and Fischer-Lichte outline may be applied to Donne's sermons as well as to Shakespeare's play. Moreover, because Donne incorporates many roles simultaneously in one person (actor/character/author/spectator), he provides a useful window onto the early modern understanding of cognitive processes and the capacity of individuals like Donne and Shakespeare to make use of that understanding in engaging their audiences.

Playgoers experience the events of *Henry V* on stage in the present tense while constantly being reminded by the Chorus (usually in the progressive aspect) to "eke out our performance with your mind" by carrying the player/kings "here and there, jumping o'er times" and large distances as the "swift scene flies" "with imagin'd wing."[21] Perhaps no other early modern play so clearly illustrates McConachie's statement that "cognitive imitation is a crucial part of spectating" (72). Past and present merge as playgoers experience the immediacy of Henry V's dramatic journey both onstage and cognitively as a journey mirrored in their minds.

Much like the mediating Chorus in *Henry V*, Donne approaches his sermons with the same sense of "presentness." Like Shakespeare, he draws upon sources presumed to be historical, but the whole point of the sermons is that they are happening *hic et nunc*. They are constructed to be immediately and personally implicating for each individual in the courtly congregation. The apparently stable sources both Donne and Shakespeare engage become transformed and transformative as they seize on dramatic, dialogic, and interrogative moments for exploration. Vividly conjuring up images and events from his text, Donne guides individual congregants in mirroring and applying the images to their own situation in such a way that they will be moved to spiritual conversion.[22] His sermons are carefully structured with split-second moral timing so that the preacher's arrows, his piercing words, hit home to an audience prepared to recognize themselves in the text and its examples and to experience the moment of calling and conversion to God, where hearers can no longer separate themselves from application of the sermon to their consciences. With the aid of the Holy Spirit, preacher and auditor join together to trouble the conscience and, through that "holy vexation," move it to recognition, catharsis, and final conformity with Christ (2.59). To this end Donne dissolves past into present when, for instance, Christ, who is at the center of the crucifixion scene in the Lenten sermon, is depicted as immediately present, speaking through the preacher from the pulpit, and immediately present to individuals whose consciences open them to conversion. Donne situates his reenactment of the events of Luke 23 in the present tense and speaks at length in the voice of the condemned thief attempting to convert his fellow thief—while simultaneously demonstrating the immediate application of the thief's words to the present congregation: "[E]very man may find some such particular condemnation in himself, and in his own crosses, if he will but read his own history in a true copy" (1.266). Immediacy is further emphasized as the audience is encouraged to look "there" (repeated four times) at the thief as preacher ("there's his Christning," "there's his Funeral," "there's his Consecration," "there's his Canonization"). That Good Friday spectacle is immediately applicable to this beginning of Lent, Donne says, as he gathers the "I" who would be "loath to think that you never fulfill the sufferings of Christ Jesus in your flesh but upon Goodfriday" with the "you" who fast and prepare for Christ's coming all through Lent until they become those whose "humiliation of ours in the text, be an Advent, a preparation to his Resurrection, and coming in glory" (1.253). Donne invokes that moment of crucifixion, Christ's passion, but only to throw into relief the present moment—"now"—to demonstrate how "powerfully," "presently," "instantly," and especially how "suddainly" God works: "This condemned person who had been a thief, execrable amongst men, and a blasphemer, execrating God, was suddainly a Convertite, suddainly a Confessor, suddainly a Martyr, suddainly a Doctor to preach to others." Donne approaches the climactic conclusion of the 1627 sermon with similar immediacy (1.254). In a scene reminiscent of *Dr. Faustus*, he leads members of his congregation vividly to imagine Satan speaking to them on their deathbed: "[T]hen when thou shalt see, or seem to see his hand turning the streame of thy Saviours bloud into another channell, and telling thee, here's enough for Jew and Turke, but not a drop for thee . . . Take heed what you heare" (7.413).

Martin Seel observes that "we yearn for a sense of the presence of our lives," and Fischer-Lichte argues that this is the attraction of theater. Playgoers "sense that the actor is present in an unusually intense way, granting them in turn an intense sensation of themselves as present."[23] Given the intensity with which Donne's sermons appeal to the spiritual presence of the congregants through the nearness of the preacher, it becomes clearer how the performative appeal of his sermons rivaled that of the theater in engaging many early modern spectators.

Characters and Perspectives

A key factor in the intense presence afforded by these performances is the palette of characters, personae, or perspectives through which the diverse court audience might access them. As McConachie has noted, the kind of engagement that evolves from empathy to sympathy requires that the audience first "consciously judge [the characters] . . . to be worthy of their concern," and this judgment requires that they have "feelings or emotions that are in concert with the interests or desires the sympathizer (justifiably) attributes to the [character] . . . Rather than stepping into an actor/character's shoes, sympathy involves the spectator in projecting her or his own beliefs and feelings onto the stage figure" (*Engaging Audiences*, 99, 202). Engaging an audience with diverse interests, desires, and beliefs therefore requires a diversity of characters to appeal to individual audience members. It is a commonplace observation to see the range of characters in Shakespeare's plays as mirroring the social microcosm of the Globe audience and the macrocosm of English society, but Donne takes a similarly polyvocal approach to his sermons—in the same style that he attributes to the Bible, an "*Opus variegatum*, a work compact of divers pieces, curiously inlaid, and varied for the making up of some figure, some representation:

and likelyest to be that which in sumptuous buildings, we use to call now *Mosaick* work: for that very word originally signifies, to vary, to mingle, to diversifie" (1.252).

Donne marvels at the range of voices brought together within the Bible, citing those of the serpent in the Garden of Eden, Balaam's ass, "prophane Poets," Caiaphas, the devil, and the good thief crucified with Christ (1.253) and appears to create a similar mosaic in his own sermons in hopes that "though a man understand not a whole Sermon, or remember not a whole Sermon, yet he doth well, that layeth hold upon such Notes therein as may be appliable to his own case, and his own conscience, and conduce to his own edification" (1.253, 7.393). The performative result of his presentation of multiple voices is a tour de force, a kind of one-man show in which the preacher presents all of the characters' perspectives and acts all of the parts.

In his Lenten sermon Donne speaks at length in the character of the thief and in the character of Christ, but he also conjures up a shorter concluding scene featuring David's confession to Nathan and his resulting forgiveness. Other parallel snapshots in the sermon focus on "extemporal" preachers such as St. Augustine, St. Bernard, and St. Basil, as well as conversions such as those of Judas and St. Paul. Even in the process of verifying the story of the thief, Donne cites from no less than seven expositors of the text (Athanasius, Origen, Chrysostom, Hilary, Theophylact, Jerome, and Augustine). As he performs all these voices, the shifting pronouns ("we," "you," "I") engage the audience by asking them to enact all of these roles as well, especially those of thieves and sinners: "[W]e see that all men are theeves in their kindes, in their courses; but yet we know, that we our selves are so too . . . We may cry out against Theft, that we may steale the safelier" (1.256). To induce sympathy with his exemplar—a preacher who was also a murderer and a thief—Donne uses the pronoun "we" to include men in all vocations, all of whom steal, and all of whom steal even from themselves—*felo de se*—and in the last lines of the sermon he deftly merges the various voices he has presented. Christ and his audience merge as "judgment is given upon you both, execution begun upon you both." From his assertion that "Thou hast no better a life then I," Donne merges his own voice with that of his audience to conclude that "we are all under the same condemnation." In the end, the voices of all three preachers—Christ, the thief, and Donne—merge in a final variation of the text: "[W]ill ye not fear the Lord, but choose still to be under the same condemnation?" (1.266–67).

For his 1627 Whitehall sermon (with the king in attendance), the text is drawn from Christ's sermon or sermons, so it is understandable that Christ's voice dominates throughout, but Donne also speaks in the voices of God, Satan, the Apostles, Isaiah, St. John, David, Solomon, Jeremy, Seneca, Tertullian, Tacitus—even the courtly earwigs or whisperers he condemns and members of his audience as he imagines them on their deathbeds. The latter scene serves to remind us that both Donne's sermons and Shakespeare's plays reflect their own mirroring or projections of the individuals and social groups in their audiences and therefore betray their level of empathy and sympathy for those individuals.[24] The characters they construct are intended to facilitate audience access to the world of the play through empathy, sympathy, and antipathy, but in a closely related effort they also attempt to determine audience response by frequently repositioning their attention from different perspectives or points of view. Again, this effect may be most obvious in *Henry V,* where scenes with the Chorus alternate with scenes at the English court and Eastcheap, with the English and French camps, or with scenes on the battlefield and during Kate's English lesson. The perspective afforded by the epic overview and imperative tone of the Chorus contrasts sharply with that of the interrogative and introverted tone of soliloquies or the raucous lead-up to Falstaff's death in Eastcheap. Speaking of Shakespeare, S. L. Bethell postulated that his work required an audience with the "ability to shift rapidly its modes of attention" to achieve "multi-consciousness in temporal succession."[25] We argue that multiconsciousness was not only a requirement but also a major attraction of early modern theater but that Donne also offers shifting perspectives to engage his audiences. For instance, the 1627 sermon is structured around the repeated refrain of the text: "Take heed what you heare." Such repetition echoes the emphatic/didactic effect of the repeated description of Henry as a "Christian king," but in Donne's sermon each section subtly repositions the audience to hear the phrase from a different perspective to the point that the phrase undergoes a shift in meaning from Christ's directive to his apostles that they listen carefully to what he said, to Donne's warning to individuals at court that they take care not to listen to malicious critique of the king, to Donne's encouragement of individuals to listen carefully to the devil to be prepared to refute him. As with Shakespeare's contrasting or parallel scenes, Donne also makes much use of antithesis by developing contrasting points of view (for example, Christ versus Satan, Catholic Church versus Church of England) to cultivate a sense of belonging or exclusion of the undesirable. Just as multiple characters in one dramatic scene afford different points of access to the action, so, too, does Donne construct his scenes using a full range of character perspectives. With the crucifixion, for instance, he focuses on Christ and the two thieves, but he also frames the scene from the perspectives of the public, the priests, the scribes, the Pharisees, the elders, the soldiers, Pilate, and other rulers (1.262–63). Offering up more immediate perspectives on the fear of God—or lack thereof—he directly addresses the broad social classes in his congregation: "Great men are above fear, no envy can reach them: Miserable men are below fear, no change can make them worse: and for persons of middle rank, and more publick feares, of plagues, of famines, or such, the abundant and over-flowing goodness of God hath so long accustomed us to miraculous deliverances, that we feare nothing, but thinke to have miracles in ordinary, and neglect ordinary remedies" (1.264).

Metaperformative Experiences

Donne's allusion to "great men," "miserable men," and "persons of middle rank" is a mild example of the metaperformative, an instance in which attention is drawn to some element of the performance text in such a way that we become particularly aware of the artificially determined conventions surrounding the performative form and/or more intensely aware of the real life "drama" in which the performative event is occurring. Donne most likely attracted people's attention when he unflatteringly singled out two social levels ("miserable men" were most likely not represented) that conformed roughly with the spatially delineated segments of the congregation, including that reserved for the king. The level of audience engagement was likely nowhere near as intense, however, as the previously mentioned instance in which he drew attention to his own personal anxieties as performer/preacher and announced that he wished the king were not there.

Contrary to the assumptions of some scholars like Chaim, who talks of metatheatrical moments as having a "distancing" effect, we argue that both Donne and Shakespeare create metahomiletic or metatheatrical moments to engage their audiences more immediately in the performative event.[26]

As with the other mechanisms of engagement previously identified, though, the metaperformative exists as one end of a continuum bounded at the other end by the simply performative, and it is invoked by degrees. Shakespeare's use of it appears far less dangerous and more conventional by comparison with Donne. Bridget Escolme argues that "Shakespeare's stage figures have another set of desires and interests, inseparable from those of the actor. They want the audience to listen to them, notice them, approve their performance, ignore others on stage for their sake. The objectives of these figures are bound up with the fact that they know you're there."[27]

Generally speaking, though, the soliloquies in which characters share their inner thoughts with the audience barely register as metatheatrical even when compared with the other form of direct address in the play, that of the Chorus, who repeatedly reminds the audience members of their participatory role and the great discrepancy between the theatrical and the historical event. However, the Chorus—as well as other self-consciously performative elements such as the spectacle of the real King James watching an actor play another king or Henry's visit with his men in disguise—tend to reinforce and advance the dramatic flow of the play. Similarly, the reflexive quality of Donne's 1627 Lenten sermon, overtly based on a sermon by Christ, focuses our attention on Donne's sermon all the more intently.

Donne makes his audience more conscious of and consequently more immediately engaged in the real-life dimension of the event when he draws attention to himself, other performers/preachers, or members of his congregation. Opening allusions in the 1627 sermon to "Every man that cometh to hear here, every man that cometh to speak here," and "any thing I say here" (7.393–94) immediately make the audience self-consciously aware of the performative venue of the event, but it is the jolt of self-recognition or recognition by others that is at the heart of his transformative objective in the sermons and the prime motivator for introducing metaperformative elements. He delivers such a jolt with his vigorous condemnation of "earwigs" or court whisperers and his oddly apposite reference (almost certainly to be applied to Henrietta Maria) to "Very religious Kings" who "may have had wives, that may have retained some tincture, some impressions of errour, which they may have sucked in their infancy, from another Church, and yet would be loth, those wives should be publikely traduced to be Heretiques, or passionately proclaimed to be Idolaters" (7.409). Yet an even greater jolt to audience engagement comes at the end of the sermon, when he itemizes character types almost certainly present as motivated by Satan. It begins simply with "youth must have pleasures, and greatnesse must have State," but he moves on more specifically to "a young man" who pursues "wantonesse"; "great officers" who "transfer their inaccessiblenesse, upon necessary State, when it is an effect of their own lazinese, or indulgence to their pleasures"; and "rich landlords" who "transfer all their oppression of tenants, to the necessity of supporting the charge of wives and children, when it is an effect of their profusenesse and prodigality." He concludes the increasingly powerful list by switching to the second person in a context calculated to implicate a much broader segment of his audience: "Nay you may heare a voice, that may call you to this place, and yet be his [Satan's] voice; which is that, which Saint *Augustine* confesses and laments, that even to these places persons come to look upon one another, that can meet no where else" (7.412–13).

Such allusions are more dangerous for integral than for accidental audiences—that is, audience members like those found at court, where the individuals know each other and are likely to meet again and will feel more vulnerable to such metaperformative moments than paying audiences, who come together for one performance but have no other relationship with each other that might bring them together again.[28] However, if his audiences were engaged by performance in part because they wanted to be made aware of their own presence, and if Donne entered the performative world of the pulpit because he wanted to effect real change in the form of conversion, the metatheatrical dimension of his sermons was essential.

The Interrogative Conscience

A final rhetorical mechanism that both Donne and Shakespeare employed to manipulate the level of audience engagement and participation is the question—not the so-called rhetorical question but genuine questions. Cognitive scientists have classified "seeking" as one of the six major systems of human emotions, and McConachie argues that "all actor/protagonists are inherently seekers" and that seeking and its related emotions underlie "audience engagement in all types of dramatic performances" (180, 203). It is not surprising, then, that questions figure prominently in each of the performances we are examining and that activating a questioning conscience emerges as one of the cumulative effects of all of the mechanisms of engagement we have so far examined. Despite their persuasive intentions, Donne and Shakespeare must have understood that questions rather than assertions paved a surer route to audience engagement and sympathy. We have already seen how, at the very beginning, the 1627 Lenten sermon situates the congregants in a seeking mode, listening carefully for something that "may be appliable to his own case, and his own conscience" (7.393). In Donne's entire performance of the sermons, in fact, he can be seen as presenting a role model, a seeking protagonist directed toward repeatedly troubling the conscience with questions. Some of these questions may simply be aimed at activating or energizing the conscience, but others derive from much more conflicted interiority and crises of conscience concerning not only personal morality but also its connection with religious allegiance, public duty, and authority. This is not to suggest that such questions were generally typical of sermons of this period. On the contrary, Donne is exceptional in this respect.

At an early phase of his preaching career, Donne is experimenting in his 1617/1618 sermon with a relatively dynamic but still uncontroversial engagement of the audience. Yet he chooses a biblical story that immediately provides him with three distinct characters and perspectives on an especially dramatic moment in the Passion sequence. For his specific text he chooses the thief's question: "Fearest not thou God, being under the same condemnation?" The question becomes a refrain repeated in variations throughout the sermon with increasing urgency to press Donne's congregation to mirror the thief's conversion and his attempted conversion of the other thief. As Donne outlines the steps that the thief/preacher takes, repeating his question, *Nonne Tu times?*, his voice modulates into the voice of the thief, and he engages his own audience in that voice with the questions the thief put to his own audience. In fact, the entire passage builds rhetorically through a radiating series of questions as Donne imagines the questions in the thief's own voice and imbued with their mutual experience of sin.

With the thief as a model, Donne argues that "every particular man, who is acquainted with his own history, may be such a Preacher to himself," and he dramatizes the questions that his hearers can ask of their own consciences, taking on the voice of the preacher/thief to effect their personal conversion. The questions that flow from this premise offer a probing examination of conscience, a series of questions (not merely rhetorical) that pierce his very circumstances—culminating in the painful question that the second thief's circumstances foreground: "[W]hat's all that [hope of the coming of a Messiah] to thee, who art going out of this world?" (1.263). We have already discussed Donne's carefully structured treatment of voices as the sermon comes to a conclusion, but appropriately these voices converge to end on the interrogative note that has dominated the whole: "Since I [Christ] have been made a man, and no man; been born, and died; since I have descended, and descended to the earth, and below the earth; since I have done and suffered so much to rescue you from this condemnation, *Nonne timetis*? will ye not fear the Lord, but choose still to be under the same condemnation?" (1.267).

Before proceeding to examine the full impact of the interrogative on audience engagement in the play as well as the sermons, it may be useful to broaden our understanding of the way questioning contributes to the making of meaning as well as to audience engagement. Using the basic elements of syntax as a model, Catherine Belsey has identified three types of texts as they relate to an audience: "declarative, imperative and interrogative." The declarative text imparts "knowledge to a reader whose position is thereby stabilized, through a privileged discourse which is to varying degrees invisible." The imperative text employs "a mode of address which invites [or compels] the reader to adopt a position of struggle rather than stability, specifically struggle vis-à-vis something which is marked in the text as non-fictional, as existing outside discourse, in the world . . . [It] exhorts, instructs, orders the reader, constituting the reader as a unified subject in conflict with what exists outside."[29] She includes sermons and various types of propaganda (political speeches, some documentary films) in this category and extends Steve Neale's perspective on propaganda to describe the imperative text more generally as causing its audience to identify "with one set of discourses and practices as in opposition to others . . . maintaining that identification and opposition, and . . . not resolving it but rather holding it as the position of closure."[30] The concept behind this type of text is similar to that of the "closed text" identified by many individuals like Marvin Carlson, who are concerned with the reception of texts in performance, to describe performances that are didactic and seek to generate "a precise response from a more or less precise" audience.[31] Belsey characterizes the third form of discourse, the interrogative text, as disrupting "the unity of the reader by discouraging identification with a unified subject of the enunciation. The position of the 'author' inscribed in the text, if it can be located at all, is seen as questioning or as literally contradictory" (*Critical Practice*, 91). It leaves its audience in "a place of uncertainty or of unresolved debate" to provide the answers to questions it may have overtly raised or implied.[32] Carlson would call this an "open text," one that provides the audience members with few specific clues as to how they should respond and encourages a variety of responses. In practice, the concepts of "open" and "closed" texts are best regarded as two extremes of a continuum, and Belsey notes that her syntactically derived categories "are in no sense self-contained and mutually exclusive" (*Critical Practice*, 91).

Belsey specifically associates the interrogative text with early modern theater, its diverse audiences, and the multiple perspectives on the action afforded by the predominantly thrust staging of that period, and this focus on multiple points of view relates well with Collinson's suggestion that Donne's phrase "all cohaerence gone" characterized the perceptions of an era and that "Shakespeare and countless others of his generation did not know what to believe or, if they did, could not tell when they might be called on to believe contrary things."[33] For such an audience the imperative character of morality plays and the earlier source text for *Henry V*, *Famous Victories*, would be less dramatically compelling than the increasingly interrogative orientation of Shakespeare's drama, with its searching, conflicting, and paradoxical perspectives. Likewise, the imperative character of the homiletic tradition connected with the morality plays would likely have been less engaging for an early modern audience than the more interrogative character of Donne's sermons. His popularity as a preacher, like Shakespeare's popularity as a playwright, may have had much to do with his capacity to engage his audiences on the common ground of a shared mindset and a sense of what mattered most to them.

Conclusion

What we discover from this introductory study is that both Donne and Shakespeare created performative venues that attracted and engaged similar audiences using some of the same rhetorical, dramaturgical, and performative mechanisms. They explored related issues that were of central concern to them and those who participated in their performance texts. Appealing to these participants from a position of nearness or distance, as individuals and as members of a collective, enabling them to mirror a variety of characters and occupy sometimes conflicting perspectives, these sermons, taken in conjunction with *Henry V*, suggest that the impulses behind attending sermons and plays were not that far apart. Both provided a medial space where audiences were expected actively to participate, where metaperformative moments both intentional and unintentional drew attention to the participants' "presence," their sense of self, and their sense of belonging to a group. As Blau has argued, the audience space was a "space of interrogation," a place where things happened, and where moments of nearness could be transformative for the individual and the collective conscience (219). Chief among these experiences was the negotiation of beliefs, values, and relative allegiances to church and king. While the cognitive chain of mirroring, empathy, and sympathy depended on value judgments derived from spectators' projecting their own beliefs, feelings, and experiences onto the performer/character, the cognitive and emotional interface of this process strengthened existing beliefs and generated new ones (McConachie, 110). From Donne's letters and his 1627 Lenten sermon we know that he was motivated by specific intentions when he exercised his "power of perswasivenesse" on his congregation's "spirit of persuasibility" (7.404). We do not know Shakespeare's intentions or the responses his play received, but we do know from Donne's experience that an engaged, questioning, and diverse early modern audience could bring more than one "horizon of expectations," more than one set of backgrounds, beliefs, and values and that they were very capable of using the medial space of performance to develop divergent meanings.[34]

The performative and interrogative engagement that Shakespeare and Donne fostered set them at the forefront of the cultural and political changes that marked their age. They share many characteristics with what Daniel Lerner identified as "Transitionals," who figure prominently in the evolution of modern nationalism.[35] Drawing heavily upon Lerner, Anthony Smith described these transitionals as educated individuals standing at the "point of 'engagement,' when they are just perceiving 'connections between . . . private dilemmas and public issues.' The Transitionals exhibit the key traits of inconsistency and ambivalence over old and new values and life-styles . . . The Transitionals are 'men-in-motion.'" They are torn by the conflict between "'new aspirations and old traditions.'" These "new" men have the capacity to empathize and identify with new aspects of their environment through "projection and introjection. So a man enlarges his identity; he incorporates new demands into the Self. His is a mobile sensibility." Additionally, these figures transfer their insights through "mass media" and literacy, which function like "an internal 'mobility multiplier'" that "greatly expand[s] the range of situations in which a man can imagine himself" and "bring the 'opinions of mankind' to bear on the self-images of individuals and nations."[36]

Although obviously accessing a range of mass-media options quite different from those available in modern society, Donne and Shakespeare reached the pinnacle of influence in the three most powerful variations of mass media in early modern England: the theater, the pulpit, and print publications. Their success had much to do with the transitional spaces they created by engaging the interrogative conscience of their age.

5. Mapping the Celestial in Shakespeare's *Tempest* and the Writings of John Donne

DOUGLAS TREVOR

Now more than fifty years ago, in "Donne the Space Man," William Empson excavated evidence from a range of John Donne's poems to suggest a preordination interest on the writer's part in space travel and the inhabitation of other planets. In this essay, Empson goes to great lengths to argue that Donne's apparent fascination with other worlds is evidence that the (somewhat) young poet "believed that every planet could have its Incarnation, and believed this with delight, because it automatically liberated an independent conscience from any earthly religious authority."[1] As a result of such an interest, according to Empson, Donne betrays hesitancy about "being a Christian" in the first place (79).

More recent work on the question of how early moderns conceived of the idea of a multitude of inhabited planets and space travel itself places enormous stress on Empson's claims. As David Cressy points out in his illuminating study of what he terms "England's lunar moment," a moment that runs—in his argument—from the publication of Nicholas Hill's *Philosophia Epicurea, Democritiana, Theophrastica* in 1601 through Aphra Behn's 1687 play *The Emperor of the Moon*, a wide range of English and continental authors entertained the question of whether the moon in particular might be inhabited and whether—often with voyages to the new world cited as precedent—Europeans might soon begin to journey to the moon themselves. These writers, it turns out, were very often ministers, and collectively they went out of their way to assure their readers that—in Cressy's words—"[b]elief in the plurality of worlds did not go against faith."[2] Such assurance seemed to have meant something, for while some authors interested in other worlds published their work anonymously, others did not, and none of these figures appear to have suffered persecution for their views. What Empson regarded as a blatant, transgressive form of heretical enterprise now appears, with more evidence at our disposal, to have been far less transgressive, far less of an indicator of anti-Christian sentiment, and far more widespread than was once thought.

Even prior to the early 1600s, however, the attention of English writers was drawn to the moon in new ways, prompted to a large degree—it seems—by the cosmological observations made by Giordano Bruno both in print and when he lectured at Oxford University in the summer of 1583.[3] Although the texts of these lectures have not survived, several contemporary references to Bruno's comments have. For example, in a letter Hilary Gatti dates to November of 1583, Alberigo Gentile—an Italian Protestant who immigrated to England and became a professor of civil law at Oxford in 1580—refers to some recent assertions he has heard, comments that likely "could only have been made by Bruno at Oxford at that time."[4] These include the idea that "*Lunam multarum urbium atque montium orbem* [the moon contains many cities and mountains]" (23). Bruno, of course, was eventually convicted of heresy and burned at the stake, but his belief in a plurality of worlds was just one of the views held against him. English Protestants were fond of extolling the virtues of victims such as Bruno and Galileo Galilei and very often regarded their opinions and discoveries with sympathy, in large part because of the Catholic censure they incurred. Thus does the narrator of John Milton's *Paradise Lost* (1667, 1674) praise Galileo even though he refrains from unambiguously endorsing his astronomical discoveries.[5]

In the Proem to Book II of *The Faerie Queene* (1590), Edmund Spenser—perhaps directly influenced by Bruno's writings[6]—poses the following string of questions:

> Why then should witlesse man so much misweene
> That nothing is, but that which he hath seene?
> What if within the Moones faire shining spheare?
> What if in euery other starre vnseene
> Of other worldes he happily should heare?[7]

The spirit of such interrogatives seems Brunonian, and yet—in England at least—Spenser's queries hardly invited an auto-da-fé. John Lyly, encouraged, as were other members of his generation, to rethink the older cosmological assumptions inherited from an intellectual tradition increasingly characterized (derisively) as Catholic, not surprisingly asks his audience, in the opening of *Endymion, the Man in the Moon* (first pub. 1591), to reconceive of the moon as a site of fantastic appropriation: "It was forbidden in old time to dispute of chimera, because it was a fiction; we hope in our times none will apply pastimes, because they are fancies. For there liveth none under the sun that knows what to make of the Man in the Moon."[8]

At the same time, then, that an increasing number of European writers and intellectuals were directing their attention to the moon, with some imagining it as possibly inhabited and even begging visitation, cartographers were producing *celestial* maps and globes in great numbers.[9] I emphasize *celestial* here because, although recent literary scholarship has made enormous strides in considering the importance of *terrestrial* maps on England's collective consciousness as a nation, less has been said about celestial maps and globes and their relation to an English world—or cosmic—view. As a result, the critical relation posed between the cartographic imaginary and questions of nationalism and colonialism in Shakespeare studies have been comfortably nestled within the earthly sphere, while in the case of Donne studies, this author's interest in the cartographic and the celestial has routinely been regarded as simply metaphoric or—as we have already seen in Empson's case—indicative of a youthful interest in atheism.

In this essay, I resituate the status of the celestial in scholarly approaches to both Shakespeare and Donne. I begin by focusing on one of Shakespeare's most exploratory plays, *The Tempest*. Commenting on the play in the context of his study of time, space, and motion, Angus Fletcher observes that "*The Tempest* is closer to the spirit of theoretical physics than [to] a description of a computer or of a weather vane" (18). In my reading, which shares with Fletcher's an interest in situating the work within a "Brunonian moment" (118), Caliban troubles the play's colonial sensibility by virtue of his own association with the moon: a site that looms beyond the reach of European imperialism. In the second section, I consider Donne's interest in the cartographic and the otherworldly as occasioned by the very epistemological limits that such discourses reveal. Rather than deploy maps, in other words, simply as props, Donne turns to them—and thinks through them—because of the interpretive desires they both foster and fail to fulfill.

What is it that prompts Shakespeare to consider lunar inhabitation? And why would Donne be inclined to see in maps the fault lines of human knowledge rather than the zenith of human intelligence? In each case,

I argue that Donne and Shakespeare exhibit significant, although oddly overlooked, debts to the writings of the French essayist Michel de Montaigne and specifically to the longest chapter of the *Essais*, translated by John Florio in 1603 as "An Apologie of Raymond Sebond" (II.xii). Although scholars have long recognized Shakespeare's obvious borrowings from Montaigne's essay "Of the Caniballes" (I.xxx) in *The Tempest*,[10] no mention has been made of "An Apologie" and the bearing this chapter—and with it Montaigne's lengthiest explanation of what constitutes his skeptical predilections—have on this play. As a result, Empson, for example, simply assumes that "scepticism in the period" would have rejected "a simple positive belief in life on other worlds" ("Space Man," 126). In fact, the opposite is true. In both Donne and Shakespeare, Montaignian skepticism powerfully emboldens an appreciation of the universe's expansive, interpretive possibilities. In our first step toward appreciating the flowering of the celestial imaginary in early seventeenth-century England and the roots of such flowering in the life-affirming qualities of Montaignian skepticism, it behooves us to turn now to *The Tempest*.

The Moon and The Tempest

One could be forgiven for missing the moon in *The Tempest*, but in fact it is everywhere in the play. The moon is also, without question, the overdetermined image par excellence of the late Elizabethan and early Jacobean eras, conjuring, as it does, a range of monarchical and medicinal tropes (to name just two). While Shakespeare does exploit the dizzying referential range of the moon in *The Tempest*, he also grants, through the figure Caliban, a singular relation to the otherworldly that speaks to this so-called monster's alienation and his fantasies both of inclusion and liberation.

According to Adam Max Cohen, of the many navigational technologies in use in the early modern era, the globe exerted the most influence on Shakespeare's dramaturgy.[11] Although Cohen mentions celestial globes in his work, his focus is principally on the terrestrial. Notwithstanding other important exceptions, including Stephen Orgel's introduction to his Oxford edition of *The Tempest* and Peter Hulme and William Sherman's introduction to their collection of essays *The Tempest and Its Travels*, our collective, scholarly attention to terrestrial globes at the expense of celestial ones would no doubt have surprised early modern Englishmen and women fortunate enough to glimpse such cartographic objects, for celestial *and* terrestrial globes were usually displayed in pairs in this period, as in Hans Holbein the Younger's painting *The Ambassadors* (1533).[12] So, too, just as terrestrial maps and globes, in David Turnbull's words, "are doubly spatial in that they create social spaces while at the same time they are modes of spatial representation," celestial maps and globes reflect the cultural investments and self-projections of their manufacturers.[13]

From the mid-sixteenth century through the first decade of the 1600s, these manufacturers were busy producing cartographic representations of the heavens. For example, the first atlas that attempted to map the entire celestial sphere, the *Uranometria*, was produced by Johann Bayer in Germany (Augsburg) in 1603. Just a year before the publication of the *Uranometria*, the cartographer Willem Janszoon Blaeu published two globes: one terrestrial and one celestial.[14] Blaeu based his globe on the work of Tycho Brahe, the Danish astronomer who—in the mid-1590s, when Blaeu visited him—was completing "the first completely new stellar catalog since that included in Ptolemy's *Almagest* more than fourteen centuries earlier" (29). Brahe's work, the *Astronomiae Instauratae Progymnasmata*, would be published in Prague in 1602.

Donne refers to Brahe more than once in *Ignatius His Conclave* (1611).[15] Shakespeare's own familiarity is less known. As has been well documented in recent years, however, Shakespeare might very well have seen the celestial and terrestrial globes produced by the Englishman Emery Molyneux in 1592 and might even have been prompted to name his company's theater the Globe by virtue of their existence (Cohen, 60). Intriguingly, any early modern English subject who examined a celestial globe and attended the theater would probably not have been surprised to see the two spheres linked, for cartographic depictions of the heavens in this period typically projected human and quasi-human forms into the sky, with the cultural situatedness of these forms very much in play. As D. J. Warner has pointed out, there were really three cartographic traditions that accounted for all star maps. "The first . . . is typified . . . by Albrecht Dürer's great woodcut star charts of 1515 . . . [t]he second tradition, following the woodcut maps made by Johann Honter in 1532, clothes the figures in contemporary styles. The third tradition is derived from Mercator's celestial globe of 1551."[16] When map- and globe makers appropriated these various traditions, they did not hesitate to impose their own particular cultural sensibilities on the cartographic objects in question. So northern European mapmakers were perfectly willing, when presented with the task of fashioning the ploughman or herdsman who customarily represented the constellation Boötes, to dress him for cold weather by giving him a fur hat, a cloak, or boots (34).

I want to underscore the projection of animate embodiments of the living into the heavens in order to propose that we take seriously the characterization of Caliban in the play as otherworldly: as one who is somewhat human but also estranged from the human. Prospero's early description of Caliban as a "freckled whelp, hag-born . . . not honoured with / A human shape"[17] has usually prompted a reading of him—often through recourse to "Of the Caniballes"—as evoking the new world Other. But as I will suggest later, this evocation is strained by virtue of Trinculo's initial response to Caliban's (largely covered) body. Likewise, Prospero's early insistence that Sycorax required Ariel to "act her earthy and abhorred commands" (I.ii.273) is an attempt to ground the powers of the "damned witch" in the terrestrial (I.ii.263). Yet such a reading is an ideologically imposing one, meant principally to exonerate Prospero for his mode of governance and to deny the unsettling implications that Sycorax was perhaps more powerful than Prospero would care to admit. At the end of the play, after having agreed to free Ariel, Prospero comes clean on the status of Sycorax. She "was a witch," he explains, "and one so strong / That could control the moon, make flows and ebbs, / And deal in her command without her power" (V.i.269–71).

In fact, it is striking to note just how closely Caliban and his mother are associated with the moon and indeed with an upwardly tending, vertical, spatial register in the play. The Neoplatonic juxtaposition proposed, for example, as recently as the last Arden edition of *The Tempest*, in which Ariel represents air and Caliban earth, is in fact not as clearly supported in the play as we might imagine.[18] The earthly dominion is available to Prospero to manipulate, often via Ariel, who functions in the play as a minor deity of nature in the Greek, mythological, pastoral tradition: "a nymph o'th' sea" (I.ii.302), as Prospero puts it at one point. But the lunar sphere is reserved for Caliban and his mother. Even Miranda's appeal is carefully demarcated by earthly bounds. She is worth, according to Ferdinand, "What's dearest to the world!" (III.i.39). Miranda, for her part, is similarly content with the terrestrial. She does not wish, she tells Ferdinand, "Any companion in the world but you, / Nor can imagination form a shape, / Besides yourself, to like of" (III.i.55–57).

Caliban, in contrast, is saturated with lunar associations, even bathed in moonlight (and moonshine) throughout most of the play. His materiality is unmistakable, but his materiality is not wholly earthly, at least as it is interpreted by some in the play. I am thinking specifically of the moment when Trinculo first stumbles upon Caliban and his own perspective shifts from the storm clouds above to the figure asleep before him:

> What have we here, a man or a fish? Dead or alive? A fish: he smells like a fish, a very ancient and fish-like smell, a kind of—not of the newest—poor-John. A strange fish! Were I in England now (as once I was) and had but this fish painted, not a holiday fool there but would give a piece of silver. There would this monster make a man; any strange beast there makes a man. When they will not give a doit to relieve a lame beggar, they will lay out ten to see a dead Indian. Legged like a man and his fins like arms!
>
> (II.ii.24–33)

It is the perceived monstrousness of Caliban here that distinguishes him *from* an Indian—and makes him potentially more lucrative as a new world (nonhuman) object. Caliban is, one might say, more interesting than a cannibal to Trinculo and fundamentally, essentially different: more exotic precisely because the likes of him, if he is indeed even a *him*, have never been seen before.

Coming now upon Trinculo and Caliban, hidden beneath the latter's gaberdine, Stephano reinscribes—now more forcefully than did Trinculo—the monstrous nature of the form that has been discovered: "This is some monster of the isle," he proclaims (II.ii.64). Then, just a few lines later, after Trinculo speaks, Stephano adds, "Four legs and two voices—a most delicate monster!" (II.ii.88–89). Once Trinculo identifies himself, Stephano exclaims, "Thou art very Trinculo indeed! How cam'st thou to be the siege of this mooncalf?" (II.ii.103–5).

Typically, editors of *The Tempest* gloss *mooncalf* as a deformed animal, citing the *OED*,[19] but in fact the *OED* cites *The Tempest* as evidence for this very definition. An alternative, seventeenth-century meaning for *mooncalf*, also offered in the *OED*, is "[a]n animal imagined to inhabit the moon."

This is what John Wilkins means by the word in *A Discourse Concerning A New World & Another Planet in 2 Bookes* (1640) when he relates a story, from Avicenna, of a calf "which fell down in a storme, the beholders thinking it a Moone-calfe, and that it fell thence."[20] Perhaps more familiar to early modern audiences was the misshapen calf born in Saxony in 1522. The birth of this so-called mooncalf was announced through the publication of a broadside shortly thereafter and interpreted as a disturbing indicator of something going awry in the world.[21] In order to establish what this something might be, clerical authorities commissioned an artist to render the mooncalf's likeness and an astrologer to cast the animal's horoscope, one that was soon taken up and commented upon by a number of scholars.[22] By the logic of sixteenth-century science, even if the mooncalf was born on the earth, it was not *of* the earth; its strangeness came from elsewhere.[23] Writing nearly a hundred years ago, the historian Preserved Smith wondered why "'[m]ooncalf' is unknown in the signification of 'monster' and is rare in any sense prior to the first years of the seventeenth century. Then, all of a sudden, in Shakespeare, Jonson, Drayton, Chapman, and others it becomes almost common. Something must have occurred to produce this change" (360). *This* something, I propose, is the emerging interest in the otherworldly, and indeed there is an association of mooncalves with the moon in Ben Jonson's masque *News from the World Discovered in the Moon* (1620), in which a mooncalf is not a monster at all but rather simply the lunar equivalent of what we on earth call a "fool."[24]

What happens to a colonial reading of *The Tempest* when we focus on Caliban's close associations with the lunar? If we permit ourselves to imagine the moon as a significant site of the spatial imaginary in the play, we are made aware of a felt desire among certain characters such as Trinculo and Stephano to reach beyond the now familiar, native American figure of New World colonization and seize upon something more exotic. But we also witness, on the part of Caliban, an energetically imagined, celestially empowered escape from Prospero's earthly dominion. The moon functions, in other words, as a rhetorical, celestial map in the play: both otherworldly and shaped by worldly concerns. Thus, in the eyes of Stephano and Trinculo, Caliban's otherness begs a lunar reading because his form does not appear to fit even in the wildness of the New World. We are invited, certainly, to dismiss their reading of Caliban as ridiculous, in that Trinculo is labeled a "*jester*" in the 1623 folio and Stephano a "*drunken butler*."²⁵ That is, the moon overshadows these two characters, linking them with another set of associations with the lunar: that it exemplifies and causes humoral fluctuation, melancholy, and irrationality in some.²⁶ Likewise, Stephano taunts Caliban's fascination with the lunar. "How now, mooncalf," he asks him at one point, "how does thine ague?" To which Caliban replies, I think hopefully, "Hast thou not dropped from heaven?" And Stephano: "Out o'th' moon, I do assure thee" (II.ii.132–35).

For Caliban, the heavens are the only realm through which he imagines escape from his servile relationship to Prospero and Miranda, and it is this capacity to imagine a kind of vertically inflected, "*high*-day freedom" (my emphasis II.ii.181) that both undercuts the colonial sensibilities of Prospero and the other Europeans in the play and registers Caliban's resistance to full interpolation as a new (terrestrial) world subject. Montaigne's skeptical regard for the capacity of Europeans to read the New World as really new empowers Caliban's imaginative energies in the play, but the Montaignian Caliban is not culled simply from "Of the Caniballes." He also emerges from a careful reading of "An Apologie of Raymond Sebond." In this essay, as rendered in Florio's translation, Montaigne asserts the following:

> Thy reason hath in no one other thing more likely-hood and foundation, than in that which perswadeth thee a plurality of worlds . . . The famousest wits of former ages have beleeved it, yea and some of our moderne, as forced thereunto by the appearance [*sic*] of humane reason. For as much as whatsoever we see in this vast worlds frame, there is no one thing alone, single and one . . . and that all severall kindes are multiplied in some number: Whereby it seemeth unlikely, that God hath framed this peece of worke alone without a fellow; and that the matter of this forme hath wholly beene spent in this only *Individuum*.²⁷

There is, in this essay, scarcely a shift between the consideration of other inhabited planets and other inhabited parts of the earth. Exploration, be it of a terrestrial or a celestial nature, is one and the same. What is essential and uniform is the spatial demarcation of plenitude. Whether one goes up into the sky or out across the sea, one encounters plurality in Montaigne—a plurality that disproves any assumption of cultural uniqueness or interpretive assurance.

In much of the two-dimensional scholarship on *The Tempest*, Shakespeare is read as having at his disposal a pair of conceptual choices: either to evoke the new world by looking west, even as the play is set in a Mediterranean surround, or to evoke other trading and cultural relations by looking east. But in the three-dimensional space of the spherical imaginary, any sea voyage west or east is a voyage through the heavens: coordinated by certain stars and (potentially) implicated by certain planetary signs. The moon provides conceptual refuge for Caliban from Prospero's autocratic power at the same time that such power is revealed to be circumscribed by the parochial sensibility of the projecting and cathecting European viewer. In this sense, Trinculo and Stephano's appropriation of the moon for their own devices is quintessentially European, and their inebriation a censure of the inelegant, even gross form that such European appropriation can take. At the same time, Prospero's acknowledgment that the globe itself "shall dissolve, / And like this insubstantial pageant faded, / Leave not a rack behind" evokes—albeit poetically—the cold, encroaching sleep of the Galilean world: one in which the examination of the heavens betrays increasing evidence of universal decay and greater reason to doubt the capacity of human inventions and achievements to continue in perpetuity (IV.i.154–56). Indeed, it is precisely such limitations—we are led to believe in Montaigne's "An Apologie"—that makes a skeptical appraisal of European reason beckon toward the heavens for evidentiary support.

John Donne and the Heavens

John Donne's most overt references to the moon occur in *Ignatius His Conclave*, when Lucifer proposes to Ignatius that he leave hell and begin a "*Lunatique Church*" on the moon (350). Scholars, most recently Anne Lake Prescott, have read Donne's prose piece mocking Jesuits and other "*Innovators*" (321) as an example of Menippean satire: a genre frequently used by Protestant writers in the Reformation to lampoon "Catholic folly or wickedness."[28] Nonetheless, we should not lose sight of the degree to which Donne's narrator assumes the likelihood of planetary inhabitation throughout the piece. When the narrator first drifts off into sleep and begins his journey to hell, where he will watch various damned figures compete for entrance into Lucifer's inner sanctum, he is granted the "liberty to wander through all places, and to survey and reckon all the roomes, and all the volumes of the heavens, and to comprehend the situation, the dimensions, the nature, the people, and the policy, both of the swimming Ilands, the

Planets, and of all those which are fixed in the firmament" (319). Of course, well before Donne, Lucian proposes the possibility—at least rhetorically—of lunar inhabitation, but Donne's *Ignatius* takes such a proposition much further. The discoveries of Galileo, Kepler, and Brahe are mentioned early in the satire, and the narrator is able to peer into hell "by the benefit of certaine spectacles" that seem clearly inspired by Galileo's telescope (320). Indeed, the offer of lunar relocation Lucifer makes to Ignatius depends upon the notion that interstellar space is a breeze to navigate: "And with the same ease as you passe from the earth to the *Moone*, you may passe from the *Moone* to the other *starrs*, which are also thought to be worlds" (350).

Ignatius declines Lucifer's proposal not because he is worried about life on the moon (or the other stars for that matter) but because he has plans to someday overtake hell himself. He wants the seat next to Lucifer's, one occupied by Pope Boniface, and the satire concludes with Ignatius throwing this nemesis aside. Nonetheless, Ignatius is certainly intrigued by Lucifer's promise that, once on the moon, he could "beget and propagate many *Hells*, and enlarge . . . [his] *Empire*" (350). Like Shakespeare in *The Tempest*, then, Donne refuses to endorse the celestial in *Ignatius* as an appropriate realm for colonization even as he is quick to incorporate the language of territorial acquisition in other works, perhaps nowhere more strikingly than in "Elegie XIX: To His Mistress Going to Bed."[29]

In her reading of *Conclave Ignati*, set within a larger assessment of the relation between skepticism and memory in the work of Donne and Shakespeare, Anita Gilman Sherman argues that the figures reviled in the text, from Copernicus to Paracelsus, are mocked "more for their noisy fixation with fashioning an artistic narrative about themselves than for their innovations."[30] I would add that it is also the prideful insistence on Copernicus's part specifically that his discoveries were unprecedented that prompts his censure. "But your inventions can scarce bee called yours," Ignatius points out, "since long before you, *Heraclides*, *Ecphantus*, and *Aristarchus* thrust them into the world" (324). Donne appears content to uncover Copernicus in hell not because of what the astronomer claimed to have known—much of which Donne, after all, seems to have believed as well—but rather because of Copernicus's presumed inability to acknowledge that others knew it before him.

In Sherman's fine account, Donne's skepticism is evinced in *Ignatius* and elsewhere by the delight he takes in "hermeneutical exploration," by which the author willfully and energetically adopts a variety of perspectives on a single subject (111). With Pyrrhonian skepticism specifically in mind, however—that is, a practice whereby its adherents profess "ever to waver, to doubt and to enquire; never to be assured of any thing, nor to take any warrant of himself" ("An Apologie," 449)—Sherman suggests that Donne might very well be aware that a series of questions that undermine philosophical positions might eventually erode theological convictions as well. It is precisely because of this awareness, it seems to me, that Donne wants nothing to do with Pyrrhonism in the first place. Rather, his interest in cartography is fueled by a Montaignian model of subjectivity that asserts itself in opposition to Pyrrhonism to the extent that the latter begins in the useful dominion of questioning and doubting but goes too far in Montaigne's opinion: denying even the value of self-examination.[31] As Tom Conley argues in his seminal *The Self-Made Map: Cartographic Writing in Early Modern France*, Montaigne's investments are in a self that

> is visible only when it achieves the effect of totality, of having engineered a world through its own labors. Yet, at the same time, in order to bear a signature, the self has to appear to be gratuitous, total, or "self-made" in a space that is granted to be its own. The self makes itself or is made to look self-alike when it appears to be simultaneous cause and effect of a creation that is both total and local.[32]

Conley's Montaigne is in fact a key piece of evidence for his thesis regarding sixteenth-century French literature, as he uncovers in the *Essais* "a topographical consciousness that gives an illusion of extension to the writer's sense of subjectivity" (251). Such a consciousness is aware of the limits of human self-understanding but nonetheless endorses such an inquiry, pairing it with other epistemological pursuits, including the study of the heavens.

In a 1604 letter to Henry Goodyer, Donne mentions his reading of Montaigne (370–71), which John Klause argues has already borne a powerful influence on Donne's *Metempsychosis* or *The Progresse of the Soule* (1601).[33] In Donne, from early in his career as a poet to well into his career as a minister, spatial extension and subjective experience commingle to an extraordinary extent, as scholars have long noted.[34] Although the presence and importance of maps in Donne's thinking have been well documented, the link between cartography and Montaignian skepticism in Donne's mind has not. Coupling in Donne is often figured hemispherically, as in "The Good-Morrow":

> My face in thine eye, thine in mine appeares,
> And true plaine hearts doe in the faces rest,
> Where can we finde two better hemispheares
> Without sharpe North, without declining West?
>
> (15–18)

Such images of completion are often accompanied by disavowals of the cartographic. Indeed, before the two loves can become one in this poem, the narrator must first abscond with an interest in a larger, more sprawling world that defies enclosure: "Let sea-discoverers to new worlds have gone, / Let Maps to other, worlds on worlds have showne, / Let us possesse one world, each hath one, and is one" (12–14). Love is appealing in part, in "The Good-Morrow," because it relieves one of the burden of trying to place oneself not only in this world but also in the cosmos more broadly.

When left alone, Donne's speakers often grope for spatial metaphors that frequently evince less a reassuring confidence in the stability of the self and the place of the self in God's creation than they do a willingness to imagine the self as in search of meaning and direction. We might consider, for example, the ventriloquized language of scholastic argumentation in the opening of "Goodfriday, 1613. Riding Westward" ("Let mans Soule be a Spheare, and then, in this / The intelligence that moves, devotion is," 1–2), or the more lengthy definition of *"Man"* in Meditation VIII of *Devotions upon Emergent Occasions* (1624):

> Let him be a *world*, and him self will be the *land*, and *misery* the *sea*. His misery (for misery is his, his own; of the happinesses of this world hee is but *Tenant*, but of misery the *Free-holder*; of happines [sic] he is but the *farmer*, but the *usufructuary*, but of misery, the *Lord*, the *proprietary*) his misery, as the *sea*, swells above all the hilles, and reaches to the remotest parts of this *earth*, *Man*; who of himselfe is but *dust*, and coagulated and kneaded into earth, by *teares*; his *matter* is earth, his *forme*, misery [425].

The Donnean self here is both bounded and boundless, constituted not only by particulate matter ("the *land*") but also by composites ("a *world*"). His most distinguishing affect, misery, is both a part of him ("his own") and distinct from him: embodied by water (water that becomes, by the end of the passage, tears) that swells in and around him. From whatever perspective we choose, the figure in question is in flux: either skirting through the heavens as a world in motion, in the Copernican model, or made of a dust that is itself "coagulated and kneaded into earth." As a being, however, that can appraise itself, Donne does not disclaim the authenticating voice of the self even as he reveals this self to be crumbling and swelling, farming and crying, all at once.

The crisis of the "new Philosophy," which, Donne memorably declares, "cals [sic] all in doubt" in *The First Anniversarie*, is in fact a crisis of the new cartography as well (205). "The Sun," we are told, "is lost, and th'earth, and no mans wit / Can well direct him, where to looke for it" (207–8). John Gillies has argued that the so-called new geography of late-sixteenth and early seventeenth-century Europe is in fact not that new; cartographers tended to borrow from their predecessors liberally and did not share the "progressivist and scientist [sic] assumptions which modern commentators too easily associate with the new geography."[35] But there is an exception to this lack of newness that Gillies notes: the sudden proliferation of double-hemispherical world maps (159). Historians of cartography have tended to regard the creation of double-hemispherical maps (maps that show us both hemispheres together, side by side) as an important step in the increasing accuracy of geographical measurement. From our perspective this is indisputable as, to give but one example, double-hemispherical maps correct the elongation of the two polar land masses that occur when a flat map represents the earth without denoting its curvature. But Donne, of course, does not share our historical perspective; for him, the proliferating ways of seeing the world—including the dizzying possibility of seeing two different views of the world *at once*—is decentering and also a visual embodiment of the perspectival relativity proposed by skepticism, perhaps most concisely in Montaigne's most famous, one-sentence consideration of double perspective: "When I am playing with my Cat, who knowes whether she have more sport in dallying with me, than I have in gaming with her?" (399).

In "Hymne to God my God, in my Sicknesse," the dying body of Donne's speaker turns into a flat map of the world. The map evoked here is expressly *not* a double-hemispherical map but rather an Ortelian one. "If cartographic accuracy is at all an issue," Gillies asks, "why authorise a type of map which must have seemed conspicuously outdated to a man of Donne's geographic literacy?" (184). Gillies suggests that Donne is drawn by the narrower rendering of the Strait of Magellan in the Ortelian version, whereas a more accurate map would have rendered the strait as broader and therefore less menacing. Certainly, in the poem, the threat posed by such a strait is of grave concern to the speaker:

> Whilst my Physitians by their love are growne
>   Cosmographers, and I their Mapp, who lie
> Flat on this bed, that by them may be showne
>   That this is my South-west discoverie
>   *Per fretum febris*, by these streights to die,
>
> I joy, that in these straits, I see my West;
>   For, those theire currants yeeld returne to none,
> What shall my West hurt me? As West and East
>   In all flatt Maps (and I am one) are one,
>   So death doth touch the Resurrection.
>
> (6–15)

What seems to me most relevant in this poem to Donne's larger project as a spatial thinker is *not* the question of what kind of map is figured at this moment but rather the process by which the speaker's body *becomes* a map and, by virtue of taking on such characteristics, quickly spawns many different readings. The "Physitians," for example, propose that the speaker is an Ortelian map, but while the speaker first endorses this reading ("and I their Mapp"), he ends up turning the Ortelian map into "*all* flatt Maps" (my emphasis). As in "Goodfriday, 1613. Riding Westward," the speaker cares little about geographical accuracy; he is rather concerned that his possible death will merit salvation: that "West" shall meet "East," at which point, of course, the flat map will become spherical, made into a globe by the hands of God.

I am suggesting here that the cartographic impulse for Donne is entwined with a skeptical impulse: that he reads maps not as purveyors of unquestionable authority but rather as further evidence that—as he says in a sermon from 1628 treating Paul's conversion—"every thing in this world is fluid, and transitory, and sandy, and all dependence, all assurance built upon this world, is but a building upon sand; all will change."[36] Montaigne anticipates and shares Donne's sense of earthly inconstancy. As he says in "An

Apologie," "*there is no constant existence, neither of our being, nor of the objects. And we, and our judgment, and all mortall things else do uncessantly rowle, turne, and passe away. Thus can nothing be certainly established, nor of the one, nor of the other; both the judgeing [sic] and the judged being in continuall alteration and motion*" (545). Like Donne, Montaigne develops his own version of skepticism not simply from a study of Sextus Empiricus but also from reading maps. Also like Donne, however, Montaigne does not read maps as empirical, scientific objects (terms we might be inclined to use in association with the cartographic) but rather as further indicators of the limits of human knowledge. "The extremities of our curious search turne to a glimmering and all to a dazeling," he observes toward the end of "An Apologie." "As *Plutarke* saith, of the off-spring of Histories, that after the manner of Cards or Maps, the utmost limits of knowne Countries, are set downe to be full of thicke marrish grounds, shady forrests, desart and uncouth places" (488–89).

When Donne decides on a career in the ministry in 1615 and agrees to become ordained, it is believed that he sat down and wrote out his *Essayes in Divinity*.[37] It is clear in reading these essays that not just the form of Montaigne's *Essais* but also their critique of Pyrrhonism influenced Donne enormously. Among the first theologians Donne glosses, in fact, is Raymond Sebond, whose natural theology he sums up in a few pithy sentences. As for Sebond's confidence, Donne offers a skeptical appraisal that is reminiscent of Montaigne's: Sebond "may be too abundant in affirming, that *in libro creaturarum* there is enough to teach us all particularities of Christian Religion."[38] Those eager for Christian "proofs," according to Donne, would do best to turn to the Bible, not to the world at large (8). When he takes on Pyrrhonism a few pages later, defending creation *ex nihilo*, his criticism is unmitigated: "*Sextus Empiricus* the *Pyrrhonian* . . . handled philosophy bravely," Donne writes, "having invented a way by which a man should determine nothing of every thing . . . who with his Ordinary weapon, a two-edged sword, thinks he cuts off all Arguments against production of Nothing" (28). In response to such an approach, Donne proposes that we "assign something of which the world was made. If it be of it self, it is God: and it is God, if it be of God; who is also so simple, that it is impossible to imagine any thing before him of which he should be compounded, or any workman to do it" (29). The retention of a divine self here buttresses the importance of self-examination, with the inalterable existence of the former justifying the exhaustive scrutiny of the latter. Just a few pages later, Donne turns back to the earth itself, reconjuring it as an object, the study of which is useful precisely because it demonstrates the impoverishment and perspectival limitations of human intelligence:

> *Earth* and *Heaven* are but the foot-stool of God: But *Earth it self* is but the foot-ball of wise men. How like a Strumpet deales this world with the Princes of it? Every one thinks he possesseth all, and his servants have more at her hand then he; and theirs, then they. They think they compass the Earth, and a *Job* is not within their reach. A busie Wit hath taken the pains to survey the possessions of some Princes: and he tells us that the *Spanish* King hath in *Europe* almost three hundred thousand miles, and in the new world seaven millions, besides the borders of *Africk*, and all his Ilands ... Yet let him measure right, and the *Turke* exceeds him, and him the *Persian*; the *Tartar* him [35].

An expansive survey is central to Donne's claim here, as it would be equally central if Montaigne were arguing a similar point. Different cases, taken from different parts of the world, devalue any single authority. Even authors who claim an exhaustive use of evidence only *"think* they compass the Earth" (my emphasis). Such voyages are actually never fully completed. Circularity here, the earth made akin to a round ball, gives the impression that varied instances will continually present themselves and that explorers will always end up failing to grasp the world in its totality. Yet such failure does not, as in the Pyrrhonian model, suggest futility. Rather, it is the humility engendered by the quest for knowledge, not knowledge itself, that is the most beneficial reward for such hermeneutic efforts.

Analyzing Jacobean skepticism, William Hamlin argues that in Donne's case, however much his doubting "draws us through anguished scrutiny—of both self and world—it leads in the end to clarification, humility, acceptance."[39] But I propose that even the ordained Donne finds his efforts toward such ends complicated by the shadows cast by Montaignian skepticism, notwithstanding Hamlin's crucial observation that "Montaigne is only one of many continental figures through whose works the ideas and practices of scepticism are channeled into Britain" (73). When we turn to the *Devotions* one final time, we see the idea of inhabited worlds gestured toward by Donne with a deliberately ambiguous degree of remove. Haunted here, in his sick state, by the specter of loneliness, Donne insists in Meditation V that:

> there is no *Phenix* [*sic*]; nothing singular, nothing alone: Men that inhere upon *Nature* only, are so far from thinking, that there is anything *singular* in this world, as that they will scarce thinke, that this world it selfe is *singular*, but that every *Planet*, and every *Starre*, is another *world* like this; They finde reason to conceive, not onely a *pluralitie* in every *Species* in the world, but a *pluralitie of worlds*; so that the abhorrers of *Solitude*, are not solitary; for *God*, and *Nature*, and *Reason* concurre against it [421].

Donne does not expressly include himself in this passage among either those who believe in a plurality of worlds or those who suffer from solitariness. He is, at least grammatically, marginal to these people ("they"). Nonetheless, he contains their sensibilities within him and within his *Devotions*. The concept of a plethora of inhabited worlds is therefore offered here as a comforting notion, but the comfort is itself slightly strained: not fully, unambiguously possessed by the author and yet transcribed and attested to in his work. We have here, in a crystallized form, the very embodiment of Donnean skepticism, whereby an idea may be endorsed as both logically and emotively compelling without necessarily being adopted in a manner that settles the question once and for all.

Montaigne's "An Apologie" impacts Donne in principally religious and eventually more narrowly devotional terms. The same cannot be said of Shakespeare, who takes from the same passages in the same text an invitation to consider the limits of European, political sovereignty writ large rather than a sovereignty that might be labeled as denominationally Catholic or Protestant, as in *Ignatius His Conclave*. A systematic doubting of *all* received opinions, the definition by which both Montaigne and Donne seek to explain Pyrrhonism to their readers, does not accurately reflect the kind of skepticism that animates the thinking of either author. Rather, with maps and exploration very much in mind, both Montaigne and Donne see knowledge as something stubbornly provisional. Yet they also see, inhering in this provisionality, not an invitation to collapse into nihilistic speculation but rather an opportunity to reimagine the self as renewed and remade when it is resituated within a cosmological perspective that reaches out beyond the normative human sphere otherwise known as earth. At least in this regard, Shakespeare's Caliban shares with Donne and Montaigne a desire to wiggle out from under the imposing limitations of his surround and pronounces this desire by insistently and stubbornly looking up into the sky, where the self may be reconstituted or reassured, at least for a time.

PART III   Names, Puns, and More

6. Inserting *Me*: Some Instances of Predication and the Privation of the Private Self in Shakespeare and Donne

MARSHALL GROSSMAN

This was at first intended to be a reading of Shakespeare's "Will" sonnets in the light of Donne's Holy Sonnets and some questions about predication. In the event, however, I have managed only the prelude to such a reading. What follows, then, is not a reading but an invitation to a reading of Shakespeare's sonnet 135.

Donne and Shakespeare share a profoundly linguistic discovery: the realization that the self can be possessed and confirmed only through and as acts of predication in which the immediacy of the self is sacrificed to the hegemony of its signifiers. One can identify with what one says and/or what is said about one, or one can resist such identification at the risk of excluding oneself from discourse. Donne and Shakespeare share an interest in discovering the consequences of resistance to or refusal of such identifications. Key to this discovery is the tension that inheres in nouns that may be used properly—that is, as what Saul Kripke calls "rigid designators"—and used commonly—that is, as floating signifiers designating objects in a class.[1] If I may begin with a very familiar example: the emotional charge implicit in this tension may be felt, for example, in the famous exchange on the threshold of Gertrude's closet: "*Gertrude*: Hamlet, thou hast *thy* father much offended. / *Hamlet*: Mother, you have *my* father much offended."[2] Gertrude refers, of course, to Claudius, while Hamlet emphatically resists the sliding of the common noun "father" from one referent to another. For him, "father" is a proper noun, a name, rigidly designating the dead King Hamlet. What is at stake between the *my* and the *thy* of this exchange is, of course, Hamlet's resistance to the sliding of the signifier "father" from old Hamlet to new Claudius. His obstinacy, from the point of view of his mother and his stepfather, resides in his refusal to accept that "father" is a linguistic placeholder, designating not a person but a position in respect to other persons. Hamlet wants "father" rigidly to designate a particular man, whom he will soon identify as precisely a man without a (human) body: "The body is with the King, but the King is not with the body. The King is a thing" (IV.ii.27–28).

That Claudius has already slipped into King Hamlet's bed and may, for all Hamlet knows, have done so even before the king was dead, sets up Hamlet's verbal conservativism; his effort to stabilize the linguistic order as it was in the old regime creates a dissonance between his language and that of the Danish court. His strategic linguistic resistance is an act at once personal and political. It is political in the same way that his black clothing is political; it calls attention to what is not to be spoken by setting up a resistance in the symbolic to the paradigmatic realignment through which Claudius tries to establish continuity of succession with the announcement that "Though yet of Hamlet our dear brother's death / The memory be green / . . . / Yet so far hath discretion fought with nature / That we with wisest sorrow think on him / Together with remembrance of ourselves" (I.ii.1–7). Claudius's first words remove King Hamlet from the public role of "the Dane" to the private role of "our dear brother" and move Claudius into that public role through his assertion of the "royal we," transforming his previously private role as the brother to assert the public will, embodied in the royal "ourselves." Claudius's second move is to absorb Gertrude into this realignment—"our sometime sister, now our queen" (I.ii.8)—and his third is to affirm that the language he speaks now is shared by his linguistic community: "nor have we herein barr'd / Your better wisdoms, which have freely gone / With this affair along" (I.ii.14–16). As he moves to control the public sphere, Claudius recognizes the public dimension of linguistic arrangements and reminds his auditors that they have agreed, for whatever political or personal reasons, to share this language with him. Hamlet, however, defines himself—as loyal son and as thwarted heir—by asserting his idiolect as a brake on the revised public language. The resistance becomes explicit when Claudius solicits his participation with the implicit promise that his status as next in line will be preserved ("But now, my cousin Hamlet, and my son"), only to be rebuked with Hamlet's characteristic use of words that make a friction against Claudius's sliding paradigms while calling attention to their own morphological and semantic plasticity: "A little more than *kin*, and less than *kind*. . . . Not so, my lord, I am too much in the *sun*" (I.ii.64–67: my emphasis).

It would be easy to multiply examples of this dialogic struggle over discrete words in *Hamlet* and in the plays in general. There is one more, very familiar instance from *Hamlet*, Act I, scene ii, that I want to recall here before I move on to the different environment of the sonnets, where the dimension of performance and the struggle of distinct voices are generally collapsed into the voice of a lyric "I" and where we can compare the peculiar interlocutions of Shakespeare's speaker and his two lovers to the strangely violent wooing of God by the speaker of Donne's Holy Sonnets:

> *Queen:* Good Hamlet, cast thy nighted color off,
> And let thine eye look like a friend on *Denmark*.
> Do not for ever with thy vailed lids
> Seek for thy noble *father* in the dust.
> Thou know'st 'tis *common*, all that lives must die,
> Passing through nature to eternity.
> *Hamlet:* Ay, madam, it is common.
> *Queen:* If it be,
> Why seems it so *particular* with thee?
> *Hamlet:* Seems, madam? nay, it is, I know not "seems."
>
> (I.ii.68–76, my emphasis)

Gertrude begins this exchange by trying, once again, to get Hamlet to admit a separation between the names *Denmark* and *father*, urging him to follow his self-interest in looking on Claudius and to stop searching for his now nonexistent father in the dust, to which the late king's body has returned. But by grounding her argument in the need to accept what is universal— what " 'tis common, all that lives must die"—she provides Hamlet with an opportunity to raise the structural underplay of linguistic predication to the level of signification itself, including its politics, that is, to turn the exchange from one about how to handle his grief for his father in the context of his present political situation into an exchange about who controls linguistic reference and whether linguistic predication has an ontological residue. He does this by picking up Gertrude's *common* and translating it to a different and much more particular context. Hamlet's "Ay, madam, it is *common*" takes the word out of its application as the opposite of "particular" and turns it instead to the opposite of "refined" or "cultured." In doing so he also removes it from its use in an adage of universal reference—all that lives must die—to a historically situated and particular context, saying in effect that Gertrude's behavior has been vulgar. He will seek his *noble* father in the dust, as an alternative to looking at the "commonness" that has befallen the court of Denmark and his own mother. Gertrude, who is second only to first gravedigger in her ability to handle Hamlet's penchant for appropriating and twisting his interlocutor's language, resists Hamlet's discursive turn by reinscribing the word *particular*. She had used the word *common* to mean "not particular," and if Hamlet is going to take it to mean something else, that is not valid usage but an idiolect *particular* to him. Hamlet's response, of course, opens into the speech in which poor Burbage must catalogue all of his actorly devices only to deny that "actions that a man might play" can ever "denote" his character truly, and the moment of Hamlet's assertion of himself as that peculiarly Shakespearean "invention," a character who is at once frankly made only of the words he speaks and yet who *seems* sometimes to know more than he says and sometimes to say more than he knows. Recognizing that literature can tell a common truth only by representing particulars, which must belie their particularized circumstances, Hamlet's "nay it is, I know not 'seems,'" like his claim to "have that within which passes show," somehow locates authentic being only in the space between two dissonant linguistic predications; the self and its signifiers cannot coincide because the "real" self is precisely what escapes signification, what is unreachable because it lies between two languages, one public and universalizing, the other private and particular. Hamlet bears his father's name, but he will be able to utter the sentence "This is I, / Hamlet the Dane" (V.i.257–58) only in the last act of the play, and the price of the utterance will be his life. With this theatrical frame in place, I want to look at a few sonnets of Shakespeare and of Donne to see how this struggle over the need to let words float between the rigid designations of proper nouns and the floating designations of common nouns plays out within the lyric voice.

A focused laboratory in which the struggle between common and rigid designation may be observed is the sonnets in which the poet discovers, through his endeavors to join words methodically, that *Will* and *will* can be separated neither from each other nor from the common welter of inchoate desires, along with the fact that words can speak the truth only by lying. Just as Gertrude's "common" fails to assert the meaning of her will when slipped free of a reciprocal "particular," the speaker of the sonnets discovers that his mistress is true only when she lies, in part, because her truth is precisely what does not stand up: "Therefore, I lie with her, and she with me" (138.13). This is a hard-won honesty, following the despair of the young man who cannot be what the poet's words designate.

The struggle to retain and signify the self in Shakespeare's sonnets is paralleled by a more specific anxiety in Donne's Holy Sonnets over the need to surrender the self to the Holy Spirit without also surrendering one's subjective voice. Curiously, both poets turn to an unsettlingly sexual, actually a sodomitical, language to express the irresolution of desire. As a way of starting a conversation about this language, I want just to glance at a couple of grammatical and prosodic wrinkles in Donne's "As due by many titles I resigne" and "Batter my heart, three-personed God" and at Shakespeare's sonnets punning on Will/will. I do not have anything decisive to say about these sonnets here, but I believe they might help us make more concrete and less gnomic what Fineman might have meant when he said that "the fundamental desire of the reader of literature is the desire of the homosexual for the heterosexual, or rather, substituting the appropriate figurative embodiments of these abstractions, the desire of the man to be sodomized by the woman."[3]

The first of Donne's holy sonnets begins a one-sided dialogue about paternity and identity with a god who remains silent. Like Hamlet, trying to articulate his filial identity to the father, whose name he bears, Donne's speaker poses himself between an originary and paternal signifier and an alien usurper:

> As due by many titles I resign
> Myself to thee, O God, first I was made
> By thee, and for thee, and when I was decayed
> Thy blood bought that, the which before was thine,
> I am thy son, made with thyself to shine,
> Thy servant, whose pains thou hast still repaid,
> Thy sheep, thine image, and, till I betrayed
> Myself, a temple of thy Spirit divine;
> Why doth the devil then usurp in me?
> Why doth he steal, nay ravish that's thy right?

> Except thou rise and for thine own work fight,
> Oh I shall soon despair, when I do see
> That thou lov'st mankind well, yet wilt not choose me,
> And Satan hates me, yet is loth to lose me.[4]

Much could be said about the "I" of this sonnet, positing himself as a son "by many titles" of God, who is usurped by the devil. What is the status of this speaker whose wish is to be spoken for or spoken through by a paternal God? In the interest of brevity, however, I am going to focus only on the couplet. What catches my ear is that the couplet as written is hypermetric. The sonnet follows the Petrarchan pattern in the octet, abbaabba, but starts to stutter in the sestet, cddccc, with eleven syllables each in lines 13–14, while the rest of the poem is pentameter. Is it simply accidental or a failure of imagination that three of the c rhymes repeat the word "me"? If one were to drop the "me" that ends lines 13–14, one would have a metrically superior or at least regular sonnet: abbaabba cddc ee, with no hypermetric lines and with no visible loss of meaning. The couplet would still be a non-Petrarchan innovation, but the sonnet would be typical in reaching the *e*-rhyme. In another poet and a less charged context, this might be a trivial observation, but Donne has a habit of making puns and metric anomalies thematic elements, such as when the energy of the speaker of "Song [Go and Catch a Falling Star]" peters out in resignation at the end of the poem, "Yet she / Will be / False, ere I come, to two, or three," or when he famously puns on his wife's name and his own: "When thou hast done, thou hast not done, / For I have more." In the sonnet at hand, moreover, Donne's representation of the self in the accusative case, "me," as the excess, the thing that disrupts the prosody but will not go away is very much to the thematic point not only of this poem but also of the "Holy Sonnets" as a group. The persistent *me* of the predicated self is precisely the *more* that keeps God, the reader, and the speaker himself from having *Don(n)e*.

The speaker in "Batter my heart, three-personed God" demands, paradoxically, that God "o'erthrow *me*" "that *I* may rise, and stand" (1–3; my emphasis). As in "As due by many titles I resign," the speaker asks God to subdue a will that is "usurped." Here, however, the language is explicitly sexual:

> Yet dearly'I love you, and would be loved fain,
> But am betrothed unto your enemy,

> Divorce *me*, untie, or break that knot again,
> Take *me* to you, imprison *me*, for I
> Except you enthral *me*, never shall be free,
> Nor ever chaste, except you ravish *me*.
>
> (9–14: my emphasis)

This speaker is indeed a divided self. The nominative speaker loves, yet never shall be free unless the accusative speaker is divorced, untied, imprisoned, enthralled, and finally ravaged. The will of the speaker toward two opposed suitors, God and the usurper, is apparently distributed along syntactic lines. The "I" of the speaker favors God, but the devil controls the "me." Why should this be, and why should the freedom of the recalcitrant *me*, which pops up five times in the sestet, depend on its being sodomized by God? I do not have a ready answer to these questions, but I note that the *me* that awkwardly rises in these poems bears a certain resemblance as concrete signifier of (masculine) desire to the thing that in Shakespeare's Sonnet 20, "by addition me of thee defeated, / By adding one thing to my purpose nothing" and which functions, in Fineman's phrase, as a "failed pointer."[5] If it were to the purpose, it would signify the desire of the other for the speaker, but it acts instead like its gender-other, pointedly taken to name "nothing" within a particular sociolinguistic alignment. If the desire of the literary reader is to be overpowered and entered by something not usurped but homologous to itself, Donne's strangled call to be anally raped by God might suggest the expectation that to make one's will God's will is the only literary way to make oneself one with one's (paternal?) signifier.

I have, in haste, tried to sketch out a context in which we might read Shakespeare's Will. Space, time, and my own limitations do not allow that reading to be carried out here, but I hope that you will join me in an attempt to test and to elaborate this context through an effort to sort out the literary specificity of Will in Sonnet 135, in which the addressee is not God and, at least in part, not homosexual and where the gathering of wills under a single proper noun is explicit:

> Whoever hath her wish, thou hast thy *Will*,
> And *Will* to boot, and *Will* in overplus;
> More than enough am I that vex thee still,
> To thy sweet will making addition thus.
> Wilt thou, whose will is large and spacious,

Not once vouchsafe to hide my will in thine?
Shall will in others seem right gracious,
And in my will no fair acceptance shine?
The sea, all water, yet receives rain still,
And in abundance addeth to his store,
So thou being rich in *Will* add to thy *Will*
One will of mine to make thy large *Will* more.
   Let no unkind, no fair beseechers kill;
   Think all but one, and me in that one Will.

Improper Nouns: A Response to Marshall Grossman

DAVID LEE MILLER

Marshall Grossman's contribution to this collection is the snapshot of a brilliant mind cut off in midstride. Marshall was, clearly, following up on his 2009 essay, "Whose Life Is It Anyway? Shakespeare's Prick," which in turn builds upon Joel Fineman's seminal work in both *The Perjured Eye* and *The Subjectivity Effect*.[1] This is characteristic: Marshall's arguments often emerged from an extended meditation on the unfinished project he calls "Fineman's short but intense career."[2] There is an oppressive irony in the way the present occasion repeats the essential structure of that dialogue, irony wrought to a higher pitch by the turn to Hamlet's exchange with Claudius and Gertrude, that opens "Inserting *Me*." If I take this occasion to speak despite the burden such irony adds to the loss of a loved friend, it is because the silence to which I am drawn would betray the lifelong commitment to language on which, and within which, that friendship thrived.

This commitment takes a powerful, characteristic form in the poststructural postulate with which Marshall's essay begins: "[T]he self can be possessed and confirmed only through and as acts of predication in which the immediacy of the self is sacrificed to the hegemony of its signifiers." Marshall offers this formulation as the "profoundly linguistic discovery" shared by Shakespeare and Donne; it is also, of course, a methodological principle shared by Fineman and Grossman. To propose that the self is irreducibly mediated by language is not, however, to deny the possibility of pre- or extralinguistic subjectivity; on the contrary, it leads to the inference that the self in its immediacy may either resist or accede to the alienating identification with its signifiers. This struggle between resistance, which carries the risk of slipping out of language into silence, and acceptance, which carries the alternative risk of finding oneself bound to an alienating self-image, is the provocation for Marshall's rigorous but unfinished argument about the subjective and political force of pronominal utterance in Shakespeare and Donne. It is also the dilemma that for several weeks has blocked my efforts to shape a response.

If Marshall were sending me this paper now ("For so to interpose a little ease . . ."), I would ask what difference it makes when we turn from the intensely carnal and secular context of Shakespeare's sonnets to the sacred context of Donne's. Early modern theology is every bit as rigorously grammatical, in its way, as modern psychoanalysis and language philosophy.[3] This is one reason we may find the emphasis on grammatical categories attractive as an approach to the poems' sexual content; in contrast to a "history of sexuality" reading of Donne's erotic matter, this approach looks first to linguistic mediation.[4] And because it shares a sense of grammar's primacy with the most searching scriptural commentaries of the period, it would seem to open possibilities for dialogue.

Luther, for example, in one of the more widely circulated Elizabethan translations of his work, argues for "a new theological grammar," a system in which words lose their accepted senses in favor of meanings derived from their relation to faith.[5] Luther's most prominent example is the word *doing*. His exegesis of it depends on the fundamental distinction between justification by works and by faith: When scripture seems to imply that a certain "doing" will lead to salvation, says Luther, it *always* assumes that the works in question flow from a prior condition of faith, so that the theological verb *doing* actually means *doing-that-arises-spiritually-from-a-prior-condition-of-faith*. It specifically does not mean *doing-that-is-in-and-of-itself-sufficient-for-justification*.

How might Luther analyze the "theological grammar" of Donne's pronouns? The *I* and *me* of the holy sonnets bear some resemblance to the Lutheran distinction between active and passive righteousness. "Active" and "passive" are themselves categories in grammar that correspond to the difference between the subject and object pronouns as they designate a self either acting or acted upon. For Luther, they set all forms of righteousness deriving from human agency—he mentions "political righteousness," "ceremonial righteousness," and "righteousness of the Law"—against "righteousness of faith," passive because it is imputed rather than achieved: "For here we work nothing, render nothing to God; we only receive and permit someone else to work in us, namely, God" (26: 4–5).

Doing nothing sounds easy, but in fact Luther argues that passive righteousness is "hidden in a mystery, which the world does not understand," and that Christians therefore repeatedly lose sight of it "in the midst of their temptations" (26: 5). When they do lose sight of it, they are in mortal danger, for as Luther asserts in a turn of phrase that would have struck Donne and Grossman both, "anyone who does not grasp or take hold of it in afflictions and terrors of conscience *cannot stand*" (26: 5, emphasis added).[6] The self that wants to "stand" is the phallic *I*, propped up by delusions of agency that must be broken down repeatedly in the holy sonnets, as Donne's speaker keeps relearning the lesson of his insufficiency: he can "stand" only if he does not attempt to do so on his own. "To do this," says Luther, "is beyond human power and thought. Indeed, it is even beyond the Law of God." Such impossibility leaves the self vulnerable to Satan, who "increases and aggravates these thoughts in us" (26: 5) just as the devil in "As due by many titles" usurps the self that ought to be "a temple of thy Spirit divine" (line 8).

It is not difficult, then, to see the pronouns in Donne's holy sonnets as markers for the kind of struggle Luther describes, the struggle to relinquish first-person agency and its attachment to works in order to let the self be acted upon by a force that arrives from elsewhere, an agency of the Other. We may see these pronouns as markers of gender and sexuality as well if we recall how thoroughly the grammatical distinction between active and passive is bound up with distinctions between masculine and feminine and between licit sexuality and the confused category of sodomy. Alan of Lille in *The Plaint of Nature* can inveigh against nonreproductive sexual practices by invoking the norms of grammar: "The active sex shudders in disgrace as it sees itself degenerate into the passive sex. A man turned woman blackens the fair name of his sex. The witchcraft of Venus turns him into a hermaphrodite. He is subject and predicate: one and the same term is given a double application. Man here extends too far the laws of grammar."[7]

Perhaps human reason clings so stubbornly to active righteousness in Luther's account because it shares the exaggerated horror of passivity that we see in Alain. Under "the law," if we may broaden this term to cover the prescriptions of grammar and sexuality as well as those of the Decalogue, passivity in the male subject is coded as solecism or sodomy. In a strong reading of "Lycidas," Victoria Silver argues that forms of incoherence—breaks in syntax, logical contradictions, inconsistencies in figuration—function for Milton as markers of the breach that separates conventional usage from an almost-unimaginable theological register in which signifiers "become completely new words and acquire a new meaning" (Luther 26: 267).[8] Applying a similar reading to the last line of "Batter my heart," we might say that the violence of Donne's figure is meant to force the accepted meanings of its terms to a breaking point, where "chaste" becomes a new word and acquires a new meaning.

Alain's diatribe does, of course, collapse sexual categories that recent criticism has been at pains to discriminate: passivity, femininity, effeminization, and sodomy are not equivalent. Nor is anal sex between men necessarily an image that provokes resistance, a point Richard Rambuss tactfully asserts when, acknowledging that his discussion of a "sodomitical Christ" has turned speculative, he adds, "some no doubt would even say wishful, an appraisal that I would not take entirely as a rebuff."[9] Donne's speaker seems at once to crave and to resist such ravishment.

.My point is not to endorse or naturalize the horror of passivity that I think Donne's speaker shares with Luther and Alain but rather to situate that horror as a conflicted attribute of the masculine *I* within the cultural norms of patriarchal society. In objecting to critical readings that "domesticate" the rhetorical violence of this poem by turning Donne and his God into a conventionally heterosexual couple, Rambuss rightly insists on "the very outrageousness that is surely its point" (52). That outrageousness, I think, lies both in language that evokes the image of anal penetration and in the suggestion that the penetration, whatever organs it involves, is at once desired *and* forced rather than voluntary. I do not, in other words, rule out a reading that regenders the masculine speaker as feminine: it is a conventional piety made readily available in religious discourse. But this regendering is not comfortable: it is a forced conversion that the masculine *I* both solicits and refuses. The reading that regenders the masculine is therefore inscribed by the poem's grammar within the perspective of a self still bound to the law, still clinging to the illusion of its own power and integrity. From that point of view, to be made passive, to be made feminine, and to be raped are indeed overlapping categories. What they have in common is the usurpation of the active self by an overmastering Other.

Marshall's reading shrewdly discovers this resistance to the demands of faith not only in the *I* of "As due by many titles" but also, residually, in the hypermetrical *me* of its final couplet. That trace of resistance Marshall associates with the refrain of "A Hymne to God the Father," with its puns on the proper name of the poet and his wife Ann: "When thou hast done, thou hast not done, / For I have more." The *I* that possesses Ann More and makes her Ann Donne is also the "more," the lingering excess of masculine self-possession that God has not yet repossessed. This trace of resistance lingers even in the *me* of "As due by many titles"—"the thing," Marshall writes, "that disrupts the prosody but will not go away."

Within the represented content of the poetry, God does not in fact ravish the speaker; he never *has* Donne. The poems close by petitioning for such an outcome, but it does not occur as an event, whether literal or figurative, in the speaker's present tense. It *happens* only in what Luther would call the "theological grammar" of the text, the interpretive moment when the force of Donne's catachresis triggers the recognition that a word like "chaste" has been translated as surprisingly as Bottom in *A Midsummer Night's Dream*. From that recognition may follow the reconstrual I have sketched for the poem's other terminology, including its conspicuous play with the pronouns *I* and *me*.

I do not know what Marshall would make of these reflections. Perhaps he would turn my own question back upon me, asking what difference comes into play when the triangle of desire is not God : Donne : Ann More but Dark Lady : Will : Young Man. The female Other of Sonnet 135 does not threaten or offer to ravish the speaker; in fact, she resembles less Donne's God than the church of his Holy Sonnet 18, "embrac'd and open to most men" (line 14).

That conversation will not happen. Marshall's concluding "I hope that you will join me" can be realized now only through the mediations of reading; in conversation Marshall can only ever be "he," not "I" or "me." Even his name no longer has the same referent; it is strangely comforting but also disturbing to write the word, for I no longer know what it means. When I first tried to imagine framing this response—and could not—I found myself returning not to Shakespeare's sonnets but to "Lycidas":

Hence with denial vain, and coy excuse;
So may som gentle muse

> With lucky words favor my destin'd urn,
> And as he passes, turn
> And bid fair peace be to my sable shroud.[10]

I have always been struck by this moment of identification, divided as it is between the living and the dead, the speaker and the spoken: whoever utters these lines, whether Milton or "the uncouth swain" of line 186, he sees himself at once in the role of the Muse, who turns in passing, and in that of the shepherd whose death brings anything but peace to the pastoral world. Not until reading the essay by Silver cited earlier did I recognize that the identification with Lycidas goes so far as to anticipate the poem's later equivocation not just about the loss of Edward King but more pointedly about the loss of his body. Here the imagined death is represented by cremation at one moment and then, two lines later, by the burial of a shrouded corpse.

Such equivocations register a failure of the imagination faced with death, and in this they resemble the inability of Donne's first-person speaker to desire "passive righteousness" as anything but a ravishing or an imprisonment. They are at odds with the sense of control conveyed by the balanced antithesis of "lucky words" and "destin'd urn." The urn will not be evaded, but the words of the passing Muse still belong to life. They and their speaker are "passing" not only in the casual sense, passing by, but also in the sense they share with Lycidas—"So passeth, in the passing of a day, / Of mortall life the leafe, the bud, the flower"—passing on to their own "destined urn" or shroud.[11] Against this inevitability the lines poise two possibilities: the Muse "may . . . turn" and the words may be "lucky." The turning, like the passing it defers, has figurative senses. To turn in grammar is to reverse a proposition: "Christe tourned Water into Wine. Turne not his miracle, make not, I meane, water of wine."[12] In poetics the "turn" of a sonnet occurs in its ninth line; the turn in "When I consider how my light is spent" arrives preemptively in the middle of the eighth line, signaling, in Silver's reading, the shift in this poem to the theological grammar that enunciates passive righteousness. If the words of the Muse in "Lycidas" are lucky enough, perhaps the "turn" that accompanies them will have prefigured a similar breakthrough.

Luck, however, implies chance, or what may seem like chance because it lies beyond the speaker's control, like the gift of inspiration—what Pope will later call "a grace beyond the reach of art."¹³ Luck escapes destiny, as the words of "Lycidas" have found a life beyond Milton's death—but is this a purely secular survival, belonging wholly to the human imagination and its works, or does it receive some radically altered sense in the grammar of faith? The history of biblical translation and commentary testify to the availability of such a sense. Joseph is called a "lucky man" because God is with him.¹⁴ The unsigned opening leaf of the Coverdale Bible (1535) records a prayer attributed to Nicholas, bishop of Salisbury, that begins, "Let my prayer ascende luckily in to thy syght lyke incense," and the 1549 translation of Erasmus's paraphrase of the New Testament contains the pronouncement "With all good and luckye woordes, blessed, magnified, and praysed bee God."¹⁵

In Milton the same phrase remains equivocal. Its semantic range asks and leaves open the question at the heart of the poem: to what extent can human words survive their speaker's purposes, giving themselves over to the unknowable force of the Other?

7. Aspects, Physiognomy, and the Pun:
A Reading of Sonnet 135 and "A Valediction:
Of Weeping"

JULIAN LAMB

What follows is a series of short sections that, in many respects, comprise different ways of grasping the same phenomenon. And though every section will fail to grasp the phenomenon in its totality, I hope that their mitigated failures will amount to something of a success. Already, though, I may have engineered my first small failure: in saying that what I consider constitute examples of "the same phenomenon," I am making an extraordinary and quite dubious claim that the phenomena I observe constitute a coherent and singular whole and one that (as my title assumes) is designated by a single word: "pun." One of the desired effects of my writing in short sections is to indicate that the term "pun" designates (or ought to designate) a family of diverse phenomena rather than pinpoints an essential similarity common to them all.[1] My method, deriving from Ludwig Wittgenstein's notion of family resemblances, is thus antiessentialist: it resists the temptation to unearth definitive criteria common to all puns and allows me (eventually) to argue that definitive criteria cannot even be ascribed to a single pun.[2] When considering the occurrence of puns in early modern texts, in the present instance, specifically in the poetry of Shakespeare and Donne, we ought to be conscious that such an umbrella term is itself anachronistic, probably developed by those eighteenth-century detractors of punning language.[3] Indeed, the homogenization of diverse phenomena under a single term would have made them a much easier target for attack: all the better for the enemies of the pun if the term itself subsequently collapses under the weight of its own equivocation, its lack of stable referent.[4] But even for champions of the pun, it is very difficult to isolate what punning actually is, to say nothing of those nagging problems as to where an act of punning takes place: in the reader, the writer, the text, or a various mixture of all three. And so this essay on poetic playwright and self-dramatizing poet begins with the premise that the pun is a slippery concept due in part to our expectations of what constitutes a firm grasp. My writing in short sections attempts a different kind of grasping.[5]

Ambiguity

Understandably, critics most often treat puns as sites of ambiguous and multiple meanings; after all, this assertion is surely where a great deal of their power and dynamism lies. Let me illustrate this with two examples from two very different critical approaches. My initial example comprises a sentence each from two deconstructionist critics—Jonathan Culler and Derek Attridge—from a collection of essays titled *On Puns*, which largely celebrates the ambiguous and often deviant quality of the pun:

> Puns present the disquieting spectacle of a functioning of language where boundaries—between sounds, between sound and letter, between meanings—count for less than one might imagine and where supposedly discrete meanings threaten to sink into fluid subterranean signifieds too undefinable to call concepts.[6]

> In place of a context designed to suppress latent ambiguity, the pun is the product of a context deliberately constructed to *enforce* an ambiguity, to render impossible the choice between meanings, to leave the reader or hearer endlessly oscillating in semantic space.[7]

Although Culler, in the first quotation, is also speaking of the deviant way in which puns produce their semantic multiplicity—through accidental phonetic resemblances—both he and Attridge, in the second, are unequivocally celebrating the pun's ambiguity under the implied gaze of those who would not. In the rhetoric of both sentences there is an inexorable teleology: in Culler's we are threatened with the unnerving possibility that puns melt "discrete meanings" into "fluid subterranean signifieds," and in Attridge's we are removed from a context designed to "suppress latent ambiguity" and are left "endlessly oscillating in semantic space." The sentences chart the course of the pun as it overflows the apparently rigid boundaries of clear, coherent sense and confounds the reader with multiple interpretations. The implication is that puns are imbued with or caught up in a teleology that makes them agents of equivocation, and they hurl us—inevitably—from the coherent and unified one to the ambiguous many.

My next example implies something similar, although it is more uneasy about the consequences of its implication. Puns come under William Empson's third type of ambiguity, in which "two ideas, which are connected only by being both relevant in the context, can be given in one word simultaneously."[8] What is revealing about Empson's treatment of this kind of ambiguity is that it comes with a stern caveat: "It is in the third type of ambiguity, when the two notions of the ambiguity are most sharply and consciously detached from one another, that one finds oneself forced to question its value . . . Thus we return to the notion I put at the beginning of the chapter, that in so far as an ambiguity is valuable, it cannot be purely of the third type" (131). Puns are of little value if their ambiguities cannot be absorbed back into the unity of the poem. A rogue pun operating outside the established ambiguities of the text will not produce any kind of ambiguity because it would be meaningless (as well as, we might infer, gratuitous and ostentatious). In fact, a pun ought not to direct meaning so much as consummate a coupling that the poem has already sanctioned: "where those who have been wedded in the argument are bedded together in the phrase" (132). Puns are effective only when they observe certain standards of civil society: "wedded" first, then "bedded." Extramarital punning ought to be discouraged.

Though less comfortable with the extreme ambiguities celebrated by Culler and Attridge, Empson is nevertheless working under the same understanding that successful puns are agents of semantic ambiguity. Deconstruction and New Criticism are here singing from the same hymnbook. And if we suppose that this similarity is too general to be revealing, then perhaps that is because the same hymnbook is still in front of us. But what are puns if not agents of ambiguity? And how else ought we to account for them if not by their multiple and complex meaning effects? In an illuminating article on puns, Catherine Bates gives urgency to these questions. She observes that when we analyze puns, we inevitably seek to work them out, unravel them, clarify the ambiguity, "put the linguistic house back in order and . . . restore the everyday, sober method of expression": "Whether the pun is cursed as a traitor to language or blessed as the welcome guest who brings two meanings for the price of one, its tendency to distort or to extend meaning is dealt with by the interpretative process which, however playfully, ultimately restores priority to the serious business of making sense, to showing what a pun finally means" (428–29). Puns, it could thus be inferred, threaten to disrupt or be disrupted by critical practices that always try to work them out. To what extent are we comfortable with "fluid subterranean signifieds" or "endlessly oscillating in semantic space" if we are always attempting to put the ambiguity perspicuously before us or if we want the "choice between meanings" to be apparent, even if impossible? But what else can we do? Is it conceivable that criticism engage with something that it must necessarily leave uninterpreted or unexplained or, in a curious way, not understood? Might not Bates's "interpretative process" come to a dead end? I contend that these questions expose areas of inquiry that are worth investigating even if they extend well beyond the scope of this essay.

In this investigation, I am interested in a family of punning phenomena that are not simply hard to understand but that cannot be understood. This is because they neither present us with an undecidable choice between readings nor melt discrete meanings into an incoherent blend. Rather, the puns I engage make us aware of the inert and unchanging homophone from which meanings emerge but which is not itself meaningful. I have chosen three poems that pun on proper names—Will, Shakespeare's given name; More, the maiden name of Ann, Donne's wife; and Donne itself—if only because, as nomenclature, their close association with individuals means that they become (as it were) saturated with their bearers such that hearing them disappear into mere sounds becomes an all the more potent experience. In order to see these phenomena correctly, we need to reverse the trajectory of our analysis. Instead of beginning with the single homophone out of which springs ambiguity, the puns I examine tend either to dissolve meaning into a single word or to present the word as something in which meaning is enfolded. I will require the remainder of this essay to clarify just what I mean here by "single word," but I will start each short section (including this one) by assuming a teleology opposite to that of those sentences I have cited by Culler and Attridge. Let me explain by using an image. When a white light is shone through a glass prism, it breaks up into the colors of the spectrum. Criticism on puns has always been very good at analyzing the way a single entity is broken up into multiple colors. By contrast, however, I am interested in the way some puns gather up the spectrum and thrust them back through the prism. We are left with a word that is analogous to that white, translucent light in which none of its constitutive colors are visible. Each section that follows works toward an albeit partial, aspectual, momentary view of this white, unambiguous, unequivocal, singular word.

Seeing Puns

Puns often go unseen by readers and/or writers. This is an obvious but vitally important aspect of their operation, and one that is frequently neglected.[9] That puns are sometimes seen means that this seeing is of a particular type; that is, they seem to elicit a different kind of seeing from words that do not pun. Question: if one reads a passage without seeing a pun and then (perhaps after having been told) reads the passage again and sees the pun, does one see anything different? In one sense, no: the words of the text have not changed; in another sense, yes: one notices that a word can be seen in a different way. This rather paradoxical situation arises as a result of the curious functions performed by the word "see." I suspect that only after clarifying the distinctiveness of these functions will we be able to understand what it means to "see" a pun: to spot one, to be struck by one, and even to miss one. I am motivated to make this call for clarity by a word of caution from Ludwig Wittgenstein: "We find certain things about seeing puzzling, because we do not find the whole business of seeing puzzling enough" (212e). It may thus be in our interests to take a few moments to be puzzled.

This remark appears in an especially labored section from part II.xi of the *Philosophical Investigations*, in which Wittgenstein isolates two different uses of the word "see": "I contemplate a face, and then suddenly notice its likeness to another. I *see* that it has not changed; and yet I see it differently. I call this experience 'noticing an aspect'" (193e). How is it that one can see something differently while also seeing that nothing has changed? The obvious answer is that the first kind of seeing is purely visual, whereas the second kind of seeing appears to involve some kind of mental activity. "Noticing an aspect" involves these two kinds of seeing. Wittgenstein's interest is in the second of these. In particular, he wonders whether it could be classed as a form of interpretation or seeing. Wittgenstein offers strenuous arguments on both sides in order to infer that aspect seeing is neither seeing nor interpretation but is situated between them.[10] I would like to give Wittgenstein's complex philosophical discussion a wide berth here and instead focus on two key features of aspect seeing, both of which can be illuminated by a visual pun: the familiar duck-rabbit.[11]

Wittgenstein presents us with a picture that we see one moment as a duck and the next as a rabbit. Countering the observation that seeing a different aspect is purely subject to the will (and therefore an intentional act of interpretation), Wittgenstein describes this experience as the "dawning of an aspect." Such a metaphor has a particular fidelity to the phenomenology of seeing the duck after having seen the rabbit (or vice versa): it dawns upon us, we are acted upon, the figure of a duck seems to emerge from the lines of its own volition. But something else happens with the dawning of an aspect: "I *see* it has not changed, and yet I see it differently." The experience of aspect dawning involves, indeed requires, our seeing that unchanged object from which the new aspect emerges.[12] As Justin Good has put it, "Not being aware of the bivalent meaning of the duck-rabbit figure, I have no basis for a distinction between the object seen and my visual impression of the object" (25). In being able to see the illustration now *as* a duck and now *as* a rabbit, we are made aware of the visual object itself, that odd configuration of lines that need not necessarily be seen *as* anything.[13]

But what exactly is this experience of aspect dawning? The first thing to establish is that this *is* an experience. Wittgenstein calls it "experiencing the meaning of a word" (214e). Because of the associations that words develop through our continuous use of them, they seem, as it were, to become "filled with their meaning" (215e). Wittgenstein uses a hypothetical situation: "Suppose I had agreed on a code with someone; 'tower' means bank. I tell him 'Now go to the tower'—he understands me and acts accordingly, but he feels the word tower to be strange in this use, it has not yet 'taken on' the meaning" (214e). Words seem to absorb their meanings such that they acquire a certain texture or rather, to use Wittgenstein's word, a certain "physiognomy": "The familiar physiognomy of a word, the feeling that it has taken up its meaning into itself, that it is an actual likeness of its meaning—there could be human beings to whom all this was alien. (They would not have an attachment to their words.)—And how are these feelings manifested among us?—By the way we choose and value words" (218e). As it happens, our experience of the physiognomy of words is especially strong when it comes to names of people: "I feel as if the name 'Schubert' fitted Schubert's works and Schubert's face" (215e). The association between a name and its bearer sometimes becomes so strong that not only does the name become filled with the person but the person comes strangely to look like his or her name.

One method that Wittgenstein uses to isolate this experience is to ask us to imagine what it would be like if we did not have it: "What would you be missing, for instance, if you did not understand the request to pronounce the word 'till' and to mean it as a verb,—or if you did not feel that a word had lost its meaning and became a mere sound if it was repeated ten times over?" (214e). Repetition sometimes has the effect of draining a word of its physiognomy such that it becomes a mere object of hearing. Stripped of its potential to be seen *as* anything, it assumes the presence of something that we merely see. Some puns may produce the same effect. If, like the duck-rabbit, they cause us to experience a fissure between our aspect seeing and our seeing, then might they not also give us an experience of that word that is not seen aspectually? Even as they present us with two physiognomies in the one body, such puns can draw our attention to that body which, as such, has no physiognomy.

Available Puns and Fatal Cleopatras

Some years ago, Stephen Booth suggested in a paper focused on the words *bear/bare* in Shakespeare that "a non-significant network of relationships among homonyms, their cognates, their synonyms, and the topics to which they pertain can—alliteration-like—give both incidental extra coherence and a 'feel' of philosophical profundity to speeches, scenes, and whole plays."[14] Booth's attention to the "non-significant" networks of relationships between words (one suspects that he is engaging in his own play on "significant" and "signifying"), tests what he sees as an erroneous assumption: that "semantically related elements in a text . . . should communicate potentially paraphrasable substance to us" ("Exit," 53). These phonetic echoes do not produce "paraphrasable substance," let alone any ambiguous meaning, but are instead the half-heard background music that produces the impression of a final unified meaning and offers the promise of complete coherence ("Exit," 53). Booth adamantly resists interpretation, preferring instead to present "close reading without readings." Such readings often involve quite virtuosic acts of aspect seeing by which insubstantial, nonsignifying connections may be drawn between, for instance, "bare" and "bear," as well as "pause" and "paws" ("Exit," 53). For Booth, the critic must not grant "import" to these aspects by actualizing them into the paraphrasable substance of an interpretation. Instead, they must be seen to create an experience of unlimited semantic possibility and signifying potential. It is in this context that Booth refers somewhat scornfully to puns, for if a language is "made rich by the mere availability of a pun," it is rendered gratuitous by an "actual" pun.[15] Dismissive of actual puns and unwilling to interpret the merely available puns that Shakespeare never makes, Booth is left attempting to account for an affect. Phonetic overlappings, echoes, and connections "generate mental circumstances of the sort that exist just before awareness of a context's potential for punning reaches sufficient intensity to trigger an actual pun. Once the pun is perceived by its discoverer, the effectively metaphysical aura of mental potential dissipates instantly. Before the pun the conditions in which it lurks—felt but unfound—give one a sense that one's wit has expanded beyond its known usual limits" ("Exit," 64). Actual puns inevitably circumscribe the impression of unlimited possibility produced by merely available puns. At times Booth almost chastises Shakespeare for using figures such as *anatanaclasis*, where one word is repeated but with different meanings each time, which allow him to make "blatantly mechanical puns" (*Essay*, 91). At other times, his analyses of phonetic echoes rather conspicuously ignore the most obvious ones.[16] Despite his brilliant accounts of the experience of language, Booth simply cannot abide gratuitous artifices that interpose their own materiality between reader and subject matter. Nor is he the only one.

Margreta de Grazia has argued that puns came to be seen as unruly only after the instantiation of lexical rules. Such rules dictated not only what words referred to but also—and more important—that they were meaningless without their power of reference.[17] By contrast, she argues, in an age before lexical standardization "puns remained largely integral rather than conspicuously peripheral to the language" (151): "What were subsequently singled out as accidental quirks might then have been integral to language, directing and encouraging associations that made sense. They literally *made sense*; that is, they constituted sense through their copious troping resources rather than representing it as something pre-existent in mind or world" (155–56). It is perhaps unsurprising that the age of the dictionary would awaken a new hatred of puns. I am compelled at this point to trot out the familiar passage in which Dr. Johnson laments Shakespeare's weakness for puns. De Grazia uses it to highlight the historical specificity of Shakespeare's prelexical punning; Culler uses it as a foil for those readers who are not put off by the "disquieting spectacle" of linguistic deviance.[18] Neither, to my mind, is alive enough to Johnson's concern to take it seriously:

> A quibble is to Shakespeare, what luminous vapours are to the traveller; he follows it at all adventures, it is sure to lead him out of his way, and sure to engulf him in the mire. It has some malignant power over his mind, and its fascinations are irresistible. Whatever be the dignity or profundity of his disquisition, whether he be enlarging knowledge or exalting affection, whether he be amusing attention with incidents, or enchaining it in suspense, let but a quibble spring up before him, and he leaves his work unfinished. A quibble is the golden apple for which he will always turn aside from his career, or stoop from his elevation. A quibble, poor and barren as it is, gave him such delight, that he was content to purchase it, by the sacrifice of reason, propriety, and truth. A quibble was to him the fatal Cleopatra for which he lost the world, and was content to lose it.[19]

The traveler Shakespeare is waylaid by a pun, which prevents him from ever completing his journey. The pun, it seems, sets him off course because it has no course; it is a diversion, and Shakespeare is easily diverted. And so Shakespeare is also Antony, distracted from his Roman thoughts, not only in thrall to Cleopatra, but also feminized by her, allowing his language to interpose between word and world. What I would like to stress is that what, for Johnson, is troubling about this is not simply (and not even largely) the pun's capacity to produce ambiguous meanings, even if in highly uncivilized and indecorous ways. Johnson is anxious that puns constitute a troubling congealment of language in which words wrest themselves free of their responsibilities to their referents: they demand to be perceived as entities of themselves. For Johnson the lexicographer, words signify the world; that world is lost when they brazenly demand to be looked at rather than looked through. He assures his readers of his own priorities in the Preface to his *Dictionary of the English Language* (1755): "I am not yet so lost in lexicography, as to forget that *words are the daughters of earth, and that things are the sons of heaven.*"[20] To become lost in words, one might infer, is to consort too freely with the daughters of the earth; to become lost in puns is positively to fall into the arms of a femme fatale and indulge in a meaningless relationship.

"Tennis Balls, My Liege"

Let me offer an example of a pun that might not actually be a pun at all. Toward the beginning of *Henry V*, the young King counters the Dauphin's "mock" of sending tennis balls by using verbal repetition to send "mock" back:[21]

> And tell the pleasant Prince this mock of his
> Hath turned his balls to gun-stones, and his soul
> Shall stand sore charged for the wasteful vengeance
> That shall fly with them; for many a thousand widows
> Shall this his mock mock out of their dear husbands,
> Mock mothers from their sons, mock castles down,
> And some are yet ungotten and unborn
> That shall have cause to curse the Dauphin's scorn.
>
> (I.ii.282–89)

Preempting the military action he will take, Henry matches his racket to the "mock" of the Dauphin's tennis balls and turns them into "gun-stones." The force of Henry's riposte is that the Dauphin's "mock" against him becomes his "mock" against the Dauphin, a reversal achieved by the powerful repetition in line 286—"Shall this his mock mock out"—through which Henry turns "mock" from a noun to a verb: where the Dauphin's mock is an inactive thing, Henry's will "Mock mothers from their sons, mock castles down." Although there is a degree of equivocation here, it is not meaning but force that predominates. Moreover, what is forceful about it is not that mock means one thing, then another, but that it is being strenuously made to mean them. We experience not ambiguity of meaning but the signifying potential of the word, as well as the power of its speaker to match his racquet to the word and make it signify something else. As in a rally in tennis, so in this wordplay we observe a single ball being hit to and fro. Thus, although this passage is compelling us to aspect-see—"mock" is seen now as a noun, now as a verb—it is also compelling us simply to see.

Although this iterative wordplay might be considered punning, it is not (strictly speaking) a pun. It is, in fact, *antanaclasis*, the gratuitous poetic figure that Booth finds so offensive. In the *Art of English Poesy*, George Puttenham describes it in these terms: "[This figure] we may call the Rebound, alluding to the tennis ball, which being smitten with the racket, rebounds back again."[22] The value of the figure is not its capacity to produce ambiguous, multiple meanings. Rather, according to Puttenham, the repetitions give the impression of profound meaning, or plausibility, or force, or—to use his word—sententiousness. Sententiousness is the effective realization of a word's signifying potential, the impression it gives of meaning something. This impression depends on the capacity of language to assert itself as what Puttenham elsewhere calls a "cognizance": a conscious display of words as objects that enfold meaning.[23] Puttenham's sententious figures are techniques by which words can be transformed into such objects, which seem to promise and withhold their significance.

And yet, and yet: are not Henry's repetitions marked by the striking way in which they do not produce anything like this effect? Though, I suspect, many puns ought to be analyzed for their sententious effects, for their capacity to freeze a word into a cognizance, this describes neither Henry's wordplay nor the punning that goes on in Shakespeare's sonnet 135, which I am about to discuss. The forceful rebounds draw attention to the single, unchanging word that, like a tennis ball, is struck back and forth. And the word, like a tennis ball, signifies nothing and gives no impression of significance. The repetitions that force upon us its status as aural object also confirm its status as mere object. Certainly, there may be significant meaning in the sound alone. One can imagine a good actor drawing out the alliteration of "mock mothers," as well as the violent, repeated, unvoiced plosive in "mock castles." But even as these inflections fill the word with meaning, the repetition has the effect that Wittgenstein intimated it would: the dissolution of the word's physiognomy.

Will, the Word

Shakespeare's sonnet 135:

> Whoever hath her wish, thou hast thy Will,
> And Will to boot, and Will in overplus;

More than enough am I, that vex thee still,
To thy sweet will making addition thus.
Wilt thou, whose will is large and spacious,
Not once vouchsafe to hide my will in thine?
Shall will in others seem right gracious,
And in my will no fair acceptance shine?
The sea, all water, yet receives rain still,
And in abundance addeth to his store;
So thou, being rich in Will, add to thy Will
One will of mine, to make thy large Will more:
    Let no unkind, no fair beseechers kill;
    Think all but one, and me in that one Will.[24]

One would be hard pressed to argue that *antanaclasis* does not equivocate here. These repetitions of "will" are markedly different from Henry's repetitions in that they do open up multiple distinct possibilities: willfulness or intention; sexual desire; male and female genitals; a male Christian name. Armed with these meanings, the critic could dutifully attend to the sonnet's ambiguities: tease them out, unravel them, clarify them, discern within them various tensions, and leave himself (in my instance) endlessly oscillating in semantic space. Heavily annotated editions of the sonnets, which present a neat list of possibilities, will certainly encourage this kind of reading. However, we ought also to be aware of a different sort of analysis that instead locates the power of this punning language not in any ambiguous meanings it produces but in the powerful, even gratuitous, manipulation of "will" to accommodate a variety of meanings. We would thus resist understanding the word as something that means this or that and instead observe its potential to mean almost anything. The problem with this line of approach is not the implausibility of its reading but the manifest absence of any kind of reading: once remarked upon, the word leaves us little to talk about. Diverted by those luminous vapors, criticism threatens to leave its task unfinished. The fatal Cleopatra is here winking at us.

Sonnet 135 is unusual and helpful because, in the trajectory of its thinking, it makes use of the pun not as a producer of meaning but as a mechanism that absorbs meanings into a single verbal object. I contend that to understand its affective argument eventually requires us to leave its "will" not understood. We should be mindful that, for all its ambiguity, the sonnet culminates in what seems like a unity. The "one Will" of the couplet indicates that which, in the course of the sonnet's equivocation, has not changed. To borrow an image from modern physics, "Will," the word, functions in this sonnet somewhat like the singularity of a black hole, into which its varied semantic matter is forcefully accommodated. After all, the sonnet is all about accommodation: Will (the name of the speaker) attempts to persuade the dark lady to accommodate his will (sexual desire, penis) in her will (sexual desire, vagina) by arguing that his will is no different from all those wills (rival sexual desirers and penises) who have found themselves, at one point or another, accommodated by her will. The success of the speaker's argument seems to rely on the degree to which the "me" of the couplet, who is called "Will" (capitalized and italicized in the Quarto), can be absorbed into her will and so be included in the group of other wills who have been. In this way, the meanings of "will" are swept up by the speaker's centripetal logic, spun around until forced into a single signifier.

But what is the intended effect of the injunction to "think all but one, and me in that one Will"? It is pretty clear what is not intended: a renewed awareness that "will" is an ambiguous word that means a whole variety of different things. The speaker does not so much plead for favor as use *antanaclasis* to argue that having sex with him would merely be a further act in a pattern of habitual behavior. The repetitions of "will" contract her rampant promiscuity into a perverse form of constancy: to be faithful to "one will" is effectively to be faithful to everyone. But the lady is constant neither to "Will" the speaker, nor to "Will" the name, nor to "will" the word with paraphrasable meanings (desire, volition, penis, vagina, a male Christian name), but "will" the word, the signifier as such, which signifies nothing in particular but brazenly flaunts its own signifying potential. In so arguing, I do not claim that "will" is without meanings. Of course, it has a dazzling panoply of meanings that no reader should be prevented from teasing out. My suggestion, however, is that the sonnet also encourages the reader to tease them back in. Gathering up the colors in a spectrum, the speaker forces them back through the prism: "Will" shines with a white, almost transparent light in which none of its constituent meanings are discernible. Nor are any of these constituent meanings present enough in the word to give it any kind of physiognomy. The repetitions have turned it to a mere material presence, something that is simply seen and cannot be seen *as* and consequently does not offer us an experience of meaning.

Over the course of the sonnet, "will" comes to resemble the censor's "beep": It becomes a nonsensical sound that stands in place of an unmentionable that would signify.

Emblems of More (I)

Donne's "A Valediction of Weeping" contains, arguably, a pun on his wife's maiden name, More. (As I hope to show, the fact that the pun is arguable is important to its operation.) Not only that, but the poem presents us with a visualization of the pun itself:[25]

> Let me pour forth
> My tears before thy face, whilst I stay here,
> For thy face coins them, and thy stamp they bear,
> And by this mintage they are something worth,
>   For thus they be
>   Pregnant of thee;
> Fruits of much grief they are, emblems of more,
> When a tear falls, that thou falls which it bore;
> So thou and I are nothing then, when on a divers shore.[26]

Those tears the speaker cries before the face of his beloved, which consequently contain her reflection, are emblems not only of his present grief and his grief to come but also of the person who is the cause of them and whose image is reflected in them. The word "more," like an empty tear, requires the proper name "More" to mint "worth" into it; the proper name is reflected in the word like More's face reflected in the tear. In this way, they are both like a blank coin impressed with the face of the sovereign. Without Ann More, the tears will be empty, and the word "more" will simply be a word, not a proper name. The tears are "emblems of more"—emblems, that is, of the homonym. The pun is visualized by the conceit, while the conceit itself is condensed by the pun into a droplet of wordplay.

Such droplets, or globes, or spheres are the imagistic currency that the poem trades on as it dramatizes the way in which such nothings are made into profound somethings. Stanza one begins with an empty tear that, minted with the face of the beloved, becomes supremely valuable. Enlarging upon this, the blank round ball in stanza two is transformed by the expert hand of the workman into the whole world. The unprepossessing "O" that begins the third stanza ("O more than moon"), itself both an aural and a visual pun, is metaphorized into the beloved and exerts a greater tidal influence over the poet's earth than does the moon. Only by presenting these objects as static, inconsequential, and of no value can the poem dramatize the way the lovers transform them. Yet the transformative power of the lovers is predicated, in the first stanza, on their physical proximity. What differentiates "A Valediction: Of Weeping" from, for instance, "A Valediction: Forbidding Mourning" is that, in the former, togetherness is all important: "So thou and I are nothing then, when on a divers shore."[27] This is why the poem begins as it does: "Let me pour forth / My tears before thy face, whilst I stay here." In order for "More" to be reflected in the poet's tears, she must be directly in front of him. However, this is a valediction, a poem whose purpose is to anticipate separation. "Whilst I stay here" carries the implication that those future tears wept on a "divers shore" will not reflectively contain More. In dramatizing the way the lovers transform nothings into somethings, the poem unavoidably tarries with the possibility that such transformations may, in the future, be undone. But might not the same be said of the pun? The word "more," which is like the empty tear, is also like the "round ball," which is blank, and the inert "O," which signifies nothing. Will "more" mean "More" after separation? I argue that this uncertainty is the very crux of the pun such that, in making the pun, the poem is also unmaking it or, at least, anticipating its potential unmaking.

The pun was first brought to critical attention by Harry Morris in 1973 and was taken up five years later by David J. Leigh.[28] Since then, almost all annotated editions of Donne's poetry offer it as a possibility. But Morris cautions: "The trouble with this sort of discovery is that once a pun is detected, others are thought to be lurking in every poem" (131). It is surprising that we would so readily ascribe this condition to ourselves and not also to Donne himself. Could he use the word "more" without also seeing "More" lurking within it?[29] Do we see any evidence of this, for instance, in the two other appearances of the word in the poem: "O more than moon" (19); "Let not the wind, / Example find, / To do me more harm" (23–25)? Possibly. But we ought to question what counts as evidence here. What need not count as evidence is either the grammatical ease with which both meanings can be inserted into the word or the pleasingly ambiguous range of readings that would result. The pun does not produce ambiguity or significant amounts of paraphrasable substance. Instead, "more" exists as a physiognomical presence, one that produces (or does not produce) the experience of the dawning of an aspect: duck and rabbit again. When the poet has been separated from his love, will "more" still be filled with her, will it still offer him an experience of her name? Or will he fail to see her name even if it is right in front of him? The "fixed foot" of this pun is not the name but the word.

Emblems of More (II)

As an answer to the question of whether Donne is punning on his wife's maiden name in "A Valediction: Of Weeping," "possibly" is unlikely to garner enthusiastic followers. It appears at best to be a prelude to an answer altogether more exact and exacting, one that would provide greater certitude and unearth those underlying criteria that give us license to lay claim to a pun when we think we see one. With "possibly," the critic's work seems hardly to have begun, let alone brought to a conclusion. Our disappointment with "possibly" registers a lack of certainty where, we feel, certainty ought to be or else a lack of analytical rigor in accounting for a phenomenon that, we think, really ought to yield greater perspicuity. The force of this "ought" is the aspiration to seek out that to which we do not have access: absolute criteria for the presence of a pun. Of course, the contingent criteria we have can ensure a pun well beyond reasonable doubt; it is possible, after all, for a pun to fulfill its criteria too strenuously, such that it becomes too obvious. (Of this variety are stale double entendres that expose their duplicity too candidly but under the false presupposition that they do so with subtlety.) My point is that Donne's use of the word "more" in "A Valediction: Of Weeping" leaves us entertaining the possibility of the pun and restlessly striving to make it more than a possibility. This textual ambivalence, which (as I have argued) is the crux of the poem, arises as a result of what we might call an ambiguity of use. This is not a semantic ambiguity—one that compels us to enumerate the multiple meanings of a word or to depict the troubling melting of apparently discrete meanings into each other—but an ambiguity that inevitably leaves us wanting more certain criteria (or a more ample fulfillment of criteria) for the meanings of a particular word. I do not intend, in saying this, to augment the range or potency of our capacity to detect puns. Rather, my hope is that it allows us to make critical use of what is sometimes the crucial ambiguity: whether a pun is actually there. We normally take this to be an inconvenient condition of reading, something that needs to be decided upon before the real analysis of ambiguous meanings can proceed. Some puns, however, encourage us to observe the way an ambiguity of use also conditions the very act of writing: to what extent in "A Valediction: Of Weeping" is Donne faced with the problem that when he writes "more," he cannot, with certainty, mean (or not mean) "More"? (To what extent can we produce a perfectly legitimate likeness of a rabbit and be absolutely certain that it will not be confused, say, for a duck?)

I would like to end with a series of observations on "A Hymn to God the Father," observations that do not amount to a reading so much as they counterpoint an existing reading by David J. Leigh. Although it was Henry Morris who first suggested that "more" in the final line of each stanza in the poem could refer to Ann, it was Leigh who has since made the most extensive use of it. He argues that the refrain in the first two stanzas—"When thou hast done, thou hast not done, / For I have more"—reveals Donne's awareness that his "excessive attachment" to his wife (or at least her memory) "must be moderated before he can be prepared for union with God the Father."[30] The refrain could thus be paraphrased: "When you, God, have finished forgiving my sins, you do not have me (Donne) because I have more sin: my earthly attachment to my wife (More)." God's having done/Donne is thus dependent on Donne's not having More. Leigh is not alone in seeing at the end of the poem a profound dissolution of its tensions: "The final resolution of the Christian paradoxes will solve all the conflicts of Donne's life and of the poem, most fundamentally that between the divine finality of 'done' and the human restlessness for 'more.'"[31] Having freed himself from his all too earthly love, Donne can finally be fully forgiven and happily attain eternity with More.

I do not disagree with this sensitive reading of the poem, but I do want to show that three puns in the poem deftly, though powerfully, qualify it. In the first two lines the poet both acknowledges original sin as his own and attempts to disown it: "Wilt thou forgive that sin where I begun, / Which is my sin, though it were done before?" Though recognizing his own complicity in original sin ("Which is my sin"), the poet attempts to distance it from him ("though it were done before"), an attempt that nevertheless punningly implicates himself in it. The pun, unintended by the poet, gives the impression of being motivated to catch him out in a brief moment of denial. Yet it asserts itself openly upon neither him nor indeed the reader; one hears it, so to speak, as a voice from a farther room. A pun in the fourth line of the same stanza has a similar effect: "Wilt thou forgive that sin, through which I run, / And do run still: though still I do deplore?" "Still" can refer either to an ongoing process or to motionlessness inactivity: the poet continues to deplore sin but does so inactively, lethargically. Once again, the speaker unwittingly confounds himself further in a sin by a momentary attempt to articulate his opposition to it. And once again, the counterpoint is something that is played out by language, not the poet, who seems unaware of what he is saying. The poem's resolution carries the poem's most subversive counterpoint. The "sin of fear" is apparently assuaged and forgiven by God's promise that his sun/Son shall shine at the poet's death: "And, having done that, thou hast done, / I fear no more." "I fear no more," which is routinely read as the poet concluding that, given God's promise, he no longer fears, cannot quite silence a contrapuntal voice: "I fear that I no longer have More."[32] In declaring his renouncement of the sin of fear, the poet continues to wallow in it.

In discussing these puns, I have consciously used the word "speaker" instead of "Donne," thus leaving open the possibility that the puns, though unintended by the speaker, are intended by Donne. Against the certitude promised by "intention," "possibility" may strike us, once more, as dissatisfying. However, attempting to establish intentions does not get us closer to certainty but merely articulates the problem. The poem works to truncate intention, to define its limits, in order to show that the criteria for meaning something often extend beyond its purview. Under the infinitely perceptive readership of God the Father, every word becomes a cognizance, an object enclosing unknown meanings, always signifying in excess of what a speaker intends, always signifying more. Awareness of the potential existence of such unknown and unlimited verbal aspects (as Wittgenstein might remind us) gives us a heightened consciousness of the object from which these aspects "dawn," in Wittgenstein's lexicon, but which itself is *seen* nonaspectually. In a fascinating chapter titled "Frozen Words," Judith Anderson shows the way early modern *sententiae* tended to "fix and reify language" into a material presence: "There are signs in the period itself—even outside creative writing, where we might expect them—of an awareness of the way *sententiae* operate as templates of meaning, freeze language, and appear to solidify it."[33] Such crystallizations of language not only make apparent the materiality of words but also turn them into objects that, like voices frozen in ice, appear to withhold their significance. But the inverse is equally true. In an age before lexical standardization, before language was (to use de Grazia's evocative phrase) "submitted to the Lockean lexical grid" upon which it "became responsible to [the] world or thoughts about the world," words appear to attain an object status because they are not always forthcoming with their meaning (151, 149).

PART IV Realms of Privacy and Imagination

8. Fantasies of Private Language in "The Phoenix and Turtle" and "The Ecstasy"

ANITA GILMAN SHERMAN

Although "perfect" and "universal" language schemes have been extensively studied, fantasies of "private language" in the seventeenth century have been neglected.[1] "Private language" is a vexed term seldom applied to the early modern period, mostly because it is anachronistic, having been coined by Ludwig Wittgenstein in the mid-twentieth century. Yet the idea of a private language would not have seemed far fetched in the Renaissance. Seventeenth-century notions of language as the privileged site of rationality derive in part from Adam's naming of the animals in Genesis 2:19. This story of origins becomes the basis for divergent but related models of language: the first involving the sovereign individual who has the power to confer identity, the second involving a fantasy of fellowship and universal language among speakers prior to Babel. The Edenic vision of perfect communication has long inspired the human mind. As a young man, Wittgenstein was attracted to mathematical logic as an instantiation of a universal language, going so far as to call it sublime, but he later repudiated it in favor of ordinary language, with its messy variations and ambiguities.[2] While his thought experiments with private language occur in his later work (sections 243–315 of his *Philosophical Investigations*), they share concerns with the universal logic of the earlier *Tractatus*. Both private and universal languages speak to a desire for perfect legibility.

Private language, while apparently the opposite of the *Ursprache* or *lingua adamica* imagined by seventeenth-century thinkers, betrays a similar yearning for transparent communication. Both linguistic models aspire to clarity and complete understanding. In a fallen world both perfect and private languages are inaccessible, simultaneously inviting and resisting translation. Both are out of reach, the one in the paradisal past, the other as a logically impossible figment lodged inside one's head. Despite this temporal and spatial disparity, both perfect and private languages aim to discover how unavailable but theoretically ideal languages signify. This essay argues that Shakespeare and Donne entertain the idea of an elusive tongue not so as to probe the cosmological mysteries of the universe and its divine order but rather so as to investigate the possibilities of Edenic intimacy. Both dream of a private language shared with an alter ego, but each represents it in opposed ways. Shakespeare's "Phoenix and Turtle" attests to the impossibility of accessing private language, insisting on our necessary reliance on linguistic practices like genre. By contrast, Donne's "Ecstasy" experiments with the thing itself, paradoxically "inventing" a private language only to turn in the end to the body to find full expression.[3]

As a preliminary to my analysis of the poems, let me sketch how seventeenth-century philosophy at once anticipates and lays the groundwork for the private language argument. The connection hinges on notions of private experience and private sensation. Descartes, for example, frames the problem of the enclosed mind with his famous *cogito* and his thought experiment about whether other people—those whom he sees out his window walking by—are mere automata. In his *Essay on Human Understanding*, Locke similarly operates with a model of an enclosed mind receiving impressions from the outside world and translating them into a private set of meanings. Although Descartes is a rationalist and Locke more of an empiricist, they share a powerful vision of humans as isolated entities, cut off from one another, busily deciphering unreliable sense data in an effort to forge connections with the world. Wittgenstein attacks the idea of private experience held by empiricists and rationalists alike. Although he avoids a historical approach, his targets are widely assumed to include Cartesian and Lockean views of enclosed minds finding words with which to label private sensations.[4] His objection to the idea of a private language is that language is by definition communal, such that it makes no sense to imagine inventing signs in isolation. When his fictional interlocutor asks, "But is it also conceivable that there be [sic] a language in which a person could write down or give voice to his inner experiences—his feelings, moods, and so on—for his own use?" (*PI* § 243), the answer is ultimately no. Before arriving at the conclusion that private language is an oxymoron and nonsense, however, Wittgenstein entertains scenarios in which something resembling a private language emerges. Because these help illuminate the

Shakespeare and Donne poems, let me mention two such scenarios of secret or hermetic language.

Wittgenstein concedes that occasions could arise when one might want to coin terms for one's private use.[5] He imagines a man keeping a journal about an intermittent pain he is feeling, proposing to jot down every experience of this mysterious twinge with the sign "S." The diarist's process would involve an intensely focused inward gaze, a quality of strained attention, which would amount to an ostensive definition—an inward finger pointing that would pick out the particular pain sensation and name it. This diarist is imagined as an Adam conferring names on his inward fauna in what Wittgenstein dubs a "ceremony" (*PI* § 258). A related scenario involves Siamese twins. In this exceptional case, the question considers how the twins would verify their shared experience of the identical sensation. What words would they use? Presumably, ordinary, everyday words.

Speaking a language, Wittgenstein is at pains to point out, involves learning to negotiate a set of practices and conventions. Language is an inherited, rule-driven, social system emerging from different forms of life (*Lebensformen*). Neither the diarist nor the Siamese twins can generate a language from scratch. This is not to deny that cryptographers can invent secret codes or that ingenious people, in the seventeenth century no less than now, have developed a plethora of elite or esoteric languages. Wittgenstein's point is that each of these special languages is always already implicated in a social grammar. As he puts it, "Much must be prepared in the language for mere naming to make sense" (*PI* § 257). Still, Wittgenstein concedes the long-standing appeal of a solipsistic model of mind even while noting its distressing result in skepticism, understood as doubt about the outside world and other people. As he puts it, "The essential thing about private experience is really not that each person possesses his own specimen, but that nobody knows whether other people also have *this* or something else" (*PI* § 272). The desire for assurance that another person shares seemingly private sensations runs deep. It can take the form of the question, how can I know with certainty what my beloved is thinking? This curiosity about others' private experience should be seen as a vital response to the solitude associated with a skeptical consciousness.

The philosopher Stanley Cavell, a gifted interpreter of Wittgenstein, suggests that skepticism and the desire for intimacy go together when he contends that "with the birth of skepticism . . . a new intimacy, or wish for it, enters the world; call it privacy shared."[6] Because skepticism is experienced as a "withdrawal of the world" in Cavell's view (a formulation that construes the individual not as a mind so much as a body poised over the abyss), one who is in thrall to a skeptical crisis will act out one's visceral need for attachment to the world by demanding perfect knowledge of the beloved (19). The skeptic in his lonely detachment craves intimacy, and the more it eludes him, the more he compensates with hyperbolic language and fantasies of ecstatic union. In other words, the Cartesian philosopher's hyperbolic doubt, whereby the world falls away and leaves only the assurance of the *cogito*, becomes transformed into a hyperbolic demand for the certainty and beauty of companionship. For Cavell, this means marriage. In an uncanny echo of Wittgenstein's use of ceremony to describe the deictic inward gaze labeling a private sensation, he describes marriage as a ceremony of single intimacy that arises as a form of defense against tragic consciousness. His phrase, "ceremony of single intimacy," captures the uneasy yoking of inherited practice with a model of relationality that seeks escape from the world (19). The problem, Cavell says, succumbing to skepticism, is that "no one knows from outside whether a marriage exists" (28). Marriage is thus an exemplary instance of the problem of other minds, eliciting doubt.

To fend off the threat of skepticism, lovers have to mythologize their love and, in so doing, resort to hyperbole.[7] As Cavell explains, "Since marriage . . . is an image of the ordinary in human existence (the ordinary as what is under attack in philosophy's tendency to skepticism), the pair's problem, the response to their crisis, is to transfigure, or resurrect, their vision of their everyday lives."[8] Intimacy thus partakes both of everydayness (*Alltäglichkeit*) and of transcendence, understood as a desire for transfiguration. Cavell interprets Shakespeare's Cleopatra and her "reinvention of marriage" at the play's end as a "quest for transcendence" involving multiple ceremonies ("coronation to religion to theater to marriage to revels to funeral") even as it invokes the ordinary (doing "the meanest chares") as its condition (*Disowning*, 28–29). That "a hallucinated marriage is an autoerotic fantasy" does not preclude the presence and anticipation of an audience (34). Not only is Cleopatra surrounded by her attendants at her suicide, but Octavius is expected as well, Antony is imagined awaiting her with open arms in the afterlife, and we are there. The theatricality of this scene, the exhibitionism of its intimacy, its invitation to voyeurs—all this supports Cavell's view that skepticism, theatricality, and the desire for intimacy go together. Hyperbole allows Cleopatra to tap into the sublime and to stage a scene that vanquishes skeptical doubt.

Like the final tableau of *Antony and Cleopatra*, both "The Phoenix and Turtle" and "The Ecstasy" conjure up ceremonies of single intimacy that disarm a skeptical consciousness.[9] Both poems present a sublime vision of ecstatic union. Both mythologize the lovers, and both invite passersby to witness the unique relationship. Yet, their contrasting approaches to the problem of intimacy reveal a fundamental difference that can be imputed to neither genre nor rivalry nor premodern notions of intimacy. The heart of this difference involves the fantasy of a private language. For Shakespeare, the game is to show how genre can be as private and impervious to interpretation as another's secret thoughts. In "The Phoenix and Turtle," he memorializes the unique love of the central pair by orchestrating a chorale of voices united in communal grief. Through metaphysical conceits and theological paradox, he dramatizes the way poetic language issues in ceremonial genres—requiem, obsequy, anthem, threnody, prayer—that mask more than they reveal. The result is a powerful but "endlessly puzzling" poem.[10] In my view, its deliberate poetic obscurity constitutes a response to the skeptical problematic at its center: the impossibility of knowing the marriage of true minds from the inside. In Donne's "Ecstasy," however, the lyric speaker gives us the inside track, pretending to offer a transparent view of the intimacy shared by the two lovers. We are invited, if qualified, to eavesdrop on their "dialogue of one" (74), a rarefied language uttered in an ecstatic state of mutuality and characterized by theological arcana and metaphysical paradox. It is as though Donne were answering the challenge of Shakespeare's lyric by selecting an ordinary pair of youths and demystifying their sublime love only to remystify it. He lets us in on shared "soul's language" (22), as though defying the unknowability at the heart of human relations. Thus, Donne offers a fiction of interanimate legibility as a way of combating the "loneliness" (44) of skepticism, while Shakespeare gives us a chorus of voices witnessing as outsiders to a relationship so ineffable that language itself is stymied. This essay, in other words, looks at these two metaphysical lyrics with their sublime flashes as instantiating problems of privacy and hyperbolic language produced by skepticism.

Cavell points out that "the fantasy of the privacy of language" is one that "Austin, Wittgenstein and Derrida are all at pains to contest."[11] Nevertheless, it persists in part because it "covers a wish that underlies skepticism," namely, the "unappeasable" wish for a perfectly transparent mode of communication that bypasses or obviates the need for speech.[12] The wish for perfect understanding bears an uneasy resemblance to omniscience and God's alleged ability to read minds, suggesting that the dream of reciprocity is uncomfortably close to a desire for possession of the beloved.[13] Regardless, the fantasy of transparency—whether construed as an ecstatic mutuality or a disguise of power—arises in response to skepticism, which Cavell describes as "a standing threat to, or temptation of, the human mind."[14] Skepticism leads to solipsism and the seductive idea that there is an unbridgeable gap between people and that no one can know what goes on inside another. To allow oneself to think this way—a dangerous delusion Wittgenstein spent a career trying to preempt—is eventually to succumb to the fantasy of a private language that will provide certain knowledge and furnish insight into the mind's hidden life. The two "ecstasy" poems, to which I now turn, confront this fantasy, exploring the affective nexus of hyperbole, the sublime, and intimacy even as they dally with skepticism.

Both "The Phoenix and Turtle" and "The Ecstasy" are philosophical lyrics celebrating an exemplary couple whose perfect love is staged for our admiration. Shakespeare's lyric is impersonal, public, allegorical, and geared toward grief even as it memorializes a once glorious love. Donne's, by contrast, is intimate, private, seemingly autobiographical, and comic. "The Phoenix and Turtle" is a social poem about a community commemorating a famous couple in traditional genres or modes; yet the poem has a long history of thwarting interpretation partly because we assume that specific contexts (*Lebensformen*) would illuminate the text. The object of our critical desire and scholarly detective work becomes those largely unknowable contexts. Yet, although its context may elude us, the poem engages familiar language games (*Sprachspielen*) that readers recognize. The poem mobilizes the public resource of ancient ritual—mourning songs of various stripes—in order to create an aesthetic object that is hermetic, knowable at best only to a select few, the cognoscenti apprised of its secret meaning. Its diction is hyperbolic and sublime, soliciting us to stake our faith on the intimacy of the couple—a demand for belief bound to produce skepticism in some. This paradoxical result is Wittgensteinian inasmuch as it instantiates the ineluctable mysteriousness of "grammar" (*der Grammatik der Sprache*).

Three overlapping voices are orchestrated in honor of the Phoenix and the Turtle. The first is the convener of the mourners. This magisterial persona speaks in the imperative voice, summoning and organizing the assembly of birds, which is not a parliament of fowls but a cortège. Even so, he requires a "Herald" (3) and dubs the occasion a "session" (9) from which "Every fowl of tyrant wing" (10) will be barred, "Save the eagle, feath'red king" (11).[15] He orders a "priest in surplice white" (13) to be the "death-divining swan" (15) and supply "defunctive music" (14). The convener also lets us know that the "troop" (8) is gathered in "obsequy" (12) and "requiem" (16) even as he announces the start of an "anthem" (21). A variety of public funeral rites are thus set in motion.

A choral anthem follows, sung it is not clear by whom but "perhaps best seen," according to William Matchett, "as expressing a general opinion held by 'chaste wings.'"[16] Its central image is one of fiery immolation: the Phoenix and the Turtle dying together in an ecstatic event described as "a mutual flame" (24). Rather than develop the erotic implications of this image, however, the anthem shifts to theology. Its second stanza descants on the couple's sublime mutuality in a vocabulary at once Scholastic and Trinitarian ("Had the essence but in one, / Two distincts, division none"). This witty view of their intimacy continues in a paradoxical vein:

> Hearts remote, yet not asunder;
> Distance and no space was seen
> 'Twixt this Turtle and his queen:
> But in them it were a wonder.
>
> (29–32)

This theological fantasy of mutual knowledge and individual interpenetration returns now to the earlier image of ecstasy and fire: "So between them love did shine, / That the Turtle saw his right / Flaming in the Phoenix' sight" (33–35). The fire of love reflected in each other's eyes mingles with the flames of the pyre. Richard McCoy describes this connection as "a blend of death and sexual consummation taking the form of a perfect communion."[17] Their wordless connection is presented to us as something wondrous and sublime.

Then a third voice emerges, a personification of skeptical Reason, who is so "confounded" (41) by this love that he interrupts the anthem of praise so as to deliver his own separate song. Reason's "threne" (49) rehearses a fideistic leap of faith in the perfect couple but regrets the absence of sex and lack of futurity resulting from their "married chastity" (61). Skeptical reason, in other words, ventriloquizes the voice of a community committed to "posterity" (59). Readers are excluded from these ceremonies until the very last stanza, when they are summoned: "To this urn let those repair / That are either true or faire" (65–66). Insofar as we feel alluded to, the illusion of connection is prolonged as we are invited into the grieving circle in the poem's final line: "For these dead birds sigh a prayer" (67). This line, as Barbara Everett comments, "may be brisk or tender or smiling or sad."[18] Its baffling tone notwithstanding, it is clear that the concluding appeal for "prayer" moves away from hyperbole into a more subdued register. Prayer, it seems, is among the most private of communal practices.

Wittgenstein, however, distinguishes prayer from other language games involving mourning: "When it is said in a funeral oration 'We mourn our . . . ,' this is surely supposed to be an expression of mourning; not to communicate anything to those who are present. But in a prayer at the grave, these words would be a kind of communication" (*PPF* § 81). He contrasts—to use the terms of speech-act theory—two types of performatives, each with its own illocutionary "style": the communication conveyed in prayer to a dead or an absent "someone" with the expressive force of communal mourning.[19] If I sigh a prayer for the Phoenix and the Turtle, I may be communicating with the dead birds—assuring them perhaps that, with their passing, Love and Constancy are dead (22). The preceding funeral songs (e.g., anthem and threne), by this logic, eschew communication and enact mourning. "But here is the problem," Wittgenstein adds, "a cry, which cannot be called a description, which is more primitive than any description, for all that, does the service of a description of the psychological" (*PPF* § 82). While Shakespeare's elaborate verse can hardly be called a cry, let alone a primitive cry, his poem imagines an occasion of ritual grief that neither describes nor communicates but instead expresses a community's bereavement in a set of interlocking songs that bear a problematic relationship to the inner life. Wittgenstein suggests that "transitions" (*Übergänge*) are key for understanding this relationship—words "may approximate" a cry more or less (*PPF* § 83).[20] Barbara Everett alludes to these verbal approximations of deep feeling when she locates "overtones of experience not merely inward but solitary" in the poem, "a tenderness, pain and pathos" belying its wit and "arcanely beautiful" conventions (15).

Yet, despite its melancholy, "The Phoenix and Turtle" resists intimacy. We have no access to the internal life of so "true a twain" (45), no purchase on their ecstatic love, no sense of their pain. The birds are silent. The best evidence we have of their sublime connection is the anthem's insistence on the shining reflection in each other's flashing eyes. The overlapping set of embedded witnesses thus presents us with the problem of other minds. As a communal ritual of consolation full of shared meanings, the poem seems to instantiate the reverse of a private language and to undo its possibility. Yet, it verges on the unintelligible by offering us the conundrum of a private language on a social scale. Saul Kripke believes that this dilemma is at the heart of the private language argument. "Wittgenstein's main problem," he says, "is that it appears that he has shown *all* language, *all* concept formation, to be impossible, indeed unintelligible" (62). While this is a contrarian take on Wittgenstein's views, Kripke's idea that private language challenges the assumptions of language more generally is useful. It allows us, for example, to think about the phenomenological effects of Shakespeare's poem, especially the way the difference between private and public language has been effaced. The collectively voiced testimonial to love in "The Phoenix and Turtle" results in a paradoxical language game of overlapping speakers and well-worn tropes so hermetic that generations of readers have felt mystified.

Cavell might ask what wish this fantasy of hermeticism covers. Two impulses may be at work: on the one hand, an effort "to illuminate something about the publicness of language, something about the *depth* to which language is agreed in," and on the other, a fear of excessive intelligibility issuing in a desire to possess one's own words and make them inalienable (*Claim of Reason*, 344). If Shakespeare is being Cavellian here and meditating on the problematic status of a public language engaged in praise, then the opacity of the poem would be more than an effect of riddling wit, Scholastic shibboleths, or the circumstantial genesis of *Love's Martyr*, the collection in which "The Phoenix and Turtle" first appeared.[21] It would be an effect of a larger meditation on language as a system.

In a sense, Shakespeare is having it both ways. On the one hand, "The Phoenix and Turtle" can be seen as a Wittgensteinian poem, showing, as

Rupert Read would say, that "language itself binds us together, closer than close" and thus that "we do not *need* the absurd acquaintance with others' fantasized 'private objects.'" As Read explains, "The Wittgenstein-style community is not defined over and against anything, not even nonhuman animals. It is a truly open field."[22] We need only acknowledge one another and so resist our solipsistic tendencies. On the other hand, as a literary artifact "The Phoenix and Turtle" seems to operate like a private object, sufficient unto itself and repelling translation. Read might say that insofar as it remains an enigma, it "blunts the possibility—the necessity—the beauty—of genuine empathy" (600). Readers who find the poem cold and aloof might agree.

Cavell might suggest instead that Shakespeare is exercising his mastery here, showing that he can negotiate and overcome competing fears of inexpressiveness and exposure. Cavell surmises that Wittgenstein's fantasy of private language conceals a fear of "inexpressiveness, one in which I am not merely unknown, but in which I am powerless to make myself known" and equally a fear "in which what I express is beyond my control" (*Claim of Reason*, 351). He dubs this elsewhere "a fantasy of suffocation or of exposure," involving both a fear of unintelligibility and a fear that my words will escape me and be stolen so that we end up "too intelligible for our good" and "being torn apart."[23] Yet I would not go that far and project Cavell's surmise about Wittgenstein onto Shakespeare. After all, what would Shakespeare be trying to conceal? Some might attribute the gnomic quality of Shakespeare's voice in "The Phoenix and Turtle" to the political conditions of censorship and self-censorship operating at the time *Love's Martyr* was published in 1601. Indeed, proscribed religious sympathies and political affiliations have often been adduced as reasons for the poem's mystery. Nonetheless, I prefer to see the turn to allegory and mourning songs not as a self-protective device but as a way of exploring the relationship of private and public language. Rather than see them as antithetical systems, Shakespeare is experimenting with a metaphysical conceit whereby public and private become conflated. The inscrutability of the miraculous pair's marriage—"Two distinct, division none"—becomes displaced onto the poem itself, which thereby replicates, in a mitigated way, the opacity always already troubling language.

By contrast, "The Ecstasy" stages a fantasy of transparent intimacy whereby the man speaks for himself and his beloved in the first-person plural. They are "one another's best" (4), he assures us in the first stanza, and have no need to talk because they share "soul's language" (22), in which "both meant, both spake the same" (26). He describes where they are in relation to the landscape and to each other: first sitting, then reclining side by side on a sloping bank with violets. They are holding hands and staring into each other's eyes, lying as still as "sepulchral statues" (18) and as silent: "All day, the same our postures were, / And we said nothing, all the day" (19–20). Yet, in this parenthesis of dilated time, while their "souls negotiate" (17) in midair, having "gone out" (16) in a reconnaissance mission "to advance their state" (15), the speaker invites the passerby to eavesdrop on their private language. The reader feels solicited and steps into the frame of the poem, happy to watch the recumbent lovers in their trance and to listen to their efforts to "unperplex" (29) the enigma of their perfect union. Using alchemical metaphors, Donne characterizes their intimate speech as a purifying agent, beneficial even to bystanders who "might thence a new concoction take" (27) if they come already initiated into the mysteries of "good love" (23). The speaker then launches into a translation, allowing us to hear the accents of their private language:

> This ecstasy doth unperplex
>   (We said) and tell us what we love,
> We see by this, it was not sex,
>   We see, we saw not what did move.
>   (29–32)

The rhythms of the stanza with its iambic tetrameter and lilting rhymes enact the motions of a changing mind despite the earlier protestations of a lull and truce " 'twixt her and me" (16). From a condition of perplexity, the couple arrives at discovery. Thanks to their ecstasy, they now understand what they love, sharing the surprising insight that "it was not sex." "We see . . . we see," the lovers repeat, transported by a quasimystical vision of their souls' bond. Yet even as they see, they fail to see "what did move." The terse sequence of assertion and denial, retracting the fullness of the insight just acquired, captures the irresolution of thought. The indeterminate reference of "what did move," seen and now unseen, suggests a speaker struggling to articulate what Wittgenstein might call "his immediate private sensations" (*PI* § 243).

In thrall to the rush of insights and discoveries, the couple continues to disclose the secrets of their sublime relation. Many literary critics have decoded Donne's specialized terminology in the last half of the poem. Catherine Gimelli Martin, for example, discusses the "voluptuous rationalism" of Nicholas of Cusa and Marsilio Ficino. Ramie Targoff focuses on Donne's invention of the term "inanimation" and the verb "interinanimate" to dispute the poem's apparent Platonic dualism, acceding that "if we were forced to identify Donne within a single philosophical school, it would almost certainly be Aristotelian." Julia Walker explores the alchemical imagery.[24] But regardless of provenance, the poem's philosophical lexicon both represents and constitutes an esoteric tongue. We are hearing a translation of the elite dialect that souls (as united as Wittgenstein's Siamese twins) might speak in an ecstatic state of sublime mutuality. This private language indulges the fantasy of overcoming the problem of other minds as skepticism dissolves in an orgy of intimacy.

Despite its exaltation of souls in a state of perfect union, at stanza 13 the poem turns to bodies with this question: "But O alas, so long, so far / Our bodies why do we forbear?" (49–50). What follows is Wittgensteinian: now no longer a hypothetical translation of the soul's private language but instead an exhibit of the body as the site of the soul's expression. When Wittgenstein declares, "The human body is the best picture of the human soul" (*PPF* § 25) or "An 'inner process' stands in need of outward criteria" (*PI* § 580), we get a secular, de-eroticized version of Donne's metaphysical conceit in his penultimate stanza:[25]

> To our bodies turn we then, that so
>   Weak men on love revealed may look;
> Love's mysteries in souls do grow,
>   But yet the body is his book.
>
> (69–72)

The lovers display themselves with theatrical self-consciousness, proffering their bodies as a text to be read: a book of revelation that will affirm the faith of the skeptical bystander.

The shift from private language to physical gesture is a concession at once to doubt and to doubters. The "lovers' souls" (65) must "descend / T'affections, and to faculties" (65–66) as a boon to the weak. Earlier, the souls' attitude to their bodies is explained disingenuously, not as a descent but as an act of condescension, as if the desire for sexual congress were a matter of *noblesse oblige*:

> We owe them thanks, because they thus,
>   Did us, to us, at first convey,
> Yielded their forces, sense, to us,
>   Nor are dross to us, but allay.
>
> (53–56)

The bodies surrender their forces to the conjoined soul in a continuation of the military metaphor broached in stanza 4, to musical accompaniment—the sibilant phoneme "us" drumming in martial beat five times. The alchemical metaphor returns with the image of an alloy as a fusion of substances, directly refuting Platonic notions of the body as dross. It is as though Donne agrees with Wittgenstein's dictum, "An inner experience cannot shew me that I *know* something."[26] To know something like ecstasy or love, the poem suggests, involves the body and all of its sensory apparatus, along with a private language game. The two go together. Private experience is neither incoherent nor reprehensible for Donne, as it is for Wittgenstein. Rather, it improves, becoming more fully legible—especially to observers—thanks to corporeal translation.[27]

The representation of each ecstatic couple in these two poems seems a study in antithesis. In "The Phoenix and Turtle" the ecstatic event transpires in a flash and ends in "cinders" (55). By contrast, in the Donne poem, the ecstatic event involves stillness and duration. Although the lovers hold hands, the central simile describes them as "sepulchral statues" (18)—no annihilating heat here. While the recumbent lovers may be dead to the world, they stare at one another in companionable silence: "And pictures in our eyes to get / Was all our propagation" (11–12), an image boding well for future consumption. In the meantime, however, their bodies lie in suspended animation. Further, the philosophical disquisition on love in "The Ecstasy" replays the Shakespearean anthem's theme of two-in-one but in a different terminological register.[28] Instead of the neo-Trinitarian vocabulary used by Shakespeare to describe "Single nature's double name" (39), Donne gives a neo-Aristotelian account of "mixed souls" (35) and "atomies" (47).[29] Donne's lexicon, in this instance, is less sacred than

Shakespeare's. It is as if, faced by Shakespeare's "opaque avian allegory" commemorating the death of a chaste and perfect pair, Donne felt compelled to respond with a poem about "married chastity" more hyperbolic than the bloodless love of the Phoenix and the Turtle (Cheney, 111). "The Ecstasy" thus ends not in cinders and wistful remembrance but in a celebration of embodied, human love.

Imagining Donne's "Ecstasy" as a response to Shakespeare's "Phoenix and Turtle" is not new. There is agreement that both belong to an "ecstasy" tradition beginning with the Eighth Song of Sir Philip Sidney's *Astrophil and Stella* and continuing through Lord Herbert of Cherbury's "Ode on a Question Moved."[30] There is also consensus that "The Ecstasy" postdates *Love's Martyr* (1601), the volume containing "The Phoenix and Turtle," whose title alone would have drawn Donne's eye even if the other contributors had not included friends like Ben Jonson. Indeed, the affinities of Donne's metaphysical poetry and "The Phoenix and Turtle" were noted long ago by Cleanth Brooks, who concluded his pages on Donne's "Canonization" by commenting on their shared language of paradox and the image of the well-wrought urn holding the ashes of the phoenix.[31] Matchett also remarks on "Donne's (conscious or unconscious) memory of *Loves Martyr*" in "The Canonization" (158). More recently, James P. Bednarz has wondered "whether or not Shakespeare by 1601 had read John Donne's poetry in manuscript" and has observed that "it is Donne who seems to be echoing 'The Phoenix and Turtle' in 'The Canonization'" (121). With respect to "The Ecstasy," however, the received wisdom holds that the Donne poem debates the Neoplatonism advanced in Edward Herbert's "Ode." In her overview of the ecstasy tradition, Everett deems that "Shakespeare's poem is surely a kind of medium, a vital Missing Link, between Sidney and Donne-and-Lord-Herbert, transitional and strongly formative" (14).

Chronology aside, both poems explore the hyperbolical desire for a sublime intimacy even while proclaiming its rarity. Both poems summon bystanders to admire and learn from the spectacle of "love revealed" (*E* 70), but the approach to audience is opposed. In "The Phoenix and Turtle," the implied audience is a community of grieving birds whose collective desire exalts the vanished pair. In "The Ecstasy," the audience is imagined as an individual who "by good love were grown all mind" (23) and who will "part far purer then he came" (28). This bystander is later pictured as "some lover, such as we" (73). Arthur Marotti argues that observer and reader are conflated, noting that the reader "is admitted into the inner sanctum of the love relationship so that his critical distance can be lost, then presented with his mirror image in the figure of the hypothetical observer, who is a docile convert by the end of the piece."[32] The poem's rhetoric is aimed at this embedded audience who needs to be convinced of "the authenticity and goodness of their love" (171).

The presence of the embedded audience produces a theatricality that is different in each poem but that in each case raises the question of skepticism since the audience's vantage point frames the action and limits knowledge. Shakespeare's poem trades in miniaturized genres and collective speech, offering us a theatricality that is ritualized and social, reminiscent as much of the playhouse as of the chancel or churchyard. Reason, after all, dubs the Phoenix and the Dove "Co-supremes and stars of love" (51) when it composes a "chorus to their tragic scene" (52). Yet this same "Reason, in itself confounded" (41), abdicates, resorting to fideism as grounds for belief in the incredible pair even while confirming the finality of their death. The theatricality of Donne's lyric is at once more intimate and exhibitionistic, challenging skepticism. We are invited to approach "within convenient distance" (24) so as to overhear the lovers and to "mark" them when they "are to bodies gone" (75–76). The teasing implication is that if we wait until they "are to bodies gone"—an ambiguous phrase suggesting both sex and death— we "shall see / Small change" (75–76), that is, little difference—as if, having "gone" to bodies, the lovers were as suspended in their ecstasy as before.[33] Regardless of what we may "see" in the poem's aftermath, however, the conceit is that we are right there, privy to the truth and beauty of this extraordinary relationship in an almost unmediated way. In the Shakespeare poem, by contrast, the embedded audiences can only sigh and sing and wonder over a relationship as foreign as it is absent. For all their efforts to know, knowledge recedes from their grasp.

Shakespeare's and Donne's contested engagements with skepticism and with deferred or incomplete knowledge inform the way these two poems parry the temptations of a private language. Both poets are masters at communicating a sense of interiority and private experience. Hamlet famously says, "I have that within which passes show" (I.ii.85). Yet the language with which they transmit their inwardness is perforce public: "public means which public manners breeds" (4), Shakespeare's Sonnet 111 notes bitterly.

Hence, the fascination with a private language, elite, apart, ideal, even sublime. As if recognizing with Wittgenstein the incoherence of such a concept, Shakespeare invents a compromise—a poetic game in resolutely public language that resists interpretation and comes across as a euphonious, stately, but slightly archaic enigma. He orchestrates the glorification of the Phoenix and the Dove but withholds the stage setting that would permit fuller comprehension. He stages a drama of inaccessible intimacy voiced through genre. If we believe in the love of the central pair, it is because we are swept up by the songs, enchanted by their magical music. Like the language of birds—a melodious, but indecipherable lingua franca—"The Phoenix and Turtle" is both public and private, intimating that genre can be the most abstruse of language games.[34]

If Shakespeare's vision of intimacy is diffident and always elsewhere, just out of reach, Donne's is defiant, vaunting his unsurpassable love as an ecstasy of mutual knowledge. Like Cavell's Cleopatra, Donne's poetic persona is bent on "transcendentalizing the domestic" and mythologizing the everyday.[35] The dream of a private language—when shared with a beloved—goes far in creating an ideal of intimacy. That ideal fostered and intensified by hyperbolical flights toward the sublime helps to offset the corrosive doubts attendant on skepticism. Christopher Johnson reminds us, "Hyperbole serves an essential psychological and narrative purpose—through it readers are urged to slake their own epistemological desire" (380). "The Ecstasy" may slake our epistemological thirst, but "The Phoenix and Turtle," although engaging in hyperbole and broaching the sublime, serves not to slake our epistemological desire but to tantalize it.

This difference in the approach to the fantasy of perfect knowledge may be partly attributable to personality: Shakespeare is self-effacing in his work, whereas Donne's persona is ostentatiously present. But I would argue that, in the case of these two lyrics, this difference has less to do with ego than with discrepant stances toward language. Shakespeare crafts a lyric that gestures toward metaphysical paradox but actually entertains a Wittgensteinian puzzle, namely, that genre, the most consensual of linguistic conventions, can resist signification and obstruct interpretation. The resulting poem is hermetic and almost private. Donne's lyric, by contrast, pretends to be ostentatiously open, soliciting all and sundry to witness that impossibility: a private language in action.

9. Working Imagination in the Early Modern Period: Donne's Secular and Religious Lyrics and Shakespeare's Hamlet, Macbeth, and Leontes

JUDITH H. ANDERSON

Like Shakespeare's Hamlet, Donne in his youth was "a great frequenter of Playes," and, in the melancholy of his maturity, he pondered the subject of self-slaughter.[1] His tonal range included irony, sarcasm, satire, and more, with a special, witty, punning emphasis on sex. Death, as dying and lying, was never far from his sight. Whether in prose or verse, he was given to a dramatic speaking voice and to expressive forms suggesting dramatic context, dialogue, and soliloquy. If imaginatively agitated, he spoke, like Hamlet, in an extravagant multiplicity of puns, figures, extensions, and amplifications. As a writer, he was intensely self-conscious. Religion was part of his world and for a good part of his life a troubled and troubling part. He, too, had a haunting family past. He was also educated, underemployed, and ambitious. But I don't offer these coincidental similarities as prelude to a whimsical characterization of Donne as tragic Dane. They are instead my *apologia* for beginning an essay on the contemporary London poets Shakespeare and Donne with Hamlet's soliloquy "O, what a rogue and peasant slave am I!" which is provoked by the recitation he shares with his "old friend" the First Player.[2] My plan, which is selective and exploratory, is to consider the workings of imagination in this Shakespearean passage and its immediate context and then in two others, Macbeth's dagger soliloquy and Leontes's abrupt shift into his own affective world—momentarily into virtual soliloquy—early in *The Winter's Tale*. I then play these workings off against those in selected secular and religious lyrics by Donne. My aim is comparison, a sharpening of definition within a cultural resemblance rather than sameness or influence. An intellectual culture whose roots, putatively like those of the imagination itself, are affective and material provides its background and referent. These roots are essentially, although not exclusively, Aristotelian.

Ann Thompson and Neil Taylor remark in their edition of *Hamlet* how, on the evidential basis of the three earliest texts (Q1, Q2, and F1), Hamlet's soliloquies seem "to be movable or even detachable" (18). This textually grounded impression further underwrites my comparison. Margreta de Grazia has earlier made a similar point about Hamlet's soliloquies, while focusing specifically on the relatively generic "To be, or not to be" (III.i.55), which is less reflexive and firmly situated than the soliloquy "O, what a rogue and peasant slave" that I have chosen to treat. De Grazia has also broadened the implications of the documentary evidence to question the very nature and function of early modern soliloquy. Although the textual histories of all Shakespearean soliloquies are not as various as those in *Hamlet*, questions such as de Grazia's and Thompson and Taylor's open this dramatic, subjective, imaginative form to comparison with like expressions in other genres.[3]

Pyrrhic Vengeance in Hamlet

The recitation Hamlet shares with the First Player prior to his third soliloquy offers a glimpse of his mental furniture and specifically of his memory, which, like imagination, is an affection or a motion—a stimulating or an agitating—of the passible (sensitive) soul in the Aristotelian tradition of faculty psychology; this is the basic, most important tradition, albeit one that mixes significantly with others in the early modern period. Summarizing salient features of Aristotelian memory images, Mary Carruthers describes them as "sensorily derived and emotionally charged"; necessarily, they are perceptual—mediated and filtered by the senses of the perceiving subject.[4] The same is true of all the *phantasmata* (phantom images) that are impressed on the faculty of imagination and stored in the memory, whose working is so closely linked to the imagination as to share the standard analogy used to illustrate it, namely the impression of a seal ring (sense datum) on wax (affected faculty). In a classic discussion of Aristotle's philosophy of mind, Franz Brentano defines the imagination, or phantasy, as simply "the capacity [capability, faculty] to have images," which it receives, combines, and recombines. Such images are in the senses and in the imagination, "the first sensory organ as such." They are not limited to representation of the visual but include all the sensory genera: for example, tone as well as color, sounded words as well as written ones.[5] Although (*unavoidably* slipping into metaphor)[6] I do not "imagine" a Shakespeare who regularly perused the works of Aristotle, I do imagine that the commonplaces of the Aristotelian and Platonic traditions—especially the Aristotelian—were as familiar in literate Elizabethan and Jacobean culture as are those of Freud in our own, and I read and watch a Shakespeare whose lexicon and concerns repeatedly signal his participation in this culture.

The historian Stuart Clark has masterfully characterized the culture of this period as visual, yet it might even more broadly and basically be *seen* as imaginative not least because of the relation of sense (eyesight) to imagination (interior impression).[7] As Clark observes, "the key beneficiary" of the interest in categorizing and conceptualizing mental powers at this time was the imagination (39–43, here 43). His slide from physical seeing to what he repeatedly designates as "seeing"—his quotes signaling perception, interpretation, spiritual vision/visions, and the like—is fundamentally translative and tropic; indeed, it is itself imaginative—a connection between outside and inside, external object and interior representation. Not surprisingly, Clark finds in the visual and verbal paradoxes of Shakespeare's *Macbeth* wonderfully "exact parallels" (254). Spoken words, like written ones and other eyesights, become *phantasmata* in an Aristotelian system before reason has access to them. As Michael Wedin explains, especially if a divine mind is bracketed, the Aristotelian interrelation of thought (*noemata*) with representation through the related processes of language and imagination (*phantasmata*) becomes ever more crucial, as it has in many a reading of *Hamlet* in recent decades (157–59). Since for Aristotle the voice is significant sound (that is, semantic in character), Giorgio Agamben even offers P/s or Phantasm/sound as a translation into Aristotelian terms of the modern (Saussurean) algorithm for a sign, namely, S/s, or Signified/signifier.[8]

When Shakespeare's Players come to Elsinore, Hamlet asks the First Player for the speech he has heard him give "once," implying "some time ago," and Hamlet repeats this word in the next line to indicate "one time only" (II.ii.372–73). He then offers the Player a surprisingly long prompt that runs to nearly thirteen lines of the requested speech. Evidently, even before Hamlet had reason to suspect his uncle of regicide, this speech about the murder of Priam by the vengeful Pyrrhus and the resulting grief of Hecuba has lodged in his memory. He now has it, in fact, by heart, a traditional, affective metonym for the mnemonic faculty (Latin *recordare*, "record, remember"; from *cor/-dis*, "heart"). As elsewhere, his "prophetic soul" might here be said really to have outdone itself, renewing the issue of the relationship between Hamlet's inside and what is outside him (I.v.40). Given the operation of imagination in Renaissance theories of mind, where a question arises as to whether something is inside or outside in this play, as in others by Shakespeare, the answer is likely "both." A clean separation is anachronistic with respect to the past and, as a matter of social and cognitive science, I should add, outdated in the present.

The length of Hamlet's prompt, not to mention the reflection of his own black guise in that of Pyrrhus, further signals his imaginative investment in the desired speech, which is by any measure rhetorically extravagant. Multiple, heightened adjectives, amplifications, and hyperboles abound, and they produce a "speaking picture" for which the word "speaking" is an understated modifier:[9]

> *The rugged Pyrrhus, he whose sable arms,*
> *Black as his purpose, did the night resemble*
> *When he lay couched in th'ominous horse,*
> *Hath now this dread and black complexion smeared*
> *With heraldry more dismal, head to foot.*
> *Now is he total gules, horridly tricked*
> *With blood of fathers, mothers, daughters, sons,*
> *Baked and impasted with the parching streets*
> *That lend a tyrannous and a damned light*
> *To their lord's murder; roasted in wrath and fire,*
> *And thus o'ersized with coagulate gore,*
> *With eyes like carbuncles, the hellish Pyrrhus*
> *Old grandsire Priam seeks.*
>
> (II.ii.390–402)

The Player, ignoring Polonius's intrusion to appreciate Hamlet's delivery, continues the speech, picking it up in midline, as Hamlet has directed him, and recounting the actual slaying of Priam for another thirty lines. The Player's sharing with Hamlet the "forms, moods, [and affective] shapes" of the speech is striking. Indeed, these are "actions that a man might play"—speech acts—into which Hamlet first enters and then to which he attends intently (I.ii.82, 84).[10]

The high point of the Player's lines about Priam's slaughter is not the actual death blow, which occupies half a line, but the conspicuously poetic suspense and deferral that precede it. The crashing to earth of Ilium's flaming tower arrests the fatal descent of Pyrrhus's sword, *"So as a painted tyrant,"* he stands *"Like a neutral to his will and matter"*—as if stilled into a painting (II.ii.418–19). Thus frozen into inaction, in a line visibly and audibly contrived with a single metrical stress to emphasize it, he does *"nothing"* (420):[11]

> *But as we often see against some storm*
> *A silence in the heavens, the rack stand still,*
> *The bold winds speechless and the orb below*
> *As hush as death, anon the dreadful thunder*
> *Doth rend the region, so after Pyrrhus' pause*
> *A roused vengeance sets him new a-work.*
>
> (II.ii.421–26)

Another three lines of epic comparison, this time mythic (the Cyclops, Mars), and then comes the death blow, which verges on anticlimax. It is followed by an outcry of five lines cursing "strumpet Fortune" (431) before Polonius again intrudes and objects to the protractedness of the speech, only to have Hamlet urge its continuation through an emotive description of Queen Hecuba's response—another fourteen lines.

Before turning to Hamlet's succeeding soliloquy, I want to pause over Polonius's third and last interruption of the performance, which finally succeeds in ending it. Just before his insistence that it end, he remarks with wonder, "Look where he has not turned his colour and has tears in's eyes." Hamlet's subsequent soliloquy makes clear that the Player actually—at least to all appearances—feels the passion he merely performs. Before this soliloquy, however, it is unclear whether Polonius's wonder arises at the Player's affective rendering or at Hamlet's response to the representation of Hecuba's grief; it could be played either way. Hamlet's focus on the Player's response could merely be a displacement of attention to his own. Polonius's insistence that the performance stop makes more sense, however, as a response to its visibly affecting the antic and erratic Hamlet. Throughout the performance, Polonius has been the intrusive voice of pedestrian reality—first interested only in the *techne* of spoken delivery, then bored by high-flown language (or "caviare to the general": II.ii.374–75), and finally disturbed by the emotional impact on the Prince of highly affective, imaginative speech, particularly about Priam's Queen. Productions that cut or radically abbreviate the Player's performance and the interruptions it evokes simplify Polonius and underplay Hamlet's youth and susceptibility to emotion in the early acts, prematurely imposing the older, more skeptical figure he will become. If the argument can be made that Hamlet is more impressionable and less cynical in the early acts than ageing actors (and critics) often render him, it can also be made that Polonius is considerably more than a staged fool.

Often, as here in the second scene of Act II, *Hamlet* recalls the comparisons of oratory, or moving, suasive speech, to professional acting in Cicero's immensely influential *De Oratore*, not least when Hamlet names the famous Roman actor Roscius, whose name peppers Cicero's dialogue (II.ii.327). A passage in *De Oratore* that addresses the conflation of the performative with the real is particularly relevant. Crassus, Cicero's major spokesman, recalls an orator's use of a series of emotive rhetorical questions asking where he can find refuge and pertinently ending, "'Home? So that I can see my mother in misery, grief-stricken and downcast?'" Crassus praises the orator's use of "his eyes, voice, and gestures to such effect that even his enemies could not contain their tears." In contrast nowadays, Crassus continues, "orators, who act in real life [*oratores, qui sunt veritatis ipsius actores*], have abandoned this entire field, while the actors, who are only imitators of reality [*imitatores autem veritatis, histriones*], have appropriated it. And no doubt, reality [*veritas*: 'truth'] always has the advantage over imitation. Yet if reality by itself were sufficiently effective in delivery, we would have no need for any art at all."[12] Conspicuously, in the speech that Hamlet first shares with the Player and with which as listener he continues to empathize to the point of tearing and pallor, the "actions that a man might play," in the form of a speaking picture, have crossed into the immediate affective reality of his own imagination.

The subsequent, self-reflexive soliloquy in which Hamlet more deliberately, if still emotionally, measures his own reality against the Player's feigning is throughout concerned precisely with this transference. Disparaging himself as a "rogue and peasant slave," Hamlet spends roughly the first third of the soliloquy asking why he cannot give himself over to affection in his actual world as could the Player "in a fiction, in a dream of passion" and "force his soul so to his own conceit / That from her working all the visage wanned . . ." (II.ii.487–89). By "soul," Hamlet refers to the imagination, which, as noted earlier, is an affection of the passible soul in its receptive working but which in its active working can be compositional and, especially as conceived in the early modern period, even generative.[13] In the course of self-assessment, Hamlet demands what the Player would do if, like himself, he had a real "motive . . . for passion" and imagines that he "would drown the stage with tears / And cleave the general ear with horrid speech . . ." (496–98). As elsewhere in the soliloquy, the familiar conflation of real ("motive") with theatrical ("stage," "speech") and of Hamlet with Player is conspicuous.[14]

Roughly the middle third of the soliloquy has Hamlet shadowboxing with himself: "Am I a coward? / Who calls me villain, breaks my pate across, / Plucks off my beard and blows it in my face . . . ?" (506–8). In this third, he, and no longer the Player, is the one in a fictive world, for he acts like a "John-a-dreams," as he puts it himself (503). Imagining the vengeance he should by now have wreaked on Claudius, he forces a crescendo of passion that climaxes in rhetorically copious name-calling, "Bloody, bawdy villain, / Remorseless, treacherous, lecherous, kindless villain," only to overhear the near absurdity of his sonically iterative speech acting and abruptly to subside into self-recognition and harsh rebuke: "Why, what an ass am I" (515–17).

All this play acting, as if both before a mirror of self-regard and within an echo chamber, actually proves constructive, however, for it issues in the reasonable plan that occupies the final third of the soliloquy. Having just experienced the affect of a *relevant* performance of Pyrrhic vengeance on his own conscience/consciousness, Hamlet wants to test Claudius with such another.[15] Well aware of his own "weakness and melancholy," he has good reason to try further whether the ghost is diabolically false or true (536). By "weakness" Hamlet obviously means something affective other than melancholy; this could simply be grief, but, where the text is unspecific, "weakness" makes better sense as the more inclusive phantasy, or imagination—an affection or agitation of the sensitive soul.[16] The ghost, which is seen by others, is visually real, but only Hamlet has heard its story, and when the ghost later appears within private chambers, only Hamlet can see it.

As Aristotle observes in *De Anima*, imagination can appear to blend perception with opinion, belief, and even judgment, and in practice it certainly influences these. In Malcolm Schofield's words, Aristotle is even "tempted to view *phantasia* [phantasy, imagination] as a form of thinking, or at least as a thought-like component of thinking."[17] Yet in *De Anima*, Aristotle also acknowledges that, whereas "sensations are always true, imaginations are for the most part false"; the qualifying phrase "for the most part" is important since imaginations (*phantasmata*, representations, appearances, sensory images) are necessary for thought.[18] As Schofield puts it, Aristotle expresses "scepticism, caution, or non-commit[ment] about the veridical character of sensory or quasi-sensory experiences . . . [i.e.,] 'it *looks* thus and so [—but is it really?]'" (251; cf. 253, 259). The *phantasmata* of imagination require direction (arguably, transformation) by the intellect lest the intellect become what Brentano calls the "plaything of the images." The active power that mediates the relation of the sensory images for the intellect is called *nous poiētikos* (productive, indeed poetic, intellect, or, in L. A. Kosman's resonant translation, "the maker mind"); this maker mind "turns the receptive intellect into something that actually thinks."[19] Given Hamlet's awareness of his own agitation and his reason, particularly in bereavement and perceived betrayal, to distrust phantom images, his choice to test further the probity of the ghost and the guilt of his uncle is at this juncture the right one.

Wither'd Murther in Macbeth

Like Hamlet, Macbeth is affected by the preternatural, and similar questions arise about the relation of what is outside to what is inside him. He is even more subject to imagination than Hamlet or, perhaps, just less conscientious in processing it rationally. In the soliloquy just before he goes offstage to murder Duncan, he famously "sees" a dagger so real that he reaches to grasp it, addressing it as "thee" and "thou." So lively is his "fatal vision"— his sight both deadly and destined—that the dagger is virtually inspirited:

> Come, let me clutch thee:—
> I have thee not, and yet I see thee still.
> Art thou not, fatal vision, sensible
> To feeling, as to sight?
>
> (II.i.34–37)[20]

"Still" means "yet" in these lines, indicating duration, but it also suggests "motionlessly" and thereby accentuates the tantalizing stability, the "thereness," of the vision, which is at once perceptually real and materially elusive or unreal. (My descriptive terms, including "virtually," just before the beginning of the preceding extract, are remarkably, not to say weirdly, like those found in theological debate about the Eucharist in this period, as, not least, is the bell signaling Macbeth that, as Marvin Rosenberg puts it, "his *drink is ready*. . . . Hot blood.").[21] Doubting, Macbeth questions the vision: "or art thou but / A dagger of the mind, a false creation, / Proceeding from the heat-oppressed brain?" (37–39). He fully recognizes that the dagger might be a hallucination caused by humoral imbalance or a fevered brain. At the same time, his words suggest the likeness of the vision to what Donne describes as the "counterfait Creation" of any turbulent imagination, one, whether lunatic's or poet's, that has escaped or exceeded rational control.[22] Such creations are generated by the affected and affecting faculties, both preconscious and fully conscious, that are relative to images.

Macbeth continues, now attributing palpability—tangibility, susceptibility of touch, the lowest of the senses—to the dagger's form, which, without bodily matter, should be intangible: "I see thee yet, in form as palpable / As this which now I draw" (40–41); he would have the dagger materialize, no matter what. He also projects his purpose onto and, more precisely, his *intention* into the dagger so that it becomes an agent actively conducting him to Duncan: "Thou marshall'st me the way that I was going" (42). Now the assertion "I see thee still" recurs more urgently, and this time the envisioned dagger is covered with blood, having become a metonym for the bloody deed itself (45–46). The increasing implication of the envisioned dagger in Duncan's murder, its increasing realization of the act itself, then triggers an even stronger return to the reality of reason. Abruptly, Macbeth recognizes that "There's no such thing." It is as if reason struggles with his wayward phantasy and for a moment regains control. Now he recognizes that "It is the bloody business which informs / Thus to mine eyes" (47–49).[23] What has been activated here without an immediate material origin is the impression of the seal ring in the wax of the sensory soul.

Had Macbeth stopped with this recognition of quotidian reality, he might never have answered the bell that summons him to murder. Instead of stopping, however, he fashions the narrative that shapes his destiny and reshapes his world forever:

> Now o'er the one half-world
> Nature seems dead, and wicked dreams abuse

> The curtain'd sleep: Witchcraft celebrates
> Pale Hecate's off'rings; and wither'd Murther,
> Alarum'd by his sentinel, the wolf,
> Whose howl's his watch, thus with his stealthy pace,
> With Tarquin's ravishing strides, towards his design
> Moves like a ghost.
>
> (II.i.49–56)

Unlike the dagger, this narrative, while highly imaginative, is controlled and consciously deliberate—at once psychopathic and culpable. It directly precedes the offstage murder and indeed might be said to enable it. Notably, Macbeth may start stealing mimetically toward Duncan's room even during its course: "*thus* with his stealthy pace" (my emphasis); he certainly could be played this way. The nearness of Macbeth's narrative to and its final distance from the function and result of the Pyrrhic narrative Hamlet chooses to hear is striking.

Macbeth's narrative, like Hamlet's, speaks of and for a heightened state of *affection* (agitation, stimulation). This landscape of death, witchcraft, murder, and lust correlates with Macbeth's psychic reality. This is the landscape of his present, murderous mind, the way the world looks to him; thus, in conception—in poetic "conceit"—it resembles Spenser's psychic landscapes, for example, those of hell and Despair, not to mention Milton's most compelling achievement in this mode, Satan's hell.[24] Like these, and also like Hamlet's Pyrrhic narrative, it is conspicuously classical and mythic.[25] In Hamlet's terminology, Macbeth forces his imagination "so to his own conceit" (II.ii.488) as to substantiate phantasy in the objective terms of narrative.

The seeming death of nature in Macbeth's "one half-world"—the death of *kind* in senses including kindred and fellow feeling, along with the ascent of wicked dreams from the realm of untrammeled affections and the influence of witches—reflectively condenses his recent past and present. "Murther" is "wither'd" not only by its implication in another's death but also by its implication in the murderer's self-destruction. Like "Witchcraft" and "Hecate" herself, the sustained personification of "Murther" further objectifies the scene, enabling its more active realization; simultaneously, this personification also abstracts the scene further from quotidian reality, thereby marking it as mind born.[26] The extensive depiction of "Murther" might thus be said at once to realize and to surrealize the scene. The comparison of "Murther's" movement to Tarquin's, then Tarquin's to a ghost's, repeats and intensifies this dual movement, this stretching—Latin *intendere*: "to stretch toward, direct to, extend to, intend"—of objective reality to its own phantasmal lack. In the final five lines cited ("Murther . . . ghost"), soldier and ravisher, paired violators, act in concert. Inhumanity and bestiality—"Murther" and "his sentinel, the wolf / Whose howl's his watch"—likewise merge in the ambiguous repetition of the possessive pronoun "his." They all mingle and blend in a playbook illustration of imagination triumphant over rational distinction and moral consciousness.

In the final nine lines of the soliloquy, Macbeth emerges decisively from his psychic landscape. Now he refers unambiguously to his own physical movement ("Hear not my steps, which way they walk") and names "fear" and "horror," which have been present but submerged in the diseased enchantment of the soliloquy's earlier lines. By its final five lines, he is no longer the fashioner of his own psychic landscape but a man of murderous action. The difference between the results of his performance and Hamlet's lies in the way each uses a psychic model and relates it to action in his real world. If Hamlet identifies with Pyrrhus or Hecuba or more complexly with both and momentarily loses control of his passion in soliloquy, his doing so involves not merely release but also exploration, and it issues in a reasonable intention that precipitates the eventual conclusion. In a word, it is productive. In comparison, Macbeth first tries to force the hallucinated dagger into material reality and then projects his desire into it so openly that his heightened expectation collapses with an audible thud: "There's no such thing." But then he consciously, deliberately makes and enters into the psychic reality of withered and withering murder. From this, he emerges with a commitment to decisive action. The ethical and moral difference between his use of imaginative potency and Hamlet's is simply enormous.

In an enlightening essay on "Scepticism and Theatre in *Macbeth*," Kent Cartwright examines Lady Macbeth's theatricalizing of herself—what he calls her "modeling" in the infanticide speech—but seems to miss that in Tarquin. Macbeth both imitates and exceeds her modeling in his own imaginative enactment (225, 230–31, 235). In other words, Macbeth indeed learns the lesson his wife would teach him. For Macbeth, Tarquin is projection and realization, not simply self-negation, the latter Cartwright's view. Yet Hamlet is, in both Protean and positive senses, more "constructive." Persisting in imaginative self-construction throughout, he inhabits, lives in, becomes it.

Affection and Intention in Leontes

The working of imagination in a crucial, puzzling passage of *The Winter's Tale* is brief but further telling. This passage occurs in the middle of a speech by Leontes to his young son Mamillius, and represents the immediate eruption of his phantasy into the quotidian world: "Affection!—thy intention stabs the centre."[27] This controversial line employs two words that I have used throughout, glossing them by cultural givens in Shakespeare's time and illustrating them with textual analysis: *affection* (stimulation, agitation) and *intention* (extension to or direction toward a thing; viewpoint). Unlike the passages I have cited from *Hamlet* and *Macbeth*, however, that in *The Winter's Tale* involves a direct, continuous fusing of intramental and extramental reality, literally a *confusion* of what is seen by the mind's eye and what by the body's. Going further, Leontes's inner reality overwhelms his outer to become it. Instead of entering a psychic world of his own making and then emerging from it into the actual world, as does Macbeth, Leontes might be said to set up shop in the psychic world even while otherwise functioning in the actual one. There is nothing preternatural about Leontes's delusion, yet it is he rather than Hamlet or Macbeth who, in Hamlet's words, cannot tell "a hawk from a handsaw" (II.ii.316). Learnedly, he knows how imagination works, but he is less aware that he is counterfeiting truth and less fully conscious and deliberate in doing so. He has become "the plaything of the images." What Leontes does may be even more dangerous than Macbeth's commitment to crime since it is done in the name of justice—a commitment to crime that is blind but self-righteous.

As previously suggested, the possibility of blurring intramental with extramental reality is present in the faculty psychology of the early modern period, especially through the workings of the interior faculties of imagination and memory upon the information they receive and make available for the intellect. With discoveries in science in the early seventeenth century, perception per se becomes inescapably more subjective, and the objective world becomes less reliably available through the unaided senses, which, notwithstanding Aristotle's noncommittal skepticism about the reliability of the *phantasmata*, are the very foundation of the Aristotelian system for knowledge of this world.[28] Of course Platonism and Neoplatonism, which were also alive and well in the early modern period, afford further complication since they are by definition more subjective, more radically privileging the mind, or more exactly the intellect in all forms of knowing. In fact, Neoplatonism, mixing with Aristotelianism, as in Sidney's *Defence of Poesy*, greatly contributes to a more positive sense of the generativity of imaginative thinking, the sense activated by the end of *The Winter's Tale*.[29]

Before engaging Leontes's speech, I want to review relevant Tudor-Stuart senses of *affection* and *intention* in the OED. My interest focuses on the more general senses rather than on those more specific. Glosses that are too specific underlie some of the perceived obscurity in Leontes's speech and the lack of consensus in understanding it. The first definition of *affection* in the OED is "The action of affecting, acting upon, or influencing; or (when viewed passively) the fact of being affected" (I.1; cf. etymology); noticeably in this definition, active and passive senses are relative to a point of view. Somewhat misleadingly, in the first edition of the OED, which I prioritize in citations, no instances of the first, broadest definition are cited before 1660, although this definition was accessible to anyone with a grammar-school knowledge of Latin and was essential for understanding classical, medieval, and early modern philosophies of mind or, more accurately, of *psuchē*, life form.[30] (In the second edition of the OED, the broadest definition has effectually and ahistorically been consigned—for many modern readers, alienated—to the Latin etymology.)[31] The OED's second definition of *affection* comes under the heading "Of the mind," belatedly suggesting why occurrences before 1660 are missing; this definition reads as follows: "*An affecting or moving of the mind in any way; a mental state brought about by any influence; an emotion or feeling*," with examples cited from medieval to modern times (II.2, my emphasis; cf. I.1.a). Notably, "mind" in this definition could mislead a modern reader insofar as it mainly pertains to the sensory, passible soul, not directly to the intellect. Additional specification brings the definition "Feeling as opposed to reason; passion, lust" (II.3; cf. I.1.b), but here the historically pertinent examples offered, all plural (*lusts* or *affections*), do not support an understanding of "lust" in its dominant modern meaning as unrestrained or obsessive sexual craving, and therefore they render "lust" a dubious gloss for Leontes's meaning. Still later in the OED entry comes a definition that shares ground with *intention*, "State of the mind towards a thing; disposition towards, bent, inclination" (II.5; cf. I.3), and arguably it would steer the influence of "Affection!" in Leontes's exclamation toward *intention*, his next noun. What most stands out in all of these definitions is a focus on the sensitive soul, in which the imagination, its most formative faculty, provides the sine qua non of any subsequent thinking from the least to the most rational. If feeling is "opposed to reason," as the simplicity of the *OED*'s third definition has it, affection needs nonetheless to rise above primary sensation to enable whatever measure of intelligible utterance is found in Leontes's speech. The most valid definition for Leontes's line, in short, is the *OED*'s second (II.2; cf. I.1.a), which I have italicized earlier in this paragraph.

Intention in the *OED* most generally signifies "*The action of straining or directing the mind or attention to something; mental application or effort; attention, intent observation or regard*" (I.1, my emphasis). The next entry reads as follows: "*The action or faculty of understanding; way of understanding (something); the notion one has of anything. Also the mind or mental faculties generally*" (I.2: my emphasis). Subsequent entries include "The way in which anything is to be understood; meaning, significance, import" (I.3); "The act of intending or purposing; volition which one is minded to carry out; purpose" and "That which is intended or purposed; a . . . design" (I.4–5; cf. I.4–5.a); "Straining, bending, forcible application or direction (*of* the mind, eye, thoughts, etc.)" and "Intensification" (I.7.b–8), which derives from the idea of stretching or tension and, like the other subsidiary definitions, returns us to the basic sense of the initial two (I.1–2). Examples contemporary with Shakespeare accompany all these definitions. Compared to the definitions of *affection*, those of *intention* are, on the whole, relatively more intellectual and purposeful. They not only reinforce the sense of "Affection" in Leontes's line but also direct it centripetally. Accordingly, while I do not deny the relevance to Leontes's speech of the *OED* entries for *intention* after the initial two (I.1–2), I consider them more limiting, less suitable, and less illuminating both for the line in question and for the rest of the speech than are the first two, which I have italicized.

Just prior to the speech at issue, Leontes, with one foot on the threshold of his dreamworld, imagines that he sees his wife, Hermione, and Polixenes making sexual overtures to one another, and at the beginning of the speech itself, he jests all too sardonically, obsessively, and disturbingly with his son about the boy's legitimacy. He focuses on the boy's obvious bodily resemblance to himself (physical, visual fact), on his nonetheless doubtful paternity (already a retreat from physical, visual evidence), on the mendacity of women (further retreat from the particular, plus distrust of verbal testimony, especially female), and on his own fancied shame as a cuckold (phantasy manifestly at work).[32] He concludes that the boy is "like" him and asks him to look him in the eye (or I?).[33] In the Oxford edition of Stephen Orgel, Leontes continues,

> Sweet villain,
> Most dear'st, my collop—can thy dam, may't be
> Affection!—thy intention stabs the centre.
> Thou dost make possible things not so held,
> Communicat'st with dreams—how can this be?
> With what's unreal thou coactive art,
> And fellow'st nothing. Then 'tis very credent
> Thou mayst co-join with something, and thou dost,
> And that beyond commission, and I find it,
> And that to the infection of my brains
> And hard'ning of my brows.
>
> (I.ii.135–45)

The third line of this passage is not about Hermione's lust or Leontes's jealousy or sensory passion specifically, as some interpreters gloss it. Such glosses do not fit the recurrent personal pronoun (thy, thou) in the lines that follow as well as does the alternative gloss "imagination," which dates back at least to Nicholas Rowe's revision in the eighteenth century.[34] Like the other Shakespearean passages I have examined, this one is about the working of imagination, which is an affection or moving of the soul that is essential to "all the passions of the mind," to borrow relevantly holistic phrasing from Edmund Spenser. More exactly, "it is that in virtue of which an image arises for us";[35] it carries an emotional charge and mixes in practice with opinion, belief, and judgment, as earlier noted. While it processes data deriving from the senses, according to Aristotle it can also take place "in the absence of both [sight and seeing], as e.g. in dreams" (428a5–8); in Leontes's words, "it communicat'st with dreams," with what is unreal, and consorts—is "coactive," or cooperates, and "fellow'st," or is associated—with nothing that is real. For some time, Leontes has been visually stalking his wife and Polixenes, his childhood friend and imagined double. Insofar as his suspicions are not brand new, a classic Aristotelian's description of the working of imagination reads as if written to illuminate both the passage now in question and Macbeth's vision of the dagger:

> [T]he agitation of the imagination often does not follow immediately after sensory perception; but even in this case it is an agitation resulting from a sensory agitation that has made a continuing impression upon the organ of sense and has left in it a certain quality, a certain persistent disposition, by virtue of which under certain circumstances, especially when other sensory representations act as stimuli, the earlier sensible form recurs within the sense.[36]

Leontes is not only expounding the working of imagination; he is also enacting this work—doing it and believing in it. While awake, he is in a dreamworld.

In the third line of Leontes's speech, the centric stab of *intention*, the straining or directing of the mind or attention to something, or intent observation (*OED* I.1), is both a mental and a physical event, like imagination itself. It is simultaneously the violent, intuitive penetration to what Leontes perceives to be real and the sharp and painful piercing of what centers his being. (As if conjured by the stab of disillusionment, the contrasting image of the child Leontes's muzzled dagger, in all its now pernicious innocence, appears within fewer than twenty lines [I.ii.155]: a telling, perversely doubled act of imagination thus combines fancied disillusionment with the illusion of innocence.) *Simultaneously,* the much-discussed "Affection" is a personification whose rhetorical status, like that of Macbeth's "wither'd Murther," marks its artificial, imaginative origin even while it realizes—projects, reifies, and objectifies—Leontes's mental processing. The possessive personal pronoun "thy" does not belong *either* to a personification *or* to Leontes himself; it belongs to them both at once—to his dream, his fiction, and his actual, existent, corporeal being.

Moreover, now Leontes is wholly *self*-centered despite his seeing and addressing those near him. That he can move, within a single speech, from addressing his son into virtual soliloquy effectively dramatizes the onset of his autism.[37] In the eighth line of his speech, "Thou mayst co-join with something," the "something" with which the imagination's *phantasmata* mingle is true in his deluded belief, that is, existent both within him and, correlatively, in the world outside him. The intention of his affection coacts and conjoins not simply with the unreality he entertains as a theoretical danger in the middle of the speech but unwittingly with the real world his senses receive perceptually. It takes over the world that he sees outside him.[38] In the ninth line, "And [dost] that [co-join] without commission," Leontes denies that he is merely imagining the sexual overtures he sees or now actually *thinks* he sees and thus denies that he has commissioned them by requesting the gracious Hermione to entice or charm Polixenes to remain in Sicilia.[39] He is effectually refusing responsibility for his own imaginings. The most likely issuer of a "commission" in this speech is the king himself, who in normal life authorizes such warrants regularly, complete with royal seal. Leontes, in his own eyes, has indeed found—the apt term in Renaissance rhetoric is "invented"—something real, and it is indeed, if also ironically, "to the infection of . . . [his] brains." His thinking is quite simply brainsick. By the end of his speech, with reason in recession, his brows are hardening into a blockhead's. Leontes is now the dupe of linguistic duplicity, an irony that he does not control, one in which he increasingly thinks he sees adultery and finally imagines a cuckold's horns sprouting on his head when he really sees only his own imaginings.

Having described Leontes as the brainsick plaything of runaway imagination, I want to stress the relative abstraction of his language, which, while full of resonance and charged with emotion, is not particularly visual or metaphorical and certainly not like the fully realized allegory of Macbeth's narrative of "wither'd Murther." It is not only "on the surface," as Carol Neely puts it in an illuminating essay, that Leontes "seeks to reason abstractly about his own passion." Our separating out, then reassembling, certain words and phrases in his speech that could make for coherent sexual allegory clarifies this potential but also overheats and oversimplifies it: "'stabs the center . . . communicat'st . . . coactive art . . . fellow'st nothing . . . may'st co-join with something . . . and that beyond commission . . . hardening of my brows.'"[40] Surface and substance are precisely not the point here: Leontes's rational surface is *continuous* with his imagination, and this is what is most frightening about it. He is awake while asleep. His condition, moreover, is finally neither Hamlet's nor Macbeth's. Discriminating their conditions brings into heightened relief the careful and urgent attention to the mind's operations in Shakespeare's writing. In this reading, Leontes also becomes less of a caricature, and what befalls him hits closer to home.

Syntactically, Leontes's speech raises other questions. Citation first of the leading modern alternative for punctuation of its most controverted lines (which traces back to Rowe more than does Orgel's punctuation in the text I have used) and then that of the historically significant 1623 folio will highlight these issues. The versions given by J. H. P. Pafford, Hallet Smith, David Bevington, Stephen Greenblatt, and others differ (see note 41, this chapter), but they are similar enough to be represented by Bevington's:

> Can thy dam?—may't be?—
> Affection, thy intention stabs the center.
> Thou dost make possible things not so held,
> Communicat'st with dreams—how can this be?—
> With what's unreal thou coactive art,
> And fellow'st nothing.
>
> (I.ii.137–42)[41]

The major differences between Bevington's punctuation and Orgel's are in Bevington's the presence of dashes on either side of "may't be," with accompanying question marks, and the presence of a comma, rather than Orgel's exclamation point and dash, after "Affection." Orgel's pointing separates "dam" from "may't be" only by a comma and does not separate "may't be" at all from "Affection" except by the unavoidable (but nonetheless significant)[42] line break. His punctuation implies that Affection, for which he admits the dubious "lust" as a possible gloss, belongs to the libidinous Hermione Leontes conjures. In some sense it must, of course, because Leontes's affected brain *engulfs* her reality; because it does so, the fact that the play text focuses attention (and "intention") on Leontes, the speaker, is all the more important. Whereas Bevington lessens the impact of "Affection" with a comma, however, Orgel heightens it with an exclamation point. Some degree of heightening seems appropriate: at this moment, more than in the succeeding lines, Leontes is agitated—affected by a stab, the painful immediacy of realization. But as I have intimated, Orgel's insertion of a dash after "Affection!" also strengthens a case for Hermione's possession of the succeeding pronoun, "thy"; as a result, "intention," which he glosses as "meaning, significance, import" and "purpose" (*OED* I.3–4), while rejecting Pafford's interpretation of "intention" as "intensification" (*OED* I.8), becomes hers as well. Of course it cannot become hers if "Affection" carries the more general sense "imagination," which is logically and culturally apt here, and if, therefore, "intention" *truly* belongs to Leontes. By the end of the speech, perhaps, the question comes down to our joining Leontes in madness or standing apart from it through reason—to our reading from the royal actor's point of view or from that of an audience whose reason is properly functioning.

The folio text is of particular interest for the pressure points that are emerging:

> Can thy Dam, may't be
> Affection? thy Intention stabs the Center,
> Thou do'st make possible things not so held,
> Communicat'st with Dreames (how can this be?)
> With what's vnreall: thou coactive art,
> And fellow'st nothing.[43]

Like Orgel's, the folio edition affords little pointing for the words between "Can" and "Affection." At the same time, by employing a question mark, it lowers the impact of "Affection" into a combination of surprise and lingering incredulity, and it extends this tonal modulation with a comma rather than a full stop after "Center." The folio's use of a parenthesis to enclose "how can this be?" likewise suggests a quieter aside—as if Leontes is recalling a logical step in a textbook *quaestio* suitable to his relatively abstract language—quite distinct from the astonishment conveyed by one or a pair of dashes. The folio's capitalization of "Affection" might even result from its position at the head of a line rather than from personification. Of additional interest is the folio's connection of "what's vnreall" with "Dreames" rather than directly with the subject's coactivity. Like the phrase "fellow'st nothing," the unreality of dreams becomes a more general observation about the cooperation of affection (imagination) with other inner and outer phenomena. In sum, the folio gives us a more thoughtful King who is less fully and dramatically subject to phantasy, albeit still clearly in its power.[44]

Pressure points (pun intended) of especial significance that are now evident involve the juxtaposed words "dam" and "may't," then "be" and "Affection," and to a lesser extent "Affection" and "thy," all of which occur early in the passage. The crucial, rational, syntactical non sequitur, which all the editions point in some way, occurs between the first of these, "dam" and "may't." It expresses both a shift in point of view and an affective jump, however best punctuated. Leontes starts an interrogative sentence and abruptly drops it between the auxiliary verb "can" and its apparently missing main verb, even as his subject shifts—"thy dam" to "it"—from objective, personalized female reference to neuter, impersonal reference. This shift facilitates a consequent shift of attention to the common noun *affection*, which, in the immediately following personal pronoun "thy," assumes agency as a personification and, as I have argued, *also* belongs to Leontes. As Leontes's nominations thus shift, their instability recalls his shifting attention when he addressed Mamillius at the outset of this same speech. Now his verbs move from fact to contingency, physical ability to imaginative possibility—"can" to "may"—all the while continuing in the interrogative mode. Either "Affection" follows "be" as predicate nominative (whether taken as forceful invention or milder speculation) or "be" is separated from "Affection" by punctuation (a dash or a question mark or a combination of these) to emphasize the interrogatory, tentative moment before "Affection's" dramatic *realization* (in both the subjective and objective, psychic and formal, senses of this word). "Thy intention" then follows from "Affection" and whatever punctuation is attached to it (exclamation point, question mark, or comma), and it belongs, I reemphasize, at once to Leontes, whose affection "thy" references, and to the personified form of an Affection to whose self-centered power he is surrendering. The movement of Leontes's interior faculties is made palpable, visible, and accessible to our own imaginative and rational faculties throughout this sequence.

Shakespeare may push the envelope of imitative form near the edge in the fascinating lines of *The Winter's Tale* that I have examined, but if the examination has succeeded, they do not deserve description as "the obscurest passage in Shakespeare" or as the " 'one [nobody] has been able to read.' "[45] Leontes is slipping increasingly out of control—for the obvious example, into virtual soliloquy in the presence of auditors on stage, of whom he should be, but now dubiously is, aware. Normative syntax orders words rationally; logical language strives for unambiguous verbal transparency and to this end employs technical terms and systematic methods. Leontes's expression, even at its most erratic, remains accessible to an analysis in touch with these norms and therefore to understanding, if not without effort. Yet in its loose structure and affective language ironically *and* positively lies the imaginative resource that will also allow his redemption.[46] In a pun much favored by Shakespeare and Donne, that it should *lie* there haunts both Donne's fictive lyrics and Shakespearean tragedy, including that in the first half of this play. The familiar pun also reflects Aristotle's ambivalence regarding the reliability yet necessity of the human imagination for thought.

Donne's "Canonization": Love, Death, and More

The power and variety of Donne's imaginings in his prose, as well as in his poetry, are vast, and space dictates a selection that is partial and exploratory, as I acknowledged before approaching Shakespeare's plays. I want to concentrate on a fairly broad, representative, and relevant choice of his lyrics: "The Canonization," "A Nocturnal upon S. Lucy's Day," "Good Friday, 1613," the Holy Sonnet "At the round earth's imagined corners," "The Dream," and the related poem beginning "Image of her whom I love."[47] In the lyrics selected, my focus will be on performance, projection, and other manifest poetic workings of the imagination, necessarily involving the cooperation of *phantasmata* with thought and especially with the higher Aristotelian *nous poiētikos* or Neoplatonized versions of it.[48] Whereas the *nous poiētikos*, by imparting a dispositive stimulus to the resources of imagination, might be said to reach down to the senses, the Neoplatonic intellect typically reaches up and away from them. Efforts to blend Neoplatonic and Aristotelian principles are also not hard to find in a Christianized context: Sidney's *Apology* and Lodowyck Bryskett's *Discourse of Civill Life* have already been mentioned as examples; Marsilio Ficino and his sometime student Giovanni Pico della Mirandola afford conspicuous Continental ones.[49] Such blends, moreover, do not stop with ontology, epistemology, poetics, and moral philosophy; they are much present in the revolutionary physics (and physiology) of optics, an anciently rooted study of light and vision obviously bearing on human sensation, perception, and imagination. In oversimplified binary terms, Platonic, like Galenic, theories of vision are dominantly active and extramissive, Aristotelian ones are dominantly passive and intromissive, and Renaissance theories readily draw on all these traditions, mixing and matching at need.[50] Even the optical theories of Aristotle and Plato are not simply opposites, however, and Avicenna and Averroës, influential interpreters of Aristotle, incorporate Galenic elements (Lindberg, *Theories*, 9, 32–33). My position, not meant to discourage the identification of precise sources where possible, remains the one with which I began: the Aristotelian tradition of faculty psychology is the basic, fullest, most important *psychological* tradition, albeit a tradition most often mixing significantly with others in the early modern period. I proceed accordingly.

"The Canonization," whose centrality to Donne's work and to its modern reception is familiar in the critical tradition, is quintessentially Donnean in its initial projection of a dramatic situation that emphatically insists it be imagined—fleshed out with personae and localized—and for this reason, I start with it. In a room, somewhere in the city, the speaker-lover replies heatedly to the worldly wise, probably older friend who has told him to get on with his career and get over his infatuation: "For God's sake hold your tongue, and let me love." The younger speaker is angry and indignant, and his heavy irony ("my palsy, or my gout") drops into sarcasm: "Or the King's real, or his stamped face / Contemplate," or, more bluntly, "Go worship power and money yourself."[51] In the second stanza, the speaker modulates his agitation into an irony that is calmer but also more hyperbolical and less close to home. He parodies the conventional exaggerations of Petrarchism, thereby denying the infatuation imputed to him, although also suffering the proximity of Petrarchism by his knowing use of its imagery: his is the contamination by ideology of resistance to it, or catch-22. While acknowledging the calamitous realities of the larger world (shipwreck, flood, plague, war, and the like), he also moves to distance and devalue them by contrast with his love, which is harmless in their larger terms. The difference here is not between body and soul or between inner and outer but between personal and impersonal, love and not-love, neither of which is without body in this poem.[52] Perhaps this is the point: without the senses the imagination is powerless, and without imagination no thought whatever, including transcendent thought, is possible. The second stanza thus prepares for the transvaluation, indeed the transfiguration, that imaginatively peaks in the third, middle stanza.

This familiar stanza performs a traditional Latin *scala*, a "flight of stairs" or "ladder," whether like one found in the contemplation of a medieval mystic, a Petrarchist, a Neoplatonized Christian humanist such as Castiglione's Cardinal Bembo, or a traditional physical scientist, categorizing substances from dense to rare. All these are laddered forms of sublation, or raising, which also continues within it something of what it cancels, some trace, part, or memory, even if only linguistic. The stanza ascends from two lowly flesh flies, through the paired extinctions of lighted candles, complete with sexual pun on "die"; to the eagle and the dove, higher and categorically more conceptual images in nature, alchemy, and classical and biblical religions; and finally to the singularity of "the phoenix riddle," an enigma and a veritable perplexity of plaited meaning, at once an archival myth and an encapsulated narrative. The phoenix riddle is a culminating figure of physical and spiritual rebirth and, as employed on tombs, a redemptive image of the fallen body that is to arise a glorified one. This riddling prophecy has a significance more witty and profound by reason of the lovers' present *realization* of it simultaneously in sexual, imaginative, and intellective expression, a consummation of it fulfilling its mystery. With the speaker's unfolding of this riddle, the language of the poem itself begins noticeably to assume the substantiality—the thingness attributed to words by Augustine—that is made explicit in the designation of sonnets as places, rooms, and, indeed, topoi, in the stanza that follows.[53]

The notion of sonnets as rooms—"pretty rooms" or Petrarchan *stanze*—in this, the fourth stanza, develops further the plaiting of natural and preternatural, physical and spiritual, in the third and fourth stages of the poem's canonizing process. In the words of the architectural historian and philosopher Dalibor Vesely, Renaissance architecture and perspective "share a sense of coherent space," embodied in "the concept of a 'room,'" and to my mind, this Euclidean conceptualizing of space bears on the imaginative process—the substantive idealizing—of Donne's poem as well.[54] Such a room, as characterized by Vesely, is an "idealized representation" expressing the "isotropic space of geometry." It is therefore analogous to the geometric circularity of the initial and final rhyme word "love" both in each stanza of "The Canonization" and in the poem as a whole, which realizes the figure of a roundel, or circle, as described in Puttenham's rhetoric.[55] The center of this roundel is the imaginative *scala* of stanza 3, its circumference bounded by love. That the word "room" is also a Renaissance commonplace for a court post or appointment is hardly irrelevant to a memory of the defiant outcry in the poem's first stanza, to the plaited fabric of the entire poem, to Donne's own life, or, for that matter, to Prince Hamlet's. The *places* of Donne's fourth stanza thus reflect and reflect on the central third, to which I will briefly return before proceeding, for the third stanza is where "we two, being one, are" said to be purely and simply "it." In terms borrowed from *King Lear*, this is truly "the thing itself," or that which is real (III.iv.106).

The third stanza is more personal in the plural sense since its initial line uses "we" rather than "me" (stanza 1) or "she and I" (stanza 2) for the first time. At this point, although there is no necessity of imagining that the speaker's initial addressee has departed, he is conspicuously silenced, and although we might choose to imagine the presence of the female lover in either a figurative or a physical sense, the speaker might as well be addressing himself. He has moved both inward and increasingly into symbolic reference. The symbols in which he speaks hover between the established value of metonyms and the creative value of metaphors, thus entities at once received or traditional and used in a novel reconstruction. That these symbolic, remembered *things* should afford the correlative terms of the associative, interior movement of the speaker's mind is itself meaningful. This kind of thing facilitates a shift into another register of meaning, or, in a word I have used earlier, it effects transformation. Donne mimes a creativity attributed to God in Christianity and extended to the poet by Sidney and his Aristotelian and Neoplatonic Italian sources, in which the poet is a maker (Greek *poiētēs*, from *poiein*, "produce, invent, create, make"). This poet preeminently uses the faculty of *nous poiētikos*; in Kosman's translation again, his is "the maker mind."[56]

The persistent punning of Donne's speaker functions simultaneously as play and serious signification, as wit and constructive exploration: "So to one *neutral thing* both sexes fit / We die and rise the same, and prove / Mysterious by this love" (25–27: my emphasis). A neutral thing is a unity of both—neither one alone rather than a cancellation of either one—Latin *ne* (not), plus *uter* (either), or *neuter*. Its biblical model is the participatory Pauline body of Corinthians.[57] For a modern reader of Donne's creative metanarrative in this poem, *neutrality* also glimpses a radical concept that affords the proper ethical option in certain historical situations, but this option, which has been broached by Roland Barthes and Maurice Blanchot, is not exclusively modern. Lowell Gallagher has suggestively explored its use in the poetry of Robert Southwell, a Jesuit martyr contemporary with Donne, and Stuart Clark has identified broadly similar features in the ethics of a moderate Pyrrhonist skepticism such as Montaigne's.[58] While neutrality hardly seems an option for a revenge play, it might better have fitted the protagonist Shakespeare fashioned for *Hamlet* than do the black-and-white choices the prince actually faces. Only with irony does it recall that moment in *Hamlet* when the decisive, vengeful Pyrrhus stands "*Like a neutral to his will and matter."* Yet it affords precisely the imaginative kind of answer that Donne's words evoke and actual circumstances tragically deny to Hamlet: "O cursed spite / That ever I was born to set it right!" (I.v.186–87).

In contrast to Donne's "neutral thing," the shift in the crucial speech of Leontes that I earlier examined also comes into view: Leontes shifts abruptly and irrationally from "thy dam" to "it," from an objective, personalized, female reference (Hermione) to the neuter and impersonal reference that facilitates his shift of attention to the common noun *Affection* and thence to his brainsick self-centricity. Donne avoids the potential danger of such movement. The *dying* and *rising* of Donne's speaker and his love fit not only both neutralized sexes but also both senses of the words "die" and "rise," which in reference are at once physical and mystical, or *soulish*, in a holistic Donnean usage capable of embracing sense, spirit, and intellect. Each "sex" itself (Latin *sexus*, "segment," deriving from *seco*, "cut, divide") in this context also implies part of a larger unity that fulfills rather than effaces selfhood. A memory of the spheroid androgyne in Aristophanes's myth about human origin in Plato's *Symposium* is hardly suppressed here, as neither is the spheroid male in all the talk of twinning in *The Winter's Tale*, especially regarding Leontes and Polixenes. For a Renaissance reading of this myth such as Leone Ebreo's, whose view of eros Helen Gardner long since associated with Donne's, the division of the androgyne results in two compound halves of a complex human whole rather than merely in simple, genital, binary opposites.[59] In the penultimate line of Donne's central stanza, even the verb "prove"—conveying "by evidential demonstration," "by actual verification," "by personal authentication"—participates in the three-line, triune, simultaneously rational, imaginative, and conclusive development of the riddle of resurrection. The Trinity is never far from Donne's wit, nor is his contemporary religious situation. Yet, while the final three lines of Donne's third stanza begin with the word "so," signifying "in this way" or "thus," "so" also signifies "to the extent that" and therefore includes a submerged qualification, a hint of the kind of imperfecting that Donne regularly maintains within an earthly vision.

A concentration and compaction, an intention and extension, a motion, an excitement, a stimulation of puns in the fourth and fifth stanzas reflect the complex, ambiguated, stereoscopic vision to which the Donnean speaker has reached. (My own multiplicities of nouns, not to mention my neologism, mime one of Donne's verbal methods of imaginatively enlarging *and* exploring in the sermons; comparatively, I think, with Arthur Marotti, of Hamlet's "wittiness" when agitated or affected).[60] Nearly all the speaker's puns in these stanzas are *images* more verbal than quasi-optical in nature: repeatedly "die" ("cease to exist," yet also "achieve sexual fulfillment"); "live" ("make a living, physically subsist," but with the construction "if not," which is inherently ambiguous in an English syntax, also glancing at the positive potential of "living forever"); "rooms" (both "physical spaces" and "verbal spaces," Petrarchan *stanze*); "becomes" ("adorns, suits," but also "turns into," ashes); and "approve" (at once "try [out]" and "consider good," a transfiguration of the same word that appears in stanza one). Each of these puns mirrors two dimensions of reality *at one and the same time*. In this way, for a moment, like a flash of light and enlightenment, each unites them. Simultaneously, however, it is notable that the pun-filled fourth stanza subsides from the climaxing third, insofar as the focus of the fourth is mainly on art (sonnets, urn, hymns), history (legend, chronicle), and death (hearse, ashes, tombs) and that the verbal unities, like the geometric ones, are, if embodied in a sense, not so in a sense that is fleshly and, in this way, living. The tone is relatively more apologetic and less intense. Again, relatively.

Not surprisingly, the final stanza is a further tonal letdown, as is typical in Donne, although not without exception.[61] The punning use of the verb "contract" primarily signifies "compress, concentrate," yet it also activates the lawyerly sense of a formal agreement, whether oral or, in Donne's time, more likely to find materially evidential expression in writing. Given this contractual sense, the punning relevantly extends to a spousal agreement as well: "You . . . Who did the whole world's soul contract, and drove / Into the glasses of your eyes" [agential, plural pun on "I"] / (So made such mirrors, and such spies . . .)" (39–42).[62] As a contract, the love expressed by the poem is also exposed to the agreement/consent of onlookers, whether within the immediate situation it performs or within that of its wider audience of listeners and readers. As simultaneously passive and agential, as a mirroring surface and an act of espying, of seeing into truth, the interaction the speaker describes bears an odd resemblance to that which Hamlet first experiences with the Player's and his own performances of Pyrrhic vengeance in Act II and then intends his *Mousetrap* to effect for himself and, extensively, for his blood relative Claudius: a societal surround of mirrorings and espyings.⁶³

In *Locating Privacy in Tudor London*, Lena Orlin treats material settings and constraints that bear suggestively on *Hamlet* and here on Donne as well. "The walls have ears" in Tudor England because of construction materials, crowded living conditions, and redesigned interiors, even aside from occasions when surveillance is specifically intended. Like Hamlet's heightened awareness of spies within the Danish court, the espying of Donne's lovers comes with the threatening undertow of suspicion that the word *spying* additionally conveys, whether in the sense of being spied upon or of seeing what is sensed, imagined, but otherwise concealed and in decency may best remain hidden, like the rotting body of a loved one, whether in London or Denmark, in artful urn or royal tomb. In Donne's final stanzas, despite an affirmation of undying exemplarity—an affirmation playful, taunting, and defiant—first the burial images, then a quieter, more telling use of the past tense, not surprisingly assert the speaker's equally abiding awareness of sacrifice and death. (The combination of courts, spies/spying, sacrifice, and death also makes it hard to ignore a memory of Lear's lyrical speeches to Cordelia just before they are taken to prison: V.iii.13–17, 20–21.) Cultural resonance compacted.

Hamlet's play within a play, like the multiple dimensions and recessive-expansive doublings in a Donne poem, is another reflection of and on the basic issue of the reliability, the necessarily hypothetical marking of imaginatively informed thought. In traditional faculty psychology, a major sticking point always already involves the relationship between the sensory nature of the imagination and the impassible nature of the intellect, which nonetheless requires the *phantasmata* to think. In the simplest terms, this is the relation of mind to matter, and at stake in it is nothing less than the immortality of the soul.⁶⁴ It is no accident that the Renaissance witnesses a pronounced uptick of interest in theories of mortalism, the temporary, partial, or total death of the soul, of which Donne, like Spenser, Milton, and, to my mind, Hamlet—along with Luther (sympathetic) and Calvin (hostile) and a range of radical sectarians—shows an engaged awareness.⁶⁵

In address, the speaker's overall performance in the "Canonization" moves inward, as already noted, then again outward ("thus invoke us": 37). This movement is compressed and controlled, seemingly deliberate, and it shares its willed quality with the otherwise contrasting narrative of darkness and death in Macbeth's soliloquy. Yet both performances also exhibit elements of spontaneity in their associative movements of mind. In Donne's lyric, the images, whether symbols or puns, are punctual and momentary stations between received metonym and live metaphor, and his speaker's mind ascends and descends by means of them. The interior landscape through which Macbeth's personified "Murther" strides with ravishing intent is allegorical narrative that displays the movement of the regicide's mind. The witty tone of Donne's lyric, simultaneously playful and serious—in its crucial middle stanza, for instance—contributes another substantive and significant difference in content: Macbeth proceeds from his inward excursion to immediate outward action. His use of imaginative potency contrasts sharply with that of Donne's speaker, as, indeed, with that of Hamlet. In the passages examined, the uses made of imaginative resources by both Hamlet and Donne's speaker are more thoughtful and far more exploratory. Both these performative personae heighten imagination with a care that is self-reflexive, intensely aware, and linguistically ironic; is to be so what a Derridean deconstructor's "always already" means nowadays? Do the awareness and consequent possibility of controlling irony themselves constitute a definitive difference? Characteristically, both Hamlet and Donne's speaker are manipulators of irony, the one an antic actor and a sponsor of staged speeches, the other a poet who builds in sonnets and fashions verbal urns. And yet Donne remains neither Danish prince nor tragic.

Psychic Modeling and Motivation: Donne's Interiorized Landscapes

As a poet, Donne makes use of physical landscapes infrequently, and, when they occur, they are typically brief and emblematic, as at the beginning of "The Ecstasy" or "The Primrose." The eight lines at the beginning of "A Nocturnal upon S. Lucy's Day" are an exception in length and, to my mind, enough of an intensification of affection to constitute a significant difference. Like the eight lines of Macbeth's murderous narrative, they are scenic:

> 'Tis the year's midnight, and it is the day's,
> Lucy's, who scarce seven hours herself unmasks,

> The sun is spent, and now his flasks
>   Send forth light squibs, no constant rays;
>   The world's whole sap is sunk:
> The general balm th'hydroptic earth hath drunk,
> Whither, as to the bed's-feet, life is shrunk,
> Dead and interred; yet all these seem to laugh,
> Compared with me, who am their epitaph.

In thus realizing a heightened state of affection, the narrative of Donne's speaker resembles those of Hamlet and Macbeth. Like these speakers, Donne's projects his imagination "so to his own conceit" as consciously here to substantiate phantasy in objective terms. The last four lines of the stanza compact disease with dying, death, and burial, all to be summed and superseded in nothingness by the ghostly speaker. He is their epitaph or the last word on them and of them, which is at once about and belonging to them or, in a pertinent Renaissance usage, "by" them.[66] In these lines, too, the figure of earth is monstrously swollen with an edematous dropsy, which, in a sonic pun, also suggests the *withering* of vital spirit ("sap," "animating lifeblood"). In an intensification of this anthropomorphic perspective, the earth swallows vital fluid as if vitality itself ("life") were draining to the edematous body's "feet" rather than only to the conventional foot of a bed; for a moment, body and bed seem to fuse grotesquely, surreally.[67] The speaker's point of view has moved from "midnight" and "spent" sun to a sickroom and beyond (more exactly, beneath) it, from dying to gravesite, from the condition of earth to individual extinction, from outside to inside, and from general objectivity to specific subjectivity.[68]

In the second stanza, the deathly speaker offers himself for study, as if for anatomy: "Study me then . . . For I am every dead thing, / In whom love wrought new alchemy." Lines later he adds, "He ruined me, and I am re-begot / Of absence, darkness, death; things which are not."[69] His meditation on his own death is a systematic application of imaginative material to it. This deliberate process enables him only in the third stanza to begin to differentiate the death of his love (inseparably "of eros per se" and "of his lover") from his own death. It is in this stanza that he uses the first-person plural pronoun and emphasizes not only its mutuality but also its plurality: "we two." This is the first time we perceive that somebody besides the speaker is involved and grasp that the death which has occurred is in all likelihood physically real. This recognition of the reality of difference, separation, loss—in a pun, the *realization* of these in poetry—in the next stanza enables explicit third-person reference to the lost lover's death and thus the distancing and extramentalizing of it, as distinct from the anguished internalizing of it in the opening stanza. What we observe in the progression of these stanzas is a poignant, moving (affective) expression of mourning that begins to come to terms with the unavoidable, necessary relation of love and physical death and not, as elsewhere, only in the verbal pun "die" that contains it. A further relation to Hamlet's struggle with subjectivity and objectivity and, inversely to Leontes's confusion of these, is certainly suggestive. Initially, Leontes's perverse, all-engulfing subjectivity is deadly, fatal to every form of love in his world, from friendship to fatherhood to marriage. He has to (re)learn, to remember and recover, the reality of difference, objectivity, and death before the redemptive resources of imagination can be employed to transfigure the world for him—astonishingly, through a sculpted figure. He has to accomplish what Hamlet at least attempts in his graveyard scene. Like Donne's speaker, Leontes has, in a sense, to die to the world before he can return to it. Unlike the fiction in which Donne's persona meditates, however, the fiction in which Leontes acts allows the recovery of a lost love, not just the "prepar[ation] towards her" that concludes "A Nocturnal" (43).

"Good Friday, 1613. Riding Westward" is another Donnean meditation: on the anniversary of Christ's death, the speaker travels west, the direction opposite the one in which he thinks, and half feels, he should be going—eastward toward Jerusalem. Figuratively, he travels away from redemptive life and in two ways toward death, the end of his mortal life and the spiritual loss of his God. Thinking imaginatively about his situation, he hesitantly, even reluctantly, begins to picture the scene of the Crucifixion in his mind's eye. Starting to pun (another characteristic form of interior excitement in Donne), he speaks conditionally and ethically of what he "should see," namely and paradoxically, a "sun, by rising set" (11).[70] Yet he is actually glad that he cannot in reality "see" the Passion, consummated in Christ's death. As the speaker's excitement (*affection*, stimulation, moving) and engagement (*intention*, straining or directing of the mind, attention, mental application or effort) increase, he asks in quick but still conditional succession, "Could I behold those hands . . . Could I behold that endless height . . . ?" (21, 23). Description of the sights he cannot behold becomes more and more specific, detailed, expansive, and intense as we realize that he is actually beholding in his mind what he says he cannot behold in the reality outside it. Of course, the poem has moved inward to achieve this intensity, and, as interior vision becomes too realistic, too detailed, it gives way to the reality of his journey on horseback: "Though these things, as I ride, be from mine eye, / They are present yet unto my memory"(34–35). More exactly, however, with the mnemonic recovery of imaginative power, the quotidian world must now share substance ("things"), as well as the present tense, with the inner one. Moreover, while the phrase "from mine eye" primarily conveys "absent from physical eyesight," subliminally it implies "arising from the mind's eye," precisely the meaning of the next line, which recalls the redemptive vision "present yet" in the speaker's mnemonic imagination. Even the rhyme of "eye" with "memory," phonically signaling "inner eye" or subjective "I," further enforces such presence. In short, interiorized vision, even when it has faded, leaves its mark, traditionally likened to the material imprint of a seal ring on wax and earlier described in my discussion of Leontes's mnemonic and present imaginings. Within a few lines, however, Donne's speaker discounts the image of Christ the Redeemer that he has realized in the poem, or he just considers it inadequate, whether too (merely) interior or too self-willed and one sided—in Hamlet's terms, too much the forcing of a conceit.[71] A seeming skeptic, he now requires direct divine intervention, Hamlet's proof: "Restore thine image."

The relevance of Donne's vision in "Good Friday" to the nigh palpable dagger of Macbeth is even clearer in the working of imagination in the first quatrain of a Holy Sonnet:

> At the round earth's imagined corners, blow
> Your trumpets, angels, and arise, arise
> From death, you numberless infinities
> Of souls, and to your scattered bodies go . . .

It would be hard to match the intensity of this imaginative flight, yet within lines, like the reality of Macbeth's envisioned dagger, it unexpectedly subsides with an emotional thud into quotidian reality, here the oppressive, prosaic enumeration of life's miseries: "war, dearth, age, agues, tyrannies, / Despair, law, chance . . . death's woe."[72] By sonnet's end, the poet is even unsure about his own election to the company of the redeemed

("As if thou hadst sealed my pardon, with thy blood"). Quite unlike the final movement of Macbeth's soliloquy, his ending is distinctly like Hamlet's distrust of imaginative test flight in his soliloquy of response to Pyrrhic vengeance. The sustained passages of such exalted vision that I know best in Donne's writing are in prose and within the embrace of an explicitly religious form, as well as of religious belief: the prayer of Donne's *Devotion 12* and the concluding vision of his second Prebend sermon, which dramatizes an ascent to heaven resembling the elation of a similar flight in the meditative context of the "Second Anniversary."[73]

Sleep and Waking: Donne's Dreams

Two poems by Donne have received the title "The Dream": one is a lyric in the *Songs and Sonnets*, and the other is the lyric beginning "Image of her whom I love," which has also been called "Image and Dream" and which was included among the elegies in the 1633 and 1635 editions of Donne's poetry.[74] In Shakespeare, Hamlet scorns the First Player's "fiction, . . . [his] dream of passion," right before briefly attempting it, and Leontes speculates about dreaming even as he dreams himself into delusion. Enclosed within mirroring walls of self-reflection, Leontes does not truly see outside them. While awake, in sum, he is in a dreamworld, as earlier observed. For my purpose, Donne's dreams bring to the fore the relation of Leontes's sovereign dreamworld to his temporal and spatial kingdom.

Both Donne's poems on dreams address the relation to waking reality of imagination's activity during sleep. In "The Dream," Donne's speaker wakens into his love's presence and actually speaks to her.[75] He attributes his waking to the strength (intensity, realism) of his "happy dream," which has been erotic. He naturally wants to see his dream, which has proved "too strong for [mere] fantasy" continued into the "true" reality of physical consummation now that he is awake (1–10). Uttering much witty and wily flattery, he wants to entice his true love, who loves truth, to make his dream history, an event truly existing in time and space (7–8, 14). He argues suasively, albeit in openly, not to say outrageously, inflated images, that, God-like, she must have known what he was dreaming since she came precisely when she knew "Excess of joy would wake me" (15–18). She anticipated the sexual ecstasy in his dreamworld and therefore kindly came to make it truly real. Summarily, the woman, who has noticeably "stayed"—

either remained long enough to cooperate or else stayed, "hesitated," been reluctant in her rejection—now departs, and the speaker has to settle for deferral and the renewed expectation that she came "to kindle, goes . . . to come" again, leaving him to his hopeful dreaming (21–30.) He ends with a dying pun ("but else would die"). I take "else" primarily to mean in a way other than merely dreaming, while, in a continuation of his earlier exaggeration, also meaning both that he would rather perish than lose hope of fulfillment and that he would welcome fulfillment, if not in truth, at least in his dreamworld. This speaker hedges his bets. The sense of "else would die" that I have deemed primary because it yields the fullest, truest sense, is also a preference for a reality that is finally subject to the limitations of real space and time. In a word, it includes death in the mortal, as well as the sexual, sense even while Donne's speaker, no matter how provoking his play, might truly be said here to die upon a pun.

Donne's "Image and Dream" is more centrally concerned with an idealized image of the woman than is "The Dream," notwithstanding the latter's playful view of her as truth, as angel, and as God-like. As if endorsing a Neoplatonic ladder of the sort found in the imaginative, ultimately contemplative vision of Castiglione's Cardinal Bembo, an ascent from bodily woman to the idea of Beauty and beyond, the speaker gets right to the point: "Image of her whom I love more than she."[76] This idealized image of an existent woman has been impressed in the speaker's heart, traditionally a metonym for memory, as earlier noted. But in a surprise twist, he finds this development too overwhelming—too pure, too intellectual, too virtuous for his weak sense and spirits, his prowess both sexual and imaginative. And so he banishes the image, along with his heart and reason, instead embracing phantasy as "queen and soul" since she offers immediate, sensual joys that better befit a natural man. His ardent wish is to be "the plaything of the images." Thus having banished the higher, truer intellectual power, the speaker reasons sophistically about the love he will now possess indulgently:

So, if I dream I have you, I have you,
   For, all our joys are but fantastical [imagined].
And so I 'scape the pain [of restrained lust], for pain is true [real];
   And sleep, which locks up sense doth lock out all [except mnemonic
     imaginings and reimaginings].

> After a such fruition I shall wake,
>   And, but the waking, nothing shall repent;
> And shall to love more thankful sonnets make,
>   Than if more honour, tears, and pains were spent.
>
> (12–20)

What he wants is a wet dream. Such a reality would be physical enough but not mutual, lasting, or conscious, as the early modern period understood this word.[77] In Donnean terms, it would truly be unreal.

In a sudden reversal, the speaker, who is presumably alarmed by his phantasy of autoeroticism, asks that his "dearest heart, and dearer image stay," adding, "true joys at best are dream enough; / Though you stay here you pass too fast away: / For even at first life's taper is a snuff" (21–24). The heart—his own, hers, her image within his, the true locus of his joys—is what passes away; day by passing day it is what time, from the instant of birth, snuffs out. By "dream enough," he encompasses "satisfying enough," "phantasy and excitement enough," and finally "unreal enough" since the heart itself is flesh and memory a sensory, passible affection fed by and feeding imagination, another sensory affection.[78] Ending the poem, the speaker clings to the contentment (the fullness) of "her love," at once loving her and being loved by her: in short, a state "Filled with her love." His brief, apostate escape to a dreamworld, a realm governed by unbridled affection, gives way to a trust in her love and a conscious embrace of it. Substituting "faith" for "trust," we are close to the end of Leontes's long winter's night.

Donne's explicit, focal use of dreams in the two poems examined never loses sight of their limited reality. Although fascinated by the phenomena of dreaming, he maintains control of them and finally resists their blurring into real time and space. Another version of this point observes the obvious generic difference between Donnean lyric and Shakespearean drama and, while avoiding unmediated biography, acknowledges that Donne's personae are typically less separate and autonomous, less exteriorized and objectified, less fully dramatized and actually embodied than are those of the playwright. Again, less fully fictive but fictive nonetheless, even while my own readings of "The Canonization" and "A Nocturnal" strike many chords with Donne's marriage and religion that are harder to ignore than are those struck by *Hamlet* with what we know, or think we know, about Shakespeare's dead son, Hamnet, his father, and his religion. Yet none of

Donne's speakers is a vengeful prince-in-waiting, an enthroned murderer, or a self-tormenting king whose mental space bad dreams tyrannize. In a paradox, Shakespeare's realer, fleshier figures (yes, figures) in the plays are more phantasied as fictions, especially as those of a common playwright, even while phantasy in them steps onto a realer stage.[79] In the soliloquies, however, Shakespeare might be said to have moved onto this stage what Donne engaged in a more intimate medium, and Donne might be said to have brought speaking fictions into contemporary life. To make such observations of more and less, of publicity and privacy, of theatricality and intimacy, is both to recognize the historical and cultural comparability of these two writers and to respect their difference. I offer these words as a conclusion to this volume on generic hybridity in the cultural imagination of Tudor-Stuart England, as well as to my own chapter in it.

Notes

Introduction / Judith H. Anderson and Jennifer C. Vaught

1. *Skepticism and Memory* (New York: Palgrave Macmillan, 2007).
2. *The Shakespearean Moment* (London: Chatto and Windus, 1954). Crutwell compares Donne's *Anniversaries* to the style of Shakespeare's later plays.
3. Oxford *DNB*, "Alleyn, Edward" (1566–1626): accessed on line 10/2/11 (Oxford University Press, 2005–2011: http://www.oxforddnb.com); see also R. C. Bald, *John Donne: A Life* (Oxford: Oxford University Press, 1970), 448–49. Donne's maternal grandfather was the playwright John Heywood, and although Donne was only six when Heywood died, he is likely to have been told of him. Aside from whatever commercial performances Donne might have frequented, his time in the university, as well as in the Inns of Court, would also have exposed him to plays.
4. Bald, *John Donne*, 72. Margret Fetzer's study of Donne and speech-act theory offers a fairly comprehensive review of relevant criticism: *John Donne's Performances: Sermons, Poems, Letters and Devotions* (Manchester: Manchester University Press, 2010).
5. William Shakespeare, *Hamlet*, ed. Ann Thompson and Neil Taylor (London: Thomson Learning, 2006), II.ii.334–36.
6. James L. Calderwood describes an Escher-like Hamlet who is "conscious of his dual identity [as actor and character] . . . almost as though he were an actor at a rehearsal": *To Be and Not to Be: Negation and Metadrama in "Hamlet"* (New York: Columbia University Press, 1983), 30, 32. Judith Sherer Herz considers Donne's illusionistic speaker "Escher-like": "'An Excellent Exercise of Wit That Speaks So Well of Ill': Donne and the Poetics of Concealment," in *The Eagle and the Dove: Reassessing John Donne*, ed. Claude J. Summers and Ted-Larry Pebworth (Columbia: University of Missouri Press, 1986), 3–14, here 5.
7. Fowler, *Kinds of Literature: An Introduction to the Theory of Genres and Modes* (Cambridge, MA: Harvard University Press, 1982), 18.

8. The odd article has afforded sustained treatment of Shakespeare and Donne only rarely in recent years, for example, Barbara Correll, "Terms of 'Indearment': Lyric and General Economy in Shakespeare and Donne," *ELH* 75 (2008): 241–62.

9. The spelling of titles and even the titles themselves of many of Donne's poems vary greatly among editions. We follow the version adopted in each essay by our contributors.

10. Michel Serres with Bruno Latour, *Conversations on Science, Culture, and Time*, trans. Roxanne Lapidus (Ann Arbor: University of Michigan Press, 1995), 103–7.

11. Daniel Lerner, *The Passing of Traditional Society* (New York: Free Press, 1964), 72; Anthony D. Smith, *Theories of Nationalism* (London: Duckworth, 1971), 90.

12. The spelling of the given name of Donne's wife varies among the authorities. We use "Ann" in this Introduction but consider "Anne" a legitimate variation elsewhere in the volume.

1. Sites of Death as Sites of Interaction in Donne and Shakespeare / Matthias Bauer and Angelika Zirker

1. See, for example, Helen Gardner, "Dean Donne's Monument in St. Paul's," in *Evidence in Literary Scholarship*, ed. James M. Osborn (Oxford: Clarendon, 1979), 29–44; and Joshua Scodel, *The English Poetic Epitaph: Commemoration and Conflict from Jonson to Wordsworth* (Ithaca, NY: Cornell University Press, 1991), 127–29.

2. "Deaths Duell," in *The Sermons of John Donne*, ed. Evelyn Simpson and George R. Potter, 10 vols. (Berkeley: University of California Press 1962), 10: 228–48, 233, 235. The phrase "exitus a morte" appears several times throughout the sermon and in different spellings. The variants in this essay follow the spellings in the edition by Simpson and Potter.

3. See, for example, Donne's "First Anniuersarie," in *The Epithalamions, Anniversaries and Epicedes*, ed. Wesley Milgate (Oxford: Clarendon, 1978):

> For though the soule of man
> Be got when man is made, 'tis borne but than
> When man doth die. Our body's as the wombe,
> And as a mid-wife death directs it home.
> (451–54)

See also Martin Luther's sermon on the preparation to die:

> [. . .] gleych wie ein kind auß der cleynen wonung seiner mutter leyb mit gefar und engsten geboren wirt yn dißenn weyten hymell und erden, daß ist auff diße welt. Alßo geht der mensch durch die enge pforten des todts auß

dißem leben; [. . .]. Eyn weyb, wan es gepirt, so leydet es angst, wan sie aber geneßen ist, so gedenkt sie der angst nymmer, die weyll eyn mensch geporn ist von yhr yn die welt, alßo zum sterben auch muß man sich der angst erwegen und wissen, das darnarch eyn groer raum und freud seyn wirt. ("Eyn Sermon von der berytung zum sterben [1519]," in *Martin Luthers Werke: Kritische Gesamtausgabe*, 120 vols. [Weimar: Böhlau, 1884], 2: 685–97).

    4. Quotation of Donne from *The Elegies and The Songs and Sonnets*, ed. Helen Gardner (Oxford: Clarendon, 1965): Unless otherwise noted, subsequent citation of *Songs and Sonnets* is from this edition. On readings of the beginning of the poem see, for example, Helen Gardner, "The Argument about 'The Ecstasy,'" in *Elizabethan and Jacobean Studies: Presented to Frank Percy Wilson in Honour of His Seventieth Birthday*, ed. Herbert Davis (Oxford: Clarendon, 1959), 279–306; A. J. Smith, "Donne in His Time: A Reading of 'The Extasie,'" *Rivista di Letterature Moderne e Comparate* 10 (1957): 260–75; Austin Warren, "Donne's 'Extasie,'" *Studies in Philology* 55 (1958): 472–80.

    5. On the separation of body and soul see, for example, Donne's *Holy Sonnet* "This is my play's last scene," in which he imagines his death: "And gluttonous death, will instantly unjoint / My body, and soul"; *The Divine Poems*, ed. Helen Gardner (Oxford: Clarendon, 1952); unless otherwise noted, subsequent citation of Donne's religious poetry is from this edition. "Donne's image of the bodies as sepulchral statues admirably portrays the alchemical idea of the dead matter lying at the bottom of the alembic. The alchemical notion of the reconciliation of warring opposites is also present in these lines. The lovers, about to merge in a *unio mentalis*, are compared to 'equal Armies,' recalling the statues of Shakespeare's lovers, also foes about to unite"; Lyndy Abraham, "The Lovers and the Tomb: Alchemical Emblems in Shakespeare, Donne, and Marvell," *Emblematica* 5 (1991): 301–20, 316. See note 43, this chapter.

    6. Cf. the meaning of the word "ecstasy": "in late Greek the etymological meaning ["insanity" and "bewilderment"] received another application, viz., 'withdrawal of the soul from the body, mystic or prophetic trance'" (*OED*, "ecstasy," *n*., etymology). The word was then used "by mystical writers as the technical name for the state of rapture in which the body was supposed to become incapable of sensation, while the soul was engaged in the contemplation of divine things" (*OED*, "ecstasy," *n*. 3.a.). See also Donne's letter to Sir Thomas Lucy on October 9, 1607, where he describes letter writing in terms of "ecstasy":

> Sir,—I make account that the writing of letters, when it is with any seriousness, is a kind of ecstasy, and a departure and secession and suspension of the soul, which doth then communicate itself to two bodies: and as I would every day provide for my soul's last convoy, though I know not when I shall

die, and perchance I shall never die; so for these ecstasies in letters, I oftentimes deliver myself over in writing when I know not when those letters shall be sent to you, and many times they never are. (John Donne, *Letters to Severall Persons of Honour [1651]: A Facsimile Reproduction* [Delmar, NY: Scholars' Facsimiles and Reprints, 1977], 11).

See also Edmund Gosse, *The Life and Letters of John Donne, Dean of St. Paul's*, 2 vols. (Gloucester, MA: Peter Smith, 1959), 1: 173.

7. Cf. Abraham, "Lovers and the Tomb." The concept goes back to Michelangelo; see Inge Leimberg, *Heilig öffentlich Geheimnis: Die geistliche Lyrik der englischen Frühaufklärung* (Münster: Waxmann, 1996), 133; and Hugo Friedrich, *Epochen der italienischen Lyrik* (Frankfurt: Klostermann, 1964), 365–70. See also Stella P. Revard, "Donne and Propertius: Love and Death in London and Rome," in *The Eagle and the Dove: Reassessing John Donne*, ed. Claude J. Summers and Ted-Larry Pebworth (Columbia: University of Missouri Press, 1986), 69–79, esp. 75–77: "Donne pictures the joy of the grave as marriage bed" (77).

8. Pierre de Ronsard, *Sonnets pour Hélène*, ed. Malcolm Smith (Geneva: Librairie Droz, 1970), 79.14 (195). See Leimberg, *Heilig öffentlich Geheimnis*, on death as topic in Donne's love poems (esp. 128–29); also Shakespeare, for example, *Romeo and Juliet*: "my grave is like to be my wedding-bed," in *Romeo and Juliet*, ed. Brian Gibbons (London: Methuen, 1980), I.v.133–34.

9. On the concept of the rehearsal of death see, for example, Kathryn Kremen, *The Imagination of the Resurrection: The Poetic Continuity of a Religious Motif in Donne, Blake, and Yeats* (Lewisburg, PA: Bucknell University Press, 1972), 100: "'[S]epulchrall statues' can be associated with the final rising of the dead body and its reunion with the soul, so these lovers imitate and prefigure on earth the resurrection to heaven." Fulfillment can either be achieved through death or experienced as death, which is, for instance, expressed in the pun on "to die": See, for example, A. R. Cirillo, "Fair Hermaphrodite: Love-Union in the Poetry of Donne and Spenser," *SEL* 9 (1969): 81–95, 82.

10. Friar Laurence explains the effect of the potion to her: "Shall stiff and stark and cold appear like death; / And in this borrowed likeness of shrunk death / Thou shalt continue two and forty hours" (*Romeo and Juliet*, IV.i.99–101).

11. This is a traditional (Neo)platonic view. See also Donne's Holy Sonnet "This is my play's last scene" for the separation of body and soul.

12. For this imagery in Donne's writings see note 49, this chapter.

13. Gibbons glosses this as "Juliet's sculptured stone-cold beauty" (introduction, *Romeo and Juliet*, 1–77, here 74). He goes on to write that "Shakespeare ironically reorders the fable of Pygmalion [. . .]: Shakespeare's lovers must undergo a metamorphosis out of Nature, into the artifice of eternity" (74).

14. This transitory state between life and death was mirrored in *transi* tombs, where a double representation of the dead person figures: The upper effigy

embodies the person as she was when alive, while the lower effigy is a portrayal of putrefaction, of the skeleton, or the person in the shroud. See Kathleen Cohen, *Metamorphosis of a Death Symbol: The Transi Tomb in the Late Middle Ages and the Renaissance* (Berkeley: University of California Press, 1973).

15. See Shakespeare's *Cymbeline*, ed. J. M. Nosworthy (London: Methuen, 1969), II.ii.31–33: "O sleep, thou ape of death, lie dull upon her, / And be her sense but as a monument, / Thus in a chapel lying."

16. "The force of this scene [in the tomb] derives from the ironic juxtaposition of Juliet's fake death, her revival, and her actual death: she is brought back to life from a false suicide only to die in earnest. Here the contrast between what might have been, had this been a comedy, and what actually takes place is made all the more striking by the fact that the scene takes place in a tomb"; Elizabeth Williamson, "Things Newly Performed: The Resurrection Tradition in Shakespeare's Plays," in *Shakespeare and Religious Change*, ed. Kenneth John Emerson Graham and Philip D. Collington (Basingstoke: Palgrave Macmillan, 2009), 110–32, 122. Williamson goes on to draw a parallel to Hero's feigned death in *Much Ado about Nothing*: She has to "die to live" (IV.i.253); William Shakespeare, *Much Ado about Nothing*, ed. Claire McEachern (London: Thomson Learning, 2006). The story continues in *Romeo and Juliet* as Juliet kills herself after she has "died to live." For a historical overview of the context of death-in-life and life-in-death see, for example, Günther Blaicher, "Die Paradoxie vom lebendigen Totsein in England: Versuch einer historischen Skizze," in *Death-in-life: Studien zur historischen Entfaltung der Paradoxie der Entfremdung in der englischen Literatur*, ed. Günther Blaicher (Trier: WVT Wissenschaftlicher Verlag Trier, 1998), 11–45; and Wolfgang G. Müller, "Die Präsenz des Todes im Leben: Erscheinungsformen eines Topos in der Literatur der englischen Renaissance," ibid., 79–96, for example, 80.

17. *The Rape of Lucrece*, in *Shakespeare's Poems*, ed. Katherine Duncan-Jones and H. R. Woudhuysen (London: Thomson Learning, 2007), 400–6: subsequent reference to Shakespeare's poems is to this edition unless otherwise noted.

18. On the various meanings of "lantern" see Gilian West, "Juliet's Grave," *ELN* 28 (1990): 33–34.

19. All biblical quotations, if not otherwise indicated, follow the *Authorized King James Version*, ed. Robert Carroll and Stephen Prickett (Oxford: Oxford University Press, 1998). See also Mt 26:29 and George Herbert's "Love (III)" as a literary elaboration on the topic of the heavenly banquet; George Herbert, *The English Poems of George Herbert*, ed. Helen Wilcox (Cambridge: Cambridge University Press, 2011), 658.

20. The idea of a resurrection might be felt to clash with Friar Laurence's view that suicide is damnable (III.iii. 107–17). When he lectures Romeo in III. iii., however, he argues that the loss of "birth and heaven and earth" (118) in Romeo's killing himself will be tantamount to "Killing that love which [he] has [. . .] vowed to cherish" (128). This is not what happens in the final scene,

226   Notes to pages 21–22

where Romeo kills himself because he believes Juliet to be dead (i.e., he joins her in love and death).

21. *Sonnets*, ed. Katherine Duncan-Jones (London: Thomson, 1997): Subsequent reference to Shakespeare's sonnets is to this edition unless otherwise noted. 1 Cor 15: 24 reads as follows: "Death is swallowed up in victory." See also *Lucrece*: "Thou death, both die, and both shall victors be" (1211). Yet another biblical reference that might lie at the background of this passage in *Romeo and Juliet* is Mt 8:22: "Let the dead bury their dead"; see also Lk 9:60.

22. See Gibbons (*Romeo and Juliet*, 224). According to him, "maw" is "gullet" and "womb" signifies "belly"; other words belonging to this semantic field are "gorg'd," "morsel," "jaws," "cram," and "food." One can also read this passage against the background of Shakespeare's Sonnet 146: "Poor soul, the centre of my sinful earth." In this case, the soul is at the body's center, in which case the "womb of death" might contain the soul.

23. See also the connection of womb and tomb elsewhere in Shakespeare's works, for example, in *Sonnets* 3.7, 86.4; *1 Henry 6* IV.v.34; *Romeo and Juliet* II.iii.5–6. On tomb puns in Shakespeare, see T. Walter Herbert, "Shakespeare's Word-Play on Tombe," *Modern Language Notes* 64, no. 4 (1949): 235–41, 235n4: Herbert refers to the "popular and pathetic elegy which Chidiock Tichborne was supposed to have 'Writen with His Own Hand in the Tower Before his Execution': 'I sought my death and found it in my womb, / I looked for life and saw it was a shade, / I trod the earth and knew it was my tomb.'" See also Doniphan Louthan, "The Tome-Tomb Pun in Renaissance England," *Philological Quarterly* 29 (1950): 375–80. John Donne also uses the rhyme womb/tomb, for example, in his "Epithalamion (Lincoln's Inn)" ("Then may thy lean and hunger-starved womb / Long time expect their bodies and their tomb" [40–41]) and in *The First Anniversarie* ("Spring-times were common cradles, but are tombs; / And false conceptions fill the general wombs" [385–86]). In the earlier passage of *Romeo and Juliet* (II.iii.5), the connection is clearly established, though with a different meaning, in order to evoke it again later in a particular context, namely that of the grave. See also Gibbons's note 137, referring to Lucretius, v. 259: "Omniparens eadem rerum commune sepulcrum," where mother nature is described as a tomb.

24. See also Henry Vaughan's "Death. A Dialogue" when the Soul says to the Body: "But thou / Shalt in thy mother's bosom sleep / Whilst I each minute groan to know / How near redemption creeps": *The Complete Poems*, ed. Alan Rudrum (New Haven, CT: Yale University Press, 1976), 27–30. While the body sleeps in the bosom of "mother Earth," its "womb," the soul awaits its reunion with the body.

25. *Richard III*, ed. Anthony Hammond (London: Methuen, 1981), IV.i.53.

26. She adds in the same passage, "Thy womb let loose to chase us to our graves" (IV.iv.54).

27. See also Friar Laurence's calling the tomb a "nest / Of death" (V.iii.150). Judith H. Anderson, *Biographical Truth: The Representation of Historical Persons in Tudor-Stuart Writing* (New Haven, CT: Yale University Press, 1984), 118, 223n23, has shown that this passage (and related ones) alludes verbally and imagistically to Spenser's Garden of Adonis, in which the boar Richard would root.

28. *Devotions upon Emergent Occasions*, ed. Anthony Raspa (Oxford: Oxford University Press, 1987), 92–93.

29. See note 23.

30. Cf. the description of Lucrece: "Her lily hand her rosy cheek lies under, / Coz'ning the pillow [. . .] Between whose hills her head entombed is, / Where like a virtuous monument she lies" (386–91). Lucrece is also compared to a "sepulchral statue"—"like a [. . .] monument." The difference between this presentation and the lovers in "The Extasie," however, consists in her being alone while the lovers interact and experience their ecstasy together.

31. The formula "defects of loneliness controls" is in itself striking. Given the etymology of "control," the formula refers to the idea of interaction: "Control" stems from Anglo-French *contreroller*, which means "to take and keepe a copie of a roll of accounts, to controll, obserue, ouersee, spie faults in" (*OED*, "control," *v.*, etymology). Loneliness is checked by adding a second part. See Donne's "La Corona," "6 Resurrection": "And life, by this death abled, shall control / Death, whom thy death slew" (5–6).

32. John Donne, *Pseudo-Martyr*, ed. Anthony Raspa (Montreal: McGill-Queen's University Press, 1993), 172. This is also the first mention of the verb in the *OED*, "inanimate," *v.* 1.

33. Robin Robbins, ed., *The Complete Poems of John Donne* (London: Pearson Education, 2010), 177n. The word "interinanimates" consists of the following elements: preposition+preposition+adjective+verb ending. Clements suggests two readings: "[W]hether we take 'interinanimates' to mean either mutually breathes life into, or mutually removes the (ordinary) consciousness of, or both (since both do apply), the lovers' love and thereby the lovers are again in this way presented as Godlike"; Arthur L. Clements, "We Two Being One, Are It," in *Poetry of Contemplation: John Donne, George, Herbert, Henry Vaughan, and the Modern Period*, ed. Arthur L. Clements (Albany: State University of New York Press, 1990), 19–79, 39. See also Ramie Targoff on Donne's use of the word "interinanimation": "Donne invented the term 'inanimation' to describe the process by which spirit gets infused into a person; his neologism conveys a sense of motion, a forward thrusting of soul into body in a manner that the ordinary term 'animation' lacks": *John Donne, Body and Soul* (Chicago: University of Chicago Press, 2008), 55.

34. Further examples from Donne that contain "inter" can be found in "inter-assured" ("A Valediction: Forbidding Mourning," 19); "interbring" ("Epithalamium at the Marriage of the Earl of Somerset," 171); "interchanged"

("Verse letter to the Countess of Huntingdon," 49); "intergraft" ("The Extasie," 9); "intertouched" ("The Progress of the Soul," 225); "interwish" ("The Curse," 26); cf. John Donne, *A Complete Concordance of the Poems*, ed. Celia Florén, 2 vols. (Hildesheim: Olms-Weidmann, 2004), 1: 409–10. An example of Donne's using the verb "inter" while evoking the meaning of the preposition is to be found in the "Obsequies to the Lord Harington, Brother to the Countess of Bedford": "Do not, fair soul, this sacrifice refuse, / That in thy grave I do inter my Muse" (255–56).

35. Cirillo ("Fair Hermaphrodite," 85) refers to Casoni's *trattato d'amore*, in which he describes a similar process: "[Love] takes the soul of the lover and infuses it into the beloved, and that of the beloved places in the lover, giving to one, and to the other mutual love and most pleasing new form" (Cirillo cites Guido Casoni, *Della Magia d'Amore*, 151).

36. A similar idea of exchange is already alluded to in the second stanza, when the speaker describes the interaction between the eyes. See also G. R. Wilson, "The Interplay of Perception and Reflection: Mirror Imagery in Donne's Poetry," *SEL* 9 (1969): 107–21.

37. Cf. "A Valediction: forbidding mourning," 1–4:

As virtuous men passe mildly'away,
   And whisper to their soules, to goe,
Whilst some of their sad friends doe say,
   The breath goes now, and some say, no.

On the identity of spirit and soul and its relation to breath, see Isidore [Isidorus Hispalensis], *Isidori Hispalensis Episcopi Etymologiarvm sive originum libri XX*, ed. W. M. Lindsay, 2 vols. (Oxford: Clarendon, 1966), Bk. 11, chap. 1, 7–10; cf. Matthias Bauer, "*Paronomasia celata* in Donne's 'A Valediction: forbidding mourning,'" *English Literary Renaissance* 25 (1995): 97–111, here 104.

38. See, for example, Stephen Gaselee, "The Soul in the Kiss," *Criterion* 2 (April 1924): 349–59. He refers to the image of kissing as an exchange or transfer of soul that can be found already in an ancient Greek fragment (in the *Anthologia Palatina* V. 78: "Kissing Kate / At the gate / Of my lips my soul hovers / While the poor thing endeavours / To Kate / to migrate") as well as in Petronius's *Satyricon*: "We clung, we glowed, losing ourselves in bliss / And interchanged our souls in every kiss." See also Targoff (*John Donne*, 25). A related image can be found in Christopher Marlowe's *Doctor Faustus* in Faustus's plea with Helen: "Sweet Helen, make me immortal with a kiss. / Her lips suck forth my soul! See where it flies. / Come, Helen, come, give me my soul again!" in *Doctor Faustus and Other Plays*, ed. David Bevington and Eric Rasmussen (Oxford: Oxford University Press, 1998), B-text, V.i.95–97.

39. This imagery can be linked to the "inanimation" of Adam in Gen 2:7: "And the Lord God . . . breathed into his nostrils the breath of life; and man

became a living soul." Cf. this passage in the *Vulgate*: "Formavit igitur Dominus Deus hominem de limo terræ, et inspiravit in faciem eius spiraculum vitæ, et factus est homo *in animam* viventem"; *Nova Vulgata: Bibliorum Sacrorum Editio*, Editio typica altera (Vatican: Libreria Editrice Vaticana, 1986) (our emphasis). Pererius, for instance, discusses the translation of "in faciem" (i.e., whether the nose or the mouth is meant); see Pererius [Benedict Pereira], *Commentatorium et Disputationum in Genesim: Continens historiam Mosis ab exordio mundi vsq ad Noëticum diluuium, septem libris explanatam. Adiecti sunt quattuor Indices, vnus quaestionum, alter eorum quae pertinent ad doctrinam moralem, & vsum concionantium, tertius locorum sacrae Scripturae, quartus generalis & alphabeticus*, 4 vols. (Lugduni [Lyon], 1592–1600), 1: 419–20.

40. See Alfred Stuiber, *Refrigerium interim: Die Vorstellungen vom Zwischenzustand und die frühchristliche Grabeskunst* (Bonn: Hanstein, 1957), 52–58. Stuiber cites Tertullian's *De Anima* (e.g., 33, 11), *Adversus Marcionem* (e.g., 4, 34), and *De monogamia* (10); the last is particularly interesting in that it deals with the notion of the rising of man and wife "to a spiritual consortship" after death; see S. Thelwall's translation in the *Ante-Nicene Christian Library (ANCL)*, vol. 18 (Edinburgh: Clark, 1870), 21–55; accessed July 11, 2011, http://www.earlychristianwritings.com/text/tertullian31.html. See also Karel Hanhart, "The Intermediate State in the New Testament" (PhD diss., University of Amsterdam, 1966).

41. Clements draws a parallel between "the lovers' love" and God as well as between "that abler soul" and divinity: "Having managed to break out of the closed ego, the lovers now know the truth about their essential selves, have essential self-knowledge, and all of this is accomplished by true love and spiritual ecstasy" (*Poetry of Contemplation*, 38).

42. See Abraham ("Lovers and the Tomb," 301). She refers to works like the *Rosarium* in *De Alchimia* (1550), the *Artis auriferae* (1593), and Daniel Stolcius's *Viridarium chimicum* (1624) and draws parallels between *Romeo and Juliet* and "The Extasie" with regard to the use of alchemy in these texts. According to her, the first and foremost alchemical feature of their union is the fact that it is immediately followed by death. Abraham speaks of the "vision of the united lovers dead on their macabre wedding bed" (ibid., 306). She explains the connection between the lovers' tomb and alchemy as follows: "The alchemical vessel as grave was clearly a place of death and putrefaction, but because the [Philosopher's] Stone was conceived there, it was also a place of conception, of renewal. In alchemical theory, conception could not take place unless there had first been a death . . . The lovers' deathly embrace inevitably led to renewal and regeneration. Their sacrificial dissolution facilitated a union at a higher level in the cycle of 'solve et coagula' " (303–4). The notion of sacrifice can be found in *Romeo and Juliet* when Capulet calls them "poor sacrifices" (V.iii.303). The way they are eventually seen by their families can be interpreted "as a dimensional tableau, a *tableau vivant*, of the alchemical emblem" (Abraham, "Lovers and the Tomb,"

307). What is more, the conflict between the families is resolved, and statues of gold are erected: "That which is base has been transmuted into gold" (ibid., 310). The monument with the statue of the two lovers now becomes a place of reconciliation and interaction between the two families (ibid., 309–10). For further alchemical readings see, for example, Angus Fletcher, *Time, Space, and Motion in the Age of Shakespeare* (Cambridge, MA: Harvard University Press, 2007), chap. 6; Gardner, "Argument"; Charles Mitchell, "Donne's 'The Extasie': Love's Sublime Knot," *SEL* 8 (1968): 91–101; Julia M. Walker, "John Donne's 'The Extasie' as an Alchemical Process," *ELN* 20, no. 1 (1982): 1–8.

43. See Abraham ("Lovers and the Tomb") and Walker ("John Donne's 'The Extasie'"). Here another parallel to Shakespeare's *Romeo and Juliet* can be drawn through the topic of the "reconciliation of foes," which is an "alchemical theme . . . closely related to the deathly union" (Abraham, "Lovers and the Tomb," 309). In Shakespeare's tragedy the reconciliation of the Capulet and the Montague families takes place after they find their children dead in the tomb and, in the wake of this, raise statues of pure gold (cf. Abraham, "Lovers and the Tomb," 309–10). Abraham points to a difference between Brooke's poem and Shakespeare's version of *Romeo and Juliet* here. In the poem, the lovers are removed from their tomb to be placed in a public monument (3018–20; cf. Abraham, "Lovers and the Tomb," 311); removal means that they are left in a tomb; "Shakespeare's version, however, foregrounds the alchemical implications, lifting the lovers into a symbolic golden state above their bodies in the grave, giving a glimpse of the possibility of true peace and harmony" (ibid.).

44. Robbins, *Complete Poems*, 175n27. The idea of "refinement" can also be found in "A Valediction: forbidding Mourning," 17–21: "But we by'a love, so much refin'd / . . . Inter-assured of the mind / . . . Our two soules therefore, which are one" (see Cirillo, "Fair Hermaphrodite," 91).

45. In *The Winter's Tale*, Shakespeare would make use of a similar image when he has Hermione—supposedly dead—transformed into a statue that then becomes alive in the end.

46. The verb "raise" is somewhat confusing—they are in fact recumbent statues; see Gibbons, *Romeo and Juliet*, 235. For examples of such statues, see, Nigel Llewellyn, *Funeral Monuments in Post-Reformation England* (Cambridge: Cambridge University Press, 2000).

47. The importance of the bodies has been noticed by Abraham, "Lovers and the Tomb"; Clements, *Poetry of Contemplation*; Stephen Farmer, "Donne's 'The Ecstasy,'" *Explicator* 51, no. 4 (1993): 205–7; Gardner, "Argument," 283; and Mitchell, "Donne's 'The Extasie.'"

48. Robbins reads the final lines—"Let him still mark us: he shall see / Small change when we're to bodies gone" (*Complete Poems*, 75–76)—as an allusion to the "spiritual body" in 1 Cor 15:44, which Donne also mentions in

one of his verse letters to Lady Bedford ("Honour is so sublime perfection," in Robbins): "You, for whose body God made better clay, / Or took soul's stuff such as shall late decay, / Or such as needs small change at the last day" (23–24). He interprets them as follows: "Here in *Ecstasy* the change will be small even if and when the lovers copulate, because they will do so for non-physical reasons" (181n76). One might also explain the lines differently: Through the purification of the soul, there is little difference between body and soul after the soul's return, which implies that yet another "interinanimation" takes place: the body profits from the soul's return there.

49. See, for example, Donne's *Holy Sonnet* "At the round earth's imagined corners": "you numberless infinities / Of souls, and to you scattered bodies go!" (3–4), in Gardner, "Argument," as well as his sermons on Job 19:26: "that soul after it hath once got loose by death . . . ambitiously seek[s] this scattered body . . . ; and yet, *Ego*, I, I the same body, and the same soul, shall be recompact again, and be identically, numerically, individually the same man. The same integrity of body and soul, and the same integrity in the Organs of my body, and in the faculties of my soul too" (*Sermons*, 3: 109–10); on Acts 2:36, preached at St. Paul's: "These two, Body, and Soule, cannot be separated for ever, which, whilst they are together, concurre in all that either of them do" (*Sermons*, 2: 14.358); and *Devotions*: "That therefore this *soule* now newly departed to thy *Kingdome*, may quickly returne to a joifull *reunion* to that *body* which it hath left, and that *wee* with it, may soone enjoy the full *consummation* of all, in *body* and *soule*, I humbly beg at thy hand" (96). See also *John Donne and the Theology of Language*, ed. P. G. Stanwood and Heather Ross Asals (Columbia: University of Missouri Press, 1986), 140; Gardner, Introduction, *Divine Poems*, xv–lv, xliv; and Ramie Targoff, "Facing Death," in *The Cambridge Companion to John Donne*, ed. Achsah Guibbory (Cambridge: Cambridge University Press, 2006), 217–31, here 221, 224–25.

50. See also Donne's poem "The Canonization":

Wee dye and rise the same, and prove
   Mysterious by this love.
. . . .
Wee can dye by it, if not live by love,
   And if unfit for tombes and hearse
Our legend bee, it will be fit for verse;
And if no peece of Chronicle wee prove,
   We'll build in sonnets pretty roomes.
               (26–32)

Here, likewise, the poem describes not only how the lovers imagine themselves to be united in death but also the poetological implications of this process.

51. Cf. Donne's "The Paradox":

> Once I lov'd and dyed; and am now become
>   Mine Epitaph and Tombe.
> Here dead men speake their last, and so do I;
>   Love-slaine, loe, here I lye.
>   (17–20)

52. John Russell Brown, with reference to Sonnet 81, points out that the "'monument' of the poem has no life in itself. It comes alive only when someone responds to its words and reads them": "Cold Monuments: Three Accounts of the Reception of Poetry," *Connotations* 9, no. 1 (1999–2000): 34–42, 38. Eynel Wardi qualifies this view: "[T]he lover does get to be resurrected from the monument-tomb that is the poem thanks to the transference of the poet's animating breath, or spirit": "Cold Monuments Animated: A Receptive Response to John Russell Brown," *Connotations* 9, no. 1 (1999–2000): 51–56, 54.

53. Cf. *Lucrece*, 679: "Entombs her outcry in her lips' sweet fold."

54. Stephen Booth, ed., *Shakespeare's Sonnets* (New Haven, CT: Yale University Press, 1977), 278, notices the pun but fails to get its point when he glosses the second meaning as "to hold another funeral for" and "to bury again," for, of course, the pun makes sense only if "rehearsing" is taken to evoke the notion of an "un-hearsing," a return to life. In Sonnet 71 Shakespeare uses the word in the same double sense, contrasting "rehearse" with the burial: "When I, perhaps, compounded am with clay, / Do not so much as my poor name rehearse."

55. "Epitaph on Himselfe," John Donne, *The Satires, Epigrams, and Verse Letters*, ed. Wesley Milgate (Oxford: Clarendon, 1967), 103: Subsequent reference is to this edition of these poems unless otherwise noted.

56. Cf. Milgate's note on fame as "discretion" (*Verse Letters*, 272).

57. See, for example, Barbara Kiefer Lewalski, "Exercising Power: The Countess of Bedford as Courtier, Patron, and Coterie Poet," in *Writing Women in Jacobean England* (Cambridge, MA: Harvard University Press, 1994), 95–123; Arthur F. Marotti, "The Social Context and Nature of Donne's Writing: Occasional Verse and Letters," in *The Cambridge Companion to Shakespeare's Poetry*, ed. Patrick Cheney (Cambridge: Cambridge University Press, 2007), 35–48; P. Thomson, "John Donne and the Countess of Bedford," *Modern Language Review* 44, no. 3 (1949): 329–40. Thomson reads Donne's "Epitaph" completely in the light of a begging letter to the Countess (336).

58. Cf. Milgate, *Verse Letters*, 272n.

59. See Rosemary Woolf, *The English Religious Lyric in the Middle Ages* (Oxford: Clarendon, 1968), 312–24, 401–4, here 402; also Scodel, *English Poetic Epitaph*, 30–31; Robbins's note to line 10 (*Complete Poems*, 719); and Inge Leimberg, "Annotating Baroque Poetry: George Herbert's 'A Dialogue-Antheme,'" *George Herbert Journal* 15, no. 1 (1991): 49–67, 59. Scott L. Newstok, *Quoting Death*

in *Early Modern England: The Poetics of Epitaphs beyond the Tomb* (Basingstoke: Palgrave Macmillan, 2009), points out that Donne, in "A Nocturnall upon S. Lucies Day" as well as in "The Paradox," presents a "particularly ingenious" variation of the dead speaker in having a living speaker present himself as his own epitaph (9, 12). To Newstok, the poems are examples of the epitaph's being "re-*cited* and re-*sited* (as in re-*situated*)" in new poetic contexts (4).

60. Robbins misunderstands the process when he glosses, "The soul is like glass in its invisibility" and contrasts the line with "A Litanie" (26), where "it is . . . the body which is glass, with the soul a candle within" (*Complete Poems*, 719). In fact, in "Epitaph on Himselfe" we read neither about the soul as glass nor about its invisibility but about its effect, which "dignifie[s] / Us to be glasse" (i.e., turns us [the whole being] into a more refined substance). In "A Litanie," it is not the soul that is a candle within "this glass lantern, flesh" but the flame of the Holy Ghost, which burns in the heart (19, 24).

61. Cf. George Herbert, "Church-Monuments": "this heap of dust; / To which the blast of deaths incessant motion, / Fed with the exhalation of our crimes, / Drives all at last" (3–6), and "The Answer": "As a young exhalation, newly waking, / Scorns his first bed of dirt, and means the sky" (8–9). On the process, see Christiane Lang-Graumann, *"Counting ev'ry grain": Das Motiv des Allerkleinsten in George Herberts "The Temple"* (Münster: Waxmann, 1997), 160–61. In contrast to the short-lived and evil exhalation of dust in the Herbert examples, Donne actually describes it as a process in which the dust of the body reaches heaven.

62. See, for example, Eluned Crawshaw, "Hermetic Elements in Donne's Poetic Vision," in *John Donne: Essays in Celebration*, ed. A. J. Smith (London: Methuen, 1972), 324–48: "Alchemy did not draw hard and fast lines between the material and the spiritual. The qualities ascribed to matter often had moral connotations, and . . . the physical process of purifying metals was thought to be paralleled by a spiritual one, the adept undergoing purgation simultaneously with the metals. Thus the significance of the work extended far beyond the confines of the crucible, and spiritual attainment might be expressed in terms of the material hierarchy" (325).

63. The inversion reverses one of Donne's other verse letters to the Countess, which begins with the line "You have refin'd mee."

64. Latin phrases from Simon Pelegromius, *Synonymorum Silva* (London, 1603), s.v. "Fame, Bruit, Rumor, or Report" (142). On the elusive and also rather puzzling history of "Epitaph on Himselfe" in the manuscripts and early editions see, for example, Milgate's note (*Verse Letters*, 271–72).

65. Anita Gilman Sherman, *Skepticism and Memory in Shakespeare and Donne* (New York: Palgrave Macmillan, 2007) regards the last couplet of the poem in which "the speaker's natural body becomes the poem itself" as an expression of Donne's skeptical attitude toward "sepulchral protocol" (158–59). While the ironical attitude toward conventions of the epitaph is palpable, we do not think

that the final lines necessarily subvert "the trope of the enduring poetic monument" because the speaker "amounts to no more than well-composed syllables" (159). The pun on "composed" rather stresses the function of poetry as a preparation for death.

66. See Scodel, *English Poetic Epitaph*, 114. When Scodel holds, however, that the speaker requests the reader to "mend himself or herself *in order* to mend the deceased" (115, our emphasis), we disagree, for there is nothing in the poem to indicate such an instrumentalization. Donne rather stresses the inevitable interconnectedness of the living and the dead.

67. Cf. George Herbert's "Deniall": "They and my minde may chime, / And mend my ryme" (29–30); "Love (II)": "All knees shall bow to thee; all wits shall rise, / And praise him who did make and mend our eies" (13–14). See also Donne's "A Litanie" XXVI:

> and invenom'd men
> Which well, if we starve, dine,
> When they doe most accuse us, may see then
> Us, to amendment, heare them; thee decline;
> That we may open our eares, Lord lock thine.
> (230–34)

On the complex interaction between speaker and listener and the notion of mending in Donne's "Litanie," see Matthias Bauer, "'A Litanie': John Donne and the Speaking Ear," in *The Senses' Festival: Inszenierungen der Sinne und der Sinnlichkeit in der Literatur und Kunst des Barock*, ed. Norbert Lennartz (Trier: Wissenschaftlicher Verlag Trier, 2005), 111–28.

68. *A Midsummer Night's Dream*, ed. Harold F. Brooks (London: Methuen, 1979), V.i.409–24.

69. See, for example, George Spencer Bower, *A Study of the Prologue and Epilogue in English Literature from Shakespeare to Dryden* (London: Kegan Paul, Trench, 1884), esp. chap. 1. For the liminal status of the epilogue between "fictional text" and "cultural reality," see also Robert Weimann, "Performing at the Frontiers of Representation: Epilogue and Post-Scriptural Future in Shakespeare's Plays," in *The Arts of Performance in Elizabethan and Early Stuart Drama*, ed. Murray Biggs et al. (Edinburgh: Edinburgh University Press, 1991), 96–112, 105. Interestingly, the epilogue is absent from Gerard Genette, *Paratexts: Thresholds of Interpretation*, trans. Jane E. Lewin (Cambridge: Cambridge University Press, 1997), and even the postclassical dramatic prologue is not accorded paratextual status by Genette "except sporadically" (166). This view is contradicted by the evidence of early modern drama.

70. Mt 9:24: "[T]he maid is not dead, but sleepeth"; cf. Lk 8:52 and Mk 5:39: "Why make ye this ado, and weep? the damsel is not dead, but sleepeth," which

is also telling with regard to the injunction "die to live" in Shakespeare's *Much Ado about Nothing*.

71. See also the Priest in Shakespeare's *Twelfth Night*: "Since when, my watch hath told me, toward my grave I have travelled but two hours": *Twelfth Night*, ed. Keir Elam (London: Thomson, 2008), V.i.151–52. On the idea of the stage as a place where the dead return to life, see Thomas Nashe's commentary on *1 Henry VI*: "How would it have joyed brave Talbot, the terror of the French, to think that after he had lain two hundred years in his tomb, he should triumph again on the stage and have his bones new embalmed with the tears of ten thousand spectators at least (at several times), who in the tragedian that represents his person imagine they behold him fresh bleeding!": *Pierce Pennilesse, His Supplication to the Divell* (1592), in *The Unfortunate Traveller and Other Works*, ed. J. B. Steane (Harmondsworth: Penguin, 1972), 113. Another example is provided by John Lyly in the "Prologue at the Court" of *Campaspe* (1584): "Appion, raising Homer from Hell, demanded only who was his father; and we, calling Alexander from his grave, seek only who was his love. Whatsoever we present we wish it may be thought the dancing of Agrippa his shadows" (10–13): *Campaspe*, ed. George K. Hunter, *Sappho and Phao*, ed. David Bevington (Manchester: Manchester University Press, 1991).

72. Sir Thomas Browne, *Religio Medici*, in *Religio Medici and Other Works*, ed. L. C. Martin (Oxford: Clarendon, 1964), II.12.

73. Cf. the chorus speaking the epilogue in Shakespeare's *Henry V* (l.1–14), referring both to the text produced by the author's "all-unable pen" (l.1) and to the stage: *King Henry V*, ed. T. W. Craik (London: Thomson, 1995).

74. Actors may leave the stage both to go inside (for example, a vault, as in Romeo's case) or to go outside. On the play on "in-" and "immortal," cf. William Shakespeare, *The Merchant of Venice*, ed. John Russell Brown (London: Methuen, 1955), V.i.63–65: "Such harmony is in immortal souls, / But whilst the muddy vesture of decay, / Doth grossly close it in, we cannot hear it," and Inge Leimberg's commentary in *"What May Words Say . . . ?" A Reading of* The Merchant of Venice (Madison: Fairleigh Dickinson University Press, 2011), 214.

75. *The Dramatic Works of Thomas Dekker*, ed. Fredson Bowers, 4 vols. (Cambridge: Cambridge University Press, 1953–61), 1: 197–98, lines 8–12.

76. Thomas Dekker, *Shoemakers' Holiday*, in *Renaissance Drama: An Anthology of Plays and Entertainments*, ed. Arthur F. Kinney (Malden, MA: Blackwell, 1999), 250.

77. *All's Well That Ends Well*, ed. G. K. Hunter (London: Methuen, 1959), 5–6.

78. For monumental Patience, see *Twelfth Night*, II.iv.114.

79. Paraphrases in annotated editions fail to do justice to the meaning of this complex expression: for example, "give satisfaction in return" (*The New Cambridge Shakespeare*, ed. R. A. Foakes [Cambridge: Cambridge University

Press, 1984]); "give satisfaction in return" (*Oxford World's Classics*, ed. Peter Holland [Oxford: Oxford University Press, 1995]); "make amends in return" (Brooks, *Midsummer Night's Dream*).

80. *OED*, "restore," *v.* 3., "To give back or recompense." In the sense of compensation, "restore" goes together with "loss," i.e., "to restore losses" means "To make amends for" (*v.* 7., and examples). In this perspective, "restore amends" is either tautological or actually implies a giving back of the improvement received.

81. *OED*, "amends," *n.* †4.a. "Improvement, betterment, amendment," with a quotation from Lyly's *Euphues*: "What I now giue you in thanks, I will then requite with amends." See also †4.b. "Improvement in health, recovery," with a reference to the Induction of Shakespeare's *Taming of the Shrew*, "Now Lord be thanked for my good amends."

82. The General Confession in the 1552 *Book of Common Prayer*, quoted in *OED*, "restore," *v.1* 5.b., where the verb is defined as "To place (mankind) again in a state of grace; to free (a person) from the effects of sin."

83. This request implies the notion that "There is nothing either good or bad, but thinking makes it so"; *Hamlet*, ed. Harold Jenkins (London: Routledge, 1993), II.ii.249–50.

84. See note 66, this chapter.

85. This is a point most expressly, perhaps, made by Donne in his first sermon on 1 Cor. 15:29 in 1626, *Sermons*, 7: 94–117.

86. Dylan Thomas, *Under Milk Wood: A Play for Voices* (London: Dent, 1974), 82.

87. See Leimberg, *Heilig öffentlich Geheimnis*, 167–68.

88. William Shakespeare, *The Tempest*, ed. Virginia Mason Vaughan and Alden T. Vaughan (London: Thomson, 1999), V.i.311–12.

89. See, for example, David N. Beauregard, "New Light on Shakespeare's Catholicism: Prospero's Epilogue in *The Tempest*," *Renascence: Essays on Values in Literature* 49 (1997): 158–74; also Stephen Greenblatt, *Hamlet in Purgatory* (Princeton, NJ: Princeton University Press, 2001), 261.

2. "Nothing like the Sun": Transcending Time and Change in Donne's Love Lyrics and Shakespeare's Plays / Catherine Gimelli Martin

1. Kathryn R. Kremen, *The Imagination of the Resurrection* (Lewisburg, PA: Bucknell University Press, 1972), 92–93.

2. See Stanley Cavell, *The Claim of Reason: Wittgenstein, Skepticism, Morality, and Tragedy* (Oxford: Oxford University Press, 1979), 494–95. Cavell explores Montaigne's essay, "On some verses of Virgil," where men are indicted for ignoring the complexity of female desire, demanding absolute female purity and

exclusivity, and their own inability to accept the inevitability of doubt, thus making monsters of themselves and deadly idols of their wives.

3. This and all subsequent quotations from Shakespeare are taken from *The Complete Pelican Shakespeare*, ed. Stephen Orgel and A. R. Braunmuller (Harmondsworth: Penguin, 1999). On this reading see, for instance, Carol Thomas Neely, "Women and Men in *Othello*," in *Shakespeare's Middle Tragedies: A Collection of Critical Essays*, ed. David Young (Englewood Cliffs, NJ: Prentice Hall, 1993), 91–116, especially 98. Neely's article—also a chapter in her monograph, *Broken Nuptials in Shakespeare's Plays* (New Haven, CT: Yale University Press, 1985), 105–35—fully summarizes previous *Othello* criticism and offers a now standard feminist alternative.

4. All references to Donne's lyrics are taken from *John Donne: The Complete English Poems*, ed. C. A. Patrides (New York: Knopf, 1985).

5. Robert Ellrodt is cited in *The Variorum Edition of the Poetry of John Donne*, ed. Gary Stringer (Bloomington: Indiana University Press, 2000), 2: 949.

6. *Variorum Edition*, 2: 949–53. Ellrodt observes that the poem's "presentiment of true love is not surprising in the poetry of a man who will marry Ann More" (952) secretly and in opposition to her father's wishes, which cost Donne his secretarial position, brief imprisonment, and considerable scandal and poverty. The most recent critic to read the elegy's conclusion nonironically is Achsah Guibbory (951); the other two are Bullough (950) and Sencourt (949).

7. *Variorum Edition*, 2: 397.

8. The minute hand on the clock first appeared in 1577, an invention of Jost Burgi, which was gradually perfected in the following century. Donne's use of the clock image in "A Lecture" is therefore conjectural (would he have seen this invention?), but the idea of noon as a point where opposing or paired physical forces meet is much older and more traditional. In the Bible, it is where Joshua makes the sun and moon stand still "in the midst of heaven" for an entire day (Joshua 10:13).

9. Jonathan Dollimore, *Death, Desire, and Loss in Western Culture* (New York: Routledge, 1998). The book's general position is that the cycle of longing and fulfillment turns passion into a simulacrum of eternal becoming, not being, because humankind's "pervasive yearning for stasis" is inevitably overcome by the "misery of mutability" (74). Dollimore then adds, "The most cosmic, most culturally necessary of all binary oppositions, life versus death, is thus subjected to collapse: the absolutely different is inseparable from what it is not, cannot be. The absolutely other is found to inhere within the self-same as nothing less than the dynamic of dissolution" (76). Dollimore has his point, but it does not seem to have prevented great poets from imagining a "blessed" end to mutability, as both Donne and Spenser most clearly do.

10. Marjorie Nicolson, *The Breaking of the Circle*, rev. ed. (New York: Columbia University Press, 1962), 47, 50, 77–80, 106.

11. Besides Cavell's reading (see note 2, this chapter), particularly perceptive treatments of this theme can be found in Katherine S. Stockholder, "Egregiously an Ass: Chance and Accident in *Othello*," *SEL* 13, no. 2 (1973): 256–72, and Kenneth Gross, "Slander and Skepticism in *Othello*," *ELH* 56, no. 4 (1989): 819–52.

12. On Donne's erotic Platonism, an underlying theme of this essay, see my article "The Erotology of Donne's 'Extasie' and the Secret History of Voluptuous Rationalism," *Studies in English Literature* 44, no. 1 (2004): 121–47.

13. Stanley Cavell, "The Avoidance of Love: A Reading of *King Lear*," in *Disowning Knowledge in Seven Plays of Shakespeare* (Cambridge: Cambridge University Press, 1987), 39–124.

14. These friends may be more "right" than they realize, given Beatrice's otherwise inexplicable refusal of Don Pedro's marriage offer.

15. Many of Donne's serious love lyrics seem to most readers to reflect on his actual marriage to Ann, particularly "A Valediction Forbidding Mourning" and "The Canonization," the former of which condoles their frequent separations; the latter, their ruined fortunes once their marriage became public. It seems unlikely that any of Shakespeare's sonnets concern his own marriage, although there are some possible, usually comic exceptions to the rule—if there is any rule in such unattributable lyrics.

16. No single person in *Othello* gets all the facts right: Iago is partly self-deluded, and Othello and Emilia belatedly piece together his plot but never his motives, which remain unknown to them.

17. See Stanley Fish, "Masculine Persuasive Force: Donne and Verbal Power," in *Soliciting Interpretation: Literary Theory and Seventeenth-Century English Poetry*, ed. Elizabeth D. Harvey and Katharine Eisaman Maus (Chicago: University of Chicago Press, 1990), 223–52.

18. It is not irrelevant that Othello's success as a general has depended on making decisive decisions, often without prior warning; see C. F. Burgess, "Othello's Occupation," *Shakespeare Quarterly* 26, no. 2 (1975): 208–13.

19. This cynicism should remind us both of Benedick's initial but mistaken attitude and of the speaker of Donne's "Song," "Goe and catch a falling star," since both male speakers declare all fair women by definition doomed to inconstancy, "beautiful fidelity" being something of an oxymoron for both.

20. This reading appears in the 1622 quarto edition rather than in the First Folio; it is used in the *Arden Shakespeare*, ed. M. R. Ridley (Cambridge, MA.: Harvard University Press, 1958).

21. G. Wilson Knight, *The Wheel of Fire* (1930; rpt. London: Oxford University Press, 1946), 107–18.

22. See Neely, "Women and Men in *Othello*," 98–99. Neely also perceptively traces Desdemona's power over all of the play's men (and most of the women) to her entire lack of any "sense of class, race, rank, and hierarchy" shared by the rest; "neither jealous nor envious nor suspicious," much less possessive (106), she

is the perfect lady and wife for a great general, as Othello himself says: "She might lie by an emperor's side and command him tasks" (IV.i.181–82).

23. Heather Dubrow, "Reconfiguring Figuring: John Donne as Narrative Poet," in *Go Figure: Energies, Forms, and Institutions in the Early Modern World*, ed. Judith H. Anderson and Joan Pong Linton (New York: Fordham University Press, 2011), 58–72, cited 66–67, 67–68; on multiple voices, see 70. Dubrow thus takes issue with Stanley Fish's view (63); for Fish's essay, see note 17, this chapter.

24. Ben Saunders, *Desiring Donne: Fantasy, Sexuality, Interpretation* (Cambridge, MA: Harvard University Press, 2006), 114, 159, 169; especially on gender, see 113–46.

25. For a fuller exploration of this strategy in Donne's elegies and minor lyrics, see my essay, "Pygmalion's Progress in the Garden of Love, or the Wit's Work Is Never Donne," in *The Wit of Seventeenth-Century Poetry*, ed. Claude J. Summers and Ted-Larry Pebworth (Columbia: University of Missouri Press, 1995), 78–100. The same essay makes a case for Donne's inherent dialogicalism.

3. "None Do Slacken, None Can Die": Die *Puns and Embodied Time in Donne and Shakespeare / Jennifer Pacenza*

1. Quotations of Donne's poetry are from *The Complete English Poems*, ed. A. J. Smith (London: Penguin, 1996).

2. Ramie Targoff, *John Donne, Body and Soul* (Chicago: University of Chicago Press, 2008), 49.

3. These word counts are based on an approximated character count, using html versions of the works. John Donne's *Songs and Sonnets* were found at http://www.luminarium.org/editions/songsandsonnets.htm and Shakespeare's sonnets were found at http://www.gutenberg.org/cache/epub/1041/pg1041.html.

4. Several sources discuss the physiological relationship between orgasm and death, including Michel Foucault's *The History of Sexuality*, vol. 2: *The Use of Pleasure* (New York: Vintage, 1990), 133–36, and Jonathan Margolis's *O: The Intimate History of the Orgasm* (New York: Grove, 2005), 72–76.

5. In *O*, Margolis argues that orgasm is just biology and that the orgasmic drive motivates individual and cultural actions. As Thomas Laqueur makes very clear in his reaction, divorcing orgasm from the emotional and intellectual pleasures that accompany it is not only impossible but also ridiculous: Laqueur, "Come Again? A History of Orgasm Completely Misses the Point," *Slate Magazine* (Nov. 15, 2004), http://www.slate.com/id/2109435/, par. 10.

6. Brian Massumi, *Parables for the Virtual: Movement, Affect, Sensation* (Durham: Duke University Press, 2002), 29–33.

7. In this paragraph, I am distilling Serres's theories as stipulated in two sources: *Genesis*, trans. Geneviève James and James Nielson (Ann Arbor:

University of Michigan Press, 1995), 71–74, and *Conversations on Science, Culture, and Time*, with Bruno Latour and trans. Roxanne Lapidus (Ann Arbor: University of Michigan Press, 1995), which contains the least ambiguous discussion of exploring the hyphen in Ju-Piter (149–66). However, the majority of Serres's works revolve around the desire to break down the binaries of traditional scientific ontology and literary/linguistic dualism.

8. For a more complete and comprehensible discussion of percolating time, see Serres and Latour's *Conversations on Science*, 57–59.

9. "Morrow," *n* 1 and 2, *Oxford English Dictionary*, Additions Series (Oxford: Oxford University Press, 1997), www.oed.com, accessed Apr. 22, 2010.

10. Anne D. Ferry, *All in War with Time: Love Poetry of Shakespeare, Donne, Jonson, and Marvell* (Cambridge, MA: Harvard University Press, 1975), 78.

11. R. E. Pritchard makes these arguments through historical and literary contextualization. He relates tantric love to the revolutionary group called the "Family of Love," which believed sex was a way to free humans from both religious and political tyranny. Plato's spheroid humans, beings made up of two gendered individuals, come from *The Symposium*. See "Dying in Donne's 'The Good Morrow,'" *Essays in Criticism* 35, no. 3 (July 1985): 215–22.

12. William Shakespeare, *Antony and Cleopatra*, ed. John Wilders (London: Thomson Learning, 2006), I.i.15.

13. "All," adj. 6, *Oxford English Dictionary*, Additions Series (Oxford: Oxford University Press, 1997), www.oed.com, accessed Apr. 22, 2010.

14. For all quotes and references from the sonnets, I have used Stephen Booth's *Shakespeare's Sonnets* (New Haven, CT: Yale University Press, 2000).

15. Bruce R. Smith, *Homosexual Desire in Shakespeare's England: A Cultural Poetics* (Chicago: University of Chicago Press, 1991) (e.g., 52, 53, 87, 112, 291).

16. Helen Vendler, *The Art of Shakespeare's Sonnets* (Cambridge, MA: Harvard University Press, 1997), 63.

17. Stanley Wells, *Looking for Sex in Shakespeare* (Cambridge: Cambridge University Press, 2004), 22.

18. For an informed and thorough source regarding the history of masturbation, see Thomas Laqueur's *Solitary Sex: A Cultural History of Masturbation* (Now York: Zone, 2004). Laqueur argues that, during the Renaissance, masturbation did not carry the heavy social stigma it does today. Solitary sex did not become masturbation, according to Laqueur, until the eighteenth century and the publication of *Onania: or, The Heinous Sin of Self Pollution* (approx. 1712), by John Marten. Prior to the publication of *Onania*, Laqueur argues, numerous classical, medieval, and Renaissance texts mention the act of masturbation but never use that term. According to Laqueur, Renaissance discourse on masturbation varied, emphasizing the ambivalent attitude toward solitary sex at the time. In two competing tales of Diogenes, masturbation is depicted as taboo, shameful, and contagious (Laqueur instances John Florio's translation of Michel de Montaigne's

An Apology of Raymond Sebond, 1603) and necessary, natural, and medicinal (Laqueur instances Galen's *De Locis Affectis*, or *On the Affected Parts*), 124–83.

19. See page 62, this chapter, for the discussion of this pun and its relationship to early modern conceptualizations of orgasm, reproduction, and creative production.

20. Philip Sidney, *Astrophil and Stella*, in *Sir Philip Sidney: The Major Works*, ed. Katherine Duncan Jones (Oxford: Oxford University Press, 2002).

21. Galen, *De Usu Partium Corporis Humani*, vols. 1–2, ed. Georg Helmreich and trans. Margaret Talmadge May (Ithaca, NY: Cornell University Press, 1968), 57, 632–33.

22. William Shakespeare, *Twelfth Night*, in *The Norton Shakespeare*, based on the Oxford edition, ed. Steven Greenblatt et al. (New York: Norton, 1997), I.v.258.

23. John 1:1, 1:14 (King James Version).

4. Donne, Shakespeare, and the Interrogative Conscience / Mary Blackstone and Jeanne Shami

1. Patrick Collinson, "The English Reformation in the Mid-Elizabethan Period," in *The Oxford Handbook of John Donne*, ed. Jeanne Shami, Dennis Flynn, and M. Thomas Hester (Oxford: Oxford University Press, 2011), 374.

2. See, for instance, Patrick Collinson, "William Shakespeare's Religious Inheritance and Environment," in *Elizabethan Essays* (London: Hambledon, 1994), 219–52; E. A. J. Honigmann, *Shakespeare: The Lost Years*, rev. ed. (Manchester: Manchester University Press, 1999); *Region, Religion and Patronage: Lancastrian Shakespeare*, ed. Richard Dutton, Alison Findlay, and Richard Wilson (Manchester: Manchester University Press, 2003); Collinson, "English Reformation," 377–78, 381–82; Dennis Flynn, "Donne's Family Background, Birth, and Early Years," in *Oxford Handbook of John Donne*, 383–94; Dennis Flynn, "Donne's Education," in *Oxford Handbook of John Donne*, 408–23.

3. On the performative dimension of Donne's preaching, see Gary Kuchar, "Ecstatic Donne: Conscience, Sin, and Surprise in the Sermons and the Mitcham Letters," *Criticism* 50, no. 4 (2008): 4. The use of the term "performative" derives from the work of John L. Austin, who initially coined the word in the context of linguistic studies of speech acts (*How to Do Things with Words* [Oxford: Clarendon, 1963], 6). Later scholars, such as Richard Schechner and Erika Fischer-Lichte, in the fields of performance theory and performance studies have extended the term to apply to a wide range of physical as well as speech acts performed for observers.

4. The intersections between pulpit and theater have been variously considered in Arnold Hunt, *The Art of Hearing: English Preachers and Their Audiences, 1590–1640* (Cambridge: Cambridge University Press, 2010); Huston Diehl, *Staging Reform, Reforming the Stage: Protestantism and Popular Theater in Early Modern England*

(Ithaca, NY: Cornell University Press, 1997); Martha Tuck Rozett, *The Doctrine of Election and the Emergence of Elizabethan Tragedy* (Princeton, NJ: Princeton University Press, 1984); Bryan Crockett, *The Play of Paradox: Stage and Sermon in Renaissance England* (Philadelphia: University of Pennsylvania Press, 1995); Jeremy Knapp, *Shakespeare's Tribe* (Chicago: University of Chicago Press, 1992); Margret Fetzer, *John Donne's Performances* (Manchester: Manchester University Press, 2010); Peter Lake, with Michael Questier, *The Antichrist's Lewd Hat: Protestants, Papists and Players in Post-Reformation England* (New Haven, CT: Yale University Press, 2002).

5. John Donne, *The Sermons of John Donne*, ed. George R. Potter and Evelyn M. Simpson, 10 vols. (Berkeley: University of California Press, 1959–62). Subsequent references to the sermons are indicated by volume and page number. William Shakespeare, *King Henry V*, ed. John H. Walter (London: Methuen, 1979). All further references to this play are to the text of this edition.

6. John Chamberlain to Dudley Carleton, *The Letters of John Chamberlain*, ed. Norman Egbert McClure, 2 vols. (Philadelphia: American Philosophical Society, 1939), 2.142 and n3.

7. See, for example, J. Dover Wilson, *The Fortunes of Falstaff* (Cambridge: Cambridge University Press, 1943); David M. Bevington, *From Mankind to Marlowe* (Cambridge, MA: Harvard University Press, 1962); Alan C. Dessen, *Shakespeare and the Late Moral Plays* (Lincoln: University of Nebraska Press, 1986); and Jane K. Brown, *The Persistence of Allegory: Drama and Neoclassicism from Shakespeare to Wagner* (Philadelphia: University of Pennsylvania Press, 2007).

8. Laurence Olivier (director), *Henry V*, 1944; A. P. Rossiter, "Ambivalence: The Dialectic of the Histories," in *Talking of Shakespeare*, ed. John Garrett (London: Hodder and Stoughton, 1954), 149–71, esp. 165; Megan Wilkinson, "Henry V: The Use of History as Propaganda," MA thesis, California State University–Dominguez Hills, 1999; Michael Delahoyde, public.wsu.edu/~delahoyd/shakespeare/henryV.1.html.

9. Peter McCullough, *Sermons at Court: Politics and Religion in Elizabethan and Jacobean Preaching* (Cambridge: Cambridge University Press, 1998). John Astington, review of *Sermons at Court*, *Shakespeare Studies* 28 (2000): 351.

10. E. K. Chambers, *William Shakespeare*, 2 vols. (Oxford: Clarendon, 1930), 2.342.

11. John Astington, *English Court Theatre, 1558–1642* (Cambridge: Cambridge University Press, 1999), esp. 75–124, 161–88.

12. Jeanne Shami, "Donne on Discretion," *ELH* 47 (1980): 50; Kuchar ("Ecstatic Donne") discusses the "nearness effect" in terms of the theatricality of Donne's externalization of conscience in the sermons.

13. The word "distance" is used here simply as the opposite end of a continuum defined by Donne's concept of nearness. It is not used in the more specialized

and conventional sense employed by theater scholars like Daphne Ben Chaim to describe the relative degree to which audiences are aware of or oblivious to the differences between the way they engage in life experiences and the way they are engaging in a theatrical performance. Although issues surrounding this other dichotomy are relevant to this discussion, they are discussed later in the context of metatheatrical and metahomiletic dimensions of the texts. See Daphna Ben Chaim, *Distance in the Theatre: The Aesthetics of Audience Response*, Theatre and Dramatic Studies, no. 17 (Ann Arbor: UMI Research Press, 1981).

14. Herbert Blau, *The Audience* (Baltimore: Johns Hopkins University Press, 1990), 218; Roger Scruton, *Art and Imagination: A Study in the Philosophy of Mind* (London: Methuen, 1974), 130.

15. Citation of Shakespeare's Chorus: Prologue, 18. For the court audience, there may well have been an alternative prologue as references to "this wooden O" and "this unworthy scaffold" would not have set the stage very well at Whitehall. Certainly they could not have lamented the lack of "monarchs to behold the swelling scene" (Prologue, 4, 10, 13).

16. This blurring of events as the court and the king moved from one performative event to the other clearly had an impact on the performance dynamics of individual performances like the sermons, masques, and plays. More exploration of these interconnections might be useful in our understanding of the performance dynamics and response to individual sermons or plays, but a full appreciation of their effect would be impossible simply on the basis of extant texts.

17. The relevant letters and documents are gathered in Potter and Simpson, *Sermons of John Donne*, 7.38–42.

18. Erika Fischer-Lichte, *The Transformative Power of Performance: A New Aesthetics*, trans. Saskya Iris Jain (London: Routledge, 2008), 33; italics in the original.

19. Peter Brook, *The Empty Space* (New York: Discus-Avon, 1968), 122.

20. Bruce McConachie, *Engaging Audiences: A Cognitive Approach to Spectating in the Theatre*, Cognitive Studies in Literature and Performance (New York: Palgrave Macmillan, 2008), 3, 18, 56, 63, 66, 18–19.

21. III.Chorus, 35; Prologue, 29; III.Chorus, 1.

22. For Donne's sermons as performances of conversion, see Jeanne Shami, *John Donne and Conformity in Crisis in the Late Jacobean Pulpit* (Cambridge: Brewer, 2003), 20, 23, 24, 259, 273, 274; Jeanne Shami, "The Sermon," in *Oxford Handbook of John Donne*, 319, 332.

23. Martin Seel, "Inszenieren als Erscheinenlassen: Thesen ueber die Reichweite eines Begriffs," in *Aesthetik der Inszenierung*, ed. J. Fruechtl and J. Zimmermann (Frankfurt am Main: Suhrkamp, 2001), 53, as cited in translation in Fischer-Lichte, *Transformative Power*, 96.

24. Largely because of the need to limit the scope of this essay we have not considered an important distinction between Shakespeare and Donne. Donne's

performative mode enabled him to construct a special "character"—a persona or mask. Understanding the connection between this persona and his shifting use of "I" would clearly contribute to our understanding of how he sought to affect audience involvement.

25. S. L. Bethell, *Shakespeare and the Popular Dramatic Tradition* (Westminster: King and Staples, 1944), 105–6.

26. Chaim, *Distance in the Theatre*, 77; Chaim's assumptions are based on the perception that audiences are aware of theater and real life as distinct entities and that a dominant awareness of the real-life context "distances" the audience from the theatrical performance. Thanks to the work of cognitive scientists, however, we now know that individuals perceive performers and what they perform as inextricable.

27. Bridget Escolme, *Talking to the Audience: Shakespeare, Performance, Self* (New York: Routledge, 2005), 16.

28. The concept of accidental and integral audiences is derived from Richard Schechner, *Performance Theory* (London: Routledge, 1988), 218–22.

29. Catherine Belsey, *Critical Practice* (London: Methuen, 1980), 91.

30. Steve Neale, "Propaganda," *Screen* 18, no. 3 (1977): 9–40.

31. Marvin Carlson, "Audiences and the Reading of Performance," *Interpreting the Theatrical Past: Essays in the Historiography of Performance*, ed. Thomas Postlewait and Bruce A. McConachie (Iowa City: Iowa City Press, 1991), 84.

32. Catherine Belsey, *The Subject of Tragedy: Identity and Difference in Renaissance Drama* (London: Routledge, 1985), 33.

33. John Donne, "The First Anniversary, an Anatomie of the World," in *The Variorum Edition of the Poetry of John Donne*, ed. Gary A. Stringer (Bloomington: Indiana University Press, 1995), 6.12, line 213; Patrick Collinson, "William Shakespeare's Religious Inheritance and Environment," in *Elizabethan Essays* (London: Hambledon, 1994), 219.

34. Phrase cited from Hans Robert Jauss, *Toward an Aesthetic of Reception*, trans. Timothy Bahti (Minneapolis: University of Minnesota Press, 1982), 22.

35. Daniel Lerner, *The Passing of Traditional Society* (New York: Free Press, 1964), 72.

36. Anthony D. Smith, *Theories of Nationalism* (London: Duckworth, 1971), 90, 92–93.

5. Mapping the Celestial in Shakespeare's Tempest and the Writings of John Donne / Douglas Trevor

1. William Empson, "Donne the Space Man," *Kenyon Review* 19 (1957); rpt. in *William Empson: Essays on Renaissance Literature*, ed. John Haffenden, 2 vols. (1993; Cambridge: Cambridge University Press, 1995), 1:78–128, here 81. I

would like to thank my colleague Valerie Traub and the editors of this volume for their generous feedback on this essay.

2. David Cressy, "Early Modern Space Travel and the English Man in the Moon," *American Historical Review* 111, no. 4 (2006): 961–82, here 967, 964.

3. In "Donne the Space Man" (82–83), Empson states that Donne became aware of the idea of the inhabitation of other planets solely from Bruno's work. In an earlier essay, Empson also mentions Copernicus, Kepler, and Galileo as sources for Donne's knowledge of the heavens. See "Donne and the Rhetorical Tradition," *Kenyon Review* 11 (1949); rpt. in *William Empson: Essays on Renaissance Literature*, 1: 63–77. In both essays, Empson fails to consider the possible influence of Montaigne on Donne's consideration of interstellar inhabitation.

4. Hilary Gatti, *Essays on Giordano Bruno* (Princeton, NJ: Princeton University Press, 2011), 23.

5. John Milton, *Paradise Lost*, ed. David Scott Kastan (Indianapolis: Hackett, 2005). Milton mentions Galileo's study of the moon's surface admiringly early in the poem (see I.287–91). Raphael cautions Adam against interstellar inquiry in VIII.167–73.

6. On Bruno's possible influence on Spenser, see Douglas Brooks-Davies, "Giordano Bruno," in *The Spenser Encyclopedia*, ed. A. C. Hamilton (1990; rpt. Toronto: University of Toronto Press, 1997), 118–19. On Donne's knowledge of Bruno and the "New Science" in general see Angus Fletcher, *Time, Space, and Motion in the Age of Shakespeare* (Cambridge, MA: Harvard University Press, 2007), 126.

7. Edmund Spenser, *The Faerie Queene*, ed. A. C. Hamilton (London: Longman, 1977), Book II, Proem, stanza 3, lines 4–8.

8. John Lyly, *Endymion, the Man in the Moon*, in *The Plays of John Lyly*, ed. Carter A. Daniel (London: Associated University Presses, 1988), 147–94, here 149. Henry Percy, the ninth Earl of Northumberland, possessed many of Bruno's publications, including *Eroici Furori* and *De Specierum Scrutinio*. Along with Hill, Donne and Thomas Hariot were known to have frequented Percy's residence, Sion House. See Daniel Massa, "Giordano Bruno's Ideas in Seventeenth-Century England," *Journal of the History of Ideas* 38, no. 2 (1977): 227–42. Hariot, best known to Shakespeare scholars as the author of *A Briefe and True Report of the New Found Land of Virginia* (1588), was also a noted astronomer and mathematician, as well as the first person to examine the moon through a telescope. See Fletcher, *Time, Space and Motion*, 117.

9. On the history of celestial maps and globes see Peter Whitfield, *The Mapping of the Heavens* (London: British Library, 1995).

10. See, for example, George Coffin Taylor, *Shakespeare's Debt to Montaigne* (Cambridge, MA: Harvard University Press, 1925), 4.

11. Adam Max Cohen, *Shakespeare and Technology: Dramatizing Early Modern Technological Revolutions* (New York: Palgrave Macmillan, 2006), 46.

12. See Stephen Orgel, ed., Introduction to William Shakespeare's *The Tempest* (Oxford: Clarendon, 1987), 1–87, here 20–23. See also Peter Hulme and William H. Sherman, Introduction to *The Tempest and Its Travels*, ed. Hulme and Sherman (Philadelphia: University of Pennsylvania Press, 2000), 3–11, here 8.

13. David Turnbull, "Cartography and Science in Early Modern Europe: Mapping the Construction of Knowledge Spaces," *Imago Mundi* 48 (1996): 5–24, here 7.

14. See D. J. Warner, "The First Celestial Globe of Willem Janszoon Blaeu," *Imago Mundi* 25 (1971): 29–38, here 29.

15. See John Donne, *Ignatius His Conclave*, in *The Complete Poetry and Selected Prose of John Donne*, ed. Charles M. Coffin (1952; rpt. New York: Modern Library, 1994), 317–57, here 319, 324. All subsequent references to Donne's prose, unless otherwise noted, are to this edition.

16. Warner, "First Celestial Globe of Willem Janszoon Blaeu," 34.

17. *The Tempest*, ed. Virginia Mason Vaughan and Alden T. Vaughan (London: Nelson, 1999), I.ii.283–84. All references to the text of the play are to this edition.

18. See Vaughan and Vaughan, Introduction to *The Tempest*, 1–138, here 28. Orgel qualifies the Neoplatonic schema in his edition of the play. See his Introduction to *The Tempest*, 22–23.

19. See Vaughan and Vaughan, *The Tempest*, 213n105; Orgel, *The Tempest*, 148n102.

20. John Wilkins, *A Discourse concerning a New World & Another Planet in 2 Bookes* (London: Norton and Hearne, 1640), 111.

21. Julie Crawford explores the religious implications of this *mooncalf*, also referred to in the period as the *monk calf*, in *Marvelous Protestantism: Monstrous Births in Post-Reformation England* (Baltimore: Johns Hopkins University Press, 2005), 27–34.

22. Preserved Smith, "The Mooncalf," *Modern Philology* 11, no. 3 (1914): 355–61, here 355, 356.

23. See Lorraine Daston and Katharine Park, *Wonders and the Order of Nature, 1150–1750* (New York: Zone, 1998), 187–88.

24. See Stephen Orgel, ed., *Ben Jonson: The Complete Masques* (New Haven, CT: Yale University Press, 1969), 292–305, here 300. In *Bartholomew Fair* (1614), *mooncalf* is explicitly associated with alcohol. Like Jonson, Shakespeare is inclined, well before *The Tempest*, to link the moon with foolish characters and irrational behavior. Sometimes these connections simply draw on conventional, pre-Copernican notions of the moon. But sometimes the valences of

these references are complicated by the astronomical discoveries and theories that were proposed in this period. To give but one example of such complexity outside of *The Tempest*, we may consider a brief moment in the *Pyramus and Thisbe* play embedded in *A Midsummer Night's Dream*. Robin Starveling, who plays "the man i' the moon," betrays no scientific sophistication in his representation of this iconic figure: *A Midsummer Night's Dream*, ed. Gail Kern Paster and Skiles Howard (Boston: Bedford/St. Martin's, 1999), V.i.242. But Bottom's veneration of the moon, performed in the personage of Pyramus ("Sweet Moon, I thank thee for thy sunny beams; / I thank thee, Moon, for shining now so bright"), *is* inflected by the language of cosmological inquiry, for early modern astronomers were not in agreement as to whether the moon reflected the sun's beams and, if it did, how this reflection was possible (V.i.254–55). In 1610, with the publication of Galileo's *Siderius Nuncius*, Bottom's praise of the moon might have sounded—to some ears—less foolish than it did in the mid-1590s. Or it might even have disconcerted some audience members. Consider a letter Donne's close friend Henry Wotton wrote to the Earl of Salisbury in 1610 referring to Galileo's work: "[T]he Mathematical Professor at Padua, who by the help of an optical instrument . . . hath discovered four new planets rolling about the sphere of Jupiter, besides many other unknown and lastly, that the moon is not spherical but endued with many prominences, and, which is of all the strangest, illuminated with the solar light by reflection from the body of the earth, as he seemeth to say. So as upon the whole subject he [Galileo] hath first overthrown all former astronomy . . . [f]or the virtue of these new planets must needs vary the judicial part, and why may there not be yet more?" As quoted by John Carey, in *John Donne: Life, Mind and Art* (1981; rpt. London: Faber and Faber, 1990), 237. On Shakespeare's apparent familiarity with Galileo, see John Pitcher, ed., Introduction to *Cymbeline* (London: Penguin, 2005), lxxii–lxxvii. I am indebted to Valerie Wayne for drawing my attention to this reference.

25. See Vaughan and Vaughan, *The Tempest*, 140.

26. See Robert Burton, *The Anatomy of Melancholy*, ed. Thomas C. Faulkner, Nicolas K. Kiessling, and Rhonda Blair, 3 vols. (Oxford: Clarendon, 1997), 1: 199–203 (part 1, sect. 2, memb. 1, subs. 4).

27. Michel de Montaigne, *The Essayes of Montaigne*, trans. John Florio (1603; rpt. New York: Modern Library, 1938), 469–70. All English translations of Montaigne are from Florio's edition.

28. Anne Lake Prescott, "Menippean Donne," in *The Oxford Handbook of John Donne*, ed. Jeanne Shami, Dennis Flynn, and M. Thomas Hester (Oxford: Oxford University Press, 2011), 158–79, here 171.

29. "My Emperie, / How blest am I in this discovering thee! / To enter in these bonds, is to be free; / Then where my hand is set, my seal shall be." John

Donne, "Elegie XIX: To His Mistress Going to Bed," lines 29–32. All references to Donne's poetry are to *The Complete English Poems of John Donne*, ed. C. A. Patrides (London: Dent, 1985).

30. Anita Gilman Sherman, *Skepticism and Memory in Shakespeare and Donne* (New York: Palgrave Macmillan, 2007), 92.

31. Carey argues, on the contrary, that "Montaigne's case is Pyrrho's: our reason is worthless because it functions only on sense data, and we have no chance of checking these against reality" (*John Donne*, 220). But Montaigne's deep investment in learning undercuts too close an association with Pyrrhonism, as does Donne's. Reason is never forwarded as worthless by either writer, just as endlessly—and intriguingly—provisional. On the generative nature of Donnean skepticism, see Richard Strier, *Resistant Structures: Particularity, Radicalism, and Renaissance Texts* (1995; rpt. Berkeley: University of California Press, 1997), 139–64.

32. Tom Conley, *The Self-Made Map: Cartographic Writing in Early Modern France* (Minneapolis: University of Minnesota Press, 1996), 6.

33. John Klause, "The Montaigneity of Donne's *Metempsychosis*," in *Renaissance Genres: Essays on Theory, History, and Interpretation*, ed. Barbara Kiefer Lewalski (Cambridge, MA: Harvard University Press, 1986), 418–43. While *Metempsychosis* is dated 1601, it does not appear in print until the 1633 *Poems*.

34. See, for example, Donald K. Anderson Jr., "Donne's 'Hymne to God my God, in my Sicknesse' and the T-in-O Maps," *South Atlantic Quarterly* 71, no. 4 (1972): 465–72; Robert L. Sharp, "Donne's 'Good-Morrow' and Cordiform Maps," *Modern Language Notes* 69, no. 7 (1954): 493–95; Jeanne Shami, "John Donne: Geography as Metaphor," in *Geography and Literature: A Meeting of the Disciplines*, ed. William E. Mallory and Paul Simpson Housley (Syracuse: Syracuse University Press, 1987), 161–67; and Noam Flinker, "John Donne and the 'Anthropomorphic Map' Tradition," *Applied Semiotics* 3, no. 8 (1999): 207–215.

35. John Gillies, *Shakespeare and the Geography of Difference* (Cambridge: Cambridge University Press, 1994), 58. See also Rodney W. Shirley, *The Mapping of the World: Early Printed World Maps, 1472–1700* (1984; rpt. London: New Holland, 1993); and Derek Wilson, *The World Encompassed: Drake's Great Voyage, 1577–1580* (London: Hamish Hamilton, 1977).

36. *The Sermons of John Donne*, ed. George R. Potter and Evelyn M. Simpson, 10 vols. (Berkeley: University of California Press, 1956), 8: 323.

37. See Evelyn M. Simpson's Introduction to John Donne's *Essays in Divinity* (Oxford: Clarendon, 1952), ix–x.

38. Donne, *Essays in Divinity*, 8.

39. William M. Hamlin, *Tragedy and Scepticism in Shakespeare's England* (New York: Palgrave Macmillan, 2005), 103.

6. Inserting Me: Some Instances of Predication and the Privation of the Private Self in Shakespeare and Donne / Marshall Grossman

1. Saul Kripke, *Naming and Necessity* (Cambridge, MA: Harvard, 1980).
2. *Hamlet*, III.iv.8–9: my emphasis, in *The Riverside Shakespeare*, ed. G. Blakemore Evans, with J. J. M. Tobin, 2d ed. (Boston: Houghton Mifflin, 1997). All citations of Shakespeare are to this edition.
3. Joel Fineman, *The Subjectivity Effect in Western Literary Tradition: Essays toward the Release of Shakespeare's Will* (Cambridge, MA: MIT Press, 1991), 37.
4. *John Donne*, ed. John Carey (Oxford: Oxford University Press, 1990), 173–74. All citations of Donne refer to this edition.
5. On the prick as failed pointer in Sonnet 20, see my "Whose Life Is It Anyway? Shakespeare's Prick," *Textual Practice* 23 (2009): 229–46.

Improper Nouns: A Response to Marshall Grossman / David Lee Miller

1. "Whose Life Is It Anyway: Shakespeare's Prick," *Textual Practice* 23 (2009): 229–46; Joel Fineman, *The Perjured Eye: The Invention of Poetic Subjectivity in the Sonnets* (Berkeley: University of California Press, 1986); *The Subjectivity Effect in Western Literary Tradition: Essays toward the Release of Shakespeare's Will* (Cambridge, MA: MIT Press, 1991).
2. *The Story of All Things: Writing the Self in English Renaissance Narrative Poetry* (Durham, NC: Duke University Press, 1998), xvii.
3. Judith H. Anderson, *Translating Investments: Metaphor and the Dynamic of Cultural Change in Tudor-Stuart England* (New York: Fordham University Press, 2005), puts Reformation theologians into dialogue with modern theorists of language in a brilliant analysis that extends to Donne's use of metaphor.
4. The contrasting approach is well represented by Rebecca Ann Bach, "(Re)placing John Donne in the History of Sexuality," *ELH* 72, no. 1 (Spring 2005): 259–89. On Donne's grammar and the holy sonnets, see Brian Cummings, *The Literary Culture of the Reformation: Grammar and Grace* (Oxford: Oxford University Press, 2002).
5. "Lectures on Galatians," delivered in 1531 and published in 1535, was first translated into English in 1575; I cite the modern translation of Jaroslav Pelikan, *Luther's Works*, ed. Pelikan and Walter A. Hansen (St. Louis: Concordia, 1955), 26: 177.
6. In Luther's Latin, *non consistet*; quoted from *D. Martin Luthers Werke* 40.1 (1911; rpt. Weimar: Nachfolger, 2006), 41. The anonymous English translation of 1575 renders this phrase "must neades be overthrown" (*A Commentarie of M. Doctor Martin Luther upon the Epistle of S. Paul to the Galathians*, sig. A4v). Donne echoes both the Latin and the English translation: "That I may rise, and stand, o'erthrow mee" (line 3).

7. Alanus de Insulis, *The Plaint of Nature*, trans. James J. Sheridan (Toronto: Pontifical Institute of Mediaeval Studies, 1980), 67–68.

8. Silver, "'Lycidas' and the Grammar of Revelation," *ELH* 58 (1991): 779–808.

9. *Closet Devotions* (Durham: Duke University Press, 1998), 61.

10. Lines 18–22, quoted from *The Complete English Poetry of John Milton*, ed. John T. Shawcross (New York: New York University Press, 1963), 120.

11. The quoted lines are from Edmund Spenser, *The Faerie Queene*, ed. A. C. Hamilton (London: Pearson, 2001), II.xii.75.1–2.

12. Andrew Kingsmill, *Godlie Advise*, in *A Viewe of Mans Estate* (1577), sig. K3v.

13. "Essay on Criticism," line 155, quoted from Pat Rogers, ed., *Alexander Pope*, Oxford Authors (Oxford: Oxford University Press, 1993), 23.

14. Genesis 39:2 as rendered in the English Bible (1540) and in Matthew Parker's 1586 translation.

15. *The seconde tome or volume of the Paraphrase of Erasmus vpon the Newe Testament*, sig. Hh2.

7. Aspects, Physiognomy, and the Pun: A Reading of Sonnet 135 and "A Valediction: Of Weeping" / Julian Lamb

1. James Brown's attempt to define eight types of pun is problematic because this kind of ostensive definition is always threatened by those examples that inevitably fall outside of its categories. See "Eight Types of Pun," *PMLA* 71, no. 1 (1956): 14–26. What I offer in this essay is wholly different. Without defining a pun or even stating what defines particular kinds of puns, I present phenomena in such a way that, I hope, clarifies similarities and differences between them.

2. See Ludwig Wittgenstein, *Philosophical Investigations*, trans. and ed. G. E. M. Anscombe (Oxford: Blackwell, 2000), §67.

3. Sophie Read draws attention to the term's absence in early modern handbooks of rhetoric: "The sort of wordplay now comprehended by the catch-all term 'pun' was described instead in the sixteenth and early seventeenth centuries with a panoply of rhetorical figures, their names taken, as was customary, from classical sources": "Puns: Serious Wordplay," in *Renaissance Figures of Speech*, ed. Sylvia Adamson, Gavin Alexander, and Katrin Ettenhuber (Cambridge: Cambridge University Press, 2007), 81–94, here 81.

4. Catherine Bates begins her fascinating article on puns by analyzing the self-consciously equivocal history the OED provides for the term. She conjectures, "The word's dubious history and unknown parentage could be seen to coincide with the pun's perfidious status as an aberrant element within the linguistic structure": "The Point of Puns," *Modern Philology* 96, no. 4 (1999): 421–38, here 421.

5. The OED entry for "pun" struggles to grasp the word in a definition: "The use of a word in such a way as to suggest two or more meanings or

different associations, or the use of two or more words of the same or nearly the same sound with different meanings, so as to produce a humorous effect; a play on words." The more specific and contained characteristics of puns offered in this entry dissipate into the vast, unmediated spaces offered by its concluding phrase: "a play on words." Even words such as "suggest," "association," and "humourous" imply modes of reception that neither puns nor their creators can definitively secure. Puns, it seems, can be almost anything and be retrospectively brought into being by almost anyone. However, in saying so, I do not mean either to belittle the task of definition or to relinquish puns entirely to the ineffable. On the contrary, the ongoing ordinary use of the word "pun," as collected and described in the *OED*, tells us something about the criteria we use to determine what counts as a pun. The *OED* definition is revealing because it implies that our criteria are ambiguous or that a pun is situated ambiguously within its criteria or that puns lack criteria. This may help to explain why we, as readers and writers, are often forced to proceed with caution when attempting to determine the presence of a pun: Our uses of the word suggest that we are often not sure of what to look for or where to look for it. The entry for "quibble" fares slightly better. Its emphasis on "evasion," "equivocation," and "uncertainty" ascribes a motivation to the phenomenon that might help us understand the elusiveness of the term. I take up this theme toward the end of the essay.

6. Jonathan Culler, "The Call of the Phoneme," in *On Puns: The Foundation of Letters*, ed. Jonathan Culler (Oxford: Basil Blackwell, 1988), 3.

7. Derek Attridge, "Unpacking the Portmanteau, or Who's Afraid of *Finnegans Wake?*" in Culler, *On Puns*, 141.

8. William Empson, *Seven Types of Ambiguity* (Harmondsworth: Penguin, 1965), 102.

9. Attridge is patently wrong to say that puns "*enforce*" ambiguity. Many of them offer ambiguity—as it were—ambiguously: Sometimes their offer goes unnoticed, or is noticed but does not seem plausible, or is noticed and refused. "Enforce" does not do justice to the way many puns may well not be seen at all.

10. Although Wittgenstein does not state this point explicitly, my reading of this section of the *Investigations* is uncontroversial. See Malcolm Budd, "Wittgenstein on Seeing Aspects," *Mind* 96, no. 381 (1987): 1–17; also Justin Good, *Wittgenstein and the Theory of Perception* (London: Continuum, 2006), 15–21.

11. Although the features I discuss are both presented as reasons that aspect seeing cannot be a form of interpretation, it ought to be made clear that Wittgenstein presents equally persuasive arguments for why aspect seeing cannot be a form of pure seeing.

12. "The expression of a change of aspect is the expression of a new perception and at the same time of the perception's being unchanged": Wittgenstein, *Investigations*, 196e.

13. This experience of the dawning of an aspect ought to be distinguished from the aspect seeing that commonly occurs whenever we read, hear, or speak words: "And I must distinguish between the 'continuous seeing' of an aspect and the 'dawning' of an aspect": Wittgenstein, *Investigations*, 194e. The continuous seeing of an aspect occurs, for instance, when we treat words as entities that mean, rather than as mere nonsensical, random gestures. Puns, however, are pieces of language that do offer this experience because they offer the seeing of a new aspect.

14. Booth, "Exit, Pursued by a Gentleman Born," in *Shakespeare's Art from a Comparative Perspective*, ed. Wendell M. Aycock (Lubbock: Texas Tech University Press, 1981), 51–66, here, 51.

15. Stephen Booth, "Shakespeare's Language and the Language of Shakespeare's Time," *Shakespeare Survey* 50 (1997): 1–17, here 12.

16. Sonnet 62 contains extremely insistent repetitions of the word "self," as well as the personal pronouns "me," "my," and "thy." Ignoring these, Booth focuses on the virtually imperceptible repetition of "for" (in lines 3, 7, and 13). According to Booth, such repetition is "inconsequential," by which he means "unostentatious," by which he means: "It tickles the reader's mind, without diverting his attention": *Essay*, 96, 94n8, 93.

17. Responding to Booth's observations, Margreta de Grazia was dissatisfied with the way he had consigned them to an aesthetic realm of their own: "[W]hile he activates these homonymic clusters by pointing them out, he resolutely refrains from and sternly warns against making them purposeful or meaningful": "Homonyms before and after Lexical Standardization," *Shakespeare Jahrbuch* (1990): 143–65, here 147. *Pace* Booth, de Grazia presents an interpretation of the *bear/bare/barne* pun in *The Winter's Tale*, which, far from treating it as "substantively gratuitous," shows its thematic relevance to the whole play.

18. Culler, *On Puns*, 6–7; de Grazia, "Homonyms," 149–50.

19. Samuel Johnson, Preface to *The Plays of William Shakespeare* (1765), in *Selected Writings: Samuel Johnson*, ed. Peter Martin (Cambridge, MA: Harvard University Press, 2009), 364.

20. *Johnson's Dictionary: A Modern Selection*, ed. E. L. McAdam Jr. and George Milne (London: Papermac, 1982), 7.

21. Henry's threat of war is couched in the tennis metaphor:

> When we have matched our rackets to these balls
> We will in France, by God's grace, play a set
> Shall strike his father's crown into the hazard.
> Tell him he hath made a match with such a wrangler
> That all the courts of France shall be disturbed
> With chases.

From *King Henry V*, ed. T. W. Craik (London: Thomson Learning, 2002), here I.ii.262–67.

22. George Puttenham, *Art of English Poesy* (1589), ed. Frank Whigham and Wayne A. Rebhorn (Ithaca, NY: Cornell University Press, 2007), 292.

23. I am informed here by Juliet Fleming, *Graffiti and the Writing Arts of Early Modern England* (Philadelphia: University of Pennsylvania Press, 2001), 118–23.

24. *Shakespeare's Sonnets*, ed. Katherine Duncan-Jones (London: Thomson Learning, 2007), Sonnet 135.

25. Such a reading is consonant with the way some critics have read Donne's conceits as emblems of the conceit itself. Speaking of "A Valediction: Forbidding Mourning," Matthias Bauer has written, "If the unexpected connection between remote points of comparison is the hallmark of the baroque conceit, then Donne's famous compasses are an image not only of the lovers but also of the very nature of the conceit itself": "*Paronomasia celata* in Donne's 'A Valediction: Forbidding Mourning,'" *English Literary Renaissance* 25, no. 1 (1995): 97–111, here 98.

26. *John Donne: The Complete English Poems*, ed. A. J. Smith (Harmondsworth: Penguin, 1996), 1–9.

27. Empson puts forward a convincing case for this reading, although he perhaps overemphasizes the poet's concerns about his partner's infidelity. "There is none of the Platonic pretense Donne keeps up elsewhere, that their love is independent of being together; he can find no satisfaction in his hopelessness but to make as much of the actual situation of parting as possible; and the language of the poem is shot through with a suspicion which for once he is too delicate or too preoccupied to state unambiguously, that when he is gone she will be unfaithful to him" (139). Doniphan Louthan has suggested, perhaps too flippantly, that "A Valediction: Of Weeping" ultimately becomes a valediction forbidding mourning": *The Poetry of John Donne: A Study in Explication* (New York: Bookman, 1951), 45–46. In the final stanza, weeping is forbidden not out of any metaphysical consolation that lovers will be together even if apart but out of a self-preserving desire to avoid a death by grief.

28. Harry Morris, "John Donne's Terrifying Pun," *Papers on Language and Literature* 9 (1973): 128–37; David J. Leigh, "Donne's 'A Hymne to God the Father': New Dimensions," *Studies in Philology* 75, no. 2 (1978): 84–92.

29. In his vast edition of Donne's poetry, Robin Robbins has included a substantial annotation to the possible puns on "done" and "more" in *To Christ*, traditionally known as "A Hymn to God the Father," outlining the proclivities for punning on "Donne" that Donne shared with several of his friends, as well as the anonymous writer of a dog Latin poem who referred to Donne as "Factus": *The Complete Poems of John Donne*, ed. Robin Robbins, 2d ed. (Harlow, UK: Longman, 2010), 577n5, 6, 11.

30. Leigh, "Donne's 'A Hymn,'" 91.

31. Ibid., 92.

32. The alternative version of this line, "I have no more," while not as overtly ambivalent, can still be read as the poet somberly reminding himself of his earthly, human loss despite his metaphysical gain.

33. Judith H. Anderson, *Words That Matter: Linguistic Perception in Renaissance English* (Stanford, CA: Stanford University Press, 1996), 35.

8. Fantasies of Private Language in "The Phoenix and Turtle" and "The Ecstasy" / Anita Gilman Sherman

1. Sixteenth- and seventeenth-century debates about biblical hermeneutics and prelapsarian languages provide a rich and germane context for a philosophical consideration of language in general and poetic language in particular, as media with varying degrees of transparency and obscurity. See, among others, D. C. Allen, "Some Theories of the Growth and Origin of Language in Milton's Age," *Philological Quarterly* 28 (1949): 5–16; Allison P. Coudert, ed., *The Language of Adam / Die Sprache Adams*, Wolfenbütteler Forschungen, Bd. 84 (Wiesbaden: Harrassowitz, 1999); Umberto Eco, *The Search for the Perfect Language*, trans. James Fentress (Oxford: Blackwell, 1995); Hugh Ormsby-Lennon, "Rosicrucian Linguistics: Twilight of a Renaissance Tradition," in *Hermeticism and the Renaissance*, ed. Ingrid Merkel and Allen G. Debus (Washington, DC: Folger, 1988), 311–41; Kristen Poole, "Naming, *Paradise Lost*, and the Gendered Discourse of Perfect Language Schemes," *English Literary Renaissance* 38, no. 3 (2008): 535–59.

2. Wittgenstein asks, "In what way is logic something sublime? For logic seemed to have a peculiar depth—a universal significance. Logic lay, it seemed, at the foundation of all the sciences" (*PI* § 89). See Ludwig Wittgenstein, *Philosophical Investigations*, trans. G. E. M. Anscombe, P. M. S. Hacker, and Joachim Schulte (Oxford: Wiley-Blackwell, 2009). This revised translation titles what was formerly known as part II of the *Investigations* as *Philosophy of Psychology: A Fragment*, abbreviating it as *PPF*.

3. All references to Shakespeare and Donne are from *The Riverside Shakespeare*, ed. G. Blakemore Evans (Boston: Houghton Mifflin, 1974), and John Donne, *The Complete English Poems*, ed. A. J. Smith (London: Penguin, 1971).

4. See, among others, P. M. S. Hacker, *Insight and Illusion: Themes in the Philosophy of Wittgenstein*, rev. ed. (Oxford: Clarendon, 1986), 246; Saul A. Kripke, *Wittgenstein on Rules and Private Language* (Cambridge, MA: Harvard University Press, 1982), 62–69, 121–22; and Avrum Stroll, *Wittgenstein* (Oxford: Oneworld, 2002), 118.

5. Commentators debate the relation of secret and private language. See, among others, A. J. Ayer and R. Rhees, "Symposium: Can There Be a Private Language?" in *Proceedings of the Aristotelian Society*, supplementary vol. 28

(1954): 63–94; Stanley Cavell, *The Claim of Reason: Wittgenstein, Skepticism, Morality, and Tragedy* (Oxford: Oxford University Press, 1979), 344–50; Stephen Mulhall, *Wittgenstein's Private Language: Grammar, Nonsense, and Imagination in* Philosophical Investigations, §§ 243–315 (Oxford: Clarendon, 2007); John Turk Saunders and Donald F. Henze, *The Private Language Problem: A Philosophical Dialogue* (New York: Random House, 1967), 6–30; Patricia H. Werhane, *Skepticism, Rules, and Private Languages* (Atlantic Highlands, NJ: Humanities Press, 1992), 22–25.

6. Stanley Cavell, *Disowning Knowledge in Six Plays of Shakespeare* (Cambridge: Cambridge University Press, 1987), 21. For a fuller argument about the dialectical relays and rhythms characterizing the experience of skepticism, see Anita Gilman Sherman, *Skepticism and Memory in Shakespeare and Donne* (New York: Palgrave Macmillan, 2007). Developing the Cavellian idea of skepticism's moods, James Conant distinguishes "the Cartesian genre of scepticism" with its discoveries that end "in a mood of disappointment" from "the Kantian genre of scepticism" with its indifference, mystery, and attendant mood of despair. See James Conant, "Varieties of Scepticism," in *Wittgenstein and Scepticism*, ed. Denis MacManus (London: Routledge, 2004), 97–136, here 107, 111.

7. Hyperbole has a complex relationship to the sublime, but occasionally, as in the two poems discussed here, it operates in tandem with it. Hyperbole is often seen as a rhetorical strategy of exaggeration used to communicate extreme experience, whereas the sublime is considered—thanks partly to Kant—an aesthetic category often issuing in the silence of wonder and awe rather than in the metaphorical protestations of hyperbole. James Noggle defines the sublime aesthetic effect as "the proximity that it establishes between absolute precariousness and absolute security—the aesthetic unification of our terror of the ocean storm with our safety on shore." See "The Wittgensteinian Sublime," *New Literary History* 27, no. 4 (1996): 605–19, here 612. That said, the sublime can be highly rhetorical, while hyperbole can drive an aesthetic, as in Christopher D. Johnson's sense that it captures "the self-conscious indecorousness of excessive figuration." See *Hyperboles: The Rhetoric of Excess in Baroque Literature and Thought* (Cambridge, MA: Harvard University Press, 2010), 329. Both terms concern the expressiveness of language: what can or cannot be said about the extraordinary and the exceptional, like ecstasy.

8. Stanley Cavell, *Cities of Words: Pedagogical Letters on a Register of the Moral Life* (Cambridge, MA: Harvard University Press, 2004), 422.

9. "Intimacy" is a vexed term. Lauren Berlant calls it an enigma, naming a range of complex attachments. See *Intimacy*, ed. Lauren Berlant (Chicago: University of Chicago Press, 2000), 3. Robert Nozick remarks that "in intimacy, we let another within the boundaries we normally maintain around ourselves, boundaries marked by clothing and by full self-control and monitoring." See *The*

Examined Life: Philosophical Meditations (New York: Simon and Schuster, 1989), 64. Since these boundaries are informed by cultural codes, notions of intimacy vary across cultures, but many agree that the concept of intimacy emerges in response to modernity. Niklas Luhmann finds "the codes" of intimacy changing in the seventeenth century. See *Love as Passion: The Codification of Intimacy*, trans. Jeremy Gaines and Doris L. Jones (Cambridge, MA: Harvard University Press, 1986), 45. Daniel Juan Gil follows Luhmann's lead, arguing that "the historically specific early modern conflict between competing social imaginaries" informs sexual interactions and discourse. See, for example, Gil's analysis of Sir Philip Sidney in *Astrophil and Stella*: "Anticipating the eighteenth-century discourse of emotional intimacy, in which emotions are the sine qua non of intimacy precisely because they seem hidden and private, Sidney finally claims that he cannot represent his joy but only point to a reality that goes beyond the words that, unlike bodies, are available to all, indiscriminately." See *Before Intimacy: Asocial Sexuality in Early Modern England* (Minneapolis: University of Minnesota Press, 2006), 9, 39. James M. Bromley historicizes intimacy, lamenting "the early modern contraction of the intimate sphere" and focusing on alternate forms of relationality in Renaissance texts. See *Intimacy and Sexuality in the Age of Shakespeare* (Cambridge: Cambridge University Press, 2012), 2.

10. Peter Milward, "'Double Nature's Single Name': A Response to Christiane Gillham," *Connotations* 3, no. 1 (1993): 60–63, here 60.

11. Stanley Cavell, *A Pitch of Philosophy: Autobiographical Exercises* (Cambridge, MA: Harvard University Press, 1994), 126.

12. Cavell states this as "a wish for the connection between my claims of knowledge and the objects upon which the claims are to fall to occur without my intervention, apart from my agreements." See Cavell, *Claim of Reason*, 351–52. Richard Rorty puts this differently: "The idea of a private language . . . stems from the hope that words might get meaning without relying on other words. This hope, in turns, stems from the larger hope, diagnosed by Sartre, of becoming a self-sufficient *être-en-soi*." See *Contingency, Irony, and Solidarity* (Cambridge: Cambridge University Press, 1989), 42.

13. But see: "If God had looked into our minds, he would not have been able to see there whom we were speaking of" (PPF § 284).

14. Stanley Cavell, *Contesting Tears: The Hollywood Melodrama of the Unknown Woman* (Chicago: University of Chicago Press, 1996), 89.

15. See Patrick Cheney, "The Voice of the Author in 'The Phoenix and Turtle': Chaucer, Shakespeare, Spenser," in *Shakespeare and the Middle Ages*, ed. Curtis Perry and John Watkins (Oxford: Oxford University Press, 2009), 103–25.

16. William H. Matchett, *The Phoenix and the Turtle: Shakespeare's Poem and Chester's "Loves Martyr"* (The Hague: Mouton, 1965), 41.

17. Richard C. McCoy, "Love's Martyrs: Shakespeare's 'Phoenix and Turtle' and the Sacrificial Sonnets," in *Religion and Culture in Renaissance England*, ed.

Claire McEachern and Debora Shuger (Cambridge: Cambridge University Press, 1997), 188–208, here 195.

18. Barbara Everett, "Set upon a Golden Bough to Sing: Shakespeare's Debt to Sidney in 'The Phoenix and Turtle,'" *Times Literary Supplement* (Feb. 16, 2001), 13–15, here 15.

19. See John Austin on "performatives" in *How to Do Things with Words* (Cambridge, MA: Harvard University Press, 1962); John Searle on "differences in the style of performance of the illocutionary act" in "A Classification of Illocutionary Acts," *Language in Society* 5, no. 1 (1976): 1–23, here 7; David Schalkwyk on speech-act theory, Wittgenstein, and Shakespeare in *Speech and Performance in Shakespeare's Sonnets and Plays* (Cambridge: Cambridge University Press, 2002) and *Literature and the Touch of the Real* (Newark: University of Delaware Press, 2004).

20. For an overview of Wittgenstein's fragmentary remarks on Shakespeare, see Peter Hughes, "Painting the Ghost: Wittgenstein, Shakespeare, and Textual Representation," *New Literary History* 19, no. 2 (1988): 371–84.

21. For a persuasive account of reasons that Shakespeare might have contributed to Robert Chester's *Love's Martyr* (1601), a volume dedicated to Sir John Salusbury and including poems by Ben Jonson, George Chapman, and John Marston, see James P. Bednarz, "*The Passionate Pilgrim* and 'The Phoenix and Turtle,'" in *The Cambridge Companion to Shakespeare's Poetry*, ed. Patrick Cheney (Cambridge: Cambridge University Press, 2007), 108–24, especially 116–19. I had hoped to consult James P. Bednarz, *Shakespeare and the Truth of Love: The Mystery of "The Phoenix and Turtle"* (New York: Palgrave, 2012), but it came out just as this volume was going to press.

22. See Rupert Read, "Wittgenstein's *Philosophical Investigations* as a War Book," *New Literary History* 41, no. 3 (2010): 593–612, here 598 and 601.

23. Cavell, *Contesting Tears*, 157, and *Pitch of Philosophy*, 126–27.

24. Catherine Gimelli Martin, "The Erotology of Donne's 'Extasie' and the Secret History of Voluptuous Rationalism," *SEL* 44, no. 1 (2004): 121–47; Ramie Targoff, *John Donne, Body and Soul* (Chicago: University of Chicago Press, 2008), 59; Julia M. Walker, "John Donne's 'The Extasie' as an Alchemical Process," *ELN* 20, no. 1 (1982): 1–8.

25. Rorty puts this provocatively: "[T]o be thoroughly Wittgensteinian in our approach to language, would be to de-divinize the world" (*Contingency, Irony, and Solidarity*, 21).

26. Ludwig Wittgenstein, *On Certainty*, trans. Denis Paul and G. E. M. Anscombe (New York: Harper, 1972), § 569.

27. Compare Ludwig Wittgenstein, *Zettel*, trans. G. E. M. Anscombe (Berkeley: University of California Press, 1967), § 227: "How curious: we should like to explain our understanding of a gesture by means of a translation into words, and the understanding of words by translating them into a gesture.

(Thus we are tossed to and fro when we try to find out where understanding properly resides.) And we really shall be explaining words by a gesture, and a gesture by words."

28. Martin comments on the difference in tone between Donne's and Shakespeare's metaphysical paradoxes, suggesting that Shakespeare's do not produce doubt in the way Donne's do: "Even the most disharmonious imagery (like for instance that found in such poems as Shakespeare's 'The Phoenix and the Turtle') may lack true metaphysical violence if its paradoxes are not 'contaminated' with a riddling logic that produces metaphysical doubt. So long as their allegorical mystery remains safely insoluble or transcendental, such poems produce complacent wonder instead of violent controversies over their missing or nonexistent keys. In contrast, Donne's *Songs and Sonets* provoke such controversies by playing with glaring inconsistencies . . . For all these works 'contaminate' spiritual and rational arguments with sensual analogies that continue to perplex, astonish, or even outrage their readers" (122).

29. See J. V. Cunningham, "'Essence' and the Phoenix and Turtle," *ELH* 19, no. 4 (1952): 265–76, here 273.

30. Critics who think each poem may owe a debt to the Eighth Song of Sidney's *Astrophel and Stella* include Barbara Everett, Helen Gardner, and Dennis Kay. See *The Elegies and the Songs and Sonnets*, ed. Helen Gardner (Oxford: Oxford University Press, 1965), 256; Dennis Kay, *William Shakespeare: Sonnets and Poem* (New York: Twayne, 1998), 82.

31. Cleanth Brooks, *The Well Wrought Urn* (New York: Harcourt Brace, 1947), 18–21.

32. Arthur F. Marotti, "Donne and 'The Extasie,'" in *The Rhetoric of Renaissance Poetry from Wyatt to Milton*, ed. Thomas O. Sloan and Raymond B. Waddington (Berkeley: University of California Press, 1974), 140–73, here 172.

33. For a reading of becalmed ecstasy as a sign of maturity, see Jorge Guillén's 1963 poem, "Al Margen de Donne," in *Aire Nuestro*, ed. Óscar Barrero Pérez (Barcelona: Tusquets, 2008), II. 58.

34. See Eco, *Search for the Perfect Language*, 184–85, and Ormsby-Lennon, "Rosicrucian Linguistics," 322–23, for the language of birds as a residue of the *lingua adamica*.

35. Stanley Cavell, *In Quest of the Ordinary: Lines of Skepticism and Romanticism* (Chicago: University of Chicago Press, 1988), 27.

9. Working Imagination in the Early Modern Period: Donne's Secular and Religious Lyrics and Shakespeare's Hamlet, Macbeth, and Leontes / Judith H. Anderson

1. R. C. Bald, *John Donne: A Life* (Oxford: Oxford University Press, 1970), 72; John Donne, *Biathanatos* (New York: Facsimile Text Society, 1930).

2. *Hamlet*, ed. Ann Thompson and Neil Taylor (London: Thomson Learning, 2006), II.ii.360, 485; unless otherwise indicated, citation of *Hamlet* is from this edition.

3. De Grazia, "Soliloquies and Wages in the Age of Emergent Consciousness," *Textual Practice* 9 (1995): 67–92, esp. 74–78.

4. Mary Carruthers, *The Book of Memory: A Study of Memory in Medieval Culture* (Cambridge: Cambridge University Press, 1990), 54, 59. Also Malcolm Schofield, "Aristotle on the Imagination," in *Essays on Aristotle's "De Anima,"* ed. Martha C. Nussbaum and Amélie Oksenberg Rorty (Oxford: Clarendon, 1992), 249–77: hereafter cited as Nussbaum and Rorty; Dorothea Frede, "The Cognitive Role of *Phantasia* in Aristotle," in Nussbaum and Rorty, 279–95; and Michael V. Wedin, *Mind and Imagination in Aristotle* (New Haven, CT: Yale University Press, 1988). Famously since the comments of Samuel Taylor Coleridge, an "overbalance of the imaginative power" has been attributed to Hamlet; see Arthur F. Kinney's Introduction, *Hamlet: New Critical Essays*, ed. Kinney (New York: Routledge, 2002), 1–68, here 30. On the Aristotelian basis of faculty psychology, see Stuart Clark, *Vanities of the Eye: Vision in Early Modern European Culture* (Oxford: Oxford University Press, 2007), 14, 16–20; also notes 7, 8 (Agamben), 9, and 29, this chapter.

5. Franz Brentano, *The Psychology of Aristotle: In Particular His Doctrine of the Active Intellect*, ed. and trans. Rolf George (1867: German; Berkeley: University of California Press, 1977: English), 67–68; also Frede, "Cognitive Role," 285. Brentano wrote four books on Aristotle and earned the distinction of having an enduring problem named after him: "Brentano's problem" is how to account for belief, desire, thought, and other intentional human attitudes in a materialistic way that is faithful to an Aristotelian view of psychology as physics (Wedin, *Mind and Imagination*, 22). Brentano's (Christian) interpretations of Aristotle (i.e., necessarily of the Aristotelian tradition) are often closer than some current ones to those of Renaissance thinkers; for discussion and examples, see S. K. Sugimura, *"Matter of Glorious Trial": Spiritual and Material Substance in "Paradise Lost"* (New Haven, CT: Yale University Press, 2009), 113, 115, and throughout.

6. Cf. *De Anima*, in *The Complete Works of Aristotle*, ed. Jonathan Barnes, 2 vols. (Princeton, NJ: Princeton University Press, 1984), 1: 428a2: "excluding metaphorical uses of the term [*imagination*]." This Aristotelian exclusion is all too easy to ignore and virtually impossible to maintain, whether in practice or theory.

7. Clark, *Vanities of the Eye*, 9–38: "In early modern culture, . . . [the] account [of perception] was largely Aristotelian in origin, transmission, and attribution (albeit with some Platonic or Neoplatonic elements), and it was socially agreed" and "deeply embedded" in the culture (14). See also note 29, this chapter. Even the average person is nowadays likely to have encountered Freudian ideas, as have many first-year college students, however popular or limited their grasp might be. The commonplaces of the Aristotelian tradition, in particular, were

similarly available in Shakespeare's time; this is why Francis Bacon is so especially exercised by their pervasive influence on *science*, "knowledge." Insofar as other traditions treat the imagination as such, they generally build on or at least include an Aristotelian basis.

8. Agamben, *Stanzas: Word and Phantasm in Western Culture*, trans. Ronald L. Martinez (Minneapolis: University of Minnesota Press, 1993): 77, 125. Pertinently suggestive essays treating the language of *Hamlet* include P. K. Ayers, "Reading, Writing, and *Hamlet*," *Shakespeare Quarterly* 44 (1993): 423–39; Jonathan Goldberg, "Hamlet's Hand," *Shakespeare Quarterly* 39 (1988): 307–27; Louise D. Cary, "*Hamlet* Recycled, or the Tragical History or the Prince's Prints," *ELH* 61 (1994): 783–805: on "the infinitely decomposible and recomposible nature of language" in *Hamlet* (784, 799).

9. Sir Philip Sidney, *An Apology for Poetry or the Defence of Poesy*, ed. Geoffrey Shepherd (1965; rpt. Manchester: Manchester University Press, 1973), 101; the metaphorical phrase "speaking picture" is ancient (160n333). Citing it in light of Stephen Greenblatt's chapter (4) on imagining in his *Hamlet in Purgatory* (Princeton, NJ: Princeton University Press, 2001), I want to stress the participle *speaking*; Greenblatt's emphasis in this chapter is strongly visual. The images, or *phantasmata*, derive from all the senses, and their representation implies language (e.g., note 8, this chapter). For examples of this broader emphasis with respect to purgatory, see Kinney, Introduction, *Hamlet: New Critical Essays*, 15–16; cf. also Christopher Tilmouth, *Passion's Triumph over Reason: A History of the Moral Imagination from Spenser to Rochester* (Oxford: Oxford University Press, 2007), 103.

10. Hamlet's engagement of the difference between mere performance and reality/authenticity has notorious relevance to the modern debate between speech-act theory and deconstruction (e.g., Jonathan Culler's *On Deconstruction: Theory and Criticism after Structuralism* [Ithaca, NY: Cornell University Press, 1982], 110–25, esp. 118–20). In contrast, see David Schalkwyk, *Speech and Performance in Shakespeare's Sonnets and Plays* (Cambridge: Cambridge University Press, 2002), esp. chap. 2, on performatives; also his *Literature and the Touch of the Real* (Newark, NJ: University of Delaware Press, 2004). For a perceptive consideration of act/action in *Hamlet*, whose protagonist "has no inner self," see Mary Thomas Crane, *Shakespeare's Brain: Reading with Cognitive Theory* (Princeton, NJ: Princeton University Press, 2001), chap. 4, here 118. But see also Alan Sinfield's persuasive consideration of character as "continuous consciousness" in *Faultlines: Cultural Materialism and the Politics of Dissident Reading* (Berkeley: University of California Press, 1992), chap. 3, here 65. See also notes 25 (character), 78 (speech acts), this chapter.

11. Michael Goldman describes Pyrrhus's arrested movement as a "'stop-action' technique," which is subsequently mirrored in Hamlet's interruption of his own soliloquy; both instances draw attention to "theatricality of gesture and

language": "Hamlet and Our Problems," in *Critical Essays on Shakespeare's Hamlet*," ed. David Scott Kastan (New York: Simon and Schuster Macmillan, 1995), 43–55, here 45–46.

12. *On the Ideal Orator (De Oratore)*, trans. James M. May and Jakob Wisse (New York: Oxford University Press, 2001), 291–92; cf. 172–75, 254–55. The Latin inserts in my text are cited from Cicero, *De Oratore*, book III, ed. G. P. Goold, trans. E. W. Sutton, completed H. Rackham (1942; rpt. London: Heinemann, 1982), LVI.212–LVII.217.

13. Carruthers, *Book of Memory*, 51–53. On a generative conception of imagination in the sixteenth and seventeenth centuries, see Janet Leslie Knedlik, "Fancy, Faith, and Generative Mimesis in *Paradise Lost*," *Modern Language Quarterly* 47 (1986): 19–47: Knedlik argues that Tasso and Mazzoni (as well as Sidney and Milton) understood and applied "the fundamental point of Aristotle's *Poetics*: that in the process of structuring the artistic mimesis, the poetic maker works in a mode intrinsically valid as a way of knowing . . . [a mode] between literal inspiration and autonomous imagination" (24–25, 27, 30); cf. Clark, *Vanities of the Eye*, 39, 43; Paul Stevens, *Imagination and the Presence of Shakespeare in "Paradise Lost"* (Madison: University of Wisconsin Press, 1985), esp. 46–79. Other relevant views can be found in Sidney, *Apology for Poetry*, 125; George Puttenham, *The Arte of English Poesie* (1589; rpt. Kent, OH: Kent State University Press, 1988), 34–35; Allan H. Gilbert, ed., *Literary Criticism: Plato to Dryden* (1940; rpt. Detroit: Wayne State University Press, 1962), 305–7, 312, 324 (Castelvetro); 360–62, 367–70, 386–88 (Mazzoni); 472, 474, 476–81, 492–94 (Tasso). On Tasso's views, see also Mindele Anne Treip, *Allegorical Poetics and the Epic: The Renaissance Tradition to* Paradise Lost (Lexington: University Press of Kentucky, 1994), 45–49 and chaps. 5–8. While the Aristotelian Pietro Pomponazzi does not address poetics in his treatise *On the Immortality of the Soul*, his argument is likewise suggestive regarding the status of imagination (thence poetic imagery): *The Renaissance Philosophy of Man*, ed. Ernst Cassirer, Paul Oskar Kristeller, and John Herman Randall Jr. (1948; rpt. Chicago: University of Chicago Press, 1956), 257–381, here 305, 319. Another review of general beliefs about the imagination can be found in K. Tetzeli von Rosador, "'Supernatural Soliciting': Temptation and Imagination in *Doctor Faustus* and *Macbeth*," in *Shakespeare and His Contemporaries: Essays in Comparison*, ed. E. A. J. Honigmann (Manchester: Manchester University Press, 1986), 42–59, here 42–46.

14. Thompson and Taylor, *Hamlet*, suggest in a note to II.ii.504 that Hamlet's inability to "say" something is ironic insofar as he "wants to imitate the Player, rather than Pyrrhus." Conversely, cf. Goldman, "Hamlet and Our Problems," 47–48, on "say" as an "intermediary step," and Inga-Stina Ewbank's positive response in *"Hamlet* and the Power of Words," in Kastan, *Critical Essays*, 56–78, here 70–71; also Kastan, "'His Semblable Is His Mirror': *Hamlet* and the

Imitation of Revenge," in Kastan, *Critical Essays*, 198–209, here 202; Kastan notes the duality of Pyrrhus as avenging son and patricide (200); James L. Calderwood describes an Escher-like Hamlet who is "conscious of his dual identity [as actor and character] . . . almost as though he were an actor at a rehearsal": *To Be and Not to Be: Negation and Metadrama in* Hamlet (New York: Columbia University Press, 1983), 30, 32.

15. The first general meaning of *conscience* that the *OED* (1933; 2d ed., 1989) recognizes is "Inward knowledge, consciousness; inmost thought, mind"; the second is "Consciousness of right and wrong; moral sense" (I–II). The conjunction of *conscience* with *consciousness* in Shakespeare's time is analogous to that of *kind*(ness) with *nature*; both assume that morality is a defining feature of human being. On conscience/consciousness in *Macbeth* and *Hamlet*, see Abraham Stoll, "Macbeth's Equivocal Conscience," in *Macbeth: New Critical Essays*, ed. Nick Moschovakis (New York: Routledge, 2008), 132–50, here 144. Tilmouth's pouncing on Hamlet's presentation of the "Mousetrap" as a new idea in his soliloquy rather than as one he has already, impulsively imagined (II.ii.74) too suspiciously dismisses the emotionally agitated, cognitive *process* of Hamlet's resolution (92–93). Tilmouth (e.g., 96–97) repeatedly criticizes Hamlet for his failure to achieve a murderous, motivational visualization (imagination)—one like Macbeth's, perhaps.

16. In *The Poetics of Melancholy in Early Modern England* (Cambridge: Cambridge University Press, 2004), chap. 3, Douglas Trevor considers Hamlet a melancholic who is reasonable, in the main, and skeptical for good reason (e.g., 66, 72–73). See also Crane, *Shakespeare's Brain*, chap. 4. Kinney, Introduction, *Hamlet: New Critical Essays*, 13–14, cites Renaissance texts illustrating that melancholy especially affects the imagination. Catherine Belsey, in "'Was Hamlet a Man or a Woman?': The Prince in the Graveyard, 1800–1920," in Kinney, *Hamlet: New Critical Essays*, 134–58, makes short, witty work of Hamlet's culturally imputed "femininity" in the nineteenth century and well into the twentieth—the inevitable offshoot of his sensitivity (cf. sensitive, or sensory, soul), poetic imagination, and thoughtfulness. Clark's chapter on apparitions, spirits, and ghosts affords valuable support for Hamlet's caution: Nobody by the opening of the seventeenth century, he indicates, could ignore the "various challenges to the veracity of seeing ghosts" (*Vanities of the Eye*, 204–35, here 205).

17. Schofield, "Aristotle on the Imagination," 274; Aristotle, *De Anima*, 427b16–24. On the various capacities of imagination, see also Schofield, "Aristotle on the Imagination," 272–74, 276–77; Frede, "Cognitive Role," 288–90; and Wedin, *Mind and Imagination*, 45–63.

18. Aristotle, *De Anima*, 428a11–12; also 427b16, 28–29; 431b2, 432a3–10. On the reliability of the images, see Schofield, "Aristotle on the Imagination," 251, and Frede, "Cognitive Role," 285, 294. See also Claudia Baracchi, "Contribu-

tions to the Coming-to-Be of Greek Beginnings: Heidegger's Inceptive Thinking," in *Heidegger and the Greeks: Interpretive Essays*, ed. Drew A. Hyland and John Panteleimon Manoussakis (Bloomington: Indiana University Press, 2006), 23–42, here 36–37: Baracchi reads Aristotle as "the thinker of unexhausted *aporia*" and "of truth as phenomenonal disclosure."

19. Brentano, *Psychology*, 106, 110; see also 115–16. Also L. A. Kosman, "What Does the Maker Mind Make?" in Nussbaum and Rorty, 343–58. For an explanation suggestively similar to the one described here, see the late Elizabethan/early Jacobean discussion of psychology by Lodowyck Bryskett, *A Discourse of Civill Life*, ed. Thomas E. Wright (1606; rpt. Northridge, CA: San Fernando Valley State College Renaissance Editions, 1970), for example, 199–203. The concept of the *nous poiētikos* is debated within the Aristotelian tradition; see Brentano, "*Nous Poiētikos*: Survey of Earlier Interpretations [ancient disciples, through Christian and Arab adherents of the Middle Ages and early modern proponents, to Brentano's present]," in Nussbaum and Rorty, 313–41. Kosman concludes that *nous* is "a principle of active consciousness" and finally "that active thinking . . . as *theōria*" is what "the maker mind makes." *Theōria* is not theory but "simply the principle of *awareness* (prior to its later thematization as interiority)," of which "the essential being of all things, the formal principle of their being what they are . . . is also a mode"; *nous* is merely "the purest form of that general power of cognitive awareness and discrimination that is increasingly revealed in *scala naturae*" (356–57); cf. Walter A. Brogan on *theoria* as "a pre-view, a viewing in advance, [and, in this way,] a seeing": "The Intractable Interrelationship of *Physis* and *Techne*," in *Heidegger and the Greeks*, 43–56, here 50. Properly speaking, moreover, even the phrase *nous poiētikos* belongs to the Aristotelian tradition rather than to Aristotle per se, as does the very text of *De Anima*: Kosman, "What Does the Maker Mind Make?" 343n2; Martha C. Nussbaum, "Introduction A: The Text of Aristotle's *De Anima*," in Nussbaum and Rorty, 1–6, here 2.

20. *Macbeth*, ed. Kenneth Muir (London: Methuen, 1984). Unless otherwise indicated, citation of *Macbeth* is from this edition. The most sustained analysis in roughly the last three decades of performances of the dagger scene is probably that of Marvin Rosenberg, *The Masks of Macbeth* (Berkeley: University of California Press, 1978), 287–316, esp. 298ff. While admiring Rosenberg's insight, my focus on imagination leads me to read the speech with considerably less emphasis on Macbeth's paralysis (300: "most testimony"; cf. 311), his unconscious (e.g., 298), and his failure of will (305). More recently, Nick Moschovakis affords a useful review of performative and critical versions of *Macbeth*: "Introduction: Dualistic *Macbeth*? Problematic *Macbeth*?" in Moschovakis, *Macbeth*, 1–72. By "dualism," Moschovakis seems to mean "with moral compass" and by "problematic," both lacking such compass and written within the past fifty years or so. See also my preceding note (and text) in connection with von Rosador on

imagination: "What is poet-like [cf. *nous poiétikos*] in Macbeth, the ability to see imaginatively into the truth of things, is at war with what is hallucinatory and produces horrid images" (48; cf. 44–46). In two essays, Arthur F. Kinney treats ideological imagination in *Macbeth*: "Imagination and Ideology in Shakespeare: The Case of *Macbeth*," in *Ideological Approaches to Shakespeare: The Practice of Theory*, ed. Robert P. Merrix and Nicholas Ranson (Lewiston, ME: Mellen, 1992), 56–85; and "Imagination and Ideology in *Macbeth*," in *The Witness of Times: Manifestations of Ideology in Seventeenth-Century England*, ed. Katherine Z. Keller and Gerald J. Schiffhorst (Pittsburgh: Duquesne University Press, 1993), 148–73, esp. 151–52.

21. Citation from Rosenberg, *Masks of Macbeth*, 311, whose description of the bell triggered my association, which persists, even if the bell is clapperless, as A. R. Braunmuller suggests in his edition of *Macbeth* (Cambridge: Cambridge University Press, 1997), 139n32. On debate about the Eucharist, see Judith H. Anderson, *Translating Investments: Metaphor and the Dynamic of Cultural Change in Tudor-Stuart England* (New York: Fordham University Press, 2005), chap. 3. In traditional philosophical/theological usage, *virtually* (Latin *virtualiter*) indicates that something possesses something else in a different (usually higher) manner than is required for a formal possession of it. Richard Wilson associates the witches of *Macbeth* both with a black mass *and* with Jesuit influences: *Secret Shakespeare: Studies in Theatre, Religion and Resistance* (Manchester: Manchester University Press, 2004), chap. 8, here 188. In "Scepticism and Theatre in *Macbeth*" (*Shakespeare Survey* 55 [2002]: 219–36), Kent Cartwright explores a theater "in which vividness [*energia*] can become a form of knowledge and performance a virtual reality" (225); in this illuminating reading, "the problem of [such] knowledge . . . haunts every corner of *Macbeth*" and "saturates its language" (220). Stephen Booth's observation that an audience sees and feels things mainly through Macbeth's point of view is particularly apt to the dagger soliloquy: "*King Lear, Macbeth, Indefinition, and Tragedy* (New Haven, CT: Yale University Press, 1983), 105–6.

22. Donne describes poetry, like math, as a "counterfait Creation" that "makes things that are not, as though they were" (*The Sermons of John Donne*, ed. George R. Potter and Evelyn M. Simpson, 10 vols. [1959; rpt. Berkeley: University of California Press, 1984], 4: 87); Sidney refers to poetry as "a representing, counterfeiting, or figuring forth" (101); Shakespeare's Theseus groups "The lunatic, the lover, and the poet" in the power of their imaginations: *The Riverside Shakespeare*, ed. G. Blakemore Evans, with J. J. M. Tobin, 2d ed. (Boston: Houghton Mifflin, 1997), *A Midsummer Night's Dream*, V.i.7; when not otherwise indicated, as in basic citation of my major Shakespearean texts, reference is to this edition. I am reluctant to join Stoll in seeing Macbeth's dagger as the conventional prick of conscience unless, perhaps, with mordant irony (136). The same applies to David

Norbrook's glossing the dagger as a "stock republican emblem of tyrannicide" and the "defense of liberty": "*Macbeth* and the Politics of Historiography," in *Politics of Discourse: The Literature and History of Seventeenth-Century England*, ed. Kevin Sharpe and Steven N. Zwicker (Berkeley: University of California Press, 1987), 78–116, here 92, 101. As Stuart Clark argues, "Stressing what visual images meant . . . once they had been interpreted is to neglect the extent to which the act of seeing itself was problematic—both in *Macbeth* and in late Renaissance culture more generally": 237–38, 256–57.

23. The gloss of "informs" is that of Muir, ed. In *The Riverside Shakespeare*, Frank Kermode gives "creates shapes" as the gloss.

24. See Judith H. Anderson, *Reading the Allegorical Intertext: Chaucer, Spenser, Shakespeare, Milton* (New York: Fordham University Press, 2008), esp. 61–69, 284–92. Also Sinfield on Macbeth's character (*Faultlines*, 62–64).

25. In *The Rhetoric of the Body from Ovid to Shakespeare* (Cambridge: Cambridge University Press, 2000), 19, 25–26, Lynn Enterline suggests that Shakespeare's Lucrece and his Hamlet use Ovid's Hecuba as a mirror "in and through which to understand and to express what they claim to be their 'own' emotions." In contrast, A. D. Nuttall, treating the formation of character, compares Hamlet and Macbeth insofar as their actions are set in motion by primitive "emissaries of blood and darkness": *Shakespeare the Thinker* (New Haven, CT: Yale University Press, 2007), chap. 7, here 289; cf. Tilmouth on Senecan protagonists as "fantasy self-images for Hamlet" (86). Stoll, "Macbeth's Equivocal Conscience," 137, finds in the evocation of Tarquin, this ravisher's "moment[ary]" dispute, with "frozen conscience" in lines 246–52 of Shakespeare's *Lucrece*; I read this connection, if valid, as a dismissal, not Stoll's assertion, of conscience in Macbeth. Cf. Norbrook, who finds in Tarquin an allusion to the demise of the Roman monarchy ("Macbeth," 101).

26. Cf. Frederick Kiefer, *Shakespeare's Visual Theatre: Staging the Personified Characters* (Cambridge: Cambridge University Press, 2003), esp. 101, 112–13, 215–20: The frequent, general interaction of personifications with embodied characters/actors upon which Kiefer comments carries specific significance in Shakespeare's Jacobean plays.

27. *The Winter's Tale*, ed. Stephen Orgel (Oxford: Oxford University Press, 1996), I.ii.137. Unless otherwise indicated, citation of *The Winter's Tale* is from this edition.

28. See note 50, this chapter. Paradoxically, perhaps, the heightened subjectivity of perception coincides with greater reliance on experiment, demonstration, scientific instruments, and the "factual" evidence that these provided.

29. This contribution is particularly conspicuous in Tasso (note 13, this chapter). Aristotle affords "the first extended analytical description of imagining as a distinct faculty of the soul," as well as of its challenges to philosophical

analysis (Schofield, "Aristotle on the Imagination," 249). Insofar as Plato treats imagination in a few late dialogues, Schofield suggests, by then he was influenced by Aristotle. The influential work of the Renaissance Neoplatonist Marsilio Ficino, who is fully aware of the Aristotelian tradition and adopts aspects of it, attends to the imagination but is suspicious of its fundamental ties to matter (e.g., *Platonic Theology*, trans. Michael J. B. Allen, with John Warden; Latin text ed. James Hankins, with William Bowen, 6 vols. [Cambridge, MA: Harvard University Press, 2001–2006]); on the deceptions of phantasy, 6: 186–93 (#6–11), 256–57 (#28); on the positive power of phantasy (anticipating Tasso's view), which Ficino distinguishes from imagination and places above it, 2: 262–71 (esp. #2–3, 7); anticipating the *scala*/ladder of Castiglione's Bembo, 1: 154–55 (#6), 3: 56–59 (#2); on the mirroring or superior iteration of the sensible phantasy in the phantastic capacity of the intellect (again anticipating Tasso), 5: 100–3 (#4–5), 106–9 (#4–6). In the last instances, Ficino is arguing speculatively as he engages the Aristotelian tradition of Averroism, an important influence in the Renaissance. On the mix of Aristotelian and Neoplatonic with other threads in Sidney's *Apology*, see Robert E. Stillman, *Philip Sidney and the Poetics of Renaissance Cosmopolitanism* (Aldershot, UK: Ashgate, 2008), 28–30, 109–10; on the medieval and Renaissance merging in "pneumophantasmology" of the Aristotelian and Neoplatonic (and other) traditions, see also Agamben, *Stanzas*, 92–96.

30. See K. V. Wilkes, "*Psuchē* versus the Mind," in Nussbaum and Rorty, 109–27, esp. 109–110. Likewise, Dale B. Martin on the Pauline body: *The Corinthian Body* (New Haven, CT: Yale University Press, 1995), 3–25. On the role of Latin in Shakespeare's time, see Judith H. Anderson, *Words That Matter: Linguistic Perception in Renaissance English* (Stanford, CA: Stanford University Press, 1996), chaps. 2–3. Nearly half a century ago, Hallett Smith glossed "affection" rightly as "a disposition or mutation happening to bodie or minde," by citing Bishop Thomas Cooper's Latin dictionary, with reference to Cicero's use of *affectio*, or "impetus, commotio, affectióque animi": "Leontes' *Affectio*," *Shakespeare Quarterly* 14 (1963): 163–66, here 163. Cicero's usage is only part of the linguistic story and part of what Leontes is doing with the term. Cicero draws heavily on Aristotelian philosophy and, as a rhetorician concerned with morals and ethics, assumes its systemic thinking (e.g., May and Wisse, *On the Ideal Orator*, 26–39).

31. I have cited the first edition of the *OED* (1933), while checking it against the latest online version, and have done so in the interest of referential stability, as well as of historical comprehension: For *Intention*, the second edition (1989), the one available online as I revise (July 2010), is virtually identical to what I cite but will likely be further altered before this essay is published. The *OED*'s first edition also corresponds to the numbering of many other sources I cite. For *Affection*, the preceding reasons also obtain. In addition, the draft revision of September 2010 that is now available to me

online, for *Affection* uses a modernized format and exhibits a modern bias less useful for the analysis of Tudor-Stuart texts, insofar as the initial, strongly Latinate usage of the first edition of the *OED*, which would have been second nature to literate contemporaries of Shakespeare, is now located in and effectually alienated into the etymology (see note 30, this chapter, on Tudor-Stuart awareness of language). Otherwise, nothing substantial in the *OED* entries has changed. To facilitate online reference, I have given the online numbering, preceded by "cf.," after that of the 1933 edition, whenever there is any difference in their numbering.

32. Cf. Stanley Cavell, *Disowning Knowledge in Seven Plays of Shakespeare*, updated ed. (Cambridge: Cambridge University Press, 2003), 193–201.

33. "In the eye" is interpretive, indeed speculative, on my part with respect to the acting and not meant as a gloss for the words "Look on me with your welkin eye" (II.ii.135). Orgel, *Winter's Tale*, offers "heavenly (or bright, shining, radiant)" as a gloss for "welkin"; in *The Riverside Shakespeare*, Hallett Smith suggests "like the sky, i.e. blue." Contextually, the presence of "kin" in "welkin" may suggest a mirroring gaze appropriate to Leontes's self-centricity.

34. Orgel, *Winter's Tale*, 9, cites Nicholas Rowe's revision of I.ii.136–37, in which Rowe substitutes "Imagination" for "Affection," thereby modernizing the line for his eighteenth-century audience. In a footnote on the same page, Orgel includes a helpful, annotated list of discussions of signification in Leontes's speech, to which, I, a belated interpreter, am indebted, as I am with respect to the other annotated texts I treat. The citation of Spenser is to *The Faerie Queene*, ed. A. C. Hamilton, with text ed. Hiroshi Yamashita and Toshiyuki Suzuki (Harlow, UK: Pearson Education, 2001), III.xi.1, vs. 9.

35. Aristotle, *De Anima*, 427b8–428a1–2.

36. Brentano, *Psychology*, 68; cf. Agamben, *Stanzas*, 76; Clark, *Vanities of the Eye*, 318–20. Also *Julius Caesar*, II.i.63–65: "Between the acting of a dreadful thing / And the first motion, all the interim is / Like a phantasma or a hideous dream" (*Riverside Shakespeare*); and *Macbeth*, I.iii.137–42: "My thought, whose murther yet is but fantastical" (139). In Leontes's speech, Charles Frey suggests that the King's line of sight moves from Mamillius, who stands before him and in whom he sees his own boyhood innocence, to Hermione and Polixenes, standing somewhat farther off, in whom he sees the inseparability of sexual maturity, lost innocence, and the violation of integrity; Leontes's view, in a Donnean word, "contracts" his own experience of growth, as both mnemonically and currently imagined: *Shakespeare's Vast Romance: A Study of* The Winter's Tale (Columbia: University of Missouri Press, 1980), 123–25. See also John Erskine Hankins, *Backgrounds of Shakespeare's Thought* (Hamden, CT: Archon, 1978), 98–101: To gloss the speech of Leontes in question, Hankins invokes the terminology of scholasticism, which traces back to Aristotle's *De Anima*.

37. Samuel Taylor Coleridge nicely describes Leontes's speech as "soliloquy in the form of dialogue": "Notes on *The Winter's Tale*," in The Winter's Tale: Critical Essays, ed. Maurice Hunt (New York: Garland, 1995), 72–75, here 72.

38. I hesitate to join Cavell in naming Leontes's basic epistemological problem *skepticism*. Leontes is instead, in his self-righteousness, all too inventive of fiction to be suffering primarily from skepticism. If warped, his imagination is powerful, not deficient, in the early acts. Yet Cavell's evolving *skepticism*, which merges, via Kant's dialectical illusion, with *fanaticism*, skepticism's radical opposite, speaks to my objection, although only by Cavell's having his argument two ways (206).

39. I do not think "unlawfully" an appropriate gloss for "beyond commission" if it attributes illegal behavior directly to Hermione without the present, transforming mediation of Leontes's imaginative processing, which is what is still being described. Hermione's behavior is here merely an effect of Leontes's imaginings. The real Hermione might (and should) be said to have disappeared.

40. Carol Thomas Neely, "*The Winter's Tale*: The Triumph of Speech," Studies in English Literature, 1500–1900 15, no. 2 (1975): 321–38, here 326. Neely's perceptive article has influenced subsequent editorial glossing and punctuation (e.g., Orgel). Neely identifies "Affection" as passion and argues that Leontes refers "in part" to himself and in part, "perhaps only half consciously," to the lust of Hermione and Polixenes (325). More recently, Jennifer C. Vaught sees Leontes's diseased affection as a cultural marker of weakness and femininity: *Masculinity and Emotion in Early Modern English Literature* (Aldershot, UK: Ashgate, 2008), 163–64. On the abstraction of Leontes's language in the speech at issue, see Maurice Hunt, "*Winter's Tale*, I.ii.135–46," *University of Mississippi Studies in English*, n.s. 4 (1983): 49–55, here 50; and Jonathan Smith, "The Language of Leontes," *Shakespeare Quarterly* 19 (1968): 317–27, here 317–18.

41. Bevington, ed., *The Complete Works of Shakespeare*, updated 4th ed. (New York: Addison Wesley Longman, 1997). Cf. Hallett Smith, *Riverside Shakespeare*: exclamation point after "Affection," parentheses, not dashes, enclosing "how can this be?" and then a comma. Cf. Stephen Greenblatt, Walter Cohen, Jean E. Howard, and Katharine Eisaman Maus, eds., *The Norton Shakespeare*, based on the Oxford edition (New York: Norton, 1997): same as Bevington. Cf. J. H. P. Pafford, ed., *The Winter's Tale* (1963; rpt. London: Thomson Learning, 2000): exclamation point after "Affection," colon rather than full stop after "centre," semicolon, plus dash, after "dreams." I do not intend the present note as an exhaustive list of editorial possibilities, but I hope it offers a fair sampling.

42. See Michael McCanles's discussion of Ben Jonson's punctuation, including his strategic use of enjambments: *Jonsonian Discriminations: The Humanist Poet and the Praise of True Nobility* (Toronto: University of Toronto Press, 1992), 4–21, esp. 18. Also George T. Wright, *Shakespeare's Metrical Art* (Berkeley: University of California Press, 1988), 213–19.

43. For the folio text, I refer to Charlton Hinman's "ideal" version of *The First Folio of Shakespeare* (New York: Norton, 1968), 296 (bottom pagination): marginal numbers 213–18; I have silently modernized long *s*.

44. David Ward cites and favors the punctuation of the folio version, arguing that Leontes "is attempting in a very positive spirit to diagnose his own psychological condition": "Affection, Intention, and Dreams in *The Winter's Tale*," *Modern Language Review* 82 (1987): 545–54, here 549, 552. My discussion shares ground with Ward's, but I find Leontes more self-fascinated and self-justifying than firmly rational and well intentioned; in this speech, his vocabulary is as philosophical/epistemological as it is medical/paramedical in origin and orientation. It is the very nature of *affection* to be both mental and physical, with all the complications this entails for ethics, agency, and judgment (from Othello's epilepsy to Macbeth's hallucinations and from Hamlet's ambivalence to Leontes's fantasies, etc.). Cf. also Laurence Wright, who calls on the medical/paramedical writings of Timothy Bright and Robert Burton and locates the crucial moment when Leontes starts trusting his imaginings in an illogical jump, namely, "Then," in line 142: "When Does the Tragi-Comic Disruption Start? *The Winter's Tale* and Leontes' 'Affection,'" *English Studies* 70 (1989): 225–32. In *Vanities of the Eye*, Clark rightly considers the fascination of melancholia in this period to be "symptomatic of much broader contemporary concerns about the rationality of seeing," perceiving, or indeed, as I see it, imagining (51–52).

45. Pafford, *Winter's Tale*, 165–66. Pafford cites the second of these comments from Charles D. Stewart, *Some Textual Difficulties in Shakespeare* (New Haven, CT: Yale University Press, 1914), 96–109. Hallett Smith assembles similar comments by editors and critics such as Dover Wilson, Horace Howard Furness, John Payne Collier, G. B. Harrison, and Northrop Frye: "*Affectio*," 163. By contrast, see Russ McDonald, "Poetry and Plot in *The Winter's Tale*," and Hunt, The Winter's Tale: *Critical Essays*, 298–318, on the artful, mutual mirroring not merely of action and utterance in *The Winter's Tale* but more precisely of perception and diction, syntax, and rhythm. Maurice Hunt, "The Critical Legacy," in Hunt, The Winter's Tale: *Critical Essays*, 3–61, more generally reviews assessments and interpretations of *The Winter's Tale* from the nineteenth century to nearly the end of the twentieth.

46. Faith, too, is affective and (within an Aristotelian system) requires the impulse of the *nous poiētikos* that enables Leontes to "see" the statue. See Sarah Beckwith's perceptive essay, "Shakespeare's Resurrections," in *Shakespeare and the Middle Ages*, ed. Curtis Perry and John Watkins (Oxford: Oxford University Press, 2009), 45–67; also Anita Gilman Sherman, *Skepticism and Memory in Shakespeare and Donne* (New York: Palgrave Macmillan, 2007), chap. 3, esp. 80–85.

47. On lyrical effects in Donne's prose, see my *Words That Matter*, 189–231 (sermons), and *Translating Investments*, 61–77 (*Devotions*). Unless otherwise

indicated, the edition I cite for Donne is *John Donne: The Complete English Poems*, ed. A. J. Smith (London: Penguin, 1996). Despite Smith's modernized English, I like his editing and annotation for the *Songs and Sonnets*—at least until the complete Donne Variorum appears.

48. See notes 19 and 29 in this chapter; also *Select Passages Illustrating Neoplatonism*, trans. E. R. Dodds (1923; rpt. Chicago: Ares, 1979), chap. 6, esp. 76, 80–81, 84, 89; cf. 57, 107–8, 110.

49. See note 29, this chapter; for Pico, see *On the Dignity of Man, on Being and the One, Heptaplus* (1940; rpt. Indianapolis: Bobbs-Merrill, 1965). Agamben locates medieval and much Renaissance phantasmology in "a convergence between the Aristotelian theory of the imagination and the Neoplatonic doctrine of the pneuma [spirit] as a vehicle of the soul" (*Stanzas*, 23). Historically, Aristotle on imagination, in all the ambiguity of *De Anima*, is something of a sine qua non. For many other examples of the merging of the Aristotelian and Neoplatonic traditions, see Sugimura (*"Matter of Glorious Trial,"* e.g., 7–8, 50, 54, and throughout).

50. See David C. Lindberg, *Theories of Vision from Al-Kindi to Kepler* (Chicago: University of Chicago Press, 1976); David C. Lindberg and Geoffrey Cantor, *The Discourse of Light from the Middle Ages to the Enlightenment: Papers Read at a Clark Library Seminar, 24 April 1982* (Los Angeles: William Andrews Clark Memorial Library, University of California–Los Angeles, 1985). Johannes Kepler's discovery of the inversion and reversal of the retinal image, which further undermined the reliability of sense-based perception, caused him "no little grief"; he declined to theorize about how the brain/spirits/soul process the retinal image (Lindberg, *Theories*, 202–3). In Lindberg's judgment, Kepler was a "medieval Scholastic manqué," a culminating figure rather than a revolutionary one; influences in Kepler's background included both visual intromission and Neoplatonism (Lindberg and Cantor, *Discourse*, vi). The tradition of Galenic medicine intersected both with the Aristotelian tradition and with the Neoplatonic one—the latter conspicuously in the instance of Ficino, himself a physician, whose interest in sympathetic magic was medical in origin. Clark notes (via Richard Tuck on Marin Mersenne) that the skeptical tropes of Pyrrhonism largely depended on optics (*Vanities of the Eye*, 270).

51. In "'An Excellent Exercise of Wit That Speaks So Well of Ill': Donne and the Poetics of Concealment," Judith Scherer Herz refuses a fictional speaker (the "invention" of Cleanth Brooks) even to the first stanza of "The Canonization" and argues instead for autonomous, successive stanzas, each having "its own voice," style, and conventions ("satire, love lyric, hermetic, coterie poetry, and hymn"): in *The Eagle and the Dove: Reassessing John Donne*, ed. Claude J. Summers and Ted-Larry Pebworth (Columbia: University of Missouri Press, 1986), 3–14, here 6–7: Does Herz's approach sound somewhat antic? Like

Calderwood on Hamlet, she describes Donne's illusionistic speaker as "Escherlike" (5) On Donne's speakers, cf. Robert N. Watson, *The Rest Is Silence: Death as Annihilation in the English Renaissance* (Berkeley: University of California Press, 1994), 167. In "No Marriage in Heaven: John Donne, Anne Donne, and the Kingdom Come," Maureen Sabine seems to take the speaker of the first stanza to be old, as well as (subsequently?) "weary, pained": in *John Donne's "Desire of More": The Subject of Anne More Donne in His Poetry*, ed. M. Thomas Hester (Newark, NJ: University of Delaware Press, 1996), 228–55, here 235, 237. Also see Dayton Haskin's review of the history of interpretation of "The Canonization" in the twentieth century and earlier, namely "On Trying to Make the Record Speak More about Donne's Love Poems" (in Hester, *John Donne's "Desire of More*," 39–65, esp. 39–44); and Hester's " 'Fœminae Lectissimae': Reading Anne Donne," which provides especially provocative background for biographical connections of Donne's poems with his marriage (in Hester, *John Donne's "Desire of More*," 17–34).

52. Richard Halpern makes the same point about love/not-love in "The Lyric in the Field of Information: Autopoiesis and History in Donne's *Songs and Sonnets*," in *Critical Essays on John Donne*, ed. Arthur F. Marotti (New York: Macmillan, 1994), 49–76, here 58–59, but enlightening throughout. Invoking the cybernetics of Niklas Luhmann, Halpern relates the opposition of love/not-love to sexuality as the ground of a self-referring, self-sustaining system that witnesses the growth of social complexity. Halpern must reject the possibility that love (or affection, eros, passion) affords "an Archimedean point from which it can grasp the whole of a social terrain" and with it any argument on the basis of early modern philosophy/theology (59; cf. his handling of traditional metonyms, 63–64).

53. Augustine, *De Doctrina Christiana*, I.ii, in *Patrologia Latina*, ed. J. P. Migne (Paris: Garnier Fratres, 1887), XXXIV, p. 19: Having identified words as signs, Augustine continues, "Quamobrem omne signum etiam res aliqua est; quod enim nulla res est, omnino nihil est [Wherefore every sign is also a thing because what is not a thing is nothing at all]. On Donne's use of narrative, see Heather Dubrow, "Reconfiguring Figuring: John Donne as Narrative Poet," in *Go Figure: Energies, Forms, and Institutions*, ed. Judith H. Anderson and Joan Pong Linton (New York: Fordham University Press, 2011); also Heather Dubrow, *The Challenges of Orpheus: Lyric Poetry and Early Modern England* (Baltimore: John Hopkins University Press, 2008), esp. chap. 5.

54. Citations in this and the following sentence are from Vesely's *Architecture in the Age of Divided Representation: The Question of Creativity in the Shadow of Production* (Cambridge, MA: MIT Press, 2004), 140–41.

55. On the figure of the roundel, see George Puttenham's chapter on figures of proportion: *The Arte of English Poesy* (1589; rpt. Kent, OH: Kent State

University Press, 1988), 111–13; Puttenham's roundel is schematically rather than visually round (i.e., conceptually and sonically so, the latter by the framing rhyme word "love").

56. See Sidney, *Apology*, 99–101, and note 13, this chapter. Stillman mentions what looks like another correlative of Aristotle's "maker mind" in Sidney's version of Melanchthon's *mens architectatrix*, "architectural mind" (162; cf. 123, 135). In *John Donne: Coterie Poet* (Madison: University of Wisconsin Press, 1986), 162–63, Arthur Marotti provides a broader summary of interpretations of the symbols in stanza 3, finding in them indeterminacy and elitism rather than imaginative excitement and plenitude; but cf. Halpern, "Lyric in the Field of Information," 66–67. Ronald Corthell's wide-ranging commentary on "The Canonization" serves to update its interpretation to the late twentieth century: *Ideology and Desire in Renaissance Poetry: The Subject of Donne* (Detroit: Wayne State University Press, 1997), 88–100; cf. Marotti, *Coterie*, 157. Margret Fetzer, *John Donne's Performances: Sermons, Poems, Letters and Devotions* (Manchester: Manchester University Press, 2010), 77–137 (secular poems), 138–84 (divine), also affords a review of recent work. For two other comprehensive, historicized, or theorized approaches to Donne's imagination in the later twentieth century, cf. John Carey, *John Donne: Life, Mind and Art* (New York: Oxford University Press, 1981), 10–11, and chap. 9: "Imagined Corners"; Thomas Docherty, *John Donne, Undone* (London: Methuen, 1986) (e.g., chap. 3, on the failure of representation).

57. See John A. T. Robinson, *The Body: A Study in Pauline Theology* (London: SCM, 1966): A body requires "more than one member"; the resurrection body of Christ is "articulated in diversity *without ceasing to be a unity*" (59–60); also Dale B. Martin's view that the Pauline body attains "identity *only* through participation" (132: my emphasis). For an Aristotelian connection, see note 30, this chapter.

58. Clark, *Vanities of the Eye*, for example, 270–74, 280; Gallagher, "The Sacramental Neuter and the Missing Body in Robert Southwell's Poetics," in Anderson and Linton, *Go Figure*, 38–57; Barthes, *The Neutral: Lecture Course at the Collège de France (1977–1978)*, trans. Rosalind E. Krauss and Denis Hollier (New York: Columbia University Press, 2005); Maurice Blanchot, "René Char and the Thought of the Neuter," in *The Infinite Conversation*, trans. Susan Hanson (Minneapolis: University of Minnesota Press, 1993), 298–307. Coincidentally, Southwell was also Shakespeare's distant cousin on his mother's side; see Richard Wilson, *Secret Shakespeare*, chap. 1, for additional Shakespearean connections. David Norbrook, invoking William Empson, defends a "genuine radical impulse" in Donne's *Songs and Sonnets*: "The Monarchy of Wit and the Republic of Letters: Donne's Politics," in *Soliciting Interpretation: Literary Theory and Seventeenth-Century English Poetry*, ed. Elizabeth D. Harvey and Katharine Eisaman Maus (Chicago: Chicago University Press, 1990), 3–36, here 13–15.

59. See Jon A. Quitslund, *Spenser's Supreme Fiction: Platonic Natural Philosophy and* The Faerie Queene (Toronto: University of Toronto Press, 2001), chap 7, here 233. By citing Quitslund rather than merely Plato's *Symposium*, I mean to invoke not only the further cultural context of *The Faerie Queene* but specifically Quitslund's discussion of Leone Ebreo (229–39). For Gardner, ed., on Leone's and Donne's erotics, see *The Elegies and the Songs and Sonnets of John Donne* (Oxford: Clarendon, 1965), Appendix D. In Leone, each male and female includes the other's sex/gender.

60. Marotti, *Coterie*, 165, compares Donne's "intense wittiness" to Hamlet's when either is "at the emotional breaking point." Cf. Patrick Grant on Hamlet: "Language at times is . . . a way of protecting himself from himself"; for example, "he plays at verbal games and riddles to temper his nerves after seeing the ghost" ("Imagination in the Renaissance," in *Religious Imagination*, ed. James P. Mackey [Edinburgh: Edinburgh University Press, 1986], 86–101, here 93). Also note 8, this chapter (language and imagination in Aristotle). Relevantly, the psycholinguist Jean Aitchison compares verbal selection and recognition to an electrical circuit board with multidirectional, reciprocal flows between semantic and phonological components, including rhythm. Her model puts both sounds and meanings in play, and it shows that the human brain, whose billions of neurons and connecting synapses are excited, agitated interactively, "is capable of massive parallel processing": *Words in the Mind*, 2d ed. (Oxford: Blackwell, 1994), 214–21, here 208. On comparing Donne's "metaphysical" style to Shakespeare's, see, for historical spread, Patrick Cruttwell, *The Shakespearean Moment and Its Place in the Poetry of the 17th Century* (London: Chatto and Windus, 1954), and Marshall Grossman: *The Story of All Things: Writing the Self in English Renaissance Narrative Poetry* (Durham, NC: Duke University Press, 1998), chap. 5. Grossman rethinks Donne as a metaphysical poet, whose "Laura idea," along with the "ontologically homogeneous," "self-signifying universe" she embodies, is gone forever (178). Cruttwell and Grossman focus on Donne's *Anniversaries*.

61. One exception is "The Good Morrow," on which see the essay by Jennifer Pacenza in this volume. More generally, on movement within a Donne poem, cf. Angus Fletcher, *Time, Space, and Motion in the Age of Shakespeare* (Cambridge, MA: Harvard University Press, 2007), chap. 7, esp. 124–26.

62. Donne was trained in law. I prefer the variant "contract" rather than "extract" in the final stanza, as does A. J. Smith in the edition I cite; extant Mss, apart from the early editions, favor "extract." Donne's use of "contracted" in "The Sun Rising," with much the same punning as that for which I argue here, however, influences my choice, as does the fuller inclusivity of "contract" (vs. "extract," alchemically distill, or, indeed, mentally abstract). "Extract" leans a little too much away from specifically *imaginative vision* for my sense of the

ending of "The Canonization." Since socio-political entities, "Countries, towns, courts," are what constitute the contraction/extraction, the pertinence of a Neoplatonic world soul would be forced, alchemical distillation silly, and a scientific, material soul, though conceivable, historically premature.

63. On such a surround, see Lena Cowen Orlin, *Locating Privacy in Tudor England* (Oxford: Oxford University Press, 2007). On spying broadly and relevantly considered in *Hamlet*, see Patricia Parker, *Shakespeare from the Margins: Language, Culture, Context* (Chicago: University of Chicago Press, 1996), chap. 7. Also, the treatment of surveillance in the Cold War productions of *Hamlet* discussed by Kinney, Introduction, *Hamlet: New Critical Essays*, 57 and 64 (Kenneth Branagh's filmed *Hamlet*).

64. For two striking examples earlier cited, see Pomponazzi, *On the Immortality of the Soul*, and Lodowyck Bryskett's *Discourse of Civill Life*, an example contemporary with Shakespeare and Donne. In the latter, the intellect maintains a functioning relation to the sensible soul subordinate to it, whose nature, capacity, or power but not whose passibility, or feeling and connection to sensation, it includes. Since the possible (receptive, potential) understanding within the intellectual soul is also "the place of the Intelligible formes," these distinctions look like an effort to reconcile Plato with Aristotle (199–200).

65. On mortalism, see Gordon Campbell, Thomas N. Corns, John K. Hale, and Fiona J. Tweedie for distinction among the three varieties within Protestantism of this ancient heresy: namely, the beliefs that the soul dies with the body until the time of the general resurrection, that the soul sleeps from death to general resurrection, and that the soul dies with the body—period: *Milton and the Manuscript of De Doctrina Christiana* (Oxford: Oxford University Press, 2007), 117–18; cf. Sugimura's revisionism regarding Milton's avowed belief in mortalism (142, 145–47, 153, 156). Also Norman T. Burns, *Christian Mortalism from Tyndale to Milton* (Cambridge, MA: Harvard University Press, 1972), for example, 14–18, 73–75, 118, 169–83. On Donne's interest in mortalism, see Watson, *The Rest Is Silence*, 166; Ramie Targoff, *John Donne: Body and Soul* (Chicago: University of Chicago Press, 2008), 8–9; also the glosses on lines 2–4 of Donne's Holy Sonnet "At the round earth's imagined corners," in *The Variorum Edition of the Poetry of John Donne*, ed. Gary A. Stringer (Bloomington: Indiana University Press, 2005), 7 (pt. 1): 409.

66. Cf. *OED* (1933, 1989), s.v. *By*, prep., adv., IV.26; and *The Yale Edition of the Shorter Poems of Edmund Spenser*, ed. William A. Oram, Einar Bjorvand, and Ronald Bond (New Haven, CT: Yale University Press, 1989), *Amoretti LVIII*. (The editor's note on "by" is tendentious; see Louis L. Martz on "by" in "The *Amoretti*: 'Most Goodly Temperature,'" in *Form and Convention in the Poetry of Edmund Spenser*, ed. William Nelson [New York: Columbia University Press, 1961], 146–68, here 162–63, 180n5.) In a reading relevant to my own, Leslie T. Duer compares "A Nocturnal" to the central figure and surroundings of a

Renaissance portrait painting: "The Poet on St. Lucy's Eve: John Donne's Portrait," in *Word and Visual Imagination: Studies in the Interaction of English Literature and the Visual Arts*, ed. Karl Josef Höltgen, Peter M. Daly, and Wolfgang Lottes (Nuremberg: Erlangen, 1988), 107–31, here 117–20.

67. Glosses on "bed's-feet" tend to underestimate the anthropomorphic compression of body and bed in this counterfactual image; see A. J. Smith, *John Donne.*, 391n7: Smith's second possibility ("a dying man's concern contracts to the limit of his bed") is more plausible than his first (vitality drains "towards the earth via the feet of the bed"). My own reading might be too free, but what the speaker projects is not a fully rational condition; the interpretive problem of this image, namely imitative form, is not without resemblance to that of Leontes's (con)fused perception.

68. For a useful summary of approaches to "A Nocturnal," see Kate Gartner Frost, "'Preparing towards Her': Contexts of *A Nocturnall upon S. Lucies Day*," in *Anne More Donne*, ed. Hester, 149–71, here 149–50. Frost treats the alchemical, liturgical, and arithmetical structure of the poem. "The Canonization" and "A Nocturnal" are often connected to one another and to Donne's marriage; in addition to Frost, see Sabine, "No Marriage in Heaven" (245–48), and Achsah Guibbory, "Fear of 'Loving More': Death and the Loss of Sacramental Love" (in Hester, *Anne More Donne*, 204–27, esp. 217–22). Guibbory compares the death of Donne's wife to his earlier loss of the (Eucharistic) body to Protestantism (221). Cf. Herz, "'An Excellent Exercise of Wit,'" 11, for the view that "A Nocturnal" is unlikely to have as referent the death of Donne's wife (or the sickness of Lucy, Countess of Bedford); also Watson, whose reading of "A Nocturnal" is as annihilative as his reading of *King Lear*, to which he compares the poem (*The Rest Is Silence*, 225–29).

69. Anthony Low observes in this stanza Donne's "remarkable capacity for suddenly . . . killing, freezing, and preserving" a situation "as if embalmed, for post mortem dissection": "Love and Science: Cultural Change in Donne's Songs and Sonnets," *Studies in the Literary Imagination* 22 (1989): 5–16, here 15.

70. Marotti's view of lines 1–14 as first "strained conceitedness" and then "smugly pat paradoxical formulae" perhaps fails to appreciate the movement within meditation (or ritual) from mere repetition and initial engagement to genuine emotion and imaginative excitement (*Coterie*, 267–68). On Donne's modal complexity and punning, see Brian Cummings's examination of the conditional tense in Donne's religious lyrics: *The Literary Culture of the Reformation: Grammar and Grace* (Oxford: Oxford University Press, 2002), 364–417. On Donne's lexical punning, see Judith H. Anderson, "Donne's (Im)possible Punning," *John Donne Journal* 23 (2004): 59–68; this essay also affords references to recent theories about punning.

71. As Ernest B. Gilman puts it, the poet's image of Christ is finally a "deformity," for the poem dramatizes "the confrontation between the poet's

image of God, and God's": *Iconoclasm and Poetry in the English Reformation: Down Went Dagon* (Chicago: University of Chicago Press, 1986), 141–47, here 146–47. Cf. Helen B. Brooks's more positive view in "Donne's 'Goodfriday, 1613, Riding Westward' and Augustine's Psychology of Time," in *John Donne's Religious Imagination: Essays in Honor of John T. Shawcross*, ed. Raymond-Jean Frontain and Frances M. Malpezzi (Conway: University of Central Arkansas Press, 1995), 284–305, here 298–99.

72. Barbara Kiefer Lewalski considers this Holy Sonnet "one of the two or three which exhibit the full Ignatian meditative structure," especially with respect to the *compositio loci* of the first quatrain: *Protestant Poetics and the Seventeenth-Century Religious Lyric* (Princeton, NJ: Princeton University Press, 1979), 268–69; Lewalski refers to Louis L. Martz, *The Poetry of Meditation* (New Haven, CT: Yale University Press, 1954). This sort of scene setting is overdetermined in the Tudor-Stuart period, within devotional writing ranging from the specifically prescribed and formulaic to what Ezra Pound would centuries later describe as more general habits of thought: in cogitation, or discursive thought, "the mind flits aimlessly about the object"; in meditation "it circles about . . . [the object] in a methodical manner"; in contemplation "it is unified with the object" (*Guide to Kulchur* [Norfolk, CT: New Directions, 1938], 77). Marotti's judgment that "Donne pridefully *over*dramatizes the self" in the opening of this sonnet (and others), while debatable, evokes for me another memory of Hamlet (*Coterie*, 256).

73. Anderson, *Translating Investments*, 74–76; *Words That Matter*, 208–13, 209n52.

74. A. J. Smith, *John Donne* also groups "Image of her whom I love" with Donne's elegies and titles it "The Dream," as in the 1635 edition. John T. Shawcross, ed., *The Complete Poetry of John Donne* (Garden City, NY: Doubleday, 1967), prints the poem with only the heading "Image of her whom I love" under *Songs and Sonnets*. Gardner also prints it with the *Songs and Sonnets* and gives it the title "Image and Dream." *The Variorum Edition of the Poetry of John Donne*, vol. 2: "The Elegies," does not include the poem.

75. I assume a female addressee, albeit cautioned by an awareness of Ben Saunders's illuminating analyses of poems by Donne that are either ambiguous on this point or involve homoeroticism: *Desiring Donne: Poetry, Sexuality, Interpretation* (Cambridge, MA: Harvard University Press, 2006), for example, chap. 2; Saunders's whole book is pertinent.

76. For example, see Baldassare Castiglione, *The Book of the Courtier*, trans. Thomas Hoby, in *Three Renaissance Classics* (New York: Scribner, 1953), 243–618, here 609–12 (ladder of love): "through the vertue of imagination, hee [the lover, progressively sundering himself from 'all matter'] shall fashion within himselfe that beautie much more faire than it is in deede" (610).

77. On conscience/consciousness, see note 15, this chapter.

78. In *John Donne's Performances*, Fetzer finds in Donne's two dream poems only the claim that "external reality . . . can be reconstructed through poetry" rather than, or additionally, their recognition of the primacy of the waking world (84–88, here 88). Her reading could make Donne Leontes. More generally, Fetzer's engaging study uses Austin's theory of speech acts to highlight the performative and sometimes specifically theatrical features of Donne's multigeneric writing.

79. On the history and theory of figures/figuration, see Anderson and Linton's introduction to *Go Figure*, 1–18.

Contributors

JUDITH H. ANDERSON is Chancellor's Professor of English at Indiana University and author of *The Growth of a Personal Voice:* Piers Plowman *and* The Faerie Queene (1976), *Biographical Truth: The Representation of Historical Persons in Tudor-Stuart Writing* (1984), *Words That Matter: Linguistic Perception in Renaissance English* (1996), *Translating Investments: Metaphor and the Dynamic of Cultural Change in Tudor-Stuart England* (2005), and *Reading the Allegorical Intertext: Chaucer, Spenser, Shakespeare, Milton* (2008), which was awarded the MacCaffrey Award of the International Spenser Society; she is also coeditor of *Will's Vision of Piers Plowman* (1990), *Spenser's Life and the Subject of Biography* (1996), *Integrating Literature and Writing Instruction: First-Year English, Humanities Core Courses, Seminars* (2007), and *Go Figure: Energies, Forms, and Institutions in the Early Modern World* (2011). Her current book project is titled *Issues of Analogy, Light, and Death*.

MATTHIAS BAUER is professor of English literature at the University of Tübingen, Germany. He has published numerous articles on early modern writers, including Shakespeare, Donne, Herbert, and Vaughan. His book on *Mystical Linguistics: George Herbert, Richard Crashaw, and Henry Vaughan* is forthcoming. He has also edited, with Angelika Zirker, *Drama and Cultural Change: Turning around Shakespeare* (2009), and he is cofounder and editor of *Connotations: A Journal for Critical Debate*.

MARY BLACKSTONE is professor emerita of theatre and director of the Centre for the Study of Script Development at the University of Regina, Saskatchewan, and former dean of fine arts, chair of the Canadian Association of Fine Arts Deans, and member of the board of the International Council of Fine Arts Deans. Both an early modern cultural historian and a professional dramaturge engaged in the development of new dramatic scripts for stage and screen, she has published numerous articles and chapters on Shakespeare and on topics such as religion, patronage, and women's writing. She is currently writing a book titled *The Performance of Commonwealth in Early Modern England*, which treats the role of various kinds of traveling performers in developing a concept of "commonwealth."

The late MARSHALL GROSSMAN was professor of English at the University of Maryland, College Park. He was the author of three books, *Authors to Themselves: Milton and the Revelation of History* (1987), *The Story of All Things: Writing the Self in Renaissance English Narrative Poetry* (1998), and the Blackwell *Seventeenth-Century Literature Handbook*. He also edited *Aemilia Lanyer: Gender, Genre, and the Canon* (1998) and *Reading Renaissance Ethics* (2007). He was working on Milton and the development of rational religion.

JULIAN LAMB completed his BA at the Australian National University and his PhD at Cambridge University; he currently teaches at the Chinese University of Hong Kong. He has published on Puttenham's *Arte of English Poesie*, early modern English dictionaries, and Wittgenstein, and he has recently coedited *Art and Authenticity* (Australian Scholarly Publishing, 2010).

CATHERINE GIMELLI MARTIN is professor of English at the University of Memphis. She is the author of *The Ruins of Allegory: Paradise Lost and the Metamorphosis of Epic Convention* (1998), which received the James Holly Hanford prize of the Milton Society of America; *Milton and Gender* (2004); and *Milton among the Puritans: The Case for Historical Revisionism* (2010). She is also coeditor of *Francis Bacon and the Refiguring of Modern Thought* (2005). Her essay "The Erotology of Donne's 'Extasie'" was awarded the essay prize of the John Donne Society in 2006.

DAVID LEE MILLER is Carolina Distinguished Professor of English and Comparative Literature at the University of South Carolina, where he directs the Center for Digital Humanities. He is the author of two books, *The Poem's Two Bodies: The Poetics of the 1590 Faerie Queene* (1988) and *Dreams of the Burning Child: Sacrificial Sons and the Father's Witness* (2003) and has coedited four collections, including *A Touch More Rare: Harry Berger Jr. and the Arts of Interpretation* (2009), with Nina Levine. His current project, with four other general editors, is a new *Collected Works of Edmund Spenser* in preparation for Oxford University Press.

JENNIFER PACENZA is currently completing a PhD at Indiana University, where she is focusing on Renaissance drama and performance, with a minor in science and literature. She has a MA in literature and a MS in library sciences from the University of North Texas. Her dissertation proposes the concept of dramatic experimentation, based on the performative nature of scientific experimentation and knowledge production, to explore how Renaissance theatrical works are themselves experiments in theater historiography.

JEANNE SHAMI is professor of English at the University of Regina, Saskatchewan. She is the author of *John Donne's 1622 Gunpowder Plot Sermon: A Parallel-Text Edition* (1996) and *John Donne and Conformity in Crisis in the Late Jacobean Pulpit* (2003), which won the John Donne Society Award for Distinguished Publication. She has also edited *Renaissance Tropologies: The Cultural Imagination of Early Modern England* (2008) and, with Dennis Flynn and M. Thomas Hester, has coedited the *Oxford Handbook of John Donne* (2011). She is currently editing Donne's verse letters for the Donne Variorum and is working on the Oxford edition of Donne's letters and on a project treating women and sermons from 1517 to 1688.

ANITA GILMAN SHERMAN is associate professor of literature at American University and author of *Skepticism and Memory in Shakespeare and Donne* (2007). She has published essays on Donne, Garcilaso de la Vega, Herbert of Cherbury, Thomas Heywood, Michel de Montaigne, W. G. Sebald, and Shakespeare in a variety of journals and edited collections. Her current book project, *The Skeptical Imagination in Early Modern England*, extends her work on skepticism in literature to authors ranging from Spenser to Marvell.

DOUGLAS TREVOR is associate professor of English at the University of Michigan. He is the author of *The Poetics of Melancholy in Early Modern England* (2004) and the coeditor of *Historicism, Psychoanalysis, and Early Modern Culture* (2000). He has published articles on early modern writers ranging from Thomas More to John Milton, and he is currently completing a monograph on charity in medieval and early modern England.

JENNIFER C. VAUGHT is Jean-Jacques and Aurore Labbé Fournet / Board of Regents Professor of English at the University of Louisiana at Lafayette. She is the author of *Masculinity and Emotion in Early Modern English Literature* (2008) and *Carnival and Literature in Early Modern England* (2012); she is also the coeditor of *Grief and Gender: 700–1700* (2003) and the editor of *Rhetorics of Bodily Disease and Health in Medieval and Early Modern England* (2010).

ANGELIKA ZIRKER teaches English literature at the University of Tübingen, Germany. She has published *Der Pilger als Kind: Spiel, Sprache und Erlösung in Lewis Carrolls Alice-Büchern* (2010) and has coedited *Drama and Cultural Change: Turning around Shakespeare* (2009). She is also an editor of *Connotations: A Journal for Critical Debate*. Her current book project is titled *Stages of the Soul in Early Modern Poetry*, with attention to Shakespeare and Donne.

Index

Abraham, Lyndy, 223n5, 229n42, 230n43
Act of Uniformity, 85
Activity, 142–44
Affection, 190–91, 194, 196–98, 200, 202–4, 214, 269n44
Afterlife, 68–69, 72
Agamben, Giorgio, 3, 187, 270n49
Aitchison, Jean, 273n60
Alan of Lille, *The Plaint of Nature*, 143–44
Alchemy, 24, 223n5, 229n42, 230n43, 233n62
Alleyn, Edward, 1
Ambiguity, 149–51, 163–64, 251n9
Anatanaclasis, 155, 158–60
Anderson, Judith H., 12–14, 165, 227n27, 249n3, 254n33
Apostasy, 2
Appearances, deceptiveness of, 49–55
Aristotelian tradition, 13, 180, 181, 186–87, 197, 200, 205, 259n7, 263n19, 266n29, 266n30, 270n49
Aristotle, 3, 62, 191–92, 196, 199, 259n5, 265n29, 270n49
Asexual reproduction, 73–75, 77–80
Aspect seeing, 152–55, 157, 252n13
Astington, John, 89–90
Atlases, 115
Attridge, Derek, 11, 149, 251n9
Audience, 7–8; addressed by theatrical/ poetic works, 31–37; at court, 89–90; engagement of, 87–110; integral vs. accidental, 105; and life/death matters, 31–37; metaperformative experiences of, 103–5, 244n26; performers and characters in relation to, 95–97, 244n26; at plays, 87, 89; presence and mediality in the theater, 97–100; at sermons, 87–89; and sites of death, 26; skepticism and, 183; speaker's relationship to, 90–94; voices and perspectives experienced by, 100–3
Augustine, Saint, 207
Austin, John L., 97, 174, 241n3
Autoeroticism, 72–81, 240n18
Averroës, 205
Avicenna, 205

Barthes, Roland, 208
Bates, Catherine, 11, 150–51, 250n4
Bauer, Matthias, 4–5
Bayer, Johann, *Uranometria*, 115
Beaumont, Francis, *The Knight of the Burning Pestle* (with John Fletcher), 32
Bedford, Countess of, 28–29
Bednarz, James P., 182
Behn, Aphra, *The Emperor of the Moon*, 111
Belsey, Catherine, 107–8, 262n16
Berlant, Lauren, 255n9
Bethell, S. L., 102

Bevington, David, 202
Bible, Donne on voices and perspectives in, 100–101
Binary oppositions, in performance, 97–98
Binary thinking, 63–65
Blackstone, Mary, 7–8
Blaeu, Willem Janszoon, 115
Blanchot, Maurice, 208
Blau, Herbert, 95, 97
Body: death and, 71–72; Donne's "Ecstasy" and, 180–81; orgasm and, 62–63; sex and, 71–72; sites of death and, 27–28; skepticism and, 180–81; soul and, 18–20, 26, 30–31, 223n5, 223n6, 231n49, 274n65
Book of Common Prayer, 35, 85
Booth, Stephen, 11, 72, 78–79, 154–55, 232n54, 252n17, 264n21
Brahe, Tycho, 115, 121
Brentano, Franz, 186, 192, 259n5
Bromley, James M., 256n9
Brook, Peter, 97
Brooks, Cleanth, 182
Brown, James, 250n1
Brown, John Russell, 232n52
Browne, Thomas, *Religio Medici*, 33
Bruno, Giordano, 112
Bryskett, Lodowyck, *Discourse of Civill Life*, 205, 263n19, 274n64
Burgi, Jost, 237n8

Calderwood, James L., 262n14
Calvin, John, 211
Carey, John, 248n31
Carlson, Marvin, 107–8
Carruthers, Mary, 186
Cartography. *See* Maps and cartography
Cartwright, Kent, 195, 264n21
Casoni, Guido, 228n35
Castiglione, Baldassare, 206, 217
Catholicism: criticism of, 113, 120; Donne and, 2, 32, 85; and heresy, 112; Shakespeare and, 2, 85

Cavell, Stanley, 3, 12, 45, 171–74, 177–78, 236n2, 256n12, 268n38
Celestial globes, 114–15
Celestial maps, 9, 113, 115–16, 118
Censorship, 178
Chaim, Daphne Ben, 103, 242n13, 244n26
Change, love and, 38–60
Chapman, George, 257n21
Charles I, 8, 88, 96–97
Chastity, 40
Chester, Robert, *Love's Martyr*, 177–78, 182, 257n21
Christ. *See* Jesus
Church of England, 85–86
Cicero, 266n30; *De Oratore*, 190
Cirillo, A. R., 228n35
Clark, Stuart, 14, 187, 208, 262n16, 265n22, 269n44, 270n50
Clements, Arthur L., 227n33, 229n41
Clocks, 43, 237n8
Closed texts, 107–8
Cognitive science, 97–98, 105, 188, 244n26
Cohen, Adam Max, 114
Collinson, Patrick, 85, 108
Colonialism, 113, 118–19
Common ground, 92–94
Common nouns, 133–40
Conley, Tom, 122
Conscience, 87, 91–92, 99, 105–8, 262n15
Consciousness, 262n15. *See also* Multiconsciousness
Control, 5–6, 56–58
Copernicus, Nicolaus, 121
Corinthians I 15:54, 21
Court audiences, 89–90
Crawshaw, Eluned, 233n62
Cressy, David, 111
Crutwell, Patrick, *The Shakespearean Moment and Its Place in the Poetry of the 17th Century*, 1
Culler, Jonathan, 11, 149–50

Dante Alighieri, 42
De Grazia, Margreta, 155–56, 166, 186, 252n17
Death: body and, 71–72; imagination and, 146; life and, 4–5, 7, 17–37; love and, 18–19, 26, 68–72, 80; modes of, 17–18; puns on, 61–81
Declarative texts, 107
Dekker, Thomas: *Old Fortunatus*, 34; *The Shoemaker's Holiday*, 34
Derrida, Jacques, 174
Descartes, René, 170
Desire, 136–37
Dollimore, Jonathan, 38, 43, 51, 237n9
Donne, Constance, 1
Donne, John: character and personality of, 185; education of, 85; generic hybridity of, 2; grandfather of, 221n3; marriage of, 59, 71–72, 237n6, 238n15; parents of, 2; as preacher, 86, 88–89, 126 (*see also* Donne, John, sermons by); and religion, 2, 32, 85; royal patronage of, 85–86; and the theater, 1–2
Donne, John, sermons by, 2, 8, 91, 97–103; on Acts 2:36, 231n49; on Job 19:26, 231n49; Lenten sermon (1617–1618), 8, 94, 95–96, 106; Lenten sermon (1627), 96, 100, 104–6, 109; on Luke 23:40, 87–88; on Mark 4:24, 8, 88; on Paul, 125; Whitehall sermon (1627), 102
Donne, John, works by: "As due by many titles," 10, 137–38, 144–45; "At the round earth's," 36–37, 215–16, 231n49; "Batter my heart," 10, 137–39, 144; "The Canonization," 13, 43, 182, 205–12, 231n50, 238n15; "Confined Love," 45–46; *Deaths Duell*, 5, 17, 20, 22, 27–28, 30–31, 33, 37; *Devotions*, 5, 22, 30, 123, 127–28, 231n49; "The Dissolution," 71–72; "The Dream," 216–17; "The Ecstasy," 4–5, 12, 18–20, 23–27, 44, 170, 173–74, 178–84, 212; Elegy III, 40; Elegy XIX, 121; Elegy XVII, 40–42, 48; "Epitaph on Himselfe," 4–5, 18, 28–29, 35–36; *Essayes in Divinity*, 126; *The First Anniversarie*, 43, 58, 69, 124, 222n3; "The Flea," 46, 60; "Goe and catche a falling star," 47, 138, 238n19; "Goodfriday, 1613. Riding Westward," 13, 123, 125, 214–15; "The Good-Morrow," 6, 9, 43, 45, 61, 65–68, 71, 74, 77, 123; Holy Sonnet III, 46; Holy Sonnets, 9–10, 13, 137–38; "A Hymn to God the Father," 10–11, 145, 164–65; "Hymne to God, my God in my Sicknesse," 9, 124–25; *Ignatius His Conclave*, 115, 120–21, 128; "Image and Dream," 216–18; "The Indifferent," 40, 45–46; "A Lecture upon the Shadow," 6, 42–45, 55, 237n8; "A Litanie," 39–40, 234n67; love lyrics, 38–46, 59–60, 238n15; "Lovers' Infiniteness," 44, 70, 78; *Loves Progress* (Elegy XVIII), 43; *Metempsychosis*, 122; "A Nocturnal upon S. Lucy's Day," 13, 212–14, 275n68; "The Paradox," 68–69; "The Primrose," 212; *The Progresse of the Soule*, 122; *Pseudo-Martyr*, 23; *The Second Anniversarie*, 43; *Songs and Sonnets*, 6–7, 48, 61–62, 64; "The Sunne Rising," 39, 44, 69; "A Valediction Forbidding Mourning," 6, 39, 42, 44, 56, 162, 228n37, 238n15; "A Valediction: Of Weeping," 11, 161–63, 253n27; "Womans constancy," 40. *See also* Donne, John, sermons by
Double-hemispherical world maps, 124
Dubrow, Heather, 59
Duck-rabbit, 153
Duer, Leslie T., 274n66
Dürer, Albrecht, 115

Ebreo, Leone, 209
Ecstasy, 18–20, 24–26, 178–82, 223n6

286 Index

Elizabeth, Queen, 85
Elizabethan Settlement, 85
Ellrodt, Robert, 40
Embodied time, 61–81
Empathy, 100
Empson, William, 11, 111–12, 150, 245n3, 253n27
Enterline, Lynn, 265n25
Epilogues, 33–34
Epitaphs, 32
Erasmus, 147
Escher, M. C., 2
Escolme, Bridget, 104
Everett, Barbara, 176–77, 182, 258n30
Extraterrestrial life, 111–29

Faculty psychology, 186, 196, 205–6, 211
Family resemblances, 148
Famous Victories, 108
Ferry, Anne, 67
Fetzer, Margret, 272n56
Ficino, Marsilio, 180, 205, 266n29, 270n50
Fickle behavior, 6, 40–41, 45–59
Fineman, Joel, 10, 11, 137, 139, 141
Fischer-Lichte, Erika, 97, 98, 100, 241n3
Fletcher, Angus, 113
Fletcher, John, *The Knight of the Burning Pestle* (with Francis Beaumont), 32
Florio, John, 114
Fowler, Alastair, 2
Frey, Charles, 267n36

Galen and the Galenic tradition, 62, 205, 270n50
Galileo Galilei, 112, 121, 247n24
Gallagher, Lowell, 208
Gardner, Helen, 209, 258n30
Gaselee, Stephen, 228n38
Gatti, Hilary, 112
Gender, sexuality and, 143–44
Generic hybridity, 2–3
Genre, 170, 173–74, 184
Gentile, Alberigo, 112

Geography, 124
Gibbons, Brian, 21, 224n13, 226n22
Gil, Daniel Juan, 256n9
Gillies, John, 124–25
Gilman, Ernest B., 275n71
Globe Theater, 115
Globes, 114–15
Gnostic Docetism, 79
God, 79, 126, 137–39, 144–45, 164–65, 208, 214
Goldman, Michael, 260n11
Good, Justin, 153
Grant, Patrick, 273n60
Greenblatt, Stephen, 202
Grossman, Marshall, 3–4, 9–10, 141–47, 273n60
Guibbory, Achsah, 275n68

Halpern, Richard, 271n52
Hamlin, William, 127
Hariot, Thomas, 245n8
Henrietta Maria, 104
Herbert, Edward, of Cherbury, 182
Herbert, George, 233n61, 234n67
Herbert, T. Walter, 226n23
Heresy, 112
Herz, Judith Scherer, 270n51, 275n68
Heterosexual reproduction, 72–75, 79
Hieros gamos (sacred marriage), 5–6, 38, 42
Hill, Nicholas, *Philosophia Epicurea, Democritiana, Theophrastica*, 111
Holbein, Hans, the Younger, *The Ambassadors*, 115
Honter, Johann, 115
Hulme, Peter, 114
Hyperbole, 172–76, 182, 184, 255n7

Imagination, 13–14, 186–219; defined, 186; Donne and, 206–19; dreams and, 198–200, 203; memory and, 186; puns and, 210; and reality, 193–95, 200–201, 203; Renaissance theories of, 188; Shakespeare and, 186–205; and thinking, 191–92, 198, 201, 211

Imitation, spectators and, 97–99
Immortality, 75–76, 76, 211
Imperative texts, 107–8
Infidelity, 45–59
Intention, 193, 195–98, 200, 202–4, 214
Interinanimation, 4, 23–25, 227n33
Interrogative conscience, 105–8
Intimacy, 171–84, 255n9

Jacobean skepticism, 127
James I, 85–86, 96, 104; *Directions to Preachers*, 91
Jesuits, 85, 120
Jesus, 79, 99, 107, 144, 214–15
Johnson, Christopher, 184, 255n7
Johnson, Samuel, 156
Jonson, Ben, 182, 257n21; *News from the World Discovered in the Moon*, 118

Kant, Immanuel, 255n7
Kastan, David Scott, 261n14
Kay, Dennis, 258n30
Kepler, Johannes, 121, 270n50
Kiefer, Frederick, 265n26
King, as audience, 95–96
King, Edward, 146
King's Men, 86, 90, 96
Kissing, 23–24, 228n38
Klause, John, 122
Knedlik, Janet Leslie, 261n13
Knight, G. Wilson, 58
Kosman, L. A., 192, 208, 263n19
Kremen, Kathryn, 38, 224n9
Kripke, Saul, 3, 11, 133, 177

Lacan, Jacques, 11
Lamb, Julian, 11
Language, 12; as arena of personal and political struggles, 134–36; materiality/objecthood of, 154, 155, 158–62, 165–66, 207; nature of, 171, 177; non-significant relationships in, 154–56; physiognomy of, 153–54; private, 169–85; religion and, 142; self and, 133–47; time and, 66–67, 81; universal, 169. *See also* Poetry; Puns
Laqueur, Thomas, 7, 62, 76, 240n18
Laud, William, 96
Leigh, David J., 11, 162, 164
Lerner, Daniel, 8, 109
Lewalski, Barbara Kiefer, 276n72
Libertinism, 40–41, 45–52
Life, death and, 4–5, 7, 17–37
Lille, Alain de, 10
Lindberg, David C., 270n50
Linear time, 62–69, 72–73, 75–76, 78, 80
Locke, John, 170
Louthan, Doniphan, 253n27
Love, 5–6; death and, 18–19, 26, 68–72, 80; desire to control, 51, 54, 56–58; fear of fickleness in, 45–59; ideal, 42–45; mutability and immutability regarding, 38–60; private language and, 174–84; sex and, 65; skepticism about, 51–54; and time, 69–70
Love lyrics, 38
Low, Anthony, 275n69
Lucian, 121
Luhmann, Niklas, 256n9, 271n52
Luke 12:37, 21
Lust, 51–52, 65, 197, 202
Luther, Martin, 10, 75, 142–43, 211, 222n3
Lying, truth and, 136–37
Lyly, John, 235n71; *Endymion, the Man in the Moon*, 9, 112–13

Maps and cartography, 9, 113, 115–16, 118, 122–27
Margolis, Jonathan, 62
Marotti, Arthur, 183, 210, 273n60, 275n70
Marriage, 172
Marston, John, 257n21
Martin, Catherine Gimelli, 5–6, 9, 180, 258n28
Masque of Mountebanks, The, 88
Massumi, Brian, 3, 6, 7, 61, 63, 65, 78

Masturbation, 65, 72–81, 240n18
Matchett, William, 175, 182
McConachie, Bruce, 97–98, 100, 105
McCoy, Richard, 175
McCullough, Peter, 89–90
Memory, 186
Mercator, Gerardus, 115
Metaperformative experiences, 103–5
Miller, David Lee, 4, 10–11
Milton, John, 10, 194, 211; "Lycidas," 143–47; *Paradise Lost*, 112
Misogyny, 48, 51
Molyneux, Emery, 115
Monophysitism, 79
Montaigne, Michel de, 9, 38, 124–27, 208, 236n2; "An Apologie of Raymond Sebond," 114, 119–20, 125–26, 128; "Of the Caniballes," 114, 115, 119
Monuments, 5, 18–20, 26–30, 35, 232n52
Moon, 9, 111–21, 246n24
Mooncalf, 117–19
More, Ann, 11, 40, 42, 71–72, 138, 145, 161–65, 222n12, 237n6, 238n15, 275n68
Morris, Harry, 162, 164
Mortalism, 211, 274n65
Moschovakis, Nick, 263n20
Multiconsciousness, 102

Nashe, Thomas, 235n71
Neale, Steve, 107
Neely, Carol Thomas, 58–59, 201, 238n22, 268n40
Neoplatonism, 116, 182, 197, 205, 217, 270n49, 270n50
Newstok, Scott L., 233n59
Nicholas, bishop of Salisbury, 147
Nicholas of Cusa, 180
Nicolson, Marjorie, 43
Noggle, James, 255n7
Norbrook, David, 264n22
Nous poiētikos (maker mind), 192, 205, 208, 263n19, 269n46
Nozick, Robert, 255n9

Nussbaum, Martha C., 259n4, 263n19
Nuttall, A. D., 265n25

Open texts, 108
Optics, 205
Orgasm, 61–81
Orgel, Stephen, 114, 199, 202, 267n34
Orlin, Lena, 211

Pacenza, Jennifer, 5, 6–7
Pafford, J. H. P., 202
Parthenogenesis, 73–74, 77–80
Passivity, 142–44
Percy, Henry, Earl of Northumberland, 245n8
Performance, 7–8, 86–110; characters and perspectives in, 100–103; for court audiences, 89–90; Donne on, 91; and the interrogative conscience, 105–8; merging of roles in, 95–97, 244n26; and metaperformative experiences, 103–5; nearness and distance in, 90–94, 242n13; presence and mediality, 97–100; and reality, 190–91, 260n10
Petrarchan conventions, 43, 46, 68, 72, 76, 138, 206
Phoenix riddle, 207. See also Shakespeare, William, poetry of: "The Phoenix and the Turtle"
Pico della Mirandola, Giovanni, 205
Plato, 39, 42, 67, 187, 205, 266n29; *Symposium*, 209
Platonism, 197
Poetry: creative power of, 264n22; death and, 25–37; virgin birth and creation of, 73–74
Pomponzaai, Pietro, 261n13
Pope, Alexander, 146–47
Pound, Ezra, 276n72
Preachers, and the theater, 86–87
Predication, 133, 135–36, 138
Prepositionality, 5
Prescott, Anne Lake, 120

Pritchard, R. E., 67, 240n11
Private language, 169–85; concept of, 169, 256n12; Donne and, 173, 178–84; perfect vs., 169–70; seventeenth-century philosophy and, 170; Shakespeare and, 173–78, 181–84; Wittgenstein and, 169–71
Privy Council, 85
Pronouns, 142–47
Proper nouns, 10, 11, 133–40
Protestantism, 112, 120
Psalm 23:5, 21
Puns, 11, 148–66; actual vs. available, 155; and ambiguity, 149–51, 163–64, 251n9; concept of, 148–49, 250n5; "contract," 210, 273n62; "die," 61–81, 207; "done" and "Donne," 145, 164–65; as images, 210; "interinanimates," 4; before lexical rules, 155; "lie," 68–69, 204–5; literary history of, 148, 250n3, 250n4; "more" and "More," 138, 145, 161–65; "neutral," 208; non-signifying character of, 154–56, 158, 160–61; seeing, 152–54, 157; signifying potential of, 157–58, 159–60; as single word, 151–52, 159–60; "son" and "sun," 78–79; "Will" and "will," 158–61
Purgatory, 32
Puttenham, George, 158, 207
Pyrrhonian skepticism, 122, 126, 128, 208, 248n31

Questions, rhetorical use of, 105–8
Quitslund, Jon A., 273n59

Rambuss, Richard, 144
Read, Rupert, 178
Read, Sophie, 250n3
Reality: art and, 190–91, 260n10; imagination and, 193–95, 200–201, 203
Religion: language and, 142; and plurality of worlds, 111–29. *See also* Catholicism; Protestantism

Reproduction. *See* Asexual reproduction; Heterosexual reproduction
Rhetoric: metaperformative experiences, 103–5; nearness/distance in relationship to audience, 90–94; presence and mediality, 97–100; and types of text, 107–8; use of questions, 105–8; voices and perspectives, 100–103
Rigid designation, 133–34, 135
Robbins, Robin, 230n48, 233n60
Ronsard, Pierre de, *Sonnets pour Hélène*, 19
Rorty, Richard, 256n12, 257n25
Roscius, 190
Rosenberg, Marvin, 263n20
Rowe, Nicholas, 199, 202

Sacred marriage, 5–6, 38, 42
Saunders, Ben, 59, 276n75
Saussure, Ferdinand de, 187
Schechner, Richard, 241n3
Schofield, Malcolm, 191–92, 266n29
Scodel, Joshua, 32, 234n66
Scruton, Roger, 95
Sebond, Raymond, 126
Second Globe Theatre, 88
Seeing, 14, 152–54, 157, 187. *See also* Aspect seeing; Vision, theories of
Seel, Martin, 100
Self, 9–10; in cosmological perspective, 128–29; Donne on, 123–24; language and, 133–47; Montaigne on, 122. *See also* Subjectivity
Sententiousness, 158
Sermons: and the interrogative conscience, 105–8; metaperformative experiences in, 103–5; nearness/distance in rhetoric of, 90–94; performative character of, 7–8; presence and mediality in delivery of, 97–100; voices and perspectives in, 100–103, 106–7, 243n24

Serres, Michel, 3, 5, 6, 7, 63–66, 80, 81
Sex: body and, 71–72; "die" puns and, 61–81, 207; gender and, 143–44; love and, 65
Sextus Empiricus, 126
Shakespeare, William: education of, 85; generic hybridity of, 2; parents of, 2; and religion, 2, 85; royal patronage of, 85–86
Shakespeare, William, plays by: *All's Well That Ends Well*, 35; *Antony and Cleopatra*, 7, 172–73; *Hamlet*, 2, 10, 13, 133–5, 183, 185–92, 194–96, 208–11, 214; *Henry V*, 8, 11, 35–36, 88–89, 91–93, 96, 98, 102, 108, 157–58; *King Lear*, 45; *Macbeth*, 185, 187, 192–96, 212; *A Midsummer Night's Dream*, 4–5, 32–33, 35–36; *Much Ado about Nothing*, 6, 45–51, 57–58; *Othello*, 6, 38–39, 49, 51–59; *Pyramus and Thisbe*, 36, 247n24; *Richard III*, 22; *Romeo and Juliet*, 4–5, 18–21, 23–28, 230n43; *The Tempest*, 5, 9, 37, 113–20, 129; *Twelfth Night*, 4; *The Winter's Tale*, 5, 6, 185, 196–205, 209, 214
Shakespeare, William, poetry by: "The Phoenix and Turtle," 5, 12, 26–27, 33, 170, 173–78, 181–84; Sonnet 2, 77; Sonnet 3, 75–76; Sonnet 7, 78–79; Sonnet 18, 27; Sonnet 20, 139; Sonnet 71, 232n54; Sonnet 81, 27; Sonnet 86, 27; Sonnet 111, 183; Sonnet 116, 38, 42, 43, 49, 60; Sonnet 135, 10, 11, 133, 139–40, 145, 158–61; Sonnet 138, 49, 51; Sonnet 146, 21; sonnets, 6–7, 26–27, 62, 64; Will Sonnets, 10, 137, 139–40; Young Man sonnets, 61, 65, 72–81
Shakespeare-Donne intersections, 1–3, 85–86, 88
Shami, Jeanne, 7–8
Sherman, Anita Gilman, 12, 121, 233n65; *Skepticism and Memory in Shakespeare and Donne*, 1

Sherman, William, 114
Sidney, Philip, 208, 271n52; *Apology*, 205; *Astrophil and Stella*, 74, 182, 256n9, 258n30; *Defence of Poesy*, 197
Silver, Victoria, 143–44, 146
Sites of death, 4–5; exchange and interaction at, 18–25; as poetic parable, 25–37
Skepticism, 12, 13, 190, 196, 268n38; about love, 51–54; and the body, 180–81; cartography and, 124–28; Donne and, 121–22, 127–28, 215; and interpersonal relationship, 171–81; Jacobean, 127; Montaigne and, 119–20, 122, 124, 126; and other worlds, 9, 114, 119–20; perspective and, 124; private language and, 171, 174; Pyrrhonian, 122, 126, 128, 208, 248n31
Sleep, 19–20, 33
Smith, A. J., 275n67
Smith, Anthony D., 8, 109
Smith, Bruce, 72
Smith, Hallet, 202, 266n30
Smith, Preserved, 118
Sodomy, 137, 139, 143–44
Soliloquies, 91–92, 104, 186
Soul: body and, 18–20, 26, 30–31, 223n5, 223n6, 231n49, 274n65; imagination and, 211; interinanimation and, 23–25
Southwell, Robert, 208, 272n58
Space travel, 9, 111
Spectators. *See* Audience
Spenser, Edmund, 194, 199, 211; *The Faerie Queene*, 112
Stoicism, 52
Stoll, Abraham, 264n22, 265n25
Subjectivity, 9. *See also* Self
Sublime, 169, 173–77, 180, 182, 184, 255n7
Sympathy, 100

Targoff, Ramie, 61, 68, 72, 180, 227n33
Taylor, Neil, 186, 261n14
Tertullian, 23–24

Theater: characters and perspectives in, 100–103; life/death analogies in, 32–37; merging of roles in, 95–97, 244n26; metaperformative experiences in, 103–5; nearness/distance in rhetoric of, 90–94; performative character of, 7–8; preachers and, 86–87; presence and mediality in, 97–100; and reality, 190–91. *See also* Performance

Thinking, imagination and, 191–92, 198, 201, 211

Thompson, Ann, 186, 261n14

Tichborne, Chidiock, 226n23

Tilmouth, Christopher, 262n15

Time: in Donne's and Shakespeare's work, 64; in Donne's sermons, 99–100; embodied, 61–81; language and, 66–67, 81; linear, 62–69, 72–73, 75–76, 78, 80; love and, 69–70

Transi tombs, 224n14

Transitionals, 8, 109–10

Trevor, Douglas, 7–8, 9, 262n16

Truth, and lying, 136–37

Turnbull, David, 115

Universal language, 169

Variorum Edition of the Poetry of John Donne, The (Stringer, ed.), 40, 42

Vaughan, Henry, "Death. A Dialogue," 226n24

Vaught, Jennifer C., 268n40

Vendler, Helen, 72–73

Vesely, Dalibor, 207

Virgin birth, 73–74

Virtual, the, 63, 65, 78

Vision, theories of, 205

Walker, Julia, 180

Ward, David, 269n44

Wardi, Eynel, 232n52

Warner, D. J., 115

Watson, Robert N., 275n68

Wedin, Michael, 187

Wells, Stanley, 73

Wilkins, John, 118

Williamson, Elizabeth, 225n16

Wilson, Richard, 264n21

Wittgenstein, Ludwig, 3, 11, 148, 152–54, 165, 169–72, 174, 176–81, 184, 257n25

Womb, 17, 21–22, 27, 226n23

Words: materiality/objecthood of, 154, 155, 158–62, 165–66, 207; non-significant relationships between, 154–56; physiognomy of, 153–54, 158

World soul, 42

Worlds, plurality of, 111–29

Wotton, Henry, 247n24

Wright, Laurence, 269n44

Zirker, Angelika, 4–5